The Right Wing in France
From 1815 to de Gaulle

The Right Wing in France

From 1815 to de Gaulle

Second American Edition

RENÉ RÉMOND
Translated from the French by
JAMES M. LAUX

Philadelphia
University of Pennsylvania Press

84916

Translator's Note to the Second American Edition

Professor Rémond's study of the French Right Wing was first published in Paris in 1954. A revised second edition appeared there in 1963 and the University of Pennsylvania Press published a translation of this edition in 1966. Late in 1968 M. Rémond presented a third French edition of his work, again revised and brought up to date, with an epilogue analyzing the crisis of May–June 1968. The first American edition having gone out of print in the meantime, it was decided to incorporate the most recent additions and revisions of the third French edition in a second American edition. The reader should note that the author revised Chapter 9, dealing with the period 1940–1968, before the events of May–June 1968, and that his discussion of those events appears in the Epilogue. The translation does not include a section of appendixes and documents contained in the French edition. In the bibliography some of the author's comments have been condensed and additional titles, primarily of works in English, have been included. The full names of organizations designated by abbreviations will be found in the index. The illustrations are unique to the American editions of this work.

Contents

Illustrations

Author's Preface to the Third French Edition

In the old days authors added to each new edition of their books a preface which celebrated the reception that had greeted the earlier edition and once again stated the reasons behind their enterprise. As the most recent of these prefaces did not replace its predecessors, one could follow in them the successive strata of the work. If we think it justifiable to do somewhat the same, it is not to revive a traditional usage but to continue a dialogue with the course of events that any work begins when it attempts to explain the contemporary world. In the five years since the preceding French edition, men, issues, and the relationships among political forces have changed, some slightly, others greatly. The reasons which in 1963 required a revision of the original 1954 edition—the progress of research and the changes in the political situation—again press for another revision on a number of points. And there are other reasons which may lead to some further considerations on the object of our study.

The progress of research can be measured by the number of additions that we have had to insert in the bibliography: after five years some 60 additional titles, even though we have not attempted to be exhaustive. These concern material in the chapters dealing with the earliest periods as well as very recent times, and foreign historians have contributed as much as Frenchmen. For the contemporary period, this growth of information reflects the stimulation given to such studies by the National Foundation for Political Science in Paris.

But the development of research cannot be measured by a quantitative increase alone. There has also been a widening of the field of observation by the use of new methods, and a deepening by the employment of investigative procedures which only recently have been used in analyzing political ideologies and traditions. Without entirely superseding the contributions of the traditional academic disciplines, the application of the methods of inquiry worked out by social psychology to the study of political opinions and behavior illuminates a whole area of reality, teaches us much more about the real content of opinions, and reveals an aspect of motivations which strongly affects fundamental choices. Here and there in the course of this book one may notice some examples of the sort of contributions that the study of ideologies may derive from such new methods. Perhaps the use of these procedures will enable us in part to overcome the logical obstacle, as yet insurmountable, that opposes to a strictly objective investigation the prior need for both a preliminary definition of the terms Right and Left, and the collection of purely empirical data on the diversity of opinions.

If the multiplication of research has enriched and sometimes altered our knowledge of some aspects of the subject, the latter has also changed somewhat. Such is one of the risks of this sort of dialogue carried on with contemporary events. It makes any work that does not try to evoke an entirely dead past a kind of serial story continued from installment to installment. When one declares at the very beginning that there is a continuity between yesterday and today, that relationships continue between a past which remains alive and a present which is not an absolutely new beginning, every event raises questions about the explanatory schema. And in the last five years there have been numerous events that have been influential and worthy of notice. To be sure, between 1962 and 1967 the Right did not experience any upheaval comparable to the changes that ensued between 1953 and 1962. Still, there were quite a few for a five-year period: in the area of general political history we have seen the end of the first seven-year presidential term, the first presidential election, the entire span of one legislature, and a general election. And for those things that directly or indirectly touch the Right Wing—delaying until later any discussion as to whether all these matters really affect it—there was the decline and fall of the extreme Right after the presidential campaign of Jean Louis Tixier-Vignancour in 1965, the strengthening of the Independent Republicans around their leader Valéry Giscard d'Estaing, the development of the Democratic Center movement which capitalized on Jean Lecanuet's campaign for the presidency, and the game of reciprocal maneuvers played by Radicalism and Christian democracy. So many names have emerged or gained greater stature in the last five years, so many shifts and changes of position have occurred, that they bring a new relevance to the enduring questions we first asked over a dozen years ago.

The big questions still are the same, although their terms may change a little. Does the two-sided division between Right and Left, assuming that it had some real importance in the past, still have meaning for the new political society that is developing? If it does, then what positive and persistent distinctions separate these two groups? And finally there are the closely related but subordinate questions—for they can be raised only after the two preceding ones have received a tentative reply—does the Right exist in the singular or the plural, and how many Right Wing groups can we detect?

The debate on the importance of the distinction between Right and Left cannot be divorced from arguments concerning the notion of the Center. In the last few years the Center has been rejuvenated and set up in the very heart of political thought and life. For one thing, it seems to exert an irresistible attraction on several political movements as much by their sincere dislike of being identified with the Right as by a calculation that the public does not vote willingly for those calling themselves Rightists. So the parties fight over positions in the middle. In the assembly, the Gaullist Union for the New Republic demands to sit on the Center benches, arguing that because it has to fight on both fronts at the same time—against the extreme Left and against the extreme Right—it can consider itself as the real center of the regime. The Independent Republicans[1] of M. Giscard d'Estaing do not intend to be outflanked on their Left by the dominant group in the governing majority. When the heirs of Christian democracy joined forces with a part of the Independents they chose the name Democratic Center, and several branches coming from Radicalism or the Right claim the same name. Doesn't this sort of competition suggest that the Center has a certain psychological and ideological reality? In addition, the purely speculative controversy over the character and role of the Center in French political history has revived. Several studies have shown how France has been governed, with some exceptions, by Center groups, that generally the Center has been as important as the two extremes, and that it deserves just as much attention from historians, even historians of ideas. Several writers have then gone beyond these objective findings to challenge the reality of the traditional dualist interpretation of our political life.

[1]Political allies of the orthodox Gaullists. Tr.

If the history of the last five years has in these ways noticeably changed the basis of this or that response, it does not seem to us that it has replaced the substance. Today as yesterday, under the Fifth Republic as under the Fourth, we believe we can recognize that the diversity of individual opinions actually displays a relative internal coherence and a long-lasting stability. These opinions extend in a regular distribution that historical events have spread out from the Right to the Left. Taken by themselves, as is too often the case, these positions are clumsy and do not hold up well against the erosion of time and experience. This has drawn frequent attacks upon them.

But from this situation spring several corollaries which give these opinions their real importance and complete significance. First, Right and Left are not isolated entities that are independent of historical situations. They are relative positions, well integrated within a system, and both define themselves in relation to the other. Except for those at the extremes, no family of thought is completely on the Right or simply on the Left; it is more to the Right or less to the Left than another. This explains why, at the same time, a group may appear on the Right for some and on the Left for others; and this disposes of the difficulties that come from such differing interpretations. The extreme Ultra Right, at the very beginning born on the Right Wing and never having been outflanked on its own right, is the only group that can be considered fully and completely on this wing of French politics. The Left can offer nothing comparable, for all the Leftist movements that have successfully risen have been outflanked, one after another, to the point that some of them have even become Right Wing groups, which confirms the essentially relative character of their identification; for

how could a Left Wing movement become Rightist if we
are dealing with timeless principles? Therefore Right and
Left are the guidelines for a comprehensive study, constituent elements of a global structure. At a time when the
idea of structure is recognized as a fundamental intellectual category and has pushed its way into most of the
social sciences as an imperious sovereign, the acceptance
of the duality Right-Left should raise few difficulties.
Isn't it an example of a structure in the political area that
predates the individual?

History should not be ruled out of the picture, however. For our second corollary is that the system changes
over time. It does this in two separate ways. On the one
hand, the whole system is affected by a slow movement
that in general pushes it from the Right to the Left. As a
result a certain intellectual tradition which initially is
located on the Left finds that later on, because it has
remained faithful to its original positions, it is on the
Right. On the other hand, the terms by which Right and
Left are distinguished change, and history acts primarily
in this way on the Right-Left polarity. The form of the
regime and the principles of its legitimacy, the religious
issue and the legal status of the Church in political life,
the rights of property and duties of the State, and finally,
decolonization, each, one after another, have divided
Right and Left. How can the content of the two terms
avoid being affected by these particular issues?

And yet we have allowed ourselves to oversimplify
just now when we used the phrase one after another.
Actually, and this is our third corollary, the emergence of
new problems does not eliminate the old ones, and new
debates do not snuff out old controversies. Earlier disagreements remain, and the most recent ones are added
to them. As a result, the same movement can be both on

the Right and the Left at the same time. This is not only a matter of appearance. Let us offer two examples which may add some flesh to this skeleton explanation. Under the Fourth Republic two families showed some analogies with each other—the Radicals and the Popular Republicans. The question often was asked, which one was to the Right of the other? Put in this way the question does not make sense because the answer would differ according to the criterion used. Should it be the religious issue? On this the Radicals, in line with political tradition, could legitimately boast of being more to the Left. If one considers the organization of the economy and the structural reforms, then the M.R.P. could justifiably judge itself to be less to the Right. But of these two criteria which was the more decisive under the Fourth Republic? The historian cannot find an acceptable answer to this question because both criteria have served alike. To prefer one over the other would indicate a personal and relative judgment. Additionally, because time multiplies meanings and complicates the variables, several political movements can coexist within the same camp where their juxtaposition reveals the historical succession of periods and issues. Consequently, there are several groups on the Right Wing and several on the Left, which demonstrate the continuity and variety of our political life. In short, to use a phrase that is going to find wider usage in our understanding of politics, Right and Left are the result and the evidence of a political culture. It is exactly because they sum up the entire national experience and describe a century or two of the past that they are indispensable to understanding our history. Far from being mutually exclusive and contradictory terms, history and structure, when they concern the Right and the Left, flow together and merge in the living and remembered reality of a culture.

The Right Wing in France
From 1815 to de Gaulle

Introduction

One or Several Right Wing Groups?

Right, Left . . . the oscillation of these two terms, indissolubly linked by their opposition, paces by its rhythmic tempo all the political history of contemporary France. Men of the Right, men of the Left, parties of the Right, parties of the Left, Leftist bloc, Rightist coalition, Right-Center, Left-Center, the persistent hammering of these twin words punctuates a hundred fifty years of political struggles. "Right, Left, by far the most vivid distinction for the mass of French voters," writes Emmanuel Berl.[1] The two rival labels stand face to face, clash with each other, blaze from the billboards, resound in schoolyards, are flaunted in black headlines in the newspapers, stir passions, generate enthusiasms, dominate debates, outlive political regimes, puzzle the foreigner, and even impose themselves on historians. A fundamental principle of French political life, this traditional division of public opinion into two great contrary points of view today remains the key which opens the door to an understanding of France's recent history. This history is bewildering and incoherent if left in an arbitrary and fortuitous disorder. If, by using the capricious power of our imagination, we abolished this basic distinction, immediately one hundred fifty years cease to be intelligible, and as if the thread which links them were suddenly broken, the events drift apart in truth there would no longer be any possible explanation.

[1] *La Politique et les Partis* (Paris, 1931), p. 195. Author.

19

What then does this distinction, which is so fundamental that it constitutes the continuing foundation of
French political evolution, really mean? The most common ideas often are the most confused and the most
banal realities the hardest to define. We shall disregard
the Left, which will concern us only in its relation to the
Right. What then is a man of the Right? Of course we
have a general concept of this term: personal experience
and memory bring to mind several characteristic examples such as a landed proprietor, an industrialist, a
simple peasant, a career officer, or even a doer of good
works. But what do these men have in common? On what
do they agree which makes them all vote for the same
ticket despite differences in background, occupation, and
condition?

Is a man of the Right *secular or clerical?* Habit answers like a echo, "clerical," but the map of France
indicates entire regions such as that of the East-Center
(departments of Aube, Yonne, Haute-Marne, and Côte-
d'Or) where at present the drift to the Right seems to
move at the same pace as the growth of religious indifference. *Authoritarian or liberal?* Next to men whose entire
program can be summed up in the desire to reinforce the
authority of the State sit others whom one does not have
to press very hard to make them admit that the State is a
kind of absolute evil. This line of argument could be continued; other examples would only uselessly lengthen the
list of variations and would add nothing to the force of
the demonstration. Each affirmation automatically gives
birth to its opposite, contradictions become the rule, and
the anomalies become so numerous that they raise
doubts even about the most commonly accepted ideas.

Thus, the more one tries to define the Right the more its outline changes, its features blur, its aspect decomposes.

Must we conclude then, that this idea of the Right is only an arbitrary invention of the mind or the conscious product of political calculation? Some people at present take advantage of the incoherence of this hybrid monster to maintain that the old distinction between Right and Left has now lost all its *raison d'être*. Such conceptions, they say, may formerly have corresponded to some reality but today they are archaic vestiges of a dead past at best good for a museum shelf. "Except for the politicians, no one understands what this means. In fact, it is a dead language."[2] So dogmatized at one point a journalist whose name later ornamented the masthead of a weekly [*L'Express*] which attempted to renovate the Left. A few years later, from quite another political sector the voice of a minister of the Fifth Republic echoed this sentiment: "France is the only country in the world which still speaks of Right and Left. But today there are no Right Wing solutions or Left Wing solutions to problems that the world has never experienced before."[3] If so, it would be proper to abandon these notions as keys which no longer open any lock. Thus the question before us is: are the terms Right and Left a permanent distinction or are they a language that today is out of date?

These supposedly outmoded conceptions are the legacy of a long history. Perhaps knowledge of the past of these conceptions will supply an answer to the riddle created by the contradictions they presently entail. If the Right appears today so complex, so disconcerting to ex-

[2]J. J. Servan-Schreiber, *Le Monde,* January 24, 1953. Author.
[3]Alexandre Sanguinetti, Minister of Veterans Affairs, in a speech at Toulouse, as reported in *Le Monde,* December 3, 1966. Author.

amine and so resistant to definition, perhaps it is because it bears the traces of successive alterations, like a building on which each age has placed its mark and which at first discourages the archeologist who wishes to date it. A general picture is always a composite image. Instead of trying to draw a picture of the Right in which all the features match all its circumstances, why not examine the past so that it may present the Right in all its diversity and thereby recreate the living unity of its historical development? I thought it would be interesting to examine this hypothesis; it is in this attempt to make knowledge of the past illuminate our understanding of the present that this study finds its *raison d'être* and its justification.

Where should we fix a point of departure for this study which corresponds to a decisive moment in political history? The date of 1815 seems the least arbitrary. Not that the Right waited until then to emerge from the limbo where political ideas sleep before their incarnation; the Second Restoration was not an absolute beginning for it. Often its birth is dated from the session of the National Assembly of September 11, 1789, when for the first time divisions of political opinion were demonstrated physically in an assembly; henceforth it became customary to have a topographical distribution of the members corresponding to doctrinal differences. One can then, in the Revolutionary period, play the game of fitting labels to men and groups, and distinguish those who lean to the Left from those who tend to the Right. Some even think they have the right to go back much further and believe they can recognize in the episodes of the Fronde or the disorders of our religious wars some characteristics of the

Right and some sensibilities of the Left. In fact, if one accepts the principle that Right and Left express a permanent opposition between two fixed systems or two temperaments, does it not follow as night the day that any political society must reproduce this eternal dialogue? Athens, in this view, had its men of the Left and its Rightist leagues. Without pretending to solve for the moment this basic debate on the nature of the Right and the Left, does not such a reduction of the opposition between Right and Left to the unchanging antagonism of two universal categories, of two timeless forms of political thought, underestimate the diversity of historical experience, and debase the peculiar originality of national political traditions?

The date 1815 marks the point after which a division was consciously understood; a division between two Frances which we can provisionally label Left and Right. To be sure, the debate which divided them is from an earlier period, since they were identified in terms of the recent past and recognized themselves either by an acceptance or rejection of the work of the Revolution. But an attempt to return to the Old Regime and the threat of a social restoration helped public opinion to realize their opposition and compelled it to choose between them. We shall begin this history, therefore, at the moment when the Right and Left became social realities and basic factors in collective psychology.

1815-1963: the bounds that limit the field of this study enclose nearly one hundred fifty years, in which parliamentary activity, collapses of ministries, regimes in crisis were in the forefront of the scene; they also were years of political thought, of meditation on doctrine, of militant activity. Within this framework of one hundred fifty

years, under changing names, we must recognize the continuity of an intellectual tradition and reconstruct the
genealogy of a family of ideas. Reconstruct the genealogy! The comparison is disturbing. We must take care
not to proceed as the genealogists who, depending on
simple homonyms, attribute flattering ancestries to their
clients. Recognize the continuity? First, we must be sure
that it existed.

To attempt to retrace the history of the Right Wing
from 1815 to 1963, does this not ascribe to the forms of
political thought an impossible and imaginary stability?
In a century and a half there is enough time for ideas to
evolve ten times as well as for loyalties to change and
bonds to unravel. One hundred fifty years are approximately five or six generations in time, and in fact it is
possible to distinguish in a general way a half-dozen successive generations among the political personalities of
this century and a half. Did these men, whose names
chronology sets down as following each other as do the
members of a dynasty, succeed one another in a straight
line, so that we may consider the Deputies of the National Bloc in 1919 as the direct and legitimate heirs of the
Ultras of the Second Restoration of 1815? Is M. Pinay
the descendant of Chateaubriand? Is not the very statement of this hypothesis enough to discard it? Then does
each generation bring a new system of thought and invent forms of political expression? Principles would be
renewed along with men. For each generation there
would be a corresponding Right, as different from its
predecessor as from its successor. At this point the issue
may be formulated in this way: was there from 1815 to
1963 one and only one Right, or were there as many as
there were generations, superimposed successively on

France's political conscience? The whole problem of the Right Wing lies in this alternative: *unity or plurality over time.* The present study tries to suggest a response.

The problem is important and has implications far beyond the question of the Right. We raise here the issue of continuity and succession, the question of the permanence of political traditions and the stability of public opinion through several regimes. Today historians rather tend to stress continuity. Studies of electoral geography and research into religious geography converge on this point. One of the most valuable contributions of the movement begun fifty years ago by André Siegfried's *Tableau Politique de la France de l'Ouest* (1913) was to have retied the threads of political continuity, at first sight broken by superficial breaks, and to have revealed the existence in France of large blocs of political and religious opinion, practice, and behavior whose territorial homogeneity interests us much less than their constancy over time. But our problem is not exactly the same; it is at once narrower and broader, and so does not lead to the same conclusions. Political or religious geography always deal with limited areas; we are concerned with the chronological continuity of one aspect of French belief throughout the country.

M. Francois Goguel, in *La Politique des Partis sous la IIIᵉ République* has replied directly to our question. He supports the thesis of continuity. In very forcefully pointing out the existence of two stable political temperaments and defining one as that of *movement,* the other as attached to the *established order,* his exposition implies the unity and continuity of the Right. From beginning to end, always the same system of values, the same groups of interests, the same meeting of minds. This interpretation of party history illuminates with unprecedented clarity the settled purposes of the Right and the Left. But it also raises some difficulties. How, for example, can one reconcile the permanence of these two temperaments with another fundamental axiom of the history of parties as stated by M. André Siegfried, that of the continual drift to the Right? By digging too deeply the trench which separates the two wings, the process by which a political group jumps across becomes incomprehensible; the gulf becomes unbridgeable, for a group does not suddenly and totally repudiate what has until then been its program. Such a total denial is possible for individuals but not likely for a group.

There is another difficulty which concerns us directly. The permanence over time and the internal unity of these two blocs are hard to reconcile with the display of doctrinal contradictions that the Right shows throughout its history. The conflicts within it do not date from today. More than once, several political groups, all on the Right Wing, have been profoundly divided on essential points. The impossiblity of determining the ideal-type of a man of the Right at the present is even more so the case in the past, when emphasized by the passage of time and by historical perspective.

Some examples will give a clearer impression of this diversity within the Right. Knowing what it has been for the last half-century, we might be tempted to define it as national or nationalistic. In fact, this word has often sufficed to define it, serving as a flag and watchword. But to this definition the history of a good part of the nineteenth century poses the contradiction of a Right friendly to peace (we would say "pacifist" if the word were not an anachronism), generally hostile to bellicose ventures,[3] and which hardly cared at that time to challenge the Left's monopoly of militaristic patriotism. In February 1871, it was still the Right which favored peace with the Prussians, and it was Gambetta who was eager to continue the war. Therefore, it is impossible to associate the Right with nationalism on a long-term basis.

To give another example, the dilemma between the liberal and the authoritarian approach is a very old one. What choice has the Right made between these two antagonistic terms? There have been deeply liberal men on the Right, attached from the bottom of their hearts to parliamentary institutions, convinced of the virtues of these institutions and as respectful of their rules as they were opposed to any regime which violated them. But there have also been men on the Right who have had only scorn and sarcasm for parliamentary assemblies and whose hopes have called for the concentration of power and the exercise of an almost unlimited authority. Yet each of these groups is as qualified as the other to represent the Right.

One Rightist tradition imbued with a strong feeling of its mission and its duty asserts the superiority of morality over politics, and subordinates the exercise of political action to higher interests. In some cases this sense of the absolute has gone so far as to eliminate from the Right the highly political sense of opportunity. This was natural to those who moved in the realm of theory. But the area of contingency was not ignored by the Right, for was there a political school more deliberately to the Right than that of "Politics First"?[4] Its theorists refused

---

[3] The expedition to Spain in 1823 and that to Rome in 1849 were exceptions and stemmed from internal political causes. Author.

[4] A reference to the Action Française, discussed in Chapter 7. Tr.

to introduce the absolute into the political realm, distinguishing jealously between morality and politics and basing political action only on considerations of strict political realism. It is hard to imagine more different points of view. How then can we consider placing them in a single Right? There are similar divergences over relations with the Church and concerning the place religious society should occupy in civil life. Gallicans and Ultramontaines sat next to each other on the benches of the Right Wing where the heir of the legists jostled the pontifical zouave.[5] Theirs and Montlosier were as unimpeachably men of the Right as were Montalembert and M. de Falloux, while in the twentieth century the Action Française reawakened the tradition of Gallican and anticlerical royalism.

If, despite everything, we agree to pass over these supposedly secondary divergences and stress the common desire to defend the established order, the history of the Right controverts us decisively on this point also. The Orleanists who accepted 1789 and the work of the Revolution did not understand the same thing by established order as the Ultras of 1815 or the Legitimists of 1873, partisans of an unlimited counter-revolution. Even for a man of the Right there was more than one way of thinking of the established order. France has established several political orders and in a country like ours there are always enough persons enamoured of the past to appeal from the most recent to the preceding and from the latter

---

[5] "Legists" refers to the medieval French scholars who, using principles of Roman law, claimed the greater authority of the monarch over the pope, while the "papal zouaves" were a military force composed of French volunteers who tried to defend the temporal power of the pope in the 1860's. Tr.

to the oldest. Thus, even on the ground of the established order where M. Goguel places the principle of the Right, the diverse nuances are not at all reconcilable, the divergences remain.

The simple problem raised by the observation of the contradictions of the present is deepened and aggravated by a consideration of the long-standing diversity within the Right. The unity of the Right, already difficult to recognize in the present, is simply impossible to make out in the past. If the Right cannot be reduced to the unity of one tradition and one way of thinking, the only solution is to admit that there were, over the course of the last hundred fifty years, not one but several Rightist traditions[6] of which we must determine the exact number, specify the characteristics, and describe the interrelations. The object of this study is to attempt this classification; by arranging the scattered elements, by bringing together the separate fragments, we hope to throw enough light to disentangle these multiple Right Wing groups.

From one end to the other of our period the number of groups in the Right Wing did not remain constant. Plainly, changes of regime and transformations of society have their repercussions on political tendencies. Each significant change brought about the appearance of a new school or caused an existing one to move to the Right, for in addition to its permanent characteristics and fundamental choices, the Right is also a relative position in a system of forces and in a debate whose subject

---

[6] In addition, doesn't the usual expression "classic Right" indicate that common sense also recognizes the existence of non-classic Rights? Author.

changes. Issues gain or lose importance; the center of gravity shifts. New groups come to take their places beside the old, altering to their advantage the balance of strengths, for the youngest captures some of the supporters of its elders but never can make the older ones disappear entirely. The older Rightist movements maintain themselves at the price of some adjustments, for nothing is more perennial than a political tradition, and our political life today resembles an amazing museum of specimens representing all the epochs of the past.

In substance then, it will be seen that we have retained and characterized out of the apparent confusion of their multiplicity three Right Wing movements, each possessing all the attributes of an authentic political tradition with its own system of thought, temperament, and clientele. They emerged at successive moments of French political development. The first borrowed its doctrine from the *Ultras* of the Restoration, counter-revolution— it was tradition made into a system and built into a policy. The second, conservative and liberal, was the hier of *Orleanism*. The third effected an amalgamation of heterogeneous elements under the sign of *nationalism*, of which Bonapartism was a precursor. Intercourse developed among these three tendencies; interferences brought them together, they were associated in coalitions; but they never fused. It is these three traditons, of unequal age and variable importance, whose conjunction forms the alliance improperly called the French *Right* in the singular. Most of the contradictions observed in the present or turned up in the past are cleared up in the light of this historical explanation; the history of the Right Wing is made up of the transformations and vicissitudes of these three Rightist factions.

Drawing its principle of explanation from history, this study will not be a connected and particularized recitation. Neither the spirit of the series of which it is a part nor the available space permits it to be a detailed summary of events. Besides, it has seemed better not to describe known events again, to repeat, for example, M. Dansette's penetrating history of Boulangism. On the other hand, an attempt to present systematically the different tendencies of the Right has a *raison d'être*, and perhaps fills a gap. The constant endeavor to synthesize will take precedence over chronological analysis. The recitation of facts will intervene only to support an attempt at explanation since explanation has no significance or justification without implicit reference to the unfolding of events.

As an essay of interpretation, the present study intends to remain faithful from beginning to end to the requirements of historical knowledge. To attempt attribute their respective parts to permanence and to change in a political tradition, is this not to do twice over the job of the historian? History is already knowledge of continuity in the succession of events. With the Right, as with all political thought, what is it if not the expression in political action of a certain meditation upon history, the practical projection of an interpretation of events, and the will, by exerting itself upon the destiny of a human society, to make or give new direction to history?

1

1815-1830: The Ultras, Extremism and Tradition

I. His Majesty's Opposition

July 1815. The parenthesis of the Hundred Days closed, King Louis XVIII re-entered his capital. A few days later, he summoned the electoral colleges, and the *pays légal*[1] was invited to send its representatives to him. The map of public opinion at this point suggests to the historian the beautiful simplicity common to all periods of conflict and discord: two clashing traditions, two defiant societies, two Frances face to face. It is useless to introduce nuances and distinctions here. One group alone had the prerogative, without restrictions or qualifications, to be called the "Right." These were the Ultra-royalists, to use a name which they accepted and by which they were known for fifteen years. Other groups

[1] Those citizens with the franchise, numbering somewhat under 100,000 at this time. Tr.

32

which were not part of the Left were said to be in the
Center or even Right-Center, but they were not the
Right. We are not concerned with the Doctrinaires,[2] for
if this group did not want to be confused with the Left
Wing Liberals, circumstances led it to oppose even more
firmly the Ultras on the Right, from whom almost everything separated them. There was nothing more foreign to
the unyielding passion of the Ultras than the Doctrinaires' conciliatory and reasonable liberalism. They were
divided even more by temperaments and moods than by
doctrines.

The situation was less simple and clear-cut for a small
group of politicians who sat on the Right-Center of the
Chamber next to the Ultras. They were brought together
by their fears and inclinations and shared the anxieties
and uneasiness of a Duke de Richelieu or a Count de
Serre. We should not incorporate these men with the
Ultras, whose immoderate excesses and verbal violence
offended their political feelings and shocked their taste,
but more than once circumstances forced a rapprochement. They feared the Jacobin peril no less acutely than
the excesses of the Ultras on the Right. In periods of
relative calm they found it possible to adopt a conciliatory position and willingly agreed to changes that they
judged inevitable. But at critical moments, they were
thrown back toward the Ultras, obliged to renounce their
generous effort to reconcile the irreconcilable. Perhaps
nothing illustrates better this unhappy dilemma than one
decision of the Count de Serre. After the crime of
Louvel,[3] out of devotion to the public interest, de Serre

[2] A small number of political intellectuals led by Royer-Collard. Tr.
[3] Louvel murdered the Duke de Berry, son of Louis XVIII's
brother, the Count d'Artois, and the only male Bourbon with a

broke his ties with friends of long standing, accepted a post in the second ministry of the Duke de Richelieu (February 1820), and became the eloquent champion of a bill which brought down upon him passionate attacks by his former political friends.[4] But these alliances developed only out of the necessity for reconciliation in the face of gains made by the Liberals on the Left. The Right-Center formed a coalition with the Ultras without marrying their sentiments and also without being pardoned by them for a supposed lack of intransigence. Richelieu and de Serre soon were judged too lukewarm and were repulsed by the more fervent Ultras. An indication of the unbridgeable gulf that separated them is the casual way in which the Count d'Artois broke his word to the Duke de Richelieu in December 1821, saying that his earlier promise of political support had been given in "less happy days." The depth and permanence of the disagreement clearly shows that the Ultras were the only Right purified of all spirit of accommodation, the integral Right.

However, the Ultras at first were not conscious of forming a party or of representing the Right in the country. For a long time they flattered themselves by assuming that they expressed the sentiment of the nation from which they excluded only, and by their own fault, a handful of those sick in mind or disappointed in ambition who were tolerated in the kingdom only by the goodness

---

chance to have an heir and thereby continue the direct family line into the next generation. However, the Duchess de Berry thereafter gave birth to a posthumous son of the murdered Duke. This child was first known as the Duke de Bordeaux and later as the Count de Chambord or Henry V. Tr.

[4] This bill tightened press censorship. Tr.

of the sovereign. The blindness of fanaticism? Not entirely, for if this was an illusion it was generally shared
by many Frenchmen who were not all Ultras. They believed that after the Revolutionary upheaval France
miraculously found herself royalist again. There was at
work here a common way of thinking to which both
mysticism and a philosophy of history brought their contributions. A cycle had finished, a new world was beginning. It was the dawn of a new era, just as it had been
after the Flood. To imaginations nourished by the Scrip-
tures, such Biblical comparisons and symbols came quite
naturally. The waters of the Revolutionary cataclysm
now having receded, the divine anger appeased, the
rainbow of reconciliation between the King and his subjects henceforth was going to guide the destinies of the
country. France, washed of her Jacobin contamination
and restored to her true Christian and royal inclinations,
was going to learn again how to love her princes. The
Ultras are not comprehensible without this sentiment of
a providential renewal, of an almost complete new beginning. And now to this certitude of faith, political
events brought a kind of confirmation. The unhoped-for
result of the elections, the surprise of the Incomparable
Chamber (*Chambre introuvable*) were quite the sort of
things to keep alive in the Ultras their reassuring illusion.
It was a tenacious illusion which, despite early deceptions, was to survive among the successors of the Ultras
for generations, for it was inseparable from a whole
group of beliefs. Ten years later it was still this mystic
conception of the monarchy which presided over the
coronation ceremony of Charles X. Once again comparison with Scripture came to the fore. France relived the
Book of Kings; it was the Lord's Annointed who came to

Reims.[5] Where liberals saw only ridiculous archaism and an unnatural resurrection of antiquated customs whose hypocricy they denounced, the Ultras, and royalist opinion with them, believed that they detected the opening stages of a renewal for France.

To become a political party and thereby consent to the consequent diminution of their importance, the Ultras had to learn that they were not all of France. The course of events soon prepared this revelation for them. In the face of a reconstituted and contentious Left that made progress year by year, the Ultras gradually came to a realization of what united them among themselves and what distinguished them from others. The quarrel of the two Frances delineated the boundaries of the party and the limits of the Ultra Right.

And yet at the beginning it was not explicitly a matter of the principles of 1789, and the significance of the Revolutionary experience was not directly involved. The issue was more simple—it revolved about the acceptance or rejection of the Charter of 1814,[6] a document conceded and promulgated by the sovereign himself, whose most faithful sons (if not the most submissive) the Ultras loved to proclaim themselves. Not the least of the paradoxes of the Ultra party, which multiplied them as the party grew older, was that its adherents were first identified by a refusal to support that royal authority, obedience to which was one of their fundamental political beliefs. It was, of course, their very fidelity that led them to

[5] In Charles X's coronation at Reims he was annointed with a long lost holy oil which churchmen announced had just been discovered. Tr.

[6] The Charter was the constitution of Restoration France, granted by Louis XVIII, which established a constitutional monarchy in France resembling that in Great Britain. Tr.

refuse to subscribe to a document which legalized a reduction of monarchical authority, but this fidelity was not enough to prevent the history of the party from opening with an act of insubordination. Loyalty and insubordination, a singular mixture, is revealed as a constant of the Ultra Right from the very outset.

From the beginning it presented itself as an opposition force, a demagogic opposition. This is exactly the meaning of the expression *Ultra-royalist*. The word "ultra" was not a novelty in the political vocabulary. The Robespierrists had already used it in overwhelming the Hébertist faction[7] but the success of the word lasted scarcely longer than the faction. It reappeared in 1815, to designate those royalists whose demands exceeded those of their king. Their contemporaries tell us that they did not object to the name, they gloried in it. It was their bad luck to deal with a sovereign whose point of view was much less absolute than theirs. In spite of the Charter and in spite of the monarch they retained their allegiance to the monarchy. This was expressed in eloquent conciseness by their cry, "Long live the king, in spite of himself!" It resounded, provocatively, in the Incomparable Chamber; Chateaubriand's pamphlet, *On Monarchy according to the Charter,* concluded with a "Save the king in spite of himself!" It was published as a daily slogan by one of the most uncompromising newspapers, *Le Drapeau Blanc.* The loyalty that the Ultras paraded was only a weak hindrance to the temptation to appeal, from a sovereign who was badly informed, badly inspired, and badly advised, to a more enlightened and more wisely guided monarch, from the reigning king to his brother

[7] The Hébertists were a radical revolutionary group in 1793-1794. Tr.

and presumptive heir. The political opposition thus became, as is common in a monarchical regime, a discreet and persistent dynastic opposition. The accession of the Count d'Artois (September, 1824) withdrew from this opposition its *raison d'être*. From the day when the Count acceded to the throne there was no longer an Ultra-royalist party in the true sense of the term, since the views of this faction henceforth coincided with those of the sovereign. This at once ended the persistent paradox of an opposition springing out of loyalty.

However, the political opposition did not completely disappear. An Ultra tendency continued. This was because the Ultra party represented by its nature an extremism which could not accommodate itself to the necessities of power nor resign itself to the servitudes of reality. It retained this character due to its members' personalities and to political circumstances.

The birth of Ultra-royalism was approximately contemporaneous with the Incomparable Chamber. The Chamber of 1814 was of slight importance; it was the old Legislative Body of the Napoleonic Empire under a different name and its majority followed a prudent opportunism that with the rapid succession of regimes could be made to appear, with a little indulgence or some artfulness, as the defense of the permanent interests of the country. It held one session without any difficulties, for points of view were not yet defined. Only some moves to restore to the clergy some unsold Church property gave a hint as to certain points of the future Ultra program.

The summer election of 1815 sent to sit at the Palais-Bourbon a completely different assembly, of an original composition, which was to give to the Ultras some of their most durable characteristics. In it the Ultras had at their disposal a literally overwhelming majority: 350 out of the 392 Deputies. Scarcely 50 of its members had sat in the Revolutionary assemblies, or in those of the Consulate or the Empire. An irreproachably royalist past hardly prepared these newcomers to understand and still less to excuse the turnabouts and recantations of the political and administrative personnel. The Hundred Days, the disavowals of the opportunists, the defections, the reappearance of Jacobinism stimulated by Napoleon's return, all exasperated them. They came fully resolved to punish those who had relapsed and perjured themselves. These lovers of justice were the first of the "just" with a rigor exempt from all indulgence. They considered it a weakness to give in to pity, it was their duty to be pitiless. (To give everyone his due, such rigor is not exclusive to Right Wing purges. In 1944-1945 it will be the turn of the Left to prove its severity against the Collaborators.) No experience in government tempered the sharpness of their intransigence. Coming late to politics, most of them had lived far from public affairs, secluded in the provinces, hoping they were forgotten. Others, newly returned émigrés, could scarcely understand the new France. Many had no other political past than bearing arms against the Republic, conducting guerilla war against it in the West, or conspiring against the usurper. Along with their deep-seated honesty and sincere conviction of doing well for their country, they brought to their new responsibilities the illusions and naiveté of beginners. Their origin also brought a hereditary distrust of the court and the political leadership. While the Legitimist historians have pinpointed the presence in their ranks of non-nobles such as Brenet, the physician from Dijon, and Billard, a landowner from Chartres, nevertheless most belonged to the small or medium provincial nobility. From them came the tone and the leadership. Included were Villèle, a gentleman from Lauraguais in the Southwest, one of the fiefs of the party. La Bourdonnaye from Anjou, whose violent remarks earned him the nickname Jacobin or the *"Conventionnel blanc,"* Clausel de Coussergues, and Baron de Haussez. This provincial nobility was hereditarily jealous of the upper nobility which it accused of leading the monarchy to its downfall. Positive personalities, unyielding characters, formed in the school of systematic and absolutist thinkers more than that of practical affairs, all the more attached to their opinions because they had suffered for them, they represented an original and new shade of opinion, a royalism which was young and vigorous, robust and combative, rural and militant. In the future this was to mark the thought of the Ultras.

To ask such men to approve the spirit and letter of a compromise between the Old Regime and the Revolution was to invite them to remain neutral between good and evil. Whether it was a matter of judging men or events, the same simple dualism inspired their appraisals. The Revolution was evil. To introduce a portion of the revolutionary heritage into the institutions of the restored monarchy was to place good and evil on a level of equality. There could be no question of setting up a compromise. Did one come to terms with evil? One either gave it all its share or one fought it without mercy. Compromise meant placing one's head in the lion's mouth.

It is easy to imagine the uncomfortable feelings of these men, split between their respect for the royal will and their horror of revolution, when confronted with the Charter. The problem was not only one of politics, it raised the matter of integrity. Through obedience most of them accepted the Charter, but with private reservations. To ease their consciences they established a restrictive interpretation to which the hastily drafted text easily lent itself. Some of them however, either more sincere or less flexible, disdained these subtleties and refused to take the oath to the Charter which was required of them. Jules de Polignac, intimate friend of Monsieur,[8] was one of these. He deemed article five, which recognized religious liberty, outrageous. Already this suggests a conjunction between the political beliefs of the Ultras and an "integrist" interpretation of Catholicism. The Chamber of Peers refused to admit Polignac so he finally gave in and took the oath. La Bourdonnaye followed a similar course.

The Liberals pretended to accept the Charter so as to embarrass the Ultras but really accepted neither the return of the Bourbons nor the Restoration. The Doctrinaires saw in the Charter an acceptable and reasonable compromise between revolution and monarchy and agreed with the desire of Louis XVIII to "nationalize the monarchy so as to monarchize the nation." But the Ultras scorned the Charter. They found no excuse for what it preserved of twenty-five detestable years and would admit its relevance only if it served to consecrate a complete restoration. Their attachment to what they believed to be absolute good in politics was so strong that they refused a relative good, and their aversion to compromise was such that in order to prepare for the best they often practiced a policy of the worst.

[8] The Count d'Artois. Tr.

This attitude led the Ultras to attack the men of the Center more often and with more vigor than their adversaries on the Left, with whom they at least had a common hostility to the current regime. Very soon, in fact, a conflict developed between the majority of the Incomparable Chamber and the king's ministers and thereby with the king himself who had expressed his confidence in them.

The debate soon raged over constitutional issues. Going beyond simple divergences over political orientation, it reached the interpretation of the Charter. Hastily drafted, the document was quite vague as to the form of government it created. It was imprecise on the power of the king to choose his ministers and on the authority of the Chamber of Deputies over them. While the Ultras had an uncontested majority in the new Chamber none of them bore any of the burdens of power. So they insisted that the king must choose his ministers from the majority. All the great names of the party forcefully maintained the rights of parliament. "To deny the prerogatives of the Chamber is to deny representative government itself," said La Bourdonnaye, who was to become a minister in the Polignac cabinet. Vitrolles wrote a pamphlet titled, *On the Ministry under Representative Government*. But the masterpiece of the abundant literature roused by this controversy was the sparkling and incisive pamphlet by Chateaubriand, *On Monarchy according to the Charter*, which explained the party's doctrine on parliamentary government. The members of the ministry, with only a minority in the Chamber, now defended the right of the king to exercise complete freedom in selecting his ministers. A paradoxical situation, where the natural supporters and the traditional adversaries of the royal prerogative fought on reversed fronts: the believers in limited monarchy pleaded for the king's initiative, while the Ultras announced the unexpected virtues of the parliamentary regime for which, quite suddenly, they became the advocates and interpreters.

We recognize here, of course, the usual effect which current interests have on doctrines: a theory of the moment which perhaps the Ultras would have developed more discreetly if they had not controlled a majority in the parliament and had not believed public opinion to be on their side. The same result came out of another debate which opposed them to the government over an electoral bill. The supporters of the ministry proposed to renew membership in the Chamber of Deputies by one-fifth each year; the Ultras favored a complete renewal every five years, a system which had served them well in 1815. The Ultras advanced arguments which sounded strange in their mouths because of their quasi-democratic character. The Ultras argued that a total renewal of the Chamber would bring a truer expression of opinion and its changes and would make elections less subject to administrative pressures. Was not the true reason for the Ultra position that the government proposal opened the way to ministerial influence on the elections and gave to the administration's agents the power to fashion a majority as they desired? Then too, if the Ultras suggested a considerable enlargement of the suffrage, was it not because they judged the middle bourgeoisie to be politically suspect and wrong-headed while they believed they would find a sure support in the lower social levels? Whether it was parliamentary responsibility, choice of ministers, or the composition of the electoral body, the Ultra positions were strongly affected by circumstances.

But however greatly the momentary situation influenced these positions, circumstances did not explain everything. The Ultras, less opportunist than anyone, would not have adopted them, despite their practical advantages, if they had not corresponded to an intellectual predisposition. Their political thought admitted of a natural tendency toward a royalism which was liberal in its fashion, parliamentary and even popular. A year of continuing conflict between an Ultra majority in the parliament and the king's ministers greatly assisted in formulating and stabilizing this inclination. Its vestiges were to last for over a century. This indicates the importance of the parliamentary year 1815-1816: it fashioned the definitive physiognomy of a group on the Right Wing.

II. Empiricism and System: A Political Romanticism

If it is true that any political organization corresponds more or less to a system of thought, then it is emphatically true of the traditionalist Right. Some of its most outstanding members were thinkers, writers, or publicists long before becoming heads of a party or men of government. Several of them, whether by taste, personal inclination, or as a result of circumstances which sometimes kept them away from political life or even from the national soil, did not play an important political role and gained renown only by their work in political philosophy. A significant proportion of these thinkers were not even of French nationality. Burke was English, Louis de Haller Swiss, and Joseph de Maistre a subject of the King of Sardinia, to cite only the most important. The emigration during the Revolution, by effacing frontiers, facilitated the introduction and dissemination of their thought. The only great French name is that of Bonald, for a time an émigré, although his stay abroad does not seem to have affected his views very much. He was also one of the political leaders of the party. His home department, Aveyron, sent him to sit in the Palais-Bourbon in 1815. He was re-elected after the dissolution of the Incomparable Chamber. Throughout the Restoration he played a double role, that of political reflection and of parliamentary practice. Perhaps he exercised a greater influence on succeeding generations than on his contemporaries, many of whom did not read him. Other monarchist writers such as Bergasse and Fiévée were more publicists than original thinkers and their works were more tracts directly inspired by current events than doctrinal studies on the nature of power or the organization of societies. Chateaubriand fits into none of these categories and should be classed as a special case.

The theoreticians of the counter-revolution are usually divided into two schools: those of the *theocratic* school who deduced the principles of their system from religious considerations such as the will of God, the workings of Providence, and the good of mankind, and the *historical* school which rested on positivist and experimental analysis and asserted that it reached its conclusions inductively from an unbiased observation of the historical experience of societies, having excluded all theological or metaphysical postulates. This distinction has its value in a philosophical examination of principles, but it loses much of its interest in a study of politics. Actually, there was a kind of common fund of postulates, convictions, and truths out of which the Ultras drew the substructure for their thinking and which constantly fed their political activity. Since average opinion interests us

as much as that of the leaders of thought, it is legitimate
to consider as a whole the basic unity of the doctrinal
system.

The use of the word system is not fortuitous. We are
dealing here with a logical construction having great
coherence, whose elements are deduced one from the
other in a rigorous progression. At the risk of some arbitrariness, let us sketch out its main lines.

The keystone of the system doubtless was the notion of
the *natural order*. It is difficult to decide which of these
two words is the more important. In this case, contrary to
the rule, perhaps it is the adjective.[9] In any case, both
are open to so many interpretations that we must avoid
any ambiguity. The idea, as indeed the whole system,
developed out of the shock of the Revolution. The spectacle of that great disturbance was the occasion of much
reflection by the émigrés, which in turn overflowed into
an abundant literature of *Essais* and *Considérations* on
the origin and causes of revolutions. The example of this
immense trench brutally cutting across the course of a
thousand-year evolution quite naturally turned political
philosophy toward the study of the evolution of institu-

[9] The idea of a natural order is found also in liberal doctrine:
the existence of natural laws, of which human intervention only
hinders the operation, is a fundamental axiom of liberalism. But
this involves neither the same nature nor the same conception of order.
The nature of the Ultras was close to the soil, and its laws had the
calm regularity of the movement of the stars or the rhythm of the
seasons. The laws of liberalism are less "natural" and more scientific.
They spring more from mechanics and political economy than from
astronomy or biology. The natural order of the Ultras was that of a
society where the "out of date rural civilization" mentioned by
M. Labrousse still dominated. The natural order of the liberals
carries the marks of a society that already has become commercial
and industrial. Author.

tions and the development of societies. In opposition to
the revolutionary event, that is, a sudden and total transformation brought about deliberately by men, they soon
advanced the idealized notion of a slow and gradual evolution developing spontaneously and in conformity with
the laws of nature. To the rational and deliberate attempt by men to modify their institutions, counter-
revolutionary thought opposed the natural course of
affairs; to a systematic effort to design politics according
to the imperatives of universal reason, it set up the empirical test of time. Against the arbitrary and abstract
regime which issued from the Revolution, the theorists of
the counter-revolution appealed to what might be called
a system of contingency, if it is not too incongruous to
couple these two words. The fundamental trait of the
Ultras' thought was its biological character and there is a
term describing this way of thinking: "organicism."

In this perspective the very idea of a constitution, the
notion of a document which would establish by a decree
of sovereign reason the nature and forms of institutions,
appeared doubly monstrous. It was an absurd denial of
the experience of centuries and even worse, it was sacri-
legious, a crime against God and king. The Abbé de
Rauzan thundered from the pulpit, "Any constitution is a
regicide" (April 1814). An anonymous pamphlet, titled
Constitution of the Times, at the same moment called
upon Louis XVIII "to reject all pedantic contrivances
which want to draw their geometric lines between the
submission of children and paternal authority." We limit
our citations to these: they tell enough of the underlying
motives which inspired the aversion of the Ultras for the
Charter, not a hostility due to circumstances nor practical reservations as to the timeliness of certain provisions,

but a basic opposition in principle to the very existence
of the document. This horror of a rational geometry, this
eulogy of living experience, such were the sentiments
and points of view which were to appear again and
again, from generation to generation until the present. At
a century's distance does not Ardéchois Thibon[10] echo
on more than one point Aveyronnais Bonald? Playing on
words as they loved to do, the Ultras opposed to these
constitutions—which they considered to be monsters of
legalism, monuments of pride, heedless of experience,
and which pretended to have universal validity—the true
constitution of each country which is its particular temperament, its own genius, and its national history. In the
name of national diversity the Ultra doctrine criticized
universalism as much as revolutionary abstraction. "Political forms," decreed Joseph de Maistre, "should be established for specific peoples." Indeed, in 1814 the Ultras
judged that France was not prepared to receive a government of the English style, an unexpected but nonetheless logical application of a doctrine that owed much to
Burke,[11] that is, that institutions cannot be similar for
different countries whose differences are the reflections
of different histories.

With this reference to *history* a second important point
of counter-revolutionary thought emerges: for to this
view history was a very significant reality. At this time,
however, its historical thought distinguished it less
clearly than its organicism. At the beginning of this century, which deserves to be called the century of history,

[10] A conservative Deputy and Senator from Ardèche in the 1930's
and 1950's. Tr.

[11] Burke's *Reflections on the Revolution in France* was published in
France several times before 1830. Author.

there was scarcely any political tradition which did not refer to historical continuity. The Doctrinaires made use of history and presented the Charter as the natural and reasonable consequence of historical evolution. The Liberals, also historians in their fashion, exalted in the Revolution of 1789 the end of a venerable effort by the Third Estate to throw off the yoke of the dominant group wrongly confused with the aristocracy. Everyone asked history for a contribution, each took what he chose. The Ultras drew a conclusion which was paradoxical only to their adversaries; in the name of history they blithely crossed out twenty-five years of history. The lessons of the past authorized them to consider the Revolution as an accident, a parenthesis after which the natural course of events returned to its accustomed path. In sum, against recent history they appealed to older history. That was what distinguished the nature of their historicism; while some turned toward the future, theirs was an exclusive desire to tie up to the past, in a word, *traditionalism*.

But there are as many traditionalisms as there are traditions. The "Old Regime" was not a singular or unique thing; that term is a kind of shorthand used retrospectively to link several quite different societies. Over the course of the centuries, the French monarchy wore more than one face. It was to the oldest that the Ultras directed their fidelity. They felt little kindness towards the absolutism or the administrative machinery of the monarchy *à la* Louis XIV. The most coherent and lucid of the Ultras were not far from acknowledging that the despotism of that monarchy strangely resembled that of Bonaparte or of the Jacobins, and that such a similarity created a responsibility for the precursor. Without it would

these rulers have been possible? It forged the tools, prepared the minds, and marked the path.

The monarchy that they cherished they imagined seeing in that of Henry IV or Saint Louis. More than the
pomp of Versailles, they liked to conjure up the good-
natured authority of good king Henry or the justice of
Saint Louis. *"Vive Henri IV!"* they cried. It was the
medieval monarchy that they wished to restore. Ultra
feelings were quite penetrated with reminiscences of the
Middle Ages. We cannot deny that there was in their
vision of thirteenth century or sixteenth century France a
large share of idealization but this embellishment on the
conventional view of the middle ages strengthened even
more its power on the imagination.

The beginning of the Ultra party was contemporary in
France with the birth of Romanticism which drew its
first inspiration from the monarchical and Christian
Middle Ages. The later development of literary Romanticism, its conversion to liberalism and certain socialist
whims, often hides the original Romanticism, Catholic
and royalist. There were, however, numerous and durable affinities between the Ultras and Romanticism.
Some young poets, hopes of the party, used the pag-
eantry of the dynasty and memories of recent royalist
struggles for their themes. Victor Hugo became known to
the *Société des Bonnes Lettres*, an organization affiliated
with the *Congrégation*,[12] through the reading of his *Ode
sur Quiberon*. The Vendée and Louis XVII were the
sources of his inspiration. Lamartine sang of the *Sacre de
Charles X*.[13] And Nodier and Vigny! In return the young
writers found many defenders among the Ultras against

[12] See below, p. 74. Tr.
[13] Coronation of Charles X. Tr.

liberals who were bound to the classical rules of poetry. (Nevertheless, more than one old royalist such as Bonald severely criticized these presumptuous innovators while retaining his preference for the literary glories of monarchical France.) The first Romanticism was an Ultra Romanticism. By repudiating Voltaire's rationalism and the formalism of classical tragedy, it tried to skip the Renaissance and resume the national and religious traditions of the Middle Ages. It agreed with the Ultra thought which denounced the spirit of the century and ministerial despotism. Literary movements and political thought went in the same direction: on both fronts the same tendencies, the same nostalgias, and the same aversions.

For the theorists of the counter-revolution there was no greater bane to the monarchy than Cardinal de Richelieu, and romantic dramas turned the protector of Laffemas and Laubardemont[14] into a rather sinister character. Ultras and romantics had a common sensibility. The same dreams haunted their imaginations: old chronicles, troubadors, and all very Christian. It happened that they could no longer clearly make out the boundary which separated these dreams from reality. *Eviradnus*[15] had his political imitators with the *Chevaliers de la Foi,* organized on the model of what was imagined to be medieval chivalry. In all this, imagination played a leading role, and this supposed historical thought was perhaps only the romanticized history of a historical novel. Many of these interpretations of the history of the French monarchy had as a basis no more nor

---

[14] Two of Richelieu's more unscrupulous agents. Tr.
[15] A chivalrous knight-errant in Victor Hugo's poem of the same name. Tr.

less than the novels of Walter Scott, known in France from 1817. These works enjoyed an immense success and assured the poet of the Stuarts the admiration of the Bourbon faithful. They contributed greatly to shape the sensibility of this Right which was as interested in romance as it was romanticist.

Whether or not they touched up history, the important thing for their politics was that the Ultras drew from their cult of the Middle Ages the picture of an ideal society which they tenaciously tried to restore. They conceived this in part as a reaction against the events which France had just experienced. France had scarcely emerged from the smothering Napoleonic despotism; thus they dreamed of *liberty*. Yes, however singular this may appear, the Ultras were quite sincerely taken with liberty, although not the same sort as their Liberal contemporaries. A distinction at once emerged which led the Ultras to oppose what they called formal liberty, qualified as abstract and deceitful, real liberty being rooted in tradition and confirmed by history. This opposition was already present in the two views of a country's constitution. Such a restriction did not prevent the Ultras of 1815 from being very real enemies of despotism. We must remember that many Frenchmen who were not ardent royalists at all hoped to find in the dynasty a bulwark against despotism or arbitrariness and hailed the Restoration as a return of liberty as well as of monarchy. A number of Liberals rallied without difficulty to the Bourbon monarchy so as to escape the imperial tyranny. The failure of the first Restoration, then the excesses of the White Terror, pushed many of them toward the Left, although, during the Hundred Days, Victor Cousin[16] en-

[16] A philosopher and educator who became a leading intellectual light in the July Monarchy. Tr.

rolled in a battalion of royal volunteers and Guizot took that trip to Ghent[17] for which he was so severely reproached later on.

Determined to restore the old liberties, the Ultras first demanded the abolition of those institutions which furnished the most effective instruments for governmental despotism. Acceding to the universal desire, Louis XVIII upon his return had announced the end of conscription, and if the Ultras' hostility to the Gouvion-Saint-Cyr law (January 1818) was so bitter, it was because, among other things, it re-established the draft and thereby maintained the military organization of the Revolution and Empire. But no Napoleonic creation unloosed so much verbal violence and roused so many curses, often odious ones, than the Imperial University.[18] Suppressed by a royal decree of February 1815 but saved *in extremis* by the return of its founder, it outlived the Hundred Days. The accusations and abuses with which it was overwhelmed gave an early example of the polemical violence which was to survive in the Ultra party and which it transmitted to its heirs. Final objects of its resentment were the principle and the agencies of administrative centralization. Local liberties found no warmer defenders than the Ultras. In every budgetary debate the Villèles, the Bonalds, the Castelbajacs pleaded the cause of the communes and departments, while some suggested the revival of the old provinces. The later history of the idea of decentralization in Rightist thought is well known. Even today few issues reveal so clearly those who belong to the Right. Regional autonomy, if it weakened the central power, restored the local aristocracy's pres-

---

[17] François Guizot, another Orleanist, had joined Louis XVIII in Ghent during the Hundred Days. Tr.

[18] The State's near-monopoly of education. Tr.

tige and authority, an essential part of the Ultra program.

However, if the Ultras could recover for themselves
the first word of the Revolutionary triad (liberty) by
using equivocation and declining it in the plural, the idea
of equality was completely incompatible with Ultra political philosophy. They believed in the basic unity of all
living things and did not believe that there were differences in nature between natural organisms and human
beings. But did not nature teach that every living orga-
nism is differentiated from others? Therefore, human societies must obey the same law of differentiation. Was
this thought historic? On this point the lessons of history
served to confirm the teachings of nature: viable societies
were founded on inequality. Finally, if one turned to the
national heritage, the society of the Old Regime rested
on a hierarchy of privileged groups where each had its
own regulations in which rights and duties were equili-
brated. It was this harmonious and cleverly-built edifice
that the Revolutionaries destroyed. Imprudently they
swept the board clear of the fruits of history and believed
they brought individual happiness by enshrining it on
the ruins of the old order. Wisdom therefore agreed with
the lessons of experience and prescribed a restoration of
the traditional system, a restoration more social than
political. This was indeed the profound significance of
the Restoration and the basic aspiration of counter-
revolutionary thought. This was why, even when the
regime had foundered and hopes of a monarchical restoration had become quite shaky, Ultra thought kept its
relevance: more than a political formula it proposed a
conception of society.

The political philosophy implied in the writings of

counter-revolutionary theorists subordinated the individual to the social group. From this principle the first and constant application dealt with the family as an institution. In 1816 it was Bonald who reported out the bill abolishing divorce. The subject of the family was also destined for a long and brilliant career in Rightist thought. The importance given to the family unit in the organization of society remains until the present one of the surest indexes by which to recognize the believers in political and social conservatism. Other social groupings, territorial, professional, and even political, were conceived on the model of the family. The ideal State for the Ultras was not the anonymous, impersonal, and administrative State of modern society; but a paternal and patriarchal monarchy whose sovereign was more the father than the head. The feelings of his subjects for him were those of sons for their father, where affection tempered respect and obedience shaded into deference. It was from their filial veneration that all the French found themselves to be brothers. This natural and familial fraternity of the inhabitants of a kingdom had little in common with revolutionary fraternity, born of a political self-consciousness with the framework of the nation. Once more the gulf dividing the two eras appears, separating the *Fête de la Fédération*[19] from the Coronation of Charles X.

Like the family where children are guided by adults, society should admit of a hierarchy of groups and authority where pre-eminence would go naturally to the nobility. The Ultras exalted the restoration of the nobility not only in its privileges but also in its duties. Certainly the

[19] A patriotic celebration of the first anniversary of the fall of the Bastile. Tr.

small provincial nobility from which a good number of
the Ultras was recruited was more interested than anyone in seeing its prerogatives recognized and its property
losses indemnified, but these kinds of desires were not
the whole story. A hereditary tradition of service and the
feeling of a special mission lost none of their powers over
nobles brought up in a worship of the past. The privileges they demanded as their right had as a counterpart a
duty to society. The king had no better servants than the
nobility. Was it not from it that he chose his ministers,
his ambassadors, and his generals? Society found in them
an element necessary to its operation and to the stability
of the social order. Scarcely changed, this conception
hung on in the second half of the century in the form of
"patronage," its base was simply enlarged to include all
the ruling classes.

To finish a survey of the system, one more essential
item must be mentioned—the Church, which the Ultras
wanted to re-establish in its rights, honors, and properties. Although the bills to return the clergy to the status
of private citizens, or to confer on the sacraments a legal
value were not passed (although the law on sacrilege did
make a legal truth of the dogma of the real presence),
others which received the force of law did have almost as
clear a significance. In less than a year the Ultra-royalist
majority decided to return the unsold national property to
the Church, to liberalize the authorization for religious
establishments to receive gifts and bequests, to appropriate five million francs to raise clergymen's salaries, and
to create a thousand scholarships of one thousand francs
each for poor seminarists. The outline of the Ultra program on religion generally included the abolition of
divorce, the control or dissolution of the University, and

the re-establishment of bishoprics suppressed by the Concordat.

But this outline scarcely reveals the spirit of that program. These proposals all tended to re-establish the Church in its material or legal status, to render it independent and pre-eminent. During the course of the century other political groups took up all or part of this program, for motives which sprang more often from political expediency or social conservatism than from religious fidelity. To be sure these considerations were not absent among the Ultras but they were animated and justified by a sincere conviction as to the beneficence of the Church's role and by a personal faith. On this point it is less suitable to speak of restoration than of renewal. Ultra thought did not directly continue that of the Old Regime, except by cutting out an entire century. A frivolous and skeptical aristocracy, sometimes non-believing, returned from emigration in a quite different frame of mind. The two brothers whose successive reigns encompassed the fifteen years of the Restoration present in this regard the striking contrast of the Old Regime aristocrat and the émigré converted to devotion. Louis XVIII was the one of the two who "had learned nothing and forgotten nothing," who remained faithful to the spirit of the eighteenth century with its elegant skepticism. Charles X was the symbol of that sincere and close relationship between royalism and Catholicism which renewed the older and forgotten traditions of the monarchy. Henceforth their alliance was to be one of the intrinsic characteristics of the conservative Right. The political doctrine and social philosophy of Ultra-royalism took on a religious perspective. Political and social conservatism were completed by religious conservatism.

In sum, the whole of these convictions or positions constituted an absolutely coherent system where practical applications were rigorously deduced from doctrinal principles. In every way it was the living antithesis of the principles which for a quarter of a century had ruled France, its government and its society. It was indeed the *counter-revolution* and it has come down to the present: in each generation, writers, theorists, and publicists tried to rejuvenate it and give it the luster and power it knew in the halcyon days of Ultra-royalism.

III. *The Ultra Country: Its Home Grounds*

Until this point in our analysis of the Ultra party doctrine and in our description of its program we have over-simplified, using the license which hindsight grants to historians. We have described the royalist Right as if it were a homogeneous reality, always and everywhere identical to itself, regularly spread throughout the French hexagon and equally distributed among all levels of the social body. It might be expected that the truth has a less geometric simplicity. Without denying the unity of its thought, there were social peculiarities, accidents of historical geography, and a variety of personalties which introduced several nuances whose description will make the physiognomy of the Ultra Right more precise.

Certain social groups had an almost natural affinity with it. Others were spontaneously against it. Sympathies and inclinations thus almost delineated an Ultra-royalist nation whose boundaries were not the same as those of the real France. The social composition of this body of opinion is poorly known, because it is very difficult to determine. Only the *pays légal*, one hundred thousand persons in a country of thirty million inhabitants, was able to express its opinion. When we adventure beyond this microcosm, we are thrown into a completely unknown area with only faint clues to bolster our conjectures. Certainly we know that the nobility, the small more than the great, was Ultra. Likewise we can see in the clergy one of the strongest supports of the Right. But both nobility and clergy were quite small minorities and the mystery still remains for the rest of the country, that is, the majority. Was France Ultra?

The Ultras who had an opinion on this subject always felt they could count on the lower classes which had remained sound, as against the commercial bourgeoisie or the liberal professions which were quite infected with the Jacobin spirit. When pointing out some of the motives of an electoral bill which was almost democratic, Villèle explained, "the middle class, envied by the lower and enemy of the upper, composes the revolutionary party in all states. If you want the upper to come to your assemblies, have it elected by the auxiliaries that it has in the lower class, go down as far as you can and thereby cancel out the middle class which is the only one you have to fear." No doubt Villèle was not wrong to suspect the monarchical sentiments of the middle class, but did he see so clearly in trusting those of the lower orders? The visible submission of the majority of the peasants to the clergy and the local notables was only a presumption. Could one infer the inner sentiment from the outward attitude? Some old traditions gave to certain urban gilds, such as the charcoal sellers, a reputation for monarchical loyalty; were these legends or the truth?

In any case a qualified answer must combine the recognition of social differences with a second dimension, the geographic, for the strength of the party varied considerably from one region to another. Besides, to construct a generalized map of royalist opinion is less presumptuous than to analyze its social composition. In this area the historian is not so completely empty-handed. Elections, even if they reflect a distorted picture, do express a continuing relationship with opinion in the electoral district. It is only prudent to bear in mind that the disproportion between the size of the electoral college and the population of the department often gave rise to significant differences between the shade of opinion represented in the Chamber and the dominant view in the *pays réel*. We should also beware of the influence of abstentions, the possible effect of administrative pressure, and, generally, of all the factors likely to falsify the true expression of opinion. In this situation, other indications fortunately may correct or complete the information given by electoral results. The circulation of the press, the activity of secret societies, the fervency of loyalty expressed at the passage of the king or the princes, or, on the other hand, the warmth of the reception given to Lafayette on his tour of 1829, are all so many spontaneous plebiscites. Even the geographic limits of a popular movement with an insurrectional tenor such as the White Terror affords valuable information. In isolation none of these investigations is very significant, but when put together they corroborate each other.

In time regional monographs will determine certain points, will specify the political nature of a district. But will they completely upset the picture that Sébastien Charléty drew some forty years ago in his history of the Restoration?[20] Our sources, poor as they are, scarcely

[20] *La Restauration* (Paris, 1921). Tr.

lead us to think so. To recall the outline of that sketch: the area of the White Terror marked off rather well the contours of a region where Ultra-royalism ruled as master, and which coincided with the two Midis, Southeast and Southwest. Marseille, Aix, Avignon, Arles were royalist cities and in the departments of Hautes Alpes and Basses Alpes the party benefited from clerical influence. The alliance of these two forces reappeared on the other side of the Rhône. At Nîmes and Uzès, political antagonisms were superimposed exactly along the traditional frontiers of religious discord. The Wars of Religion were not yet over. Bordeaux drew some glory from having been the first large French city to open its gates to the princes. The Duke d'Angoulême entered it even before the Emperor's first abdication (March 12, 1814). The royalist party there included, in addition to the nobility, some merchants who counted on the return of peace to enable them to resume their fruitful trade (there was a similar phenomenon at Marseille; the port cities leaned toward royalism, perhaps because they had suffered more from the blockade), some winegrowers who for centuries had had business relations with England, and some artisans. From Montpellier to Bordeaux, the whole country, cities and countryside, constituted a region of ardent loyalty. It was at Toulouse that, after the Hundred Days, the Duke d'Angoulême formed a kind of semi-autonomous government. The Ultras placed great hopes in it to foil the Parisian intrigues that imprisoned the king. Volunteers flooded in, those *Verdets* whose very name[21] proclaimed that their loyalty was addressed more to Monsieur than to his brother. It was an ephemeral affair because the Duke d'Angoulême was a submis-

[21] Green (*vert*) was to remain the color of fidelity to the legitimate princes after 1830. Author.

sive prince and obeyed, after a short period of hesitation, the king's order to dissolve this pseudo-government, but it left some regrets behind it. In the 1816 election, the departments of the Midi gave the Ultras a majority. Then in 1827 the Garonne Valley, mainstreet of the party, still voted Right, contrary to the general trend.

There also was the West: Brittany which the Duchess de Berry visited in June 1830, and the Vendée. The latter, however, had lost its royalist primacy to the Midi, for in the Hundred Days the Western departments scarcely budged. Manuel[22] was a Deputy from the Vendée, and the Duchess de Berry in 1832 found only a handful of the faithful there ready to share her adventure.[23] The Southern royalist bastion sent extensions up into the Center: they flowed around the periphery of the *Massif Central* into Aveyron, Lozère, and the Haute Loire, climbed the valley of the Rhône, reached Lyon, encompassed the Beaujolais. Lyon kept its reputation as a city faithful to its princes, but did it not owe this to memories of 1793[24] rather than its sentiments in 1815? On his return from Elba, Napoleon received a triumphal reception there. In 1818 the voters chose some Liberals: Corcelles and Camille Jordan. Elsewhere there were other Ultra-royalist strongholds, here and there some faithful areas: Franche-Comté, parts of Lorraine, but these were no more than islands, squeezed in and besieged by Jacobinism or Liberalism. Ultra-royalism was rather diluted in the vast areas where the majority escaped it. This was pagan ter-

[22] A Liberal eventually expelled from the Chamber. Tr.

[23] She vainly attempted to rouse the West to overthrow the July Monarchy. Tr.

[24] In 1793 Lyon rebelled unsuccessfully against the Convention in Paris and was ruthlessly punished. Tr.

ritory. The faithful areas, namely the West, Aquitaine, Languedoc, Provence, Lyonnais, Franche-Comté, appear then as a large arc on the nation's periphery.

IV. The Divisions within the Opposition

Along with social and regional peculiarities, a third factor of diversity brought differences into the apparently solid bloc of Ultra-royalists: the variety of temperaments. Inside the party in a tumultuous collaboration there sat together theoreticians and men of action, irreconcilables and compromisers, extremists and moderates, Gallicans and Ultramontaines. As much as by differences of dispositions, they were separated by diverging views on methods, a different understanding of the chances of the party and of the possibilities of success. Events were going to reveal these discords and sometimes accentuate them to a break. The brusque alternation, during the Restoration, of periods in power with those in opposition emphasized these disagreements. Forming their party among the Rightist opposition, the Ultras held power on two occasions, first with the Villèle cabinet, from December 16, 1821 to January 3, 1828, second with the Polignac ministry from August 8, 1829, to the fall of the Bourbons, or seven years out of fifteen, split by an interval of nineteen months (the Martignac ministry) and preceded by six years of expectation. General histories, fully occupied with the struggles between the Ultras and their adversaries, don't always have the leisure to pause over the episodes of their internal relations. Yet these have at least an equal interest, for we can watch the gradual development of points of view, and thereby the formation of the interpretations of Ultra-royalism which were to survive the circumstances of their appearance, survive the regime and the Ultra party, interpretations whose extensions have been inscribed ever since in the history of the Right.

The sudden dissolution of the Incomparable Chamber quickly brought about some rather divers consequences. The decree of September 5, 1816, first brought consternation to the ranks of the Ultras, whose hopes it prostrated. Powerful with an absolute majority in a Chamber whose normal duration was to extend to 1820, they felt themselves assured of the morrow, masters of the future. The King shared neither their ideas nor their feelings but he was growing old and Monsieur was their leader. The next reign would be an Ultra reign, where the concurrence of the monarch, ministers, and Chambers would establish a true Restoration. But in the stead of these comforting perspectives, now suddenly everything was called into question. We can imagine their bitter astonishment. The nostalgic memory of this period when they thought they were approaching success was never to leave them.

Moreover, from year to year their situation became more precarious. The general election of October 4, 1816, sent only a minority of them to the Palais-Bourbon. Their party was reduced to an opposition that became slimmer with each partial renewal of the Chamber. In October 1818, none of those whose terms expired was re-elected, in 1819 of 54 seats in contention only 4 went to the Ultras. The day did not seem distant when their parliamentary representation would consist of a handful, powerless to make themselves heard. The government spared them neither from its rigor nor from humiliations. Chateaubriand lost his title of Minister of State; *On Monarchy according to the Charter* was seized like the pamphlet of a vulgar libeler. The nomination of the liberal university professor Villemain to head the censorship portended a difficult future for their press and publications. Why shouldn't they be angry at seeing renegades and men without spirit prevail over those faithful to the monarchy?

For an entire year the Ultras had based their program on the dictum of Fiévée, who defined monarchy as "the alliance of royalty and liberties." Were these liberal views going to survive the sudden change in their situation and the reversal of the parliamentary majority? This depended on personalities. The liberal evolution of some was accentuated and their sympathies eventually developed into a system, others threw themselves body and soul into intrigue.

At first illegal action seemed to be the more significant. Quite naturally it took the front of the stage. Blunt and simple characters, plungers, those also who found in the memory of their militant opposition to the usurper the two-fold attraction of youth and adventure, wantonly and vigorously intrigued, plotted and conspired. Then there followed a series of affairs, some complete fabrications, others greatly inflated, all of them bearing the marks of turbulent spirits who tended to confuse politics with intrigue and were incapable of disciplining themselves to the rules of the parliamentary game: the Grenoble affair, the Lyon conspiracy,[25] the "riverbank" plot.[26] Different places, different methods, but with the same idea. At Grenoble in 1819, in order to defeat a min-

[25] This was an attempt by royalists in Lyon secretly to stir up a popular revolution so they could point to the danger France was in from that quarter. Tr.

[26] The riverbank (*bord de l'eau*) plot was simply a discussion among some officers to kidnap Louis XVIII and force him either to abdicate in favor of his brother or change the ministry. Tr.

isterial candidate, the Ultras gave their votes—eighty-eight of two hundred twenty—to the former Constitutional bishop Grégoire despite the horror inspired by his name. Again and again it was that same policy of the worst with its erroneous calculation that out of an excess of evil the good of the country would emerge. The results scarcely proved these bold predictions: the conclusions of an inquiry on the troubles in Lyon, the uncovering of the "riverbank" plot, the affair of the secret note sent to the Allied powers[27] cost Monsieur his command of the National Guard and cost the party the most effective apparatus of its "occult government."

Other men, more prudent, did not wait for the failure of clandestine action to utilize less risky methods. Demanding for themselves the advantages of freedom of the press, they appealed to public opinion and wagered on it to regain power. By trying to regain the majority through the normal exercise of the freedoms of opinion and expression, they implicitly rendered homage to parliamentary institutions. To those veterans of the royalist press, the *Gazette de France, Quotidienne,* and *Journal Royal,* all of which went back at least to the first Restoration, were added the *Conservateur* whose first issue carried the date of October 3, 1818, and the *Drapeau Blanc,* which appeared in January 1819. In the provinces the newspapers had only limited funds and ordinarily restricted themselves to echoing those of Paris. However, two of them stood above the rest by the quality of their

[27] Vitrolles sent a secret note to the Allied sovereigns, denouncing the growing liberal spirit in France and imploring them not to evacuate French territory but to stand ready to crush the Revolution. When Decazes discovered and published the note the Ultras were not helped. Tr.

content, the *Gazette Universelle* at Lyon, with its un-compromising expression of ultra-Catholicism, and the *Echo du Midi* at Toulouse.

The most brilliant of all certainly was the *Conservateur*. It originated as a reply to the *Minerve*, a liberal journal which appeared at the beginning of 1818. It was important to correct the legend which asserted that the Ultra party was one of ignorance and anti-intellectualism. This was the first attempt to make the Right the "party of intelligence." Chateaubriand played a decisive role in the origin of the enterprise and gathered a team with great prestige, including all the great names of the party: Bonald, Villèle, Martainville, and the young priest de La Mennais, who the day before had been still unknown and on whom his *Essay on Indifference* (1817) suddenly focused a new-found glory. The attempt was interesting from several aspects. It was the first time that some great names became professional publicists and Chateaubriand's later *Mémories d'Outre-Tombe* reflect the legitimate pride of the enterprise's instigator. But the *Conservateur*'s originality was not lessened by its political line. It made the Charter the basis of its fight against the government which it denounced day after day for its arbitrariness and arrogation of power. Was this is a true conversion or a tactical position taken only to embarrass the ministry? The amount of sincerity doubtless varied with the individual. Nevertheless, the enterprise was an obvious success. Three thousand five hundred copies of the first number were printed; a few months later the circulation reached 8500, exceptionally high at a time when the total newspaper circulation did not exceed 50,000. Vitrolles even insisted that the circulation climbed to 25,000 but presented no proof that this figure was not inflated. For a year and a half the *Conservateur* waged a merciless war on the government. It passed out of the picture in March 1820 when Chateaubriand, faithful to the principle of freedom of the press, preferred to cease publication rather than submit articles to the censor without whose approval newspapers could no longer appear.

Such differences of method and temperament were closely repeated on the parliamentary level. In the last months of the year 1819, faced with the Left's alarming gains, two views developed which led to disagreement after the election of November 19, 1819. One side, including those who at Grenoble preferred to vote for Grégoire rather than elect a Constitutionalist, made "all or nothing" their principle and the policy of the worst their method. They opposed any compromise with the ministers in power and anticipated only one solution, the substitution of an Ultra government for the Dessoles-Decazes cabinet. The others, more conciliatory or more realistic, either because of simple opportunism or because of a more lucid appreciation of the political situation, suggested the imprudence of continuing a single-minded opposition, and accepted Decazes' advances rather kindly. In December 1819, Villèle saved the ministry by having his friends vote in favor of six months of provisional appropriations. The failure of this bill would have required Decazes to resign.

With Louvel's crime and Decazes' resignation (February 1820), a new chapter opened in which problems took on different shapes and which by steps was going to bring the Ultras to power. The situation allowed them to impose their conditions on a government which depended on them and sought on its right an indispensable parliamentary suppport. Villèle hoped his political friends would decide to support the new ministry: the Ultras' place was no longer in opposition, the future of the party was to become a governmental party. But if five years of parliamentary practice revealed an informed political sense in this man who was made for power, the prolonged sojourn in opposition did not have the same effect on all his colleagues. Their intransigence remained as pure as on the first day. They had relinquished none of the demands of the Incomparable Chamber and did not expect to indulge in half-measures. It is never easy for a group sworn to combat to repudiate its original character. A situation which seemed to bear out the gloomy predictions of the most pessimistic confirmed the intransigence of the theorists and sharpened the appetite of the greedy.

The Ultras' accession to power was in two steps. Until the end of the year 1820 their attitude toward the Richelieu ministry was that which present-day parliamentary language would call support without participation. Just after the election of December 1820 in which they won 198 of 220 seats,[28] Richelieu, who wanted to strengthen his parliamentary position, offered the heads of the party places in his government. After delicate negotiations for which the author of *Mémoires d'Outre-Tombe* claims the chief credit, Villèle, Corbière, and Laîné entered the government as ministers without portfolio; Chateaubriand got the Embassy in Berlin. This was only a temporary solution. The Ultras were not slow to decide that what had been given to them was far from corresponding

[28] In addition to a fifth of the Deputies normally required to run for election, the law of the Double Vote (June 1820) created 172 new seats. Author.

to their importance. Their support became conditional. Part of them, "the spearhead," even moved into open opposition. Pressed by their friends, the Ultra ministers stopped attending cabinet meetings. Then, after the election of October 1821 further reinforced their predominance in the Chamber of Deputies, they withdrew. Chateaubriand resigned as ambassador. Richelieu, disavowed by the Ultras and betrayed by Monsieur, resigned in December 1821. The way was open for an Ultra government. After waiting seven years the Ultras finally commanded the majority of the Chamber and all the ministerial portfolios. Two years later the 1824 election gave them another Incomparable Chamber. In this "Comparable Chamber" 413 of the 430 Deputies claimed kinship with Ultra principles. Finally, the arrival on the throne in the same year of the head of the party promised a peaceful reign in which the sovereign, ministers, and Deputies would think alike on the necessity and methods of restoring in France the customs and institutions of a Christian and monarchical society.

In fact, the attainment of governmental responsibilities was going to divide the party more deeply than its period in opposition because of the difficult transformation it made necessary. Would the men of yesterday's opposition be able to mature into men of government? From the former opposition party, several oppositions were successively to detach themselves.

A first disagreement, whose antecedents already were old, developed between opportunists and theorists, realists and idealists. Villèle represented the first. Several years of parliamentary practice had made his rigidity more tractable and enlarged his political horizon at the same time as they had revealed his real ability in matters of public finance. If it is true that the Ultras were political romantics, Villèle was a very unorthodox Ultra. His tastes leaned more toward debates on technical matters and laws on business than toward measures of principle and symbolic acts. He was more interested in converting the *rentes* than punishing sacrilege. He was not a man who, for the sheer beauty of the gesture, would oppose the evolution of customs or push back the inevitable. Mme. de Boigne declared, "He also believed in the *juste milieu* and had all the extremists of the Ultra party as his active enemies." Villèle was not a free agent. He had to reckon with his majority which pressed him to undertake immediately the complete realization of the restoration program. Since his policy was a permanent compromise between the demands of his friends and the possibilities of the moment, the consequent half-measures never succeeded in satisfying the extremists, whose suspicions were waxing. The dissension even grew into an open conflict with a small group of Ultras who, behind La Bourdonnaye, carried on an extreme Rightist opposition against Villèle.

A second opposition, of quite a different sort, soon crystallized around Chateaubriand. Its origin sprang from personal motives: Villèle and Chateaubriand were certainly poorly equipped to understand or even respect each other; their characters were too different. We may imagine wounded pride, galling jealousies, and shocked vanities. Villèle was surrounded by a handful of ambitious men who demanded positions. He himself acted like a prime minister and insisted upon directing everything himself. Chateaubriand, who had political sense, followed his own personal diplomacy and dreamed up grandiose schemes. At the Congress of Verona (December 1822) he went beyond Villèle's moderate instructions and obtained "his war" in Spain. His receipt of the portfolio of Foreign Affairs established the triumph of his policy. Perhaps he intrigued to become Villèle's successor; secretly he opposed some of his proposals and was not completely innocent of the failure of a government bill to convert the *rentes*. The principle of ministerial solidarity required a punishment for this break. "Chateaubriand has betrayed us," declared Louis XVIII, who signed the dismissal ordinance. Then came the famous scene on Whitsunday, 1824, when the lack of formalities rendered the discharge insulting, "fired like a lackey!" Villèle had made an enemy of a rival in power who would make him pay dearly for the insult he had received. Chateaubriand carried the *Journal des Débats* with him in his "defection" and placed at the service of this new opposition the brilliance of his pen, the authority of his talent, and the prestige of his name.

Such a quarrel over disappointed ambitions, that only the important interests in question and the style of Chateaubriand saved from being a mediocre personal intrigue, would not merit two lines of recollection if it had not had important results for the destiny of Ultra thought. The passage of Chateaubriand into the *counter-opposition* suddenly breathed new life into the ferment of liberal ideas that the Ultras had embraced so fervently at the time of the Incomparable Chamber and in the great days of the *Conservateur*. To tell the truth they had rather forsaken them in recent years. For whoever passes quickly from the fetters of opposition to the satisfactions of power, there is the strong temptation to take advantage of this to bring about a long-desired revenge, and having formerly pleaded, even with eloquence, for the rights of the minority does not always guarantee against the seductions of victory. Perhaps it was the same Ultra who had invoked the rights of the majority against the government, and then those of the minority against the majority, who now advanced this unexpected argument in support of a bill giving the Chamber the power to silence one of its members: "The sovereignty of speech of an individual opposed to the majority which the Chamber recognized as sovereign is a veritable revolt that this sovereign majority must suppress." That such views were not those of an isolated member is clearly proved by the expulsion of the Liberal deputy Manuel at the beginning of the 1823 session.

Against these perjurers, who repeated to each other the phrase, "to be arbitrary is bad, but anarchy is worse," Chateaubriand again took up his campaign for civil liberties, that of the press first of all,[29] often with support from the majority of the Peers. "While the Chamber of Deputies was servile as well as childishly aristocratic, the Chamber of Peers showed itself independent and liberal," (Mme. de Boigne). His fiery polemic restored the old alliance of royalism with a certain "liberalism." He thereby prepared for the advent of a form of monarchism sincerely attached to parliamentary liberties. He also anticipated the subsequent evolution of the Legitimist Right toward the idea of a monarchy resting on the people and renewing, this time with the lower classes and against the ambitious bourgeoisie, the traditional alliance of the Old Regime monarchy with the Third Estate and especially with the bourgeoisie against the insolence of the great lords.

[29] He supported a Friends of Freedom of the Press Society. Author.

To the extremist counter-opposition of a La Bourdonnaye, to the liberal "defection" of a Chateaubriand, in
this picture of the factions which tore apart the Ultra
party and progressively shrank the ministerial majority,
we should add a third dissident group, of Gallican inspiration. It went back to a fundamental tradition of the
Old Regime monarchy, the anti-Ultramontaine tradition
of the king's lawyers,[30] and was to continue beyond the
Restoration to the present. A century later this was the
source of the anticlericalism of the Action Française.

It had more than one point of agreement with the liberal and parliamentary royalism of the *Journal des Débats*: the distaste for arbitrariness, the aversion for the
tyranny of a faction or a sect. This point of view was
unique in that the inobtrusive domination of the regime
by the Church roused some of its most tenacious opponents within the very precincts of the royalist party. The
expression *priestly party* which began to appear at this
time was not the monopoly of the liberals on the *Constitutionnel*. More than one authentic royalist deplored that
the civil power seemed subordinate to the ecclestiastical
authorities. From this feeling of a utilization of the government by the "men in black" was born the famous
myth of the *Congrégation*. Here fable was mixed so
closely with incontestable truth that for a long time the
legend presented an enigma to probing historians and
until the recent labors of Father Bertier de Sauvigny[31]
some despaired of deciphering the secret. For a century,
in fact, two completely contradictory explanations confronted each other. The liberal thesis denounced the exis-

[30] See p. 28. Tr.
[31] G. Bertier de Sauvigny, *Le Comte Ferdinand de Bertier et
l'Enigme de la Congrégation* (Paris, 1948). Author.

tence and all-powerful influence of a mysterious secret
society, known as the *Congrégation*, a sort of Catholic
and royalist freemasonry, a veritable state within a state
controlling the administration, causing prefects, generals,
and the king's ministers to tremble. The great novelists,
Stendhal (*The Red and the Black*) and Balzac (*The
Priest of Tours*) did not disdain to draw from this occult
government some ideas for their stories. The Catholic or
royalist historians[32] said it was a pure legend overflowing from the too-fertile imaginations of the liberals. What
was called the *Congrégation* was only a pious and in-
offensive association in piety whose membership was
never more than several hundred. Father Bertier de
Sauvigny found a way to reconcile these divergences. His
explanation indeed seems to present the key to the
enigma. The *Congrégation*, properly speaking, was quite
innocent of the crimes imputed to it, but another secret
society, the *Chevaliers de la Foi,* existed partly in its
shadow and did indeed try to place at the service of the
Church and the monarchy the powers of secrecy and organization. As its recruitment in many cases was in common with that of the *Congrégation,* it is easy to see how
the two societies were confused with each other.

Although its contemporaries did not know its exact
nature, they suspected the existence of a fearful and
powerful Catholic freemasonry, which wrongly or rightly
they likened to "Jesuitism," and whose enemies were not
only on the Left. The ever-increasing pretentions of the
Church and the government's docility in the face of clerical demands soon awakened Gallican susceptibilities.
Survivors of the old Parlements, heirs of their spirit or

[32] Geoffroy de Grandmaison, *La Congrégation (1801-1830)* (Paris,
1889). Author.

their functions such as judges and the Royal Courts, and the Peers as well, who considered themselves in some respects as guardians of the fundamental laws, all wished to protect the kingdom from the enterprises of the priestly party. This political and monarchical opposition was paralleled by a religious and Catholic opposition, even within the Church. There were many among the clergy who, nurtured on a certain intellectual tradition of the Church of France, often close to Jansenism, grew alarmed at the intrusion of Ultramontaine orders and deplored the changes that this new aspect of Catholicism brought to traditional piety as well as to religious discipline. Because of its position in the Church, this opposition acted with the greatest discretion. Members of Parliament and aristocrats were not obliged to be so cautious.

As early as 1824, Dumesnil warned against the clerical danger; but the most resounding denunciation came from Montlosier, a unique old Auvergnat gentleman whose seventy years had not weakened his fighting spirit. But don't imagine here some stubborn and narrow-minded fanatic. During the emigration he had courageously defended middle-of-the-road ideas against those who were then dreaming of an impossible restoration of absolute monarchy, and he had drawn down a rebuke from the Count d'Artois for writing that, "Revolutionary France will indeed become a monarchy again but only by saving part of the institutions and forms of the Revolution." His horror of despotism inspired his two letters to the *Drapeau Blanc* (July–August 1825), and then the famous *Memorandum to be Consulted on a Religious and Political System Tending to Overthrow Religion, Society and the Throne* (eight printings in the year 1826), and finally a *Denunciation addressed to the Royal Courts*. The majority of the Peers agreed with him (117 votes against 73) and sent his indictment to the government for an investigation.[33] The government's embarrassment was exceeded only by that of the Church. In the Chamber Mgr. Frayssinous offered an inept defense with imprudent admissions which the Liberals exploited. We should point out that at the same moment the most single-minded doctrinaries of Ultramontanism, dissatisfied with the policy of half-measures followed by the government, moved in the opposite direction. La Mennais, one of these, at this time published *Religion and its Relations with the Political and Civil Order* (1826) which showed his detachment from the regime and which was a step toward the idea of a separation between Church and State.

Thus three distinct views, each corresponding to a differing shade of thought, breached the party's unity and split up Villèle's majority. The story of how these dissensions first brought the fall of the ministry and then the doom of the regime belongs to general history. The November 1827 election which followed the dissolution of the Comparable Chamber brought about the defeat of Villèle's ministry and confirmed the fate of the single lasting (six years) experience of Ultra government. The Polignac ministry of August 8, 1829, cannot be considered as such. No doubt it included men whose career attached them to the most intransigent Ultra-royalism (La Bourdonnaye, the fire-eater of 1815 and the incitor of the Rightist counter-opposition, Polignac who in 1814

---

[33] On his death in 1838 the Bishop of Clermont refused his body the last rites of the Church. Author.

refused to swear an oath to the Charter) but they could not agree on any program and the eleven months this government was in power were empty of action. In November 1827, the voters re-elected only 130 supporters of the ministry but a close examination of the results shows that the government succumbed more to the party's divisions than to the blows of the Liberals. The Rightist opposition itself won seventy seats.

The Ultra party came out of these six years in power profoundly divided. This disunion was to outlive the circumstances which produced or aggravated it, as the party itself would survive the loss of power, the downfall of the dynasty, and the collapse of the regime. As men passed on and as time healed wounds, grudges waned and personal resentments were appeased, but points of view and divisions of opinion remained. Periodically, the antagonism between a Gallican royalism and an Ultramontaine royalism, between an Ultracism with liberal tendencies and a fighting Ultracism, unyielding and absolute, was to reappear.

The fifteen years of the Restoration were only a first chapter in the history of the Ultra Right. Henceforth there existed a congeries of views strongly rooted in French political life. The course of events usually kept it burning low but from time to time, the sudden upheaval of the normal conditions of political life, the collapse of a regime, or a national disaster would bring it into full illumination—witness 1871 and 1940. Seen in this perspective, the history of the Ultras takes on its true significance. It was not an unsuccessful episode in an abortive reaction, it was the birth of a Right.

2

1830-1848: Legitimism, Old Regime France and New France

I. From Ultracism to Legitimism

The period of the July Monarchy brought a prompt demonstration of the permanence of the Ultra Right through the vicissitudes of political history. If it had only been an ephemeral combination, without roots in public opinion, the July Monarchy would have swept away everything but its memory. The 1830 Revolution came exactly fifteen years after the Second Restoration whose undertakings it rejected, and it ruined the hopes of the Ultra party, condemning it to a legal death, for the Revolution deprived it of its *raison d' être*. How could one be more royalist than the king with the king in flight or exile and the Bourbons dethroned? Suddenly all the quarrels over which political line to follow were meaningless, since the very principles of dynastic legitimacy and hereditary succession in a direct line were ridiculed by the usurpation of the cadet branch of the royal house. In fact, the official existence of the Ultra party ended with the refusal of a minority of the members of parliament to ratify the transfer of the crown and to approve the revised Charter. Its last public act was the noble oration in which Chateaubriand stated the reasons for his fidelity to Henry V (August 7, 1830). At this point the Ultra faction disappeared. It dissolved into the broader stream which reconciled all nuances of the royalism that remained faithful to the fallen princes. The defeat had the virtue of appeasing controversies, for a while at least. With Charles X's fall, silence descended on the quarrels. Martignac was the living symbol of the reconciliation of differences as he spent a part of what little remained of his life pleading the cause of his maladroit and unlucky successor, Jules de Polignac, in the case brought by the new regime against the last cabinet of the legitimate monarchy. Ultracism gave way to Legitimism.

But they resembled each other in several ways and the extent of their similarities suggests that Ultracism perpetuated itself under the flag and colors of legitimacy. The same names reappeared. Unquestionably the cause of the legitimate princes rallied families and groups which always had obstinately refused to adopt Ultra intransigence. The case of Martignac was not unique; others confirmed it. Still, the line which henceforth separated Legitimists from Orleanists coincided in a general way with that which, in the preceding regime, had divided Ultras from Constitutionalists. It is vain to search for former Doctrinaires who did not rally to the July Monarchy, just as one can find few Ultras who moved into the Orleanist camp. The Ultras formed the nucleus of a new Carlism[1] and furnished its cadres. It more or less borrowed its doctrine from the Ultra Right. A political tradition strongly established and deeply rooted in opinion as was the counter-revolutionary tradition was scarcely at the mercy of the vicissitudes of history. It did not suddenly vanish because the regime on which it leaned had just collapsed. Ultra-royalism was a way of thinking, a system, almost a theology, and there is nothing that resists the contradictions of experience or the inroads of time more strongly. Far from shaking its dogmatic certainty, the failure, segregation, and retreat into the opposition were to strengthen its intransigence and idealism. The Ultras were even confirmed in their faith by the misfortunes of their princes: was not fidelity the keystone of their whole system? Fidelity was the practical expression of the Legitimist principle. To the Ultras it was at the same time a traditional way of thinking, an obligation of conscience, and an act of faith, the basis of their convictions and the very marrow of their life. Where better to demonstrate this fidelity than in adversity? Legitimism was, first of all, the party of fidelity. Powerful bonds stretched across the accident of 1830 to unite the Legitimists of the moment to the Ultras of yesterday: a common way of thinking, a harmony of feelings demonstrated by the continuity of a tradition whose guardians sometimes forgot its origins but continued to think and feel "Ultra." Deprived of the means to carry out its policy, Ultra-royalism kept its motives and aims intact. The faithful were to see their army thin as time

---

[1] Carlist was the pejorative term used by enemies, while the name Legitimist was that adopted by those faithful to the senior branch of the royal house after the accession of the cadet branch. Author.

passed and age and death cut holes in it, but the body of
their doctrine survived without losing its brilliance.

The vitality of this tradition under the July Monarchy
raises a certain problem. We have seen how, during the
Restoration, this faction had the power to dispute successfully the possession of power. It would seem that,
enlarged with new elements, it should have been a source
of continuing preoccupations for the regime as a result of
its defeat and eviction. But the story of its intrigues and
plots is quite a minor one in the history of the July Monarchy. Ordinarily we move rather quickly over this chapter in which it is customary to see only bungling agitation and whose interest seems to be purely anecdotal.
Perhaps we are duped in this by the historian's mirage
which retrospectively judges the importance of events by
the volume of their consequences and grants to them an
attention strictly proportional to the size of these developments. Because the Carlist conspiracies did not overthrow the regime and since we know that it did give way
to the Republic, are we not inclined to overestimate the
importance of the Republican party and underestimate
that of the Legitimist opposition? Perhaps those in control of the new regime did not hold the same estimate of
this danger. A regime is naturally more suspicious of the
one that it has just overthrown than of the proponents of
a regime which has not yet appeared and whose hopes it
holds to be chimerical. It is quite possible that at least in
the beginning the Legitimist opposition, numerous, powerful, and earnest, raised unfeigned fears among the
Orleanist leadership. But they were soon allayed; the
Carlist opposition never was a serious danger to the
regime.

How then can we explain why this party never succeeded in shaking the stability of the regime? A party which included in its ranks the elite of society, which had at its command the unreserved support of influential and respected families, and whose faithful had an inherited habit of facing danger when they had not already learned to do so through personal experience in bearing arms. At the same time some thousands of workers or artisans without education, without resources, and without leaders were able on several occasions and at divers places to resist the combined government forces and make the regime tremble. This is an enigma. The explanation of this surprising ineffectiveness is to be found in both the psychology and social composition of the party. The history of the Legitimist opposition is that of a conception quite sure of its truth, but powerless to find means of expression appropriate to its time, and of a social group with dwindling influence, greatly weakened by changing mores, and which, overcome by discouragement, step by step gives up the fight.

II. The Weight of the Past: Old France

More and more, Legitimism turned to the past. Progressively the field of political action became closed to it. In a few weeks after the July Revolution, all those faithful to the fallen princes were removed from their positions and the places from which they would have been able to play a role and especially maintain contact with political life. As a matter of honor and so as not to acknowledge the *fait accompli*, 52 Deputies resigned, a courageous gesture whose nobility seemed quite natural to them, for disinterestedness was in their family tradition. This only anticipated the steps the new regime was

preparing to take against them. The mandates of 68
Deputies were invalidated and 75 Peers were expelled
including all those named by Charles X. Immediately
then, the party lost its parliamentary representation.
Build it up again? Indeed, they could try by appealing to
the voters against the result of 1830, and some of them
did this, but in general they were paralyzed by the loyalty oath requirement demanded of all candidates. This
scruple is significant; for them it was a matter of conscience and honor, while those who took the oath saw in
it merely a matter of political opportunity. Taking the
oath would appear to be perjury to the Legitimists. Their
fidelity imposed political abstention upon them. The feelings which required their resignations in the first weeks
of the regime now forbade them to return to political life.
Only a few, such as Berryer, who, because he was not a
noble perhaps felt less need for consistency, worked to
rebuild a parliamentary group.

It was not only in parliament that abstention was the
rule: the movement was contagious and those who did
not join it drew down upon their heads the reproach of
their friends. It gradually spread through all branches of
the public service. It was not only the new government's
dismissals of the principal administrative officials—76
prefects, 196 sub-prefects, almost 400 mayors, 65 generals—but, in a few weeks, hundreds of officers, embassy
secretaries, and magistrates resigned their careers and
salaries, and sometimes the loss was important, for
dynastic fidelity. Their defection opened great holes in
the rather small bureaucracy of that day although they
were quickly filled as place-seekers were not lacking. The
most devoted, most compromised, or most inclined to
despair of the future crossed the frontier and shared the

exile of the princes; these were not the most numerous. The rest remained in France awaiting the king's return. But they took the road to the provinces, retiring to their estates and shutting themselves up in their rural residences. They tried to isolate the Orleanists, they held themselves aloof from the prefects' receptions, snubbed the servants of the regime, and organized a matrimonial blockade which would deprive of alliances and dowries all those implicated in the usurpation, from the Orleans princes to the lowliest functionary of the July Monarchy.

These men expected in this way to weaken the regime and prepare its downfall; but abstention, which in their case perhaps corresponded less to a tactic than to a natural inclination of their characters, was a two-edged sword. This internal emigration doubtless brought them a renewed influence among their peasants (and significant progress to French agriculture, for these men who understood the soil and loved to work it also knew their own economic interest and counted on their rents to compensate for the loss of salaries). But also, in town, at the Court, they lost some of their influence and they relinquished a part of their authority. Above all, in expecting to isolate the regime they actually isolated themselves from public affairs. Their point of view poorly prepared them to understand their era. Withdrawn to their lands, separated from Paris and linked to it only by the *Gazette de France* or *La Quotidienne* which sent back to them a reflection of their own prejudices, they were scarcely fearsome. Their political experience, already brief, grew still poorer; we remember in *Lucien Leuwen*[2] the amusing portrait of those officers who

[2] An uncompleted novel by Stendhal. Tr.

turned in their commissions and who died of boredom
after they lost the great, priceless obligation of maintaining the color of the piping on their uniforms or on the
regimental mace. The little that they understood of politics (it may be summed up as an unhealthy fear of a new
'93 and a nostalgia for the Old Regime), made up, along
with horses and the price of oats, all their conversation.
Of course, we should not take Stendhal's suggested picture of provincial *Henricinquism* literally;[3] he sometimes
drew caricatures, but he never hid the deep integrity and
dignity of these characters. He caught the resemblance
almost too well for the picture not to be faithful to the
model. Besides, his description of Legitimist circles in
Nancy was not so far from the Ultra-royalist society
depicted ten or twenty years earlier.

In fact, Legitimism was too close to this society not to
resemble it, in its virtues as well as its absurdities. Marvelously ignorant of the century in which it lived, incuri-
ous about movements of ideas, infatuated with the nobility's prejudices as well as its highest traditions, it
penitently performed the rituals of worldly politeness,
religiously observed all the rites and jealously preserved
the secrets of fashionable speech and of society life. It
poked fun at the ignorance of correct usage and of what is
proper displayed by the new men in power with the
nuance of scorn we reserve for barbarians, hicks, or foreigners, without seeing that perhaps this was less ignorance of usages than the observance of different ones.
Often, too often for the success of the cause that this
aristocracy passionately embraced, it was a difference of
customs or inequality of conditions which delineated the
frontier between the parties. Legitimist society still

[3] Henry V-ism. Tr.

counted on ridicule to kill the regime it laughed at. It did not realize that ridicule was about to change sides and was to catch up with the outdated customs of a society which gradually ceased to be in harmony with its century.

The Legitimists were in the position of becoming internal émigrés in the middle of their country and their century. Moreover, they already had those afflictions of émigrés, the lost feeling, the sudden bursts of enthusiasm followed by spells of depression, the weary and quarrelsome moods. Controversies which the catastrophe of 1830 had suspended for a time soon reappeared. Polemics over the causes and those responsible for the dis-- aster raised tempers. Everyone took up the old arguments again. Those at the top set the example. Charles X held a grudge against Chateaubriand for having, like a "useless Cassandra," predicted the misfortunes which came. Those who err don't pardon others for having been right. Chateaubriand continued to call the Duke de Blacas[4] unlucky. Factions revived, for others are always more intransigent than oneself. The princes decided to consider the Rambouillet abdications in favor of the young Duke de Bordeaux as invalid.[5] At the death of Charles X at Goritz on November 4, 1836, his elder son, the Duke d'Angoulême, took the name of Louis XIX and his wife was saluted as Queen by the small exile court. Until 1844, when his uncle died, the young Duke de Bordeaux was simply called Monseigneur. In France, how-

---

[4] A leading Ultra and tutor of the young Henry V. Tr.

[5] On August 2, 1830, at Rambouillet, Charles X abdicated and his son, the Duke d'Angoulême, renounced his rights to the throne. Charles' ten year old grandson, the Duke de Bordeaux, thereby inherited the throne and was proclaimed Henry V by the faithful. Tr.

ever, the opposite situation prevailed. Except for a handful of the faithful and the newspaper *La France,* organ of
this supposed royalty, the royalists, the party, and opinion generally recognized only the Duke de Bordeaux[6] as
Henry V. The disagreements between Charles X and the
Duchess de Berry, along with the pretensions of the
Duke d'Angoulême brought divisions into the party and
aggravated the misunderstanding which separated the
Bourbons from the national sentiment. When the young
Duke de Bordeaux came of age, on September 29, 1833,
and a Legitimist delegation went to Prague with presents
for him, Charles X received it rather coldly.

Neither the princes nor their partisans could clearly
distinguish between dream and reality anymore. Instead
of acting they plotted. When they thought they were
analyzing events they really were putting novels together. They believed they were making the future when
they dreamed of the past. These were the sincere but
powerless royalists that Chateaubriand described as "full
of fine qualities . . . always believing that they were re-
establishing legitimacy by wearing a tie or flowers of a
certain color." By turns their opposition took on all the
sentimental or romantic forms that were suggested by
the inventiveness of their fidelity, often touching, sometimes ridiculous, but always sincere. They wore the
colors of the fallen line. They piously commemorated the
annals of the monarchy, the sometimes happy and sometimes sad anniversaries of the royal family: January 21,[7]
February 14 (assassination of the Duke de Berry), birth-
days of young Henry V (September 29), of his sister, of

---

[6] Not until 1843, when he went to London in his first gesture as the
pretender, did he take the title of Count de Chambord. Author.

[7] Execution of Louis XVI. Tr.

St. Charles, St. Louis, St. Henry. In the person of Henry V everything coincided to affect a sensibility which grew with the cult of misfortune: his youth, the circumstances of his birth, his exile, and his present adversities. For some avid readers of Walter Scott (and if the Legitimists were not great readers, they at least read the novels of the bard of legitimacy), the sojourn of the royal family at Holyrood completed the identification of the Bourbons with the Stuarts,[8] of confusing history and fiction. Engravings everywhere popularized the picture of the *Young Scotsman.*

Many Legitimists never escaped from this dangerous confusion of species. Almost all their schemes bore evidence of poor preparation or of the most fantastic imagination. The Prouvaires Street Plot[9] is an example and even the escapade of the Duchess de Berry, although better prepared than commonly believed, cannot fully escape these criticisms. Rarely did the Legitimists analyze their chances, coldly calculate the strength of forces,

[8] Family ties associated the memory of the Stuarts with the Bourbon cause: more than one old Jacobite family, in exile in France since 1688, was represented among those faithful to the elder branch. An ancestor of Vicomte Walsh, director of *La Mode,* equipped the ship of the pretender Charles Edward. From the same origin came the manager of the newspaper *L'Union,* Lieutenant-Colonel MacSheeby, who resigned his command in 1830. Isolated in their own country, the Legitimists often found themselves closest to foreigners, with whom a common belief in legitimacy united them: the Carlists eagerly welcomed the remnants of Don Carlos' armies in France (1839-1840). Others went to fight in Portugal for Dom Miguel: young Henry de Rochejaquelein met death at Lisbon. These relationships thus suggest a kind of internationale of legitimacy. Author.

[9] A Legitimist conspiracy in 1832 to stage a coup d'état by seizing the royal family during a ball at the Louvre. The leaders were arrested after enjoying a dinner in a restaurant on the rue des Prouvaires. Tr.

and begin an action which was fully thought through. Their activity, oscillating between sullen abstention and blundering agitation, displayed all the faults of Ultraroyalism, increased by the misfortunes of a new emigration.

III. The Promise of the Future? Young France

This picture presents only one aspect of Legitimacy, and the most somber one: that which drew it toward the past. The other side of the coin offers a striking contrast to it. In contrast to a society slowly drifting into oblivion and diehards who sought a refuge in abstention and fed on chimeras, it also presented men who renounced nothing, who lucidly enumerated the chances that the future still offered to Legitimacy, and who, at the price of a renovation, proposed to reconcile it with contemporary society.

They were convinced that Legitimacy had not said its last word. The elder branch of royalism still could count on great resources; it retained imposing reserves in the country. Entire regions, especially in the West and South, kept their fidelity to the Legitimate princes. The Gard was estimated as two-thirds Carlist. If Marseille's abstention frustrated the projects of the Duchess de Berry and if the plan for the Vendean insurrection led to the well-known fiasco of 1832, this double failure simply taught that it was a mistake to expect a provincial uprising to re-establish the king on his throne.[10]

[10] The failure of the attempt owed much to divisions within the party. The Paris Legitimist Committee formally disapproved the Duchess' project. May 24 was the date set for taking up arms. It was expected that this would catch the troops on both sides of the

Moreover, a menacing unknown hung over the fidelity of these regions: the attitude of the Church. The map of the Carlist regions generally coincided with that of the dioceses where the clergy's influence was not yet attacked too seriously by the new ideas. This agreement was the strength of Legitimacy. It could be precarious too. If the bishops rallied to the new regime, the princes risked seeing the integrity of their domains breached. But, just after the Revolution of 1830, the most compromised prelates such as Mgr. Forbin-Janson, Bishop of Nancy, put the border between themselves and their dioceses, and the chief concern of the others, corresponding to the wish of the Holy See, was to live on good terms with those in power. For one Mgr. de Quélen, Archbishop of Paris, who remained obstinately faithful to the exiled princes, how many bishops were there who henceforth intended to busy themselves only with the religious life of their dioceses! Therefore it was important to renew and enlarge the bases of Legitimacy. To appear as the party of fidelity to the past was no longer a sufficient *raison d'être*, it had to present new reasons for hope.

At this time the party had a double advantage. First, it had as leaders a certain number of well-balanced men, with wide experience, too informed to confuse the requirements of action with the fancies of imagination. They tried to keep the party out of adventures which only led up blind alleys. We alluded earlier to the respectful but very formal disapproval that Berryer, Cha-

---

Loire napping. But Berryer extracted a counter-order from Marshal de Bourmont. The uprising was then postponed to June 4. In the interval, seizure of papers and leaks alerted the authorities. Failure to synchronize the uprisings ended by ruining the slight chances of a badly begun affair. Despite much valor and even some heroic exploits such as the seige of Pénissière, the insurgents were easily overwhelmed. Author.

teaubriand, and the leading figures of the Carlist committee of Paris had expressed for the Duchess de Berry's
enterprise. Left under their influence alone, the party
doubtless would have lacked boldness. In private several
of them let it be understood that they held no illusions
about the chances of a third Restoration. But the enthusiastic support of a group of young men, full of fire and
often of talent, teamed rather happily with the slightly
timid skepticism of the older men. An original feature of
the 1830's was the important role which youth played,
and the sometimes considerable part that it took in all
sorts of intellectual movements. Liberal Catholicism,
Saint-Simonianism, and the Republican party were movements of young men which borrowed from their youth
an enthusiastic and contagious fervor. The same was
true of Legitimism.

Since only those parties which accepted the inevitable
had a future, the Legitimists had to come to terms with
modern society and first of all use the methods that it
offered. The Revolution of 1830 had established the freedom of the press and the political power of journalism.
Legitimists therefore had to revive the earlier attempt of
the *Conservateur* in 1818 and become journalists. Between 1830 and 1848, the young Legitimists wrote one of
the most brilliant chapters in the history of the royalist
press. The older generation of newspapers such as the
Gazette de France continued its rather tranquil career.
La Quotidienne was enlivened by young editors who
dreamed of a "monarchical 20th of March,"[11] of a
princely "return from Elba." In 1847 it merged with *La
France* and *L'Echo Francais* to produce a new organ,
L'Union Monarchique, which gave promise of a long

[11] The date of Napoleon I's triumphal return to the Tuileries in
1815 after his exile on Elba. Tr.

future. In addition to these older newspapers, some new-comers quickly found an honorable place: *Le Populaire,* edited by A. Nettement from 1837 to 1839, and especially *La Mode.* The latter, an organ of the fashionable world, had been founded by Emile de Girardin in 1829 as a review of fashions and foreign literature. He had cleverly won the patronage of the Duchess de Berry. After 1830, Alfred du Fougerais proposed to make it a journal of the political opposition. It kept its articles and engravings on fashion to serve as a front, but *La Mode* was henceforth read for its carping political criticism. It carried on a war of epigrams against Louis-Philippe, the royal family, and the servants of the new regime in a tone half-way between society gossip and political satire. It gained immediate success, finding three thousand subscribers despite a high subscription price. By turns Edouard Walsh and Alfred Nettement headed it. In the provinces the party made a comparable effort. Each important city had its Legitimist newspaper whose title often took the old provincial name—*Gazette de Normandie, de Bretagne, d'Anjou, de Languedoc, d'Auvergne*—as a symbol of fidelity to the old regime and a sign of adherence to administrative decentralization. In sum there were a good forty newspapers which kept alive, in the town houses of the nobility as in the provincial salons, the country estates, and the rectories, the flame of attachment to the princes and fed the mockery of the Château.[12]

Resolved to make use of recognized liberties, the Legitimists tried their electoral chances. They ignored the prohibition against taking the oath and several of them entered the Chamber. While some were obscure—Dugabé, Hennequin — others were better known — Falloux, Benoist d'Azy, and in 1842 the Vendée elected

---

[12] A reference to Louis-Philippe and his family. Tr.

the Marquis de Rochejaquelein. Legitimism again found a parliamentary voice, becoming eloquent when Berryer exercised his great talent.

Rejuvenation did not stop with the means of action; from methods it spread to the program. The success of the 1830 Revolution and the Bourbons' unpopularity quickly convinced the most discerning Legitimists that it was vain to insist on the monarchy against public opinion and that they should first reconcile the monarchy with the people. There is an analogy with the newspaper *L'Avenir,* which at the same time proposed to reconcile the Church and the people, God and liberty—the inspiration was identical. Besides, it had precedents even in royalist history: the Incomparable Chamber also tried to establish a parliamentary and popular monarchy. The Legitimists spontaneously picked up the tradition of the Ultras of 1815. In 1830 as in 1815 they needed liberty; they tested its advantages. Without it they could no longer express themselves, nor organize themselves, nor continue to fight. It was the necessary condition of their existence and survival.

One name brought together these two successive attempts at a liberal royalism: Chateaubriand. The author of *Monarchy according to the Charter,* the founder of the *Conservateur,* the writer for the *Journal des Débats* (that of the Restoration) denied his liberal tendencies not at all. Shortly after the Revolutionary days he declared his sympathy for the people of Paris who had acclaimed him as a defender of freedom of the press. If he retained for the old king a veneration accentuated by the latter's age and misfortune, if he extended to the young king— "Madame, your son is my king"[13]—a fidelity whose

[13] The famous concluding line of an address to the Duchess de Berry. Tr.

knightly grandeur so well fitted his character, the historian in him recognized how the natural development of
societies led them toward democracy. He was not one of
those who took alarm at this. He saluted its arrival in
advance and hoped one day to see a union of Legitimacy
and liberty, those two great causes to which he had devoted his political life. Republicanism did not terrify
him; he wished several of its apostles well. He esteemed
Armand Carrel[14] and he extended the same affectionate
admiration to the condemned priest,[15] inspired prophet
of *Words of a Believer,* which had gone to the author of
the *Essay on Indifference.* This mixture of fidelity to the
past and confidence in the future, this deep attachment
to legitimacy associated with a spontaneous sympathy
for the people, already foreshadowed the sentiments of
an Albert de Mun. Chateaubriand's liberal Legitimacy
anticipated, a half-century before the fact, the conservative Republicanism of the *ralliés* of Liberal Action.[16]

These neo-Carlists formulated a rather liberal program
in which a leading element was extension of the suffrage.
Berryer in the Palais Bourbon, Dreux-Brézé in the Lux-
embourg, proposed that all Frenchmen paying real estate
taxes vote in the electoral colleges. This was the old Ultra
program of 1815. Genoude threw his *Gazette de France*
into the campaign for a democratic and popular royalism. Already some social issues were becoming sharp.
The Legitimists quite early became interested in the
labor question, pitying the Lyon workers bombarded by

[14] A liberal journalist and fiery advocate of freedom of the press.
Tr.

[15] Lamennais, whose *Words of a Believer* was condemned by the
Pope in 1834, and who thereupon betook himself to the Republican
political faction. Tr.

[16] See pp. 221-222.

Louis-Philippe,[17] and busily tried to win the workers'
sympathy. From 1831 on, tracts were distributed to the
laboring population in an attempt to win them to Carlism. The party faithful included men from all social
strata. There was a considerable lower class support for
Legitimacy, lavish in its obscure devotion but most often
unrecognized by the Legitimist leaders themselves. The
famous names may have done more harm than good to
Legitimacy; they tended to identify the Legitimist party
with the faubourg Saint-Germain. Here and there Legitimists and Republicans sketched out a rapprochement and
temporary alliances were constructed to defeat an Orleanist candidate. In Marseille, the Republicans voted for
Berryer and at Perpignan Arago owed his re-election to
royalist votes. Several times Legitimists paid the heavy
fines levied on Republican newspapers. Meeting each
other in prison, they were on cordial terms. Collaboration
once went beyond this level and brought about a curious
experiment. To prepare a reconciliation between monarchical Legitimacy and democratic liberty the Abbé de
Genoude, along with Arago, Laffitte, and with the support of Chateaubriand, established a Left-Wing newspaper titled *La Nation*. Individually, several Legitimists
improved upon the democratic evolution of their party
by going bag and baggage over to the Republican opposition. The political travels of a Cormenin[18] are a significant example.

---

[17] The Lyon insurrection of 1834 was brutally suppressed by the
army, using artillery. Tr.

[18] A legist who moved from royalism to Bonapartism under the
First Empire, then to Legitimism under the Restoration, then Re-
publicanism under the July Monarchy, and finally he served under
Napoleon III. Tr.

Even the events and accidents of the royal family seemed to favor this attempt at royalist regeneration. The death in exile at Goritz of the old king who had never understood the new France ended the resentment against him as the rash leader who had been responsible for the July Days. The new pretender was a young man of sixteen who did not have to carry the burden of too heavy a past. His graceful charm added a new elegance to the prestige of centuries. Why couldn't this young prince seal the monarchy's alliance with modern society? Many writers and journalists viewed this eventuality with sympathy. Would Legitimism, long a synonym for the past, become one for the future?

The dawn of this monarchical renaissance was not followed by a high noon. The chronic dissensions of the royalists promptly withered such promise. Far from rallying the party, the program of renovation aggravated its divisions and a veritable schism split the Legitimists. At Lyon two newspapers carried on an unceasing war: the *Gazette du Lyonnais* recognized Louis XIX and represented "Old France," while *Le Réparateur* favored "Young France" and demanded the necessary liberties. After fighting each other for a long time *La Quotidienne* and the *Gazette de France* became reconciled and staged a campaign against Berryer, setting up the Marquis de Rochejaquelein as his rival in the Chamber. This dissension was inevitable for it simply demonstrated the fundamental ambiguity of a political group torn from the first day between total restoration and adaptation, between pure reaction and liberal inclinations. In addition, the hints of renovation fell before the too heavy weight of traditions. History drew Legitimism backward and the generous efforts of its younger partisans were powerless to uproot it from a superannuated society. Decidedly, Legitimism was of the past.

Whatever the fidelity of its disciples, despite the influence and authority of its notables, it is clear that Legitimism was unable to threaten the regime that benefited from its defeat. It had nothing to do with Louis-Philippe's fall in 1848. Although Legitimism was incapable of overthrowing the July Monarchy, it was able to draw something out of its collapse. Its inertia then became a force. In the general confusion and with the Republicans unprepared, royalist society made its appearance with the innate superiority given to it by the stability of its cadres, the experience of its members, and the reputation of its leaders. At each upheaval which was to break the political continuity: 1848, 1871, royalism again would profit from its permanence. Faithful to the legitimate sovereign, it easily survived the accidents of history. Perhaps the only happening capable of hurting it to the roots of its existence would be a dynastic event: the death of the Count de Chambord. The critical date for Ultra royalism in this nineteenth century which was so disastrous for the French monarchy was ultimately neither 1830 nor 1848 nor 1875, but the year when, in an Austrian castle, the man died who throughout his life had symbolized monarchy's grandeur and majesty to thousands of Frenchmen (1883). For all of them the Count de Chambord had truly been the king. With Henry V, the king died. The royalists then faced a new problem: could royalism survive the king? Did the monarchical idea have any *raison d'être*, any reality outside the person of the monarch?

3

1830-1848: Orleanism, Liberalism and Conservation

I. A Center Leaning toward the Right

Although the Revolution of 1830 overthrew the legitimate sovereign and pushed those faithful to him into the opposition, its greatest effect was not on the destiny of Ultra traditionalism. More important was the Rightward gravitation, enacted in a few months, of a political group which since its formation had followed a firm rule and principle to remain halfway between the extremes and had even tried, with more perseverence than success, to reconcile them. This group was to hold power for the next eighteen years and identified itself so closely with the regime that it subsequently bore its name: Orleanism.

At first its relative position placed it on the Right. This was not because it had to face on the Left an anti-dynastic opposition—the Republicans—for at this time the Legitimists on the Right were a symmetrical opposition. By re-establishing the equilibrium, such symmetry put the Orleanists in the geometric center, halfway between the two extremes. They were exactly in the position of the former Doctrinaire group, to which some of the leading personalities of the new regime had belonged. It was a different conflict, of an internal nature, which pushed Orleanism to the Right. After the cordial unanimity of the first few months, the victors of July split over the interpretation of their conquest and the consequences to be drawn from it. Two factions appeared: resistance and movement. As early as November 2, 1830, when Casimir Périer and the Duke de Broglie resigned from the ministry, the breach was opened. But these men were liberals who always had fought Ultra policies. For the first time in their political lives they found themselves in an opposition group which threatened the government from the Right. The dividing line between Left and Right henceforth passed between these men and the ministers whom they fought, between resistance and movement, between the Right-Center and Left-Center. It left them on the Right; they remained there until the end, and the regime with them, for they soon returned to it. Their sojourn in the opposition was brief. After four months, on March 13, 1831, their return to the ministry definitively swept the party of movement from power. As a result of this long cohabitation, Orleanism was to identify itself with the party of resistance to the point of borrowing its color, its spirit, and its program.

Where a group sat in the semicircular Chamber did not necessarily determine whether it belonged to the Right or the Left, for, except for those on the extreme Left, any group was always to the right of another. At the most its position was a presumption, which doctrines, inclination, and orientation were to confirm, deny, or qualify. In this case they confirmed it. The men who entered the ministry in March 1831 and were to guide the destinies of the regime for the next seventeen years followed a resolutely conservative policy. Their best thought was to limit the consequences of 1830, to stabilize its results. Their constant preoccupation was to maintain and conserve. For all the rest, they relied on the natural course of events and labeled anyone who proposed reforms, even partial ones, or suggested a remodeling of society, either as dangerous or visionary.

Others before them had already made respect for the natural order into a political maxim—the Ultras. There was between the Ultras and the Orleanists a difference which time has somewhat diminished but which in 1830 was large enough to open an unbridgeable abyss between them. The Ultras held that the natural course of history was arbitrarily interrupted and reversed in 1789. The Orleanists judged that it was the attempt at restoration which introduced arbitrariness into the course of historical evolution and that 1830 re-established its continuity. Such diverging views on the meaning of the forty previous years forever limited any mingling of the Orleanist Right with the traditionalist extreme Right. This was the great novelty in the political situation created by 1830: that it included two groups on the Right which were going to follow parallel but separate destinies.

II. *The* Juste Milieu

The name of this new political force—Orleanism—may be misleading. It suggests a kind of necessary and natural harmony between it and the dynasty, where there really was only an accidental alliance. It is one of those anomalies of historical terminology that the name Ultra does not at all hint of the attachment to the person of the king, while in Orleanism the dynastic reference seems intentionally to underline an attachment which hardly existed with the reigning branch.

The feelings that Louis-Philippe's person inspired, despite his own elevated conception of the crown and his house, despite the theory of quasi-legitimacy, had nothing in common with the almost religious devotion which surrounded the legitimate king. To be sure, governmental personnel were flattered to be on familiar terms with the sovereign and the bourgeoisie were more than ordinarily proud to be received at the Chateau de Neuilly and invited to balls at the Tuileries, but it was a long way from this sort of satisfaction of vanity to the reflection of God which haloed round the semi-sacred majesty of the legitimate monarch! The recent change of sovereigns was not the only thing at issue; in the eyes of even the most loyal Orleanists the king was no longer the king. If the present sovereign transfered his attributes to someone who discharged the same functions under another title would the change be so great? The relative facility with which a majority of Orleanists converted to the Republic forty years later tells us much. To the Orleanists the person meant less than the regime and the name of the regime less than its institutions. Such a development was unthinkable for a Legitimist. The *Ralliement*[1] became possible, and only at the cost of great soul-searching, for a small minority of Legitimists obedient to a holy authority—the pope and the Church—only ten years after the death without children of the Count

[1] A movement sponsored by Pope Leo XIII in the 1890's to encourage French Catholics to support the Republic. Tr.

de Chambord, who had properly made the Orleans princes his heirs. Monarchical sentiment died with the king. So, while fidelity to the sovereign constituted a valid and nearly sufficient definition of Legitimism, attachment to the Orleans branch did not characterize Orleanism and still less exhausted its program. There was much more than the Orleans family in this new political force.

And yet, Orleanism perhaps owed a heavier debt to the Orleans family than the extent of its gratitude would indicate. The family brought more than its name. With another sovereign than Louis-Philippe on the throne, things certainly would have been different. The former Duke d'Orleans[2] had more than one claim to sponsor the new political tradition. He inherited a family tradition that already suggested Orleanism and its program—his father had impetuously embraced the principles of the Revolution; the young Duke d'Orleans never denied them. He fought at Valmy and Jemappes and this record of bearing the colors of the nation into battle was a valuable argument for him in 1830. After 1815 the well-ordered and calm life of the Duke and his family, the simplicity of their style, the decision to send their sons to school with bourgeois children while tradition required tutors for the princes and for the young Duke de Bordeaux, all this suggested a bias favorable to the times and a desire to mix with contemporary society, the exact opposite of the old-fashioned etiquette and archaic style of the elder branch. In sum, a discreet but deliberate outline of Orleanism before the fact.

However, there was infinitely more in Orleanism after 1830 than the contributions of a family tradition. There

[2] Louis-Philippe's title before attaining the throne. Tr.

was even much more than a regime, or it would not have
survived the fall of the July Monarchy. As Ultracism was
more than the Villèle government, the succession of ministries from 1831 to 1848 offers us only a very shallow
approximation of the nature of Orleanism. Does the
study of its institutions tell us more? Two characteristics
defined it: monarchy and parliamentarism. Neither of
these was unique to the July regime. Even their combination was not new, for already in the Restoration a monarch and a parliament had been associated in the exercise
of power. To be sure, the balance of forces was slightly
modified by the revised Charter but we suspect that
there were more differences between Ultracism and Orleanism than this minor nuance in the adjustment of the
institutional machinery. Describing the constitutional
framework of a regime is not a good method of penetrating to its essential nature. Orleanism was not the July
Monarchy, it was its idea, its interpretation, the notion as
conceived by its theoreticians, the ideal which the regime approached in its happy days, what the July Monarchy tried to be. Orleanism was to the regime as a novel
proposal is to its active realization, which becomes de-
formed and cumbrous through use and age, or as the
justification is to an act which it explains and excuses.

Considered in this wise, Orleanism can be defined as a
certain *monarchical system*. The contemporary existence
of another monarchical tradition suggests that there are
monarchies and there are monarchies, and nothing demonstrates better the originality of the Orleanist idea than
comparing it with Ultra and Legitimist doctrine. To the
religion of Reims, still quite bathed in a reflection of the
divine mystery, 1830 substituted a secular monarchy.
Charles X, God's lieutenant, was the last king for whom

the age-old pomp of the coronation unfurled; Louis-Philippe began a legal and parliamentary type of ceremony. He took the oath to the revised Charter in the presence of the Chambers. To the Lord's Annointed succeeded the chief executive of the nation, to the king of France, legitimate heir of the kingdom by the grace of God and right of birth, a king of the French assigned to the executive authority by virtue of a contract between the candidate for the throne and the Deputies representing the *pays légal*. Here then was the revolution of the *jurists*: one ceremony drove out another, the legal prescription replaced the liturgical rite *et antiquum documentum novo cedat ritui. . . .*[3] From the coronation at Reims to the oath of the Palais Bourbon, only five years elapsed between these two ceremonies, but they separated two worlds. 1825: an age-old tradition expired; 1830: another was born. Two conceptions went parallel to each other but did not mix in the slightest degree. Orleanism first of all was this: a modern and secular image of monarchy.

It was also a *parliamentarism*. The Republican affiliated with a secret society doubtless thought it a peculiar parliamentarism, while the Legitimist saw only monarchy shamed by the travesty of a sacred concept. Parliamentary regimes, like monarchies, admit of several varieties. In the final analysis the nature of Orleanism was determined by the spirit which animated the operation of its parliamentary institutions. It is less easy to find this spirit than that of Ultra-royalism. The doctrine of the Orleanists did not have the beautiful and simple precision of the Ultra system. It seemed to define itself in rather a negative fashion. It can be delineated little by

[3] "And let the old law give way to the new ordinance." (From the *Pange Lingua*, a Latin hymn by St. Thomas Aquinas.) Tr.

little as we show what it opposed. This fact springs from the position of Orleanism between two oppositions. The regime spent its first ten years on the defensive, fighting on two fronts. Its doctrine bore the consequences: Orleanism developed its own ideas less than it repulsed those of others. As Albert Thibaudet said of it, "It did not represent an idea, it was only against ideas."

This was an inconvenient position and one hardly propitious for the elaboration of a system of thought. However, from this rejection of the ideas of the extreme Right and the extreme Left, a rather negative attitude, a positive position gradually emerged at an equal distance from the extremes, as between the hollows of a mold there rises the form that separates them. Forced to explain what they didn't want and to give motives for their refusal, the Orleanists ended by making of this middle position, at first forced upon them by their opponents, their *raison d'être* and their justification. Consequently, the most exact definition of Orleanism, that which is most consistent with its intentions, is the nickname with which its enemies derisively decked it out: the *juste milieu*. A regime of the *juste milieu,* rule by the third force, search for the middle road, truly this was Orleanism. All its program was composed of dicta like these, an ambiguous program which inextricably mixed grandeur and weakness and whose composite nature explains the rather contradictory estimates of the regime which came from its friends and its adversaries. Its partisans took account of its intentions, its detractors chose to see only the pettiness and deceptions of its daily practice.

To hold to the *juste milieu* was a worthwhile national project for a France torn by factions and still bleeding from internal quarrels. It was to proclaim the will to reconcile all Frenchmen. In doing it, the Orleanists were indeed the heirs (and often the same men) of the Doctrinaires of the Restoration, dreaming of uniting the king and the nation around the compromise of the Charter. Some small minded persons made fun of Guizot's magnifying the July regime into the culmination of French history. But after all, it did constitute an acceptable compromise. In any case it was a less adventuresome historical view than the medieval utopias of the Ultras or the chimerical proposals to make a *tabula rasa* of the past. This will to conciliation gave Orleanism its highest justification. It inspired the regime's symbolic gestures: the return of Napoleon's ashes and the dedication of the restored Chateau of Versailles to all the glories of France. The July Monarchy was neither the shameful monarchy denounced by the Legitimists nor a caricature of the best of the republics. It offered itself as a *modus vivendi* appropriate to reforge national unanimity.

Such was the plan and such also was the official version. There was, of course, the other side whose ugliness is revealed to us by satires, pamphlets, and lampoons. We end up better informed about the underside and all the pettiness of the regime than about the large and generous ideas which redeem it. All political regimes face the menace of debasing themselves in a parody of their intentions, but a regime of the *juste milieu* is exposed to this more than any other. Its natural inclination leads it toward an inglorious opportunism. The July Monarchy too often was the reign of self-satisfied and triumphant mediocrity: peaceful compromise turned into surrender, conciliation was transformed into sordid deals. There were some extenuating circumstances for the regime in the conditions of political life of that day: the smallness

of the *pays légal,* a cramped and artificial parliamentary
life, debates where the insignificance of the issue did not
always justify the talent, eloquence, and passions displayed. What cause could make up for the narrowness of
parliamentary activity? The policy of peace and moderation which the regime followed in foreign affairs seemed
the height of banality to a people who had grown up
amid the cult of the Napoleonic epoch, and even more, to
a romantic generation. It neither acquired nor could give
glory. The heroes of July 1830 did not die for it, and the
return of Napoleon's ashes bathed it only in borrowed
glory. Thus its adversaries had an easy time in denouncing this regime as without an ideal, without convictions,
and without grandeur.

Between these two faces of the regime where did the
truth of Orleanism lie? In order to reply we must first
examine two other dimensions of any political system: its
constituency and its ideology.

III. Orleanist Society: the Elites

If any commonplace is well established, it is the axiom
that identifies the July Monarchy with the reign of the
bourgeoisie. The year 1830 rung in the political arrival of
this class. Already possessing of wealth and a monopoly
over education, from this point forth, it held in its hands
all the signs and attributes of power. The myth of a
bourgeois king, symbol and trustee of the domination by
one class, topped off and completed the picture. From
this perspective Orleanism was nothing but the politics
and thought corresponding to the reign of the bourgeoisie: by definition a regime of self-interest and of thought
subordinated to the justification of it. Contrary to those

regimes which emphasize doctrine over all other considerations, it understood and spoke only the language of self-interest. "Reign of the vile bourgeoisie," our modern Saint-Simons would surely say. Those anxious to be logical continue the chain of reasoning with a diagram showing Orleanism, the triumphant expression of bourgeois ambitions, victorious over Ultracism, the bitter demands of a declining nobility.

Is this interpretation as just as it is simple? Clearly, in no wise could the regime have done without the support of the bourgeoisie. If it had not been granted spontaneously, the regime would have had to seek its favor. A majority of the nobility did remain faithful to the elder branch, to the old regime, and pulled out. The clergy, if it in general accepted the change of regimes, renounced the active political role that it had formerly played with such calamitous results. Soon the education issue and the renewal of the struggle against the University's monopoly impaired its relations with the government. The peasants? Could one probe this ignorant mass whose political consciousness was scarcely awakened and which ordinarily followed the discreet or imperious suggestions of the clergy and other social authorities? As for the industrial proletariat, still numerically weak, its sympathies went to the Republic. Thus, despite any preference it may have had, the regime had no choice. As if by elimination, the bourgeoisie was indeed the only element in French society on which a regime which had just pushed the nobility into the opposition might rest.

Now, all evasion aside, it has been demonstrated a hundred times that the July Monarchy did serve the interests of the bourgeoisie. Neither the ministers nor parliament permitted the slightest detraction from the interests of the dominant class. The constant unanimity of the Chambers in preserving the integrity of tariff protection often has been pointed out; the coalition of landed proprietors and manufacturers, iron masters and cotton spinners, nipped in the bud any attempts to relax the rigor of the prohibitionist system. This is only one example of a possible ten. In the course of these eighteen years everything points to and verifies the close agreement, the constant solidarity, what the ill-disposed would call the complicity, of the regime and the bourgeoisie.

The accuracy of the equation, July regime equals bourgeoisie, stands out in a perhaps newer and still more striking fashion when we examine their political ideas. The idea of the State, the definition of its competence and attributes were the typical views of the bourgeois society of the time. We are astonished more than once at the repeated spectacle of majorities, basically supporters of the regime, nonetheless quibbling with Louis-Philippe over the modest increases he requested for his civil list. Generally the frequency and acrimony of these disputes is imputed to the avarice of the sovereign and the meanness of the Deputies. These do not explain everything, however. In particular, they don't take account of the symbolic importance that the Chamber gave to such debates. In contrast to the pomp of the traditional or restored monarchy, in opposition to the despotic State of Napoleon, the French bourgeoisie, whose Deputies faithfully reflected its prejudices and tastes, conjured up the ideal of *cheap government*. This expression occurred regularly in contemporary discussions. It was a prudent precaution to forestall an accumulation of power and governmental despotism, but more than that a transposition of bourgeois practice in the management of personal

affairs to the conduct of public business. They expected
the maxims of thrift, prudence, and balance that they
successfully applied in their own firms or trade to prevail
in the public finances, . . . unless it came to trimming
some bounty from the budget or of soliciting for a relative a tobacco license or a job as tax collector or postmas-
ter. In this way saving, a peasant habit which became a
bourgeois practice, was becoming the business of the
State. Honor, the principle of monarchical or aristocratic
societies, sank before the importance of money saved.
Even today it is to this form of bourgeois and peasant
thinking that we owe a belief about public finance according to which the State should follow the practice of
a prudent family man, that the government should manage the *House of France* as a commercial enterprise.

Along with its political beliefs the bourgeoisie imposed
its customs, its rights, and its style of living. The political
date 1830 thus also marks a decisive step in the history of
mores: another regime, another society. The change can
even be seen in the displacement of the locale of society
life: the center of gravity moved from the Left Bank
to the Right Bank, from the faubourg Saint-Germain to
the Chausée-d'Antin. Thiers built on the Place Saint
Georges, the Leuwens lived on Place de la Madeleine,
and the Dambreuse's town house was on the Rue
d'Anjou. After the sittings of the Chamber the ministers
now went to their bankers; at the doors of their town
houses there were lines of brilliant carriages; their homes
displayed a luxury that the noble faubourg confidentially
mocked for its ostentation and bad taste. This new society did not forget the scorn with which it had been humiliated for so long. So lively was its antinoble resentment that many Orleanists felt it political wisdom to

agree to the abolition of the hereditary peerage, whose privileges seemed an affront to the bourgeois who was not highly born. Its disappearance removed the last official trace of aristocratic society. Instead, the National Guard, that citizen's army where the officers were elected and which flattered the vanity of the bourgeois, proud of his epaulette, consecrated and symbolized the equality of the new order. Clearly, 1830 was the definitive revenge of bourgeois society on the hierarchical and hereditary society of the Ultra-royalist Restoration.

Thus a great number of resemblences verifies the equation July Monarchy equals bourgeois regime. Still we must beware of arriving too hastily at a conclusion. This formula calls for some observations which will qualify its oversimplification. Firstly the notion of bourgeoisie needs precision. In nineteenth century society it corresponded to several distinct realities. French society, the product of a very old history, a long political evolution, and an already complex economy, was sharply differentiated. The steps were many in the scale which went from the small shopkeeper with his groceries or dry goods selling his cloth or his candles, to the great bourgeois who lived in a mansion and dealt on equal terms with government ministers. César Birotteau and the senior M. Leuwen have almost nothing in common. One toiled daily to escape poverty and win an uncertain security for his old age, the other was one of the powers of the times. Yet each had an equal right to the title of bourgeois.

Among these separate bourgeoisies where the distinctions small, middle, and upper do not exhaust the differences, it very clearly was the oldest and, at first, the richest which maintained the closest relations with the regime. This group, then, provided the features and attributes of Orleanism. To be assured of this it is enough to enumerate the outstanding personalities of the regime, its political notables (this method, quite dubious as a general rule, is quite appropriate here, because Orleanism was primarily a party of personalities). Most belonged to families of the old and rich bourgeoisie: Guizot, Casimir Périer, and so many others, members of those "bourgeois dynasties" of which M. Beau de Loménie has made himself the public prosecutor.[4] To list them all we would have to return here to the inventory compiled by the author of this Gotha of Orleanism. The unexpected presence of·an Adolphe Thiers, a petty bourgeois without name or fortune, with an irregular birth, a scholarship holder at the Marseille lycée, and symbol of the upstart, is a case of a brilliant exception whose uniqueness emphasizes the universality of the rule.

The Orleanist leadership was recruited from the upper bourgeoisie then, but we must not be misled by words, the permanence of which, when applied to changing realities, is often deceiving. We do not refer to large scale industrial capitalism. First, nothing could be farther from the economic reality of the time then to cite American prosperity as an ideal for the leadership of the bourgeois monarchy. Industrial firms were family enterprises. Above all, land remained the principal wealth; income from real estate furnished the capital for a growing industry. When Thiers wanted to rise in the social scale he did not buy shares but secretly acquired real estate. The true sign of wealth was not a portfolio of securities but landed property. This bourgeois society still remained by its customs, tastes, and ideas, very close to the world of

---

[4] *Les Responsibilités des Dynasties Bourgeoises*, 4 vols. (Paris, 1943-1963). Tr.

the soil. Perhaps this is even true today: certain character traits, certain modes of thought that we call bourgeois, aren't they rather the tenacious survivals of a peasant psychology? In fact this Orleanist bourgeoisie was
only in part a business bourgeoisie. Two names, always
the same ones, come to mind in reference to this bourgeois regime—Laffitte and Casimir Périer. But the first
went over to the opposition after eight months and the
second died in the second year of a regime which was to
survive him by sixteen years. On December 2[5] when
business circles, the moneyed bourgeoisie, could do nothing faster than rally to the new regime, the Orleanist
leaders observed a marked reserve toward the authors of
the coup d'état.

If Orleanism was not all the bourgeoisie—and the
upper bourgeoisie's monopolization of power explains the
growing disagreement between the regime and the more
modest social levels—the bourgeoisie was not all of Orleanism either. Orleanism clearly spread beyond the
frontiers of the bourgeoisie. There was an Orleanist aristocracy in which the nobility of the Empire, military as
well as administrative, held a high place: Soult, Gérard,
Mortier, Sébastiani, Maret. There was also an aristocracy
of birth, both the nobility of the bench—the Molés, the
Pasquiers—and families of the oldest nobility who served
the regime as a family tradition: often these were the
heirs of that fraction of the liberal nobility that in 1789
took a stand against the interests of their own order.
Their fathers having refused to emigrate in 1792, they
refused in their turn to join the new interior emigration.
The most famous example, by reason of the celebrity of
the family, was the Broglie family, two generations of

[5] Date of Louis Napoleon's coup d'état in 1851. Tr.

which identified itself for half a century with the destinies of Orleanism: Duke Victor, premier during the July
Monarchy, who began his career as Auditor at the *Con-
seil d'Etat* under the Empire, and Duke Albert, his son.

Finally, one of the most original traits of this society,
more receptive to new men than it appeared, was the
significant proportion of those who owed admittance
solely to intelligence or talent. Thiers had neither birth
nor fortune in his favor. He arrived through his merit, as
the first of the publicists who found that journalism
opened the door to power. The Restoration governments,
Ultra or not, would not have conceived the idea of bringing academic personnel into the ministry or the upper
bureaucracy. The July Monarchy did this regularly; it
borrowed from the Sorbonne so extensively that Thibaudet has spoken of a monarchy of professors. The three
who were suspended in 1827—Guizot, Villemain, and
Cousin—had their revenge in 1830. We shall not re-
hearse Guizot's career; he ended by identifying himself
with the regime. Victor Cousin was a member of the
Royal Council on Public Instruction, director of the
Ecole Normale, and Minister of Public Instruction in the
Thiers cabinet of 1840. He exerted an unchecked intellectual and administrative domination over the University. A kind of osmosis developed between politics and
the University, between the ministries and the academies. The regime lavished honors on the talented: the
king made peers of a number of professors, Villemain,
Cousin, Sylvestre de Sacy, of writers and artists. The
property qualifications for voting were set aside for
members of the *Institut.* In return the *Institut* elected the
notables of the regime to its ranks: illustrious men of
politics filled the *Académie Française:* Guizot, Thiers,

Molé, Pasquier, Dupin, Rémusat, Salvandy. It was the beginning of a close connection between the regime and the *Institut,* comparable to that at the end of the Directory, and which for half a century was to make Orleanist salons of the *Académie Française* and even more so of the *Académie des Sciences Morales et Politiques.*

From the composition of its personnel the true nature of Orleanism may be more clearly seen. It was not simply the egotistic defense of its own interests by a commercial or financial bourgeoisie. Wealth was not the sole definition of legitimacy nor the single measure of individual rights. In fact, it was taken into consideration only as a sign of personal merit, an index of intelligence, or as an indication of moral virtues. This was the real meaning of the dictum of Guizot which is so often considered a crime because it is generally parodied and misinterpreted, "Get rich by labor and thrift." Some see in this the insolent assertion of a moneyed materialism, but really a twofold conviction was expressed—that achieving wealth was the natural return for labor, and that the self-generating evolution of political conditions is surer than improvised transformations and revolutionary upheavals.

At this point we are surely in a better position to make out the distinctive nature of Orleanism. It was a government by the elites. To be sure, every regime has its elite, only the method of recruitment changes. Thus Ultraroyalism had its, constituted naturally by the aristocracy of birth. That of Orleanist society had another origin and another name: *the notables.* Orleanism, while it withdrew its traditional sway from the hereditary nobility, did not contest the existence and utility of social influence. It handed over to its own notables political power, local administration (the mayors and their deputies were not elected but appointed), social authority, the privileges of education and patronage of the lower classes. Against the Ultras who reserved for the aristocracy of birth power, prestige, and priority, against the Republicans whose success would have brought forth a clean sweep of acquired situations and social superiorities (at this time Tocqueville was showing how democracy signified leveling), later against the Second Empire, a regime of new men, of upstarts without ancestors or titles, Orleanism, with its doctrine of the *juste milieu*, represented rule by the notables, by the managerial classes, by all the aristocracies—those of birth, wealth, and intelligence.

IV. A Political Philosophy: Liberalism

The preceding observations about the role of professors in the governmental leadership, the very close relations which united the world of politics and academic circles, suggest that Orleanism was not, as its opponents thought, the party of interest groups only. It is also contrary to historical truth and to justice to paint it in black as a coterie completely preoccupied with compromise and opportunism. If Orleanism was able to survive long after the regime from which it took its name and tradition, it was because it rested on convictions, it related to a doctrine, it even admitted of an ideology. The idea of an Orleanist ideology may sound surprising but nevertheless it is not incorrect. It was Thibaudet who said, "Orleanism was not a party, it was a state of mind."

With the July regime an intellectual school achieved power—the Doctrinaires. They had retained their reflective habits, and certain characteristics such as the taste for philosophical and political speculation, a tendency to systematize their views, kept even the attitude of cool superiority which made them so unpopular with those who did not agree with them. Before gathering in the councils of the government they had worked together in editorial offices. The entire team of the *Globe* of 1826 came together again in the leadership of the new regime. In 1828 a group of young men had founded *La Revue Francaise* as a means of expression. We read in it the signatures of Guizot, the Duke de Broglie, Barante, Villemain, Cousin—all men whom a few years later we find holding the highest positions in the State. The July regime offers the first example of the power of the press; for the first time, excepting the brief Revolutionary episode, political journalism opened the way to power and became a method of carrying on a political career. The Ultra-royalist attempt—the *Conservateur*—shows the opposite movement. There political leaders, the leading lights of the party and all quite well known already, on occasion became publicists. With Orleanism the political press played an official role. For eighteen years the *Journal des Débats* was to be, with sober dignity, the semi-official spokesman of Orleanist doctrine.

However, a doctrine needs more than a press and a means of expression. The Orleanist doctrine formed a system of philosophical thought with its own metaphysics. We can speak of a religious Orleanist as fifty years later we can speak of a religious Republican during the period of the Opportunist Republic. But there can be nothing religious without a spiritual authority to spread its precepts. The Third Republic was to have the primary school and freemasonry. Orleanism had the University.

The press and education were the two pillars of Orleanism as a doctrine. Journalists and professors were its ministers. Supported jointly by the Sorbonne and the *Journal des Débats,* the July Monarchy gave the appearance of an enlightened regime in contrast to the Restoration which controlled the University and extended the kind of solicitude toward the press that the latter would have been pleased to do without. Orleanism simply did not have the same reasons for being suspicious of civil liberties—it was liberal, or better, it was liberalism.

Before expressing itself in a political position its liberalism had originated in a philosophical conception which made individual reason the measure and judge of truth. This relativism permitted a dash of anticlericalism, even anti-Catholicism, which came as much from the relative positions of the philosophical systems and of religious orthodoxies as from the internal logic of the system. The relativism of any statement of the liberal view directly offended the absolute position of Catholicism and seemed a defiance of its authority. This was the modern form of the old struggle between the Church and the spirit of free examination. Also there were personal links between liberalism and Protestantism which emphasized their doctrinal affinities. Guizot was a pillar of Protestantism, the Duke de Broglie married Albertine de Staël, granddaughter of Necker. By them and by Benjamin Constant, the highest authority of liberalism, Orleanism was connected with Coppet[6] and was grafted onto the trunk of liberal Protestantism. Finally, anticlericalism remained an elementary defensive reflex for the University which had to defend its independence of thought

[6] The Swiss estate of Jacques Necker and his famous daughter, Germaine de Staël. Tr.

and its very existence against the sometimes artful and
sometimes brutal encroachments of a Catholicism which
was ultra in two ways—Ultramontaine and Ultra-royalist.

But in this period there were several varieties of anticlericalism. Orleanism never followed the coarse style of
the *Constitutionnel*. Its liberalism made it abhor what
was only another kind of sectarianism and it had too high
a regard for itself to stoop to the vulgarity of such low
conduct. Rarely was it aggressively anticlerical. Usually
it was led to it in responding to campaigns against the
University. The political authorities did not wish to be on
bad terms with the Church. After 1832, once the popular
explosion of anticlericalism which marked the beginning
of the regime had become more temperate, the public
authorities put a damper on official anticlericalism.
Thiers' violent attacks on the Jesuits in 1845 did not represent the government's point of view. High society was
beginning to recede from its Voltairianism of the Restoration. The facts are not clear, as always in the matter of
religious sensibility, but it seems that dating the bourgeoisie's conversion from the morrow of the June Days[7]
is too late and too abrupt. The shift was neither so hasty
nor dictated by such selfish motives. Sudden conversions,
even when collective, are the culminations of long pro-
cesses; the slow evolution of customs through unnoticed
changes makes for unexpected about-faces. Rather early
in the July regime the change appeared. Queen Marie-
Amélie was very pious. If it was still ridiculous for a man
to be devout, a pious woman was respectable. Anticlericalism went out of fashion, it ceased to indicate good
breeding and became a sign of vulgarity; it savored of
the "petty bourgeois."

[7] The Parisian revolutionary upheaval of June 1848. Tr.

Finally, this Orleanist rationalism was quite the contrary of a materialism that it considered coarse; it was a spiritual rationalism. Victor Cousin's eclecticism, promoted to the dignity of the official philosophy of the University and the regime by the administrative power of its founder, was a system of thought infinitely respectful of what the heirs of Orleanism would later call the "spiritual values." It took account of the beautiful, the good, and the true. This discreet, tolerant, and enlightened liberalism drew down the episcopal thunderbolts but got along rather well with a certain Catholicism of the Gallican and Jansenist tradition, stricter concerning ethics than philosophy. The absence of an official Catholic philosophy permitted and explained on the intellectual level a freedom or even flexibility of thought that the restoration of Thomism was to restrain. The higher administration of the University then included several sincere Catholics as full of respect for their faith as they were precise in fulfilling their professional duties.

As the Orleanist monarchy divorced itself from theocracy and became secularized, Orleanist philosophy achieved its separation from theology and also became secularized. Indeed it was the philosophy of this modern, rationalist, and liberal society whose principles political Orleanism accepted and whose institutions it justified. But just as the regime attempted a compromise, Orleanist thought also tried a conciliation—to the *juste milieu* corresponded *eclecticism*.

V. *Order and Liberty*

We now have all the components with which to determine the true significance of parliamentary Orleanism. For an Orleanist parliamentary institutions represented much more than a practical solution to the problem of the relations among the branches of political power. They went far beyond procedures and exalted less the technical regulations than the spirit of the institution. Parliamentarism was compromise erected into a rule of government, the application to the operations of the State of that spirit of conciliation that was the essence of Orleanism. Ministerial changes replaced the wars of religion and revolutions. Through them the natural evolution of societies might be carried on without accidents, a principle of the Orleanist philosophy of history.

All the political history of the July Monarchy revolved about this axis: the Revolution of 1830 broke out over a disagreement between Charles X and the Chamber concerning the responsibility of the ministers. The success of the Revolution established once and for all the parliamentary interpretation of the Charter, although groups still fell out over this question and it indirectly brought the fall of the regime when the latter paralyzed the free play of the system.

Orleanism, when necessary, was to take little account of the name of a regime, but it would never compromise on the parliamentary liberties. It was severe against Napoleon III, less for preventing a dynastic restoration than for suppressing the parliamentary regime. Many Orleanists later on willingly rallied to an Empire which had become parliamentary. It was not in 1830, 1840, or 1849 that Thiers enunciated the pure Orleanist doctrine; it was in 1864 when he was a Deputy in the Legislative Body, when he demanded the "necessary liberties." The attachment to parliamentarism was so strong that for Orleanists it became a way of life, a form of behavior. The heirs of the great Orleanist families were to find it at their birth as if it were a family property and cherish it as the most sacred inheritance of all.

Of course this intellectual and parliamentary liberalism did not have much in common with democracy. Liberalism and democracy have no other point of contact than appearing, from historical hindsight, as two successive steps in the political history of the nineteenth century. Taken by themselves they are two ill-assorted and even contradictory notions. Democracy means equality, and Orleanist liberalism implied the necessary superiority of the social elites. The democrats looked toward the United States and the Orleanists toward England. British institutions inspired a lively admiration which was reinforced by Protestant affinities, by the political rapprochement of the two countries, by the imitation of customs and infatuation for British fashions, and by the proximity of Normandy to England. The Broglies, Tocqueville, and even Guizot by electoral adoption were from Normandy where Orleanism seems to have found its favorite territory. Liberalism dreamed of a powerful and honored landed aristocracy which was receptive to merit, to talent, and to young ambitions, master of local power by means of administrative decentralization and superior to the central power by parliamentary control of it.

Such a conception of liberalism made it quite possible for Orleanism to be fundamentally conservative. Government by the elites and the managerial classes, party of the notables, wasn't this enough to pull it toward the Right? Its only chance, and it was limited, of a democratic evolution consisted in the door open to "ability." The only republic the Orleanist would accept would be a conservative republic. Political liberalism and social conservativism, these were the two pillars of the program, the two sides of Orleanism, inseparable as the opposite slopes of a mountain. The unbreakable alliance of these two factors defined the original appearance of Orleanism but it also led to the ambiguity which brought so many contradictory analyses of it. The alliance was signed on the day when Orleanism identified itself with the program of *resistance*. It is quite possible to imagine an Orleanism which in 1830-1831 would have seized the hopes of those favoring *movement;* we would have had an Orleanism of the Left, resting on the small and middle bourgeoisie, a precursor of a sort of Radicalism. But these are empty conjectures that the historian rejects. Orleanism, originating on the Right, was to remain there, although it pretended to be in the Center.

Indeed it could, according to the circumstances, sometimes emphasize its liberalism and sometimes its social conservatism, depending on whether it faced the Right or the Left, or whether it was in the opposition or in power. What remains is that this unprecedented mixture of order and liberty, this balancing of social stability and natural evolution characterized an original inclination and tradition of the Right, the second of the nineteenth century. The events of 1848, by introducing new partners and revamping the conditions of political life, were to interrupt the hitherto well regulated relations of these two already traditional Right Wing groups.

4

1848-1870: Bonapartism, "Classic" and Authoritarian Rightist Groups

I. The Party of Order

The suddenness of the Revolution of February 1848 was such a great surprise for the Orleanist leadership, ensconced as it was in the certitude of its security, that there is nothing else to compare it to than the stupor of Charles X's entourage eighteen years earlier. The Legitimists were scarcely less surprised and hardly less uneasy than their Orleanist adversaires over this unforseen stroke which avenged them on the men in power and on the "faithless tutor." Was it possible to limit the repercussions of a disturbance whose shock waves threatened to spread beyond governmental circles to the entire society? The February Days threw everyone in the governing classes into a confusion which is movingly reflected in the correspondence of Montalembert, although he was not a beneficiary of the regime, since he had been the soul of the Catholic party's campaign against the University's educational monopoly.

For 1848 was not 1830 all over again. The break was more brutal and the repercussions were of much greater significance. In July 1830 the crisis had been settled in a few days, the succession assured without a great upheaval, and the change, although not unimportant, was registered on a clear-cut balance sheet whose limits were presumably well-defined. At the price of some alterations of detail, the Charter had remained the constitution of the new regime as of the old. The members of the *pays légal* had been approximately doubled, but each of the full citizens could indulge himself in the reassuring feeling that he still was among friends. Political life had remained the privilege of a limited elite; the power of the notables had continued intact.

In the months following the 1848 Revolution the situation was far from resembling this happy settlement. Nothing was left to safeguard a semblance of continuity. The Charter was swept away along with the throne and the ministers. There was no longer constitution, legality, or regularized political power. The houses of parliament themselves were gone. It was the clean sweep which the notables of all opinions had so dreaded for two generations. In the forefront of the people, carried to power by the revolutionary upheaval, appeared a handful of men who made no mystery of their intention to reconstruct the State on new foundations. There was, if possible, something even worse, because it bore more fateful implications: the promise of an appeal to universal suffrage. It is difficult to imagine today, after a century of electoral practice scarcely interrupted by the Vichy episode, what it meant to move without any transition from a padded, insulated, and attenuated political life to the uproar of popular passions, and from an electoral body of some two hundred thousand voters to a mass of nine million electors. The *pays légal,* abruptly multiplied by fifty, was dilated to the dimensions of the nation. An entirely new experience was going to begin, which no other great European country had as yet attempted and which in France had only one precedent—the Great Revolution—something well calculated to redouble the anxiety of the notables. They experienced the anguish of a passenger setting out in a frail skiff for a peaceful excursion on the calm waters of a harbor, who suddenly finds himself exposed to the perils of a passage on the open sea in stormy weather. The unknown was dreadful. What was really known of this mass, as yet silent, in whose hands were now placed the destinies of the nation? Its political education, never yet attempted, was made up of legends and was nourished almost exclusively on an oral tradition. The majority could not read, and realized only imperfectly what it wanted. In any case, the abrupt and prodigious enlargement of the electoral body deprived the political and social authorities of the hope of controlling the elections. Formerly a clever prefect might sway some dozens of votes on which the result generally depended. Now, on the scale of an entire department, this became impossible.

In addition, in 1830 there was a team ready to take over. A staff which was not at all unpracticed quickly filled the vacuum left by the Legitimist emigration. In 1848 there was nothing comparable. The revolution that turned out the Orleanist personnel did not recall to service the cadres of the preceding regime. The successive elimination of two groups of leaders increased the administrative confusion and left no replacement team. What great nation would have been able, with such a limited *pays légal* and a secondary education still reserved to a small minority, to find in quick succession three governmental teams ready to take over, one after another, every fifteen years?

It was indeed precisely this scarcity of qualified men, this dearth of competent personnel, that made inevitable an appeal to the experience of the traditional leaders and facilitated the return of the old parties to importance. After the very first weeks, when they had had no other wish than to achieve oblivion, they began a discreet return. They did not yet openly proclaim themselves for what they were, and most called themselves Republicans, even if this tardy support made them only "morning-after Republicans."[1] For the recovery of their power the notables counted on the solidity of their local positions, the long period of their local family dominance, their influence as large landholders, and the obligations that a constituency of protégés owed them. Their calculations did not seem erroneous, for their adversaries followed the same reasoning and in Paris organized demonstration upon demonstration to postpone the election. They judged that a year's delay was necessary to take care of the political indoctrination of the country and to remove the provincials from the custody of their traditional leaders. The hopes of one group and the fears of the other led to an identical prediction of the probable results of the first electoral experiment. The general election of April 23 and 24, 1848, confirmed it on every point. Of the nine hundred victors who met on May 4 in the temporary building constructed in the courtyard of the Palais Bour-

---

[1] Already in March 1848, a discreet regrouping of conservative interests began to form around a *Republican Club for Free Elections.* Author.

Charles X: the Ultra leader.
(Documentation Française)

Berryer: the Legitimist spokesman.

(Documentation Française)

François Guizot: Orleanism, from liberal to conservative.

(Documentation Française)

Duke Victor de Broglie: the aristocrat as Orleanist.
(Documentation Française)

Thiers: the self-made man as Orleanist.
(Documentation Française)

L'ÉLU DU PEUPLE

DIEU LE VEUT

VOX POPULI — VOX DEI

7,481,231 VOIX

NAPOLÉON III EMPEREUR DES F[RANÇAIS]

DÉPARTEMENTS	OUI	NON
AIN	81819	3472
AISNE	137062	5383
ALLIER	70450	614
ALPES Bᵉˢ	34215	1338
ALPES Hᵗᵉˢ	24745	1665
ARDÈCHE	67033	7136
ARDENNES	75248	3603
ARIÈGE	53930	2419
AUBE	75427	3000
AUDE	57660	10214
AVEYRON	85351	2171
Bᵉˢ ᵈᵘ RHÔNE	51288	12753
CALVADOS	108743	5688
CANTAL	40472	1377
CHARENTE	94746	4120
CHARENTE Iᵉ	114343	6503
CHER	67827	2486
CORRÈZE	59838	4022
CORSE	51876	372
CÔTE D'OR	88427	12854
COTES ᵈᵘ NORD	109195	2853
CREUSE	54518	3048
DORDOGNE	112790	5729
DOUBS	60123	3695
DRÔME	65799	10279
EURE	103310	8376
EURE ᵉᵗ LOIR	68782	6515
FINISTÈRE	74683	4053
GARD	70529	15949
GARONNE Hᵗᵉ	93414	12345
GERS	64449	8588
GIRONDE	123110	15223
HÉRAULT	60356	14311
ILLE ᵉᵗ VILAINE	71792	3626
INDRE	58948	4399
INDRE ᵉᵗ LOIRE	77952	12637
ISÈRE	114501	8348
JURA	61656	2409
LANDES	62061	5293
LOIR ᵉᵗ CHER	55965	7917
LOIRE	78763	1943
LOIRE Hᵗᵉ	48313	5231
LOIRE INFᵉ	62094	5076
LOIRET	74900	4233
LOT	65583	7909
LOT ᵉᵗ GARᵉ	79576	2222
LOZÈRE	27663	5995
MAINE ᵉᵗ LOIRE	105880	4369
MANCHE	119791	5202
MARNE	92076	5646
MARNE Hᵗᵉ	67106	2746
MAYENNE	76187	5157
MEURTHE	101943	2010

Bonapartist propaganda: the Plebiscite of 1851.

The Duke d'Aumale: brightest light of the Orleans family.
(Documentation Française)

Paul Déroulède: *fin de siècle* nationalism.
(Documentation Française)

Raymond Poincaré: the Orleanist Republic in the 1920's.

(Documentation Française)

Colonel de La Rocque: the leaguer of the 1930's.

Jacques Doriot: fascism *à la française.*
(Documentation Française)

Charles Maurras: the traditionalist Right at Vichy.
(Documentation Française)

Paul Reynaud: Orleanism up to date.

(French Embassy)

Antoine Pinay: the Orleanism of the provincial middle class.

(Documentation Française)

Charles de Gaulle: Bonapartism at mid-century?
(French Embassy)

bon to house their deliberations, there was a high proportion of former members of parliament who had sat in the
Chambers of the Restoration or the July Monarchy. The
pays réel did not disavow the choice of the *pays légal;* it
had not yet dissociated itself from its traditional leaders.
Consulted, the nation chose its notables as its representatives.

Avowed or disguised, the presence of some two hundred Orleanists attested that Orleanism had survived the
regime and the dynasty. Rising from the past after a long
eclipse, a hundred representatives gave to Legitimism a
parliamentary expression more closely proportional to its
national importance than the few personalities which the
official pressures of the July Monarchy had not been able
to unseat. The results of 1830 and 1848 had different
effects on the destinies of these two groups. In 1830 the
passage to the opposition of the strong Ultra tradition
had been followed by a rightward tendency of the new
Orleanism. The Revolution of 1848 did not modify these
relative positions. They were both on the Right and they
stayed there, with the innovation that the Orleanists
joined the Legitimists in the opposition. Universal
suffrage now made visible the true proportions of
strength. The Orleanists, yesterday still in power, not yet
completely dislodged from their positions by the revolution, directed the fight. By natural disposition they were
more clever than the Legitimists in buying votes, manip-
ulating interest groups, and pushing advantages. Orleanism gave the tone to the double opposition on the Right,
it furnished the decisive impetus to the common policy,
and its leaders were the strategists and orators of the
Right. The Legitimists harvested the bitter fruits of their
long separation from public life. Out of their element,
baffled, whether they liked it or not they had to accom-

modate themselves to second place. Side by side the two Rights waited, suspicious and distrustful, for nothing was forgotten between them. Nevertheless, for a time their common misfortune brought them together in the opposition.

The June Days precipitated their return to power. Before the social danger the two Rights silenced their ill-feelings and for the moment recognized enemies only on the Left. They organized themselves for conquest and formed the *Party of Order,* whose name clearly expressed the preoccupation which cemented the coalition, the spirit which animated it, and the theme of its campaign. It was the new watchword for action engraved on the façade of the two allied Right Wing groups. It married their efforts, amalgamated their influences, and totalized their gains. In a few months the coalition, which included as its leaders those from both traditions, Berryer, Molé, and Thiers, seized power. In the election for President of the Republic for a four-year term (December 10, 1848), its candidate, Prince Louis-Napoleon Bonaparte, won over his opponents in a runaway with a total vote which placed him in an unassailable position. The new president took from the ranks of the party the members of his first cabinet led by Odilon Barrot (December 20). Five months later, on May 13, 1849, the election for a three-year term in the Legislative Assembly of a majority of the "respectable and moderate" candidates completed the conquest of power.[2]

Master of the situation, the Party of Order then began a policy that it is rigorously correct to call reactionary,

---

[2] The Right, which won more than 3,300,000 votes, took two-thirds of the 713 seats. The Legitimists won almost 200 of these seats. Author.

since the measures that it included tended, if not always in their letter at least in their spirit and application, to re-establish by degrees the state of affairs so brutally abol-ished by the revolutionary accident of February 1848. Directly or not, these measures aimed to return the nota-bles to their pre-eminence. For the Orleanists also it was now a matter of *restoration*.

Two measures, both passed in the year which marked the mid-century, show the progress of the restoration and underline its spirit. One of these could not disguise its re-strictive character: the Law of May 31, 1850, which re-quired as a condition for voting three years residence in the same place. At a time when artisans and day laborers made up a floating population subject to continual move-ment, when the fluctuations of employment forced masses of men seeking work to migrate frequently, when the roads still flowed with artisans making their tour of France, and when new roads—the railways—already employed in their construction a numerous and neces-sarily mobile labor force, to draw up a requirement of this sort was to reduce the electoral body by a good third of the citizens and to tacitly abolish the principle of uni-versal suffrage. This also eliminated its risks, for only the stable, docile voters remained, supposedly the most re-ceptive to the suggestions of the political, social, or reli-gious authorities.

And, notably enough, the second measure began an unexpected rapprochement between the religious au-thorities—the Church—and Orleanism, whose liberalism formerly implied a dash of anticlericalism. This was the great novelty of the Falloux and Parieu Laws, passed in March 1850, one of the major events of French politi-cal history in the nineteenth century. An assembly with an identical social composition and very similar political views to the Chambers of the July Monarchy which on four occasions had rejected very similar bills, now passed a law whose principal points satisfied the Catholics. Historians have argued for a long time over the motives for such a hasty turnabout. Certainly the case for social safeguards was decisive, or to repeat the apothegm of a conservative historian, Pierre de la Gorce, "fear of the Jacobins won out over fear of the Jesuits," dread of revolution spoke louder than fear of clericalism. However, all of the inner divisions did not magically disappear. Ultramontaines and Gallicans, Legitimists and Orleanists, anticlericals and Catholics, all mutually sacrificed their preferences of principle. Thiers and Mgr. Dupanloup, Victor Cousin and the Count de Falloux could agree only at the price of reciprocal concessions. The text of the Law was a compromise, and the noisy dissatisfaction of extremists in both camps clearly underlined its character as a bargain. Nonetheless, it represented a first step toward a rapprochement of the two Rightist groups.

Was this a prelude to a fusion of these two traditions, until then more accustomed to fight each other than to concur, and for a longer time enemies than allies? Not at all; the vote on the Falloux Law did not commit the future. The fundamental disagreement continued. The death of Louis-Philippe in the summer of 1850 seemed to eliminate the main obstacle to a reconciliation of Bourbons and Orleanists. However, the tentative negotiation for a dynastic fusion led only to failure. Was the fault for this the resentment by the Count de Chambord of the pretensions of the Orleanist princes? Assuredly, neither the tenacious grudges of a too-recent past nor the rival ambitions of two groups whose experience made them competitors facilitated the rapprochement. But the decisive cause was elsewhere. The two movements remained irreconcilable because in them two traditions, two conceptions of society, and two histories confronted each other. They were two societies jealous and distrustful of each other. It was the Orleanist historian Barante who stated that the party of the Count de Chambord still preferred a Republic, an Empire, or even socialism "to the vexation of being governed by the men of modern France." The Legitimists remained the heirs of the men of the policy of the worst. The fear of disorder and subversion, the necessity to face the Left in a common front would have led them in time to compromise, but two years were not enough to fill in the gulf produced by a half-century of history. Doctrine soon took its revenge over tactics. Already, under the apparent unity of the Party of Order, we can discern, alive and trembling, our two Right Wing groups, faithful to what defined and constituted them and hence to what separated them and opposed them to each other.

II. A New Political Force

Thus, after several months of confusion, the political situation in 1850 included a Right Wing coalition, the Party of Order, which embraced without any basic changes a majority of Orleanists and a minority of Legitimists. It linked the Bourbon faithful and those of Orleans, the leaders of the Restoration and the personnel of the July Monarchy associated together to contain the menace of radicalism. But this was very close to the basic equilibrium of political forces before 1848. The year 1850 was the extension of 1845 or 1840, as if 1848 had

not occurred: Orleanism still in power. Once again continuity prevailed over upheaval, and the expected
changes were forgotten, annulled, and sent back to oblivion, like the fragile castles built on the seashore that the
ground swells from the open sea destroy and wash away
forever.

However, the France of 1850 was no longer that of
1848. The 1850's were in her history like the lines of the
height of land which were the main preoccupation of the
ancient geographers: they separated two watersheds. In
many ways the France of 1840 prolonged the Old Regime; the France of the Second Empire turned its back
on it and was further from it than from the end of the
nineteenth century. Politically, 1848 planted a seed
which gave only a hint of its distant consequences: universal suffrage, the principle behind all later transformations. In consequence of this the Party of Order had to
determine its policy even before the end of 1848, on the
occasion of the election of the first president of the new
republic. The political heads of the party, the Thiers and
the Molés, believed they had found a candidate whose
personal mediocrity seemed to make him safe enough.
In fact, the election of December 10, 1848, unleashed a
new political force, radically different from its predecessors, and whose millions of voters then and there established its importance in the country. Along with the
exercise of universal suffrage appeared an unexpected element—a Bonapartist party, whose intervention was to
bring profound alterations in the equilibrium of political
forces. From 1849 on, in addition to their initial and still
present concern for a defense against a return in force of
the Left, the leaders of the Party of Order experienced
another anxiety. For it was inherent in the destiny of
Orleanism that it had to fight on two fronts. The growing

autonomy of the president and his party confronted the political experiences of these clever tacticians with the delicate problem of the relations of the two traditional movements on the Right with the new force of Bonapartism.

And it was definitely of Bonapartism, and not of Louis-Napoleon Bonaparte. The game played between December 10, 1848, and December 2, 1851, should not be minimized by assuming that it was between a man on the make, eager to play his own cards, and the party which staked his entrance. It was quite another matter: a political force which had its own doctrine, program, and supporters soon clashed with the Party of Order. Their collaboration lasted scarcely beyond the first objective which they proposed to reach in common: the victory of December 10, 1848. Quickly Bonapartism emerged from its initial association with the Rightist coalition. Quite probably it broke away at the time of the May 1849 election to the Legislative Assembly. The Prince-President can no longer be described in the months following his election as a general without troops, seeking supporters which he could recruit only from the ranks of the Party of Order. The excellent thesis of M. Louis Chevalier[3] has focused an entirely new light on this period, for it clarifies the beginnings of the Bonapartist party and its relationships with the "Classic" Right Wing groups—for the first time we can risk the use of this epithet that later became standard. Almost all of the following details and some of the conclusions come from the research of M. Chevalier.

The elections to the Legislative Assembly are a good

---

[3] Louis Chevalier, "Les Fondements Economiques et Sociaux de l'Histoire Politique de la Région Parisienne, 1848-1851," Thèse de doctorat, Paris, 1950, typewritten copy. Author.

point of reference, for this was the first time the Bonapartist party fought under its own colors in several constituencies, although it did not everywhere break with
the traditional Rightist movements. The situation varied
according to the region. For example, in the Aube and
the Marne, departments where the social structure was
relatively simple and where for the moment fear of the
"reds" eclipsed every other consideration, the Bonapartist
central committee recommended voting for the lists of
the Party of Order and did not set up any rival candidates. On the contrary, in the departments with a more
complex social structure, like those which adjoin Paris, the
dissociation between Bonapartism and the Right Wing
movements was already more advanced. Everywhere
that the relative voting strengths of Right and Left did
not advise against it, each party entered the campaign
and tried its luck separately. That it was a conflict between two distinct political forces and not rival individual personalities is emphatically demonstrated by the
rigorous and penetrating analysis of M. Chevalier.

Let us follow our guide across Seine-et-Marne, Seine-et-
Oise, and Eure-et-Loir. These three departments had a
very similar make-up although in Eure-et-Loir the Orleanists were relatively stronger. If we listen to the
speeches of the candidates of the two parties we can
learn much. In what terms, for example, did the men of
the Party of Order speak of the Prince-President less than
five months after the election in which they had joined
their fortunes? They scarcely mentioned him, or if so in
terms which hardly disguised their distrust. They dwelt
with more pleasure on the victory of Cavaignac in June[4]
than on that of their candidate in December. As for the

---

[4] General Cavaignac suppressed the uprising of Parisian workers
in the "June Days" of 1848. Tr.

Bonapartists, they observed an absolute silence regarding the Party of Order. While the notables, supported by the Rue de Poitiers,[5] willingly called themselves "friends of order," the Bonapartists seem to have made a rule never to even pronounce the name. The professions of faith of the Rightist candidates rang the changes on family, property, and religion, while the Bonapartists expounded on local roads, canals, and railways. Two vocabularies, two languages, whose differences clearly reveal that they were addressed to two quite distinct groups whose votes they hoped to win.

The personalities of the candidates confirm these conjectures suggested by an examination of their political positions. The men of the Party of Order are already familiar to us. We have known them since their first appearance in our study of Ultra-royalism and of Orleanism, even in those cases where the Rightist coalition included some moderate Republicans. Nothing is more revealing than the method of nomination of those candidates who represented the cause of order and property; with few exceptions the identical process was followed. In general the initiative came from the general council of the department. It organized in each canton a committee which sent delegates to a central committee which made up the slate of candidates. In Seine-et-Oise choices were made in conjunction with the Central Agricultural Committee. In the three departments here considered the men finally selected were the urban or rural notables, from those classes whose heritage was participation in government and acting as the spokesmen, representatives, and protectors of their localities. If a final proof was needed that the Party of Order was indeed the legit-

---

[5] The street in Paris on which the headquarters of the Party of Order was located. Tr.

imate and recognized heir of the two societies to which
the two traditional groups on the Right corresponded,
this scrutiny of its membership on the departmental scale
confirms it.

From this date Bonapartism represented an original
political force no longer to be confused with the movements described earlier. It was more than the timely invention of an ambitious man interested only in justifying
his attempt to seize power; it rested on a doctrine. Louis-
Napoleon declared this unequivocally in the presidential
message which accompanied his announcement of the
cabinet revision on October 31, 1849: "An entire system
triumphed on December tenth, for the name Napoleon
is itself a program." An entire *system,* an entire *program*: the meaning of these words is clear, their use was
too insistent not to be deliberate. Louis-Napoleon wanted
to contrast system to system, and program to program.

Of what did this system consist? How did it differ from
the system of the Ultras or the Orleanist program? Or, to
consider the question in terms of our benchmark, was it
Right? was it Left? This question is of capital importance
for this study: in one case it would become another Right
in our gallery, in the other we could portray it only obliquely. But if the question is an essential one, its answer
is not simple and can be given only after an investigation.

The first exhibits in the case are the declarations of
those involved. The higher authorities of official Bonapartism had a ready reply here. Essentially, this was that
the question was not relevant. Bonapartism was neither
Right nor Left. It took exception to these labels and refused to be pigeonholed in a classification which it definitely wanted to go beyond and abolish. Taking up his

uncle's plan, the Prince-President planned to suppress the parties which divided the nation and wanted to reconcile Frenchmen with one another by turning them toward the work of the future. Bonapartism has never varied on this point. We must admit that this resolution has been many times expressed and never denied.

But we need not give up so easily on the basic issue. No political force for one hundred fifty years has been able to evade the question which orients French political life: Right or Left? Every movement must, sooner or later, reenter the confines of this area which admits of only two known dimensions—Right and Left. The question still remains for Bonapartism. If it refuses to answer, we have ways of interrogating it, others may speak for it: its friends, its supporters, its program, its opponents, its successors, and its heirs whether they be legitimate or not.

Guizot, whose historical ability quite as much as his political experience made him better able than anyone to appraise the nature of Bonapartism, characterized it in a sentence which gives us perhaps its most revealing definition: "It is quite a feat to be at one and the same time a national glory, a guarantee of the Revolution, and a principle of authority." This description is both penetrating and comprehensive. In a few words it enumerates the decisive strengths and reveals the secret of the remarkable success of the Second Bonapartism. A *guarantee of the Revolution:* this drew it to the Left, making it the heir of the new France. *Principle of authority:* after 1900 with this testimonial no one would hesitate to place it on the Right. But in 1850 the principle of authority was not yet a Rightist one. The Ultras demanded the free exercise of liberties against an authority which always smacked of despotism. And parliamentary liberalism had become second nature to the Orleanists. Neither of these two Rightist traditions had yet annexed the force of the State to its system. Authority was the badge of Jacobinism, the stamp of Napoleon, and Louis-Napoleon had found it in the heritage of Napoleonic ideas. To the message of October 31, 1849, proudly replied the echo of the proclamation of December 2, 1851: "My name is a pledge for strong and stable government and good administration." Finally, *glory* placed Bonapartism well above the political parties and eclipsed the pettiness of their quarrels in the radiance of national grandeur. The novel union of these three themes sounded an unusual chord to which neither Ultra-royalism and the Restoration nor Orleanism and the July Monarchy had accustomed France.

Was Bonapartism on the Left then, despite its temporary alliance with the Right in the Party of Order? In fact, similarly to philosophical systems, contrary streams develop from certain political movements. Hegelianism knew its rightist and leftist derivations; Comtism nurtured the thought of Maurras[6] as well as that of Littré.[7] For a moment there appeared the imaginary vision of an Orleanism on the Left. Bonapartism also is open to several interpretations: Janus-like politically, its ambiguity permitted, within certain limits, several tendencies. In 1849 it could have given birth with almost no difficulty and with equal probability to a Bonapartism of the Left or of the Right.

That of the Left had in its favor the explicit and categorical reference to the great principle of national sovereignty, the deliberate acceptance of the work of the Revolution, and the Napoleonic Legend. This popular and

[6] The Rightist discussed at some length in Chapter 7. Tr.

[7] A 19th century philosophical positivist, lexicographer, and linguist. Tr.

democratic version of the Bonapartist principle was what some of the most devoted servants of the Emperor tried for twenty years to make prevail, although with more perseverance than success. Persigny's surliness toward the notables, the fidelity of the soldiers, as well as Prince Jérôme's anticlericalism and republican sympathies all can be placed in the Left Wing of Bonapartism.

But on the other side of the balance weighed the voters of December 10 and the motives for their votes: fear of the reds, fear of the unknown, terror of a second Terror, defense of order. All these, which played a determining part in winning rural and bourgeois votes, drew Bonapartism to the Right. The vocabulary that the Prince-President used, even after the break with the leaders of the Party of Order was consummated, appealed to those feelings that one can summarily label Right Wing. The famous phrase, "The time has come to reassure the righteous and make the wicked tremble," already foreshadowed the speeches of MacMahon in the days of moral order.

Thus in 1850 Bonapartism was open to two interpretations. It could as easily have given birth to a Left Wing Bonapartism, popular, democratic, and anticlerical, as to a Right Wing Bonapartism, conservative, defender of the social order, and on good terms with the notables and the Church. The orientation which was to prevail depended basically on the nature of the regime's relations with the three forces, classes, or institutions which (except for the urban workers) then composed French society: the mass of peasants, the notables, and the Church.

The support of the peasants, except for rare occasions on a regional scale, never failed the regime. Rural Bonapartism was a permanent factor in the Second Empire, a

stable and constant ingredient of the system. The faithful
adherence of these supposedly conservative masses sometimes is interpreted as pulling Bonapartism to the Right,
certainly the official candidates played on the fear of the
"sharers."[8] But the countryside's attachment to the
nephew of the great Emperor signified something else
also: for an ill-informed mass with little political education but which was not mistaken as to its own true interests, the Second Empire also meant the maintenance of
the Revolution's victories over the evil designs of the
nobles. It was the guarantee of equality, it was the peas-
antry's revenge against the age-old domination by the
notables. Already in the elections of 1849 Louis Chevalier believes he can recognize that the success of the
Bonapartist party in the countryside was a revolt of rural
democracy against the oligarchy of the departmental
notables. In the same fashion, to vote for the official candidate in 1852 or 1857 signified quite simply a blow
against the notables or the priest. The peasant who followed the prefect's recommendation was not performing
an act of dependence, on the contrary, he was asserting
his independence from close and ancient guardians. He
found no other way to challenge the social authorities or
"put one over" on the spiritual authorities. Interpreted in
this manner, rural Bonapartism marked in certain of its
aspects a step in the slow emancipation of the peasants.
It primed the political education of the countryside and
unknowingly prepared the latter's rapid adherence to the
Republic twenty years later. Perhaps it was even the unrecognized and unconscious precursor of rural Radicalism. Bonapartism and Radicalism were for two succes-

[8] A contemporary term for Communists. Tr.

sive generations two related ways of expression, two
original methods of translating the permanent preoccupations of the peasant mentality. To vote Bonapartist in
1849 or 1869 and to vote Radical in 1902 (as to vote
Socialist in some regions in 1936 or even Communist in
1945) was still voting against the "lords." Therefore we
should not be too hasty about cataloguing rural Bonapartism among the conservative forces.

Such prudence is not at all necessary for the Bonapartism of the notables or the Church. There can be no doubt
about the weight of their influence, which pulled the regime to the Right. But their force, contrary to the support of the countryside, was not constant. It varied considerably from one period to another, in direct relation to
the changes of their connection with the regime. It was
simply that neither the traditional governing classes nor
the religious hierarchy had as decisive reasons as the
peasants did for supporting the Empire. For the notables
an underlying suspicion balanced the advantages they
gained from the regime; as for the Church, it never deviated from its traditional principle of basing its attitude
toward those in power on that of the latter toward the
Church. The history of these two groups' relations with
the regime followed two almost parallel curves, with almost the same crises and ordeals. A knowledge of Orleanism does not at all require a narrative account of the July
Monarchy, whose crises and quarrels never touched the
heart of Orleanist doctrine. For Bonapartism, on the contrary, a discussion of its relations with the two classic
Right Wing groups is of essential importance, for variations in these relations modified its political position.
Therefore, the following pages borrow their outline and

rhythm from the history of these relations. Two events were landmarks in the twenty years 1850-1870. The first was a single date on the calendar, December 2, 1851. The second is harder to localize; it was the crisis the development of which extended over more than a year in 1859-1860.

III. Bonapartism of the Notables

We shall resume our narrative with the spring of 1849 when the election led us to suspend it because it began to reveal the disagreement between the allies of December 10, 1848. For thirty months the dissension grew until it reached open conflict: the monarchists scarcely hiding their intention of restoring the monarchy, the Prince-President not intending to be ousted. The contrast of their social circles amplified the antagonism between their plans. Louis-Napoleon gave the appearance of an adventurer and his entourage of upstarts inspired only contempt or disgust among those whose solemn dignity earned them the nickname, *the Burgraves*.[9] The opposition between the two systems blazed higher everyday. Legitimists and Orleanists, especially the latter whose preponderance gave the tone to the Assembly, were both attached to parliamentary liberalism. Bonapartism was authoritarian and antiparliamentarian as well as equalitarian and appealing to the lower orders. Its pretension to be the direct emanation of the national will, without admitting the intermediary of political parties, carried the germ of a break-up of the traditional structures in which the two Rightist groups placed the only guarantee of social stability. Conservative liberalism, authoritarian

[9] A term taken from Victor Hugo's play of this name and applied to elderly people with old-fashioned ideas. Tr.

democracy, the two systems each linked two ideas whose combination only aggravated their incompatibility.

The Assembly violated the application of universal suffrage; the President proposed its re-establishment. Clever people saw in this move of the President only a maneuver, good at best to delude only the naïve, but his proposal actually corresponded to the underlying thought of Bonapartism. The tension grew. On October 31, 1849, by discarding from his ministry several men whom he had chosen from the Party of Order just after his election, *i.e.,* Odilon Barrot, Falloux, and Tocqueville, Louis Napoleon wiped out the remnants of the alliance and demonstrated his independence. The Coup d'Etat resolved the conflict. It was a declaration of hostility against the two Rights. Directed against the Assembly which it dissolved, it hit *the Burgraves,* decapitated the Party of Order, and settled accounts with the monarchists. The democratic Left was not at first a direct target, its leaders were arrested only to balance off those on the Right. The people of Paris understood this well, and made no move to defend a conservative Assembly which had despoiled them of some of their political rights. The victims that the "fusillade of the boulevards"[10] stretched out on the sidewalks doubtless had voted Orleanist. Everything in the Coup d'Etat worked to create an unbridgable gulf between its authors and the notables, as a half-century before the execution of the Duke d'Enghien did between the first Napoleon and the royalists. By crushing the Rightist groups it interrupted their long rivalry with Bonapartism. The normal consequences of such an operation would have been to push the new regime toward popular Bonapartism, radical and authori-

[10] A skirmish between troops and bourgeois citizens of Paris two days after the Coup d'Etat of December 2, 1851. Tr.

tarian, resting firmly on mass support against the former governing classes.

In fact the Coup d'Etat of December 2 had quite different results. The regime first risked its future on the uncertain chances of a Bonapartism of the notables, conservative at the same time as authoritarian. This unexpected tack had several causes. In the first place there was the manifest desire of the Bonapartist leadership, of men who themselves belonged to the governing classes, with Morny at their head, to attract the notables. Morny was not far removed from the Orleanists, as much by sympathy for parliamentary institutions as by his own material interests. Locally the prefects used all their zeal and skill to establish good relations with the leading provincial families. In return the social authorities were grateful to the regime for removing threats of disorder. Finally, an accident did much to precipitate the rapprochement: the sequel of the Coup d'Etat in the provinces. Although Paris remained quiet, in several areas the Leftist Republicans took up arms and marched on the departmental capitals. The vigor and unexpected size of this resistance, together with the firmness of the repression which followed, gave credence to the myth of social war which had been predicted for 1852, and retrospectively furnished a reason and an excuse for the fear of it by property owners, both large and small. From this repression the Coup de'Etat took on new meaning. Its character as a police operation to defend public order relegated to a secondary importance its aspect as a forceful and illegal seizure of power by an ambitious man. At once the conditions were recreated for an alliance between Bonapartism and the traditional leaders of society; the political situation of the Party of Order in the period after the June Days was restored. At this point the conditions of the alliance which was to associate the two forces for eight years were laid down. Setting themselves firmly against the Left, the laws of political mechanics forced the system and the regime to the Right.

During these eight years, its happy years, the Empire had few worries about the Right: few men resisted its force, repulsed its advances, or remained unaffected by its prestige. The business world was conquered by the vigorous stimulation afforded to the economy; the peasants turned away from the older parties. As for the Church, whose support was almost unanimous (to salute the *new Constantine* some prelates found new forms of verbal exaggeration), the regime lavished honors and advantages on it. The government employed a persistent zeal in those regions of France where a long tradition had united allegiance to the Church with allegiance to the Bourbons, as in the West, where the non-voters in the plebiscite of December 1851 had been especially numerous, 40 per cent in the Vendée, 50 per cent in the Morbihan. Thus an entire chapter of the religious policy of the regime was directed toward these departments: the creation of a new bishopric at Laval, the promotion of that in Rennes to an archbishopric. Finally the trip of Their Imperial Majesties to Brittany during the summer of 1858 and their presence at the great pilgrimage of Saint Anne of Auray established the good relations between the regime and the Church. The regime could flatter itself with having won over practically all the social groups which, in other circumstances, had or would have given their support to the two Rightist traditions.

Bonapartism won the masses, it did not need their leaders; but it was by these leaders that political traditions were maintained and carried on. Their situation now was similar to that of the Legitimist opposition under the July Monarchy, but transposed, for the Orleanists this time joined the Legitimists in the opposition.

The Legitimists returned quite naturally to silent or fault-finding abstention from politics; this was less a matter of tactics than of habit for them. They had not evaded the clever schemes of the men of July only to yield to the advances or fall into the clumsy traps of this regime of upstarts. Just after the Coup de'Etat the Count de Chambord again ordered his followers to refuse to take the oath of loyalty to the new government.[11] After slightly more than three years of participation in public life his faithful supporters once again took the road to their provincial retreats, with dignity and without complaint. This was their third emigration, this time lasting for eighteen years. All in all, owing to the decisions of their prince, they were able to serve their country actively only three years out of forty. The generation that came of age about 1830 thus lived out its entire existence outside of public life. Obedience to the commands of the prince cost something to some of them, but they would not have been themselves if they had ceased to be faithful. Resigned to their bad luck or retaining hope and confidence against all expectation, they simply took up again the peaceful and monotonous routine of an existence devoted to managing their estates, hunting, and reading the *Gazette de France* or *L'Union*. Their discreet and sullen opposition hardly embarrassed the government, and not until the noticeable stiffening of the regime after the assassination attempt of Orsini did Persigny suppress one of their newspapers, the *Spectateur*. A single event could have rendered their opposition dan-

[11] Nevertheless, four Legitimists were elected to the Legislative body in 1852. Author.

gerous to the regime: a rapprochement with the Church, which, with the support of the clergy, would have given them some powerful forces. Such an eventuality then seemed improbable, for it did not take long to count the prelates who remained faithful to Henry V. Only one, Mgr. Baillès, bishop of Luçon, refused to order prayers for the new regime. The government got rid of him by having the Vatican call him to the Curia in Rome. Two others did not hide their Legitimist sympathies: Mgr. Pie and Mgr. de Dreux-Brézé, bishops of Poitiers and Moulins.[12] But Ultramontaine Catholicism, uncompromising, anti-liberal, the natural and traditional ally of Ultraroyalism, was also that which had the greatest reason to be won over by the authoritarian character of Bonapartism. In resounding articles Veuillot[13] saluted the success of the Coup d'Etat.

The Orleanists had not had such a long experience in the opposition. Recently thrown out of power, they still had to do their apprenticeship. Therefore the defections were proportionally larger in their ranks, although the leadership held firm. Opposition even had on them an effect analogous to that which the persecutions in the early Church had on the faith of the Christians, it reaffirmed their liberal convictions. While after June 1848 they had given in too often to demands that they defend the social order, they now rediscovered the virtues of liberalism. The open antiparliamentarism of the Empire irritated these parliamentarians; this "regime of brass hats" (the phrase is Thibaudet's) offended these thoroughly civilian men; the muzzling of the University and

---

[12] The bishop of Moulins received a warning from the government in 1857. Author.

[13] Louis Veuillot was a militant Ultramontaine Catholic propagandist and journalist. Tr.

the scorn expressed for intelligence wounded these "intellectuals." Finally, the somewhat vulgar magnificence of the Imperial court, the flashy luxury of the new masters, shocked these men in whom were united the intellectual discrimination of the Doctrinaires, the cold politeness of the Orleanist aristocracy, and a hereditary sense of moderation. As if the regime's mixture of despotism, police pressure, and demagoguery did not contain enough to repel them, its confiscation of the property of the House of Orleans besmirched its beginning with a spot of dishonesty which compelled the resignation of some men such as Rouher and Fould who later on were to be among the best servants of the Emperor.

The Orleanists did as the Legitimists had done twenty-two years earlier. They resigned from positions in the army and diplomacy the occupancy of which had been a family tradition. Prince Albert de Broglie abandoned his career. It is interesting to point out that many writers insist on depicting this Orleanist opposition as one of the bourgeoisie, while in fact it was one of the aristocracy: Broglie, Haussonville, Meaux, Montalembert, these were the leaders of the Orleanists who did not rally to the regime. But the forms of their opposition distinguished them greatly from the Legitimists. The latter returned to the provinces, the Orleanists stayed in Paris. To go away would have been too cruel a deprivation. Life in society was as indispensable to them as it was to Madame de Staël. They could not give up entertaining and discussing. The Orleanist opposition was one of the salons. It had all their glitter, brilliance, and pungency. It adopted their weapons: irony, sarcasm, allusion, and it also revealed their weaknesses. This intellectual and high-toned criticism did not worry the Minister of the Interior

nor keep the Prefect of Police awake at night. The regime
was not bothered by such pinpricks. Sainte-Beuve
laughed at "this general-staff of the salons." However,
this opposition had nothing to do with the frivolity often
associated with society life. These were academic salons,
these were serious men with an inherited taste for reflection. Pushed back to their studies by political inactivity,
they spent their forced leisure on erudite research, scholarly efforts, and huge historical works. With them history
was a tradition and a family property. For example,
Albert de Broglie worked on a *Histoire de l'Eglise et de
L'Empire Romain au IVe Siècle* in six volumes. Their contributions formed the character and reputation of the
Journal des Débats and the *Revue des Deux Mondes*.

This opposition of the pen was matched by an opposition of the rostrum. Parliamentary eloquence was one of
the attributes of Orleanism, and now ejected from the
Chamber, they found in the *Académie Française* a thea-
ter for their oratorical exploits. This was the finishing
touch in the composition of that curious picture which
identified the Orleanist opposition with a few salons,
some newspapers and periodicals, and the academies.
For at least a half a century the *Institut* became an Orleanist salon. The Orleanists guarded it well; only those
candidates who had given clear proofs of their liberalism
were privileged to enter. All varieties of liberalism were
represented: Montalembert and Berryer, Mgr. Dupanloup, the two Broglies—father and son, Duke Victor, the
former minister of Louis-Philippe, and Prince Albert, the
future minister of MacMahon—Duvergier de Hauranne,
Sylvestre de Sacy, Lacordaire, Prévost-Paradol. For a few
hours the addresses of welcome for a new member made
these political or religious orators forget their nostalgic

regrets for parliamentary debates. They expressed quiet audacities, allusive defiance, as when Lacordaire gave, in the *Institut,* an encomium on American liberty.

The list of those received in the academies, whose Orleanist orthodoxy carefully rejected any of uncertain leanings, includes some names the presence of which indicates the importance of the readjustment made since the last years of the July Monarchy. Memories of the sharp quarrels became blurred. Already the Falloux law had initiated a rapprochement between moderate Catholics and conciliatory Orleanists. Their parallel opposition to the Second Empire strengthened their relations and revealed numerous affinities, for they had the same opponent. Those liberal Catholics who surprisingly assented to the Coup d'Etat of December 2, 1851, quickly repented. Montalembert, who in a moment of weakness stood as a government candidate in Doubs, soon became himself again. In June 1852 he went into open opposition and cried out in the Legislative Body, "What are we then, a kind of departmental council at the mercy of the prefectural council over there?" pointing to the State Councillors attending the session. Six months later he published his pamphlet, *Some Catholic Interests in the Nineteenth Century.*

Their common opposition to an authoritarian regime led the liberal Catholics and Orleanists to recognize their equal attachment to liberty. Their agreement went even further, for the same goals of principle and the same fundamental choices were at the bottom of their political attitudes. Orleanism did not agree to throw out all of the new society which had emerged from the Revolution; liberal Catholicism did not subscribe to the anathemas hurled against the nineteenth century. In both there was the same favorable disposition toward movement and innovation, an equally optimistic view of life, and an identical belief that conciliation was more fruitful than inflexibility. These feelings of thought and mood were characteristic of a type of man and of a type of Catholic who at the same moment found their living antithesis in the symbolic figure of the Ultramontaine Legitimist.

It seems that history, having a taste for symmetry in these years 1852-1859, created two directly opposed forms of Catholic sensibility, and their contrast revived, with some original aspects and with an exceptional sharpness, a conflict of views within the Church perhaps as old as the Church itself. To draw the portrait of one of the two it is enough to outline, stroke for stroke, the other's opposite.

Modern society inspired in liberal Catholicism sympathy, good-will, indulgence, and a desire for understanding; in intransigent Catholicism it created only defiance and suspicion. The first stressed the variety and complexity of factual situations, the second wanted to know only the absolute and unchanging simplicity of principles. The former suggested flexible adaptations which conformed more to the spirit than the letter while the latter insisted on total and literal application.

This antagonism extended to the political realm where two opposed factions appeared. For the evolution which broke down the barriers between liberal Catholicism and Orleanism also tended to bring together authoritarian Catholicism and the Legitimists. The fusion of the latter two was not yet consummated, but affinities between them opened the road to the imminent alliance. These two forms of thought both led to emigration during the century, as they honored total allegiance to principles more than attempts at conciliation. It was not a simple coincidence that the faithful followers of the exiled

prince were also the most ardent servants of the pope
who lived on the other side of the mountains and who
was soon to be dispossessed of his kingdom. They even
had the same soldiers, for the Legitimists furnished the
papal zouaves and Louis Veuillot was one of the favorite
writers of the Count de Chambord.

This shifting of positions, by associating the two ultra
traditions, Ultra-royalism and Ultramontanism, isolated
and condemned to decay a tradition which had thrived
for many years while closely linked to the monarchical
idea: royal Gallicanism. Where would be the place of a
Montlosier in the Legitimism of 1860? Would the Comte
de Chambord have permitted one of his followers even to
express ideas which his grandfather had tolerated thirty
years before? Nevertheless, political or religious Gallicanism was not dead, for its representatives moved into
the liberal Catholic and Orleanist camp. This was true of
Sylvestre de Sacy and Mgr. Dupanloup; the latter's name
is inseparable from this chapter of the history of liberal
Catholicism.

The opposition of these two religious temperaments
attained the grandeur of an antithesis with the duel of
two newspapers which symbolized the two points of
view: *L'Univers* and *Le Correspondant*. The first was the
paper of Veuillot; the second after 1855 brought together
Montalembert, Albert de Broglie, the Vicomte de Meaux,
Mgr. Dupanloup, Foysset, and Cochin. This small team
of liberal Catholics steadily followed its search for a
concordat between principles and facts, dogmas and
modern thought, the Church and society, its class and
the nation.

Still, brilliant and intelligent it was, the Orleanist opposition was too intellectual to appeal to the general public. It was too careful to keep the tone and observe the

usages of good society to reach a large audience and rouse public opinion. It was too much the work of an elite to worry a regime which was based on the support of the masses, as expressed through the manipulations of universal suffrage. Academic criticism, scoffing in salons, sulking by intellectuals, this opposition lacked the plebeian vigor of a Veuillot. Basically the government tolerated it because it did not fear it at all. Nevertheless, when the response of the Duke d'Aumale to Prince Napoleon was suppressed[14] or when Haussonville was forbidden to become an editor of a newspaper, Persigny dealt with them without tenderness.

Seven years of authoritarian government and a meaningless political life reduced the numbers of the two classic Right Wing groups to their leaders, and their opposition to impotence. One deliberately withdrew and practiced abstention, the other was involuntarily isolated in a rarified atmosphere and lived imprisoned within the circle of a worldly society.

IV. Toward an Orleanist Empire

To this double opposition which was slowly wasting away and becoming anemic, the regime, suddenly and in the least expected way, gave hope, troops, and a political part to play. In fact, the years 1859 and 1860 were not only a turning point for the regime, but they markedly altered its relationship with the traditional governing classes.

Businessmen grew worried about the uncertainty and hazards of foreign policy and agreed with the warning of Baron James de Rothschild, who echoed the Bordeaux

[14] His reply to Prince Napoleon's attack on the Bourbon family was suppressed and the publisher was imprisoned for a year. Tr.

speech, "The Empire is peace; no more peace, no more Empire."[15] Other groups withdrew from the regime the confidence which only under certain conditions they had granted it. These were industrialists menaced or who feared they were menaced by the new tariff policy, and members of parliament bruised in their self-esteem or their feeling of political responsibility by the casual manner in which the Emperor outflanked their resistance by negotiating the free trade treaty of January 23, 1860, without consulting them. Their conditions of support ignored, these men lent willing ears to the proposals of the opposition, not of course the Legitimist opposition but that of the liberal Orleanists. Some fondly remembered the policy of peace carried out by Louis-Philippe, others recalled that under that regime the Chamber of Deputies had always successfully opposed governmental initiatives to soften the protectionist rigor; both suddenly discovered the advantages of a parliamentary regime and envisaged without distaste the prospect of defending their interests under the banner of liberalism. In a word, we see the reforging of that coalition of interests and convictions, of ideas and business, which had created the solidity of the July Monarchy. The Empire had been able to dissolve it in its own favor, but the close understanding between the notables and the regime always had rested on an ambiguity in which the notables lent their support more than they gave it. From that point on they did not mean to overthrow the regime—that would have opened the door to Heaven-knows-what adventure—but to supervise it more closely. The re-establishment of certain liberties and the normal operation of a parliamentary

[15] At Bordeaux in 1852 Louis-Napoleon had proclaimed, "The Empire is peace!" Tr.

regime would forestall a new coup d'état in tariff policy
or another Italian adventure.

Simultaneously, the Italian crisis and its repercussions
detached another conditional support from the regime,
that of the Church. The French Catholics were severe
with Napoleon III for having thoughtlessly stirred up the
Roman question and permitted the amputation piece by
piece of the holy territory of the Papal States. Without
appearing to retain the slightest gratitude to the Emperor for past favors, the bishops hurled anathemas at
the Empire's foreign policy. With that genius for verbal
excess which seems one of the attributes of religious eloquence, Mgr. Pie conjured up Herod and Pontius Pilate.
This bishop, to be sure, was a monarchist. But the liberal
Catholics, suspect at the Holy See for their liberalism,
were quite happy with this opportunity to atone for their
lukewarm Ultramontanism and raised the issue to a boil.
The diocesan letters of Mgr. Dupanloup did not lag behind those of Mgr. Pie. Liberals and irreconcilables,
Ultramontaines and Gallicans all had in common their
opposition to the policy of the regime.

The political authorities, who had never been troubled
by the hostile reserve of a handful of liberal Catholics
without much influence, worried more about this development which threatened to carry most of the faithful
into open opposition. The government replied sharply:
Mgr. Pie was accused before the Council of State of en-
croaching on the powers of the temporal authority, and
on January 30, 1860, *L'Univers* was forbidden to publish.
The Catholics, who under the authoritarian Empire were
the only ones to enjoy certain liberties, lost them and saw
themselves made subject to the common law. The executive committee of the *Conférences de Saint-Vincent de*

Paul which, in the absence of any law guaranteeing freedom of association, appeared to be a nucleus of opposition, was dissolved for refusing to permit its president to
be chosen for it. Relations turned sour. More than one
high government official was not unhappy to make the
Church feel the weight of civil authority and remind it
that the organic laws[16] were still in effect. At this time
many Catholics carried their unattached political allegiance over to the legitimate monarchy, with which
bonds of blood had already been established by the sacrifice of the Papal troops. While waiting for Providence
to deign to enlighten the Emperor or arrange a restoration, they began to demand the liberties they considered
necessary to the Church.

Thus *liberty* became the rallying cry and the common
banner for all the oppositions. Some invoked it by conviction, others as a tactic, the former as a matter of principle, the latter for their immediate advantage. When the
Alsatian Keller, a former official government candidate,
took the floor in the Legislative Body as one of the Catholic opposition, he declared that he did so in the name of
"Catholic and liberal France." This was an unusual marriage of terms. It no longer referred to the small fraction
of liberal Catholics with Orleanist sympathies, but signified a regrouping in the opposition of almost all Catholic opinion. This marked the failure of Catholic Bonapartism. And so, by the loss of its two borrowed allies,
the notables and the Church, Bonapartism found itself
reduced to its own proportions.

This official and public reconstitution of the Rightist
opposition was accomplished in two steps marked by
election years. Until this time, the system of official can-

---

[16] Certain regulations of the secular government concerning the
exercise of religion in France which dated from the First Empire. Tr.

didates and administrative pressure left practically no chance for opposition candidates; now suddenly the field of public life was reopened to them.[17] The Orleanists, who did not have thirty years of abstention in their past as did the Legitimists, had not yet lost the taste nor forgotten the rules of the parliamentary game. In each election, 1863 and 1869, there was an Orleanist gain.

Once again the irritating problem of the oath of loyalty to the regime came up for the victorious opposition candidates. Each of the two groups on the Right Wing responded in a way conforming to its past, its mood, and its way of thinking. A majority of the Legitimists submissively complied with the *non expedit* maintained by the Count de Chambord. The only ones who ignored it were a few of the more resolute or better informed like Berryer or Falloux whose political intelligence, independence of mind, and lively sense of opportunity separated them from the rest. The Orleanists also were divided, but in reverse proportion. In their case a minority followed the advice of Dufaure and abstained. The majority, excepting two of those elected, agreed to take the oath.

The opposition included four shades of opinion, among which the slogan liberty, the only common denominator, was the sign of recognition: the small fraction of Legitimists who followed Berryer and Falloux, the Orleanists, the Catholics, and the protectionists. The last two groups, united under the name *Independents,* included a strong contingent of former official candidates who had lost the government's favor. This was the case of the Alsatian Keller and of Clichon from Roubaix, two spokesmen for the new Catholic opposition. A more exact

[17] In 1860 and 1861 the Legislative Body was granted greater power by the government. Tr.

analysis of the strength of forces in the new assembly than that of the official statistics adds to the 32 members of the quadruple opposition a number of official candidates who were elected only with the support of the bishops. Beholden to the Church for their seats, each time that they had to choose between official policy and that of the "Catholic interests," the compliance of the "cathedral candidates" determined their choice. At the beginning of the 1866 session in the discussion on the speech from the throne, there were 63 votes in favor of an amendment offered by two Catholics well known for their liberal and Orleanist sympathies, Buffet and Daru. Thus there developed a *third force,* too much the enemy of adventure to want the regime to fall, too conciliatory not to want an accord, but firmly resolved to force the Empire to move in a liberal direction and bring safe men into the government. This policy conformed closely to the Orleanist tradition of accommodating itself to what existed rather than trying to change it, and it was Thiers who announced its minimum program by demanding the five necessary liberties. Liberalism was the key word and noble idea of this moderate opposition. The old theme of local liberties against the often heavy-handed authority of the Imperial prefects reappeared, witness the decentralization program of Nancy, which was signed by Berryer, Falloux, Guizot, and Montalembert.

A large part of the monarchist opposition spontaneously took up the tradition of an alliance with the Republican Left which the Legitimists had inaugurated against the July Monarchy. This was not merely an occasional collaboration. At Marseille, Berryer was elected with the help of Republican votes. A year later (1864) Berryer, Dufaure, and another Orleanist lawyer, Hébert, defended the Republicans in the Committee of Thirteen affair.[18] Some of the money used to launch the *Revue Politique*, a journal of Republican tendency, was advanced by Orleanists. The Orleanist presiding judge of a court permitted Gambetta in November 1868 to continue his impetuous indictment of the men of December Second without gavelling him to order. Among the subscribers for a monument to the Republican Deputy Baudin[19] were Berryer and Odilon Barrot.

The elections of 1869 were decisive for the regime and were not less so for the rapidly growing liberal Orleanist Right. Historians, preoccupied with what was to come, have usually pointed out the considerable gains of the Republicans. Contemporaries noticed quite as much the important progress accomplished by the Rightist opposition since the previous election. Forty-five Catholics were elected without official support and perhaps as many more with it. The Minister of the Interior counted the latter as supporting the government until a debate developed when he found them against it. On the first occasion 116 names were on a request for an interpellation.[20] Henceforth the regime had to take account of some 150 liberal deputies on which its majority depended: 110 or 120 on the Right-Center, and a Left-Center of 40 stanch Orleanists. After eighteen years the Party of Order was ready to gather the fruits of its long patience and pay off its former protégé for his ingratitude.

But the liberal Right did not want the sinner's death; it

---

[18] A trial of Republicans growing out of the 1863 elections. Tr.

[19] Killed in the Coup d'Etat of 1851, for political reasons Baudin was hailed as a martyr in 1868. Gambetta's speech came at the trial of the organizers of the Baudin affair. Tr.

[20] An interpellation is a Deputy's rather peremptory question of a government minister. It requires a debate and a vote on the issue. Tr.

did not want the regime to collapse; it judged it more prudent and politically wise to reorganize it. It was even inclined to renew its former alliance with the aging Emperor if he would subscribe to its conditions: a liberal evolution and the elimination of the personnel of the authoritarian Empire. He gave them complete satisfaction. Duruy, the anticlerical Minister of Education, and Haussmann, the authoritarian Prefect of the Seine, were dropped; Rouher himself, the faithful Rouher, was sacrificed; and Imperial institutions were profoundly changed. At this price the return of the liberal Right was not only possible but glorious. It had its revenge for the Second of December.

The ministry formed January 2, 1870, marked the Right Wing's return to power. Six of the eight ministers were devoted to the interests of the Church. Buffet and Daru themselves agreed to enter the cabinet. The signs of a reconciliation of the Rights and the Empire multiplied. For the first time in eighteen years veterans of the July Monarchy such as Guizot and Odilon Barrot were seen at the receptions for the new ministers. Finally, the admission of the principal minister Emile Ollivier to that sanctuary of liberal Orleanism, the *Académie Française*, had a symbolic value: the notables had pardoned the Second of December and granted an amnesty to the Empire. Parliamentary liberalism was quite willing to retain the framework of a regime whose contents it had emptied and replaced. Except for the name, the classic Right Wing had made an Orleanist monarchy out of the Empire. Their thought was to accept the constitution in order to change the legislation. Seconded by Ultramontaine Catholicism, Orleanism won a stunning revenge over Bonapartism. The young *Rue de Poitiers* did more than regain the positions taken from its parent, it reconquered them in the name of that universal suffrage which Bonapartism formerly had used against it.

Nevertheless, this reconciliation would have had no future, even if the regime had not collapsed at Sedan eight months later. The great concessions made by the Empire had not disarmed the intransigence of the haughtiest Orleanists. The Centrist majority supporting Emile Ollivier against a Republican Left and a Bonapartist Right once again proved the rule that the Center must move to one side or the other. It fell apart. On the Left-Center 40 irreconcilables threatened to desert it. The two ministers representing this shade of opinion in Ollivier's cabinet, Buffet and Daru, resigned in April 1870. They alleged that the regime created by the new constitution was not fully parliamentary. Above all Orleanism could not support the regime's request for a new mandate by plebiscite, thereby returning to the democratic and popular source of its authority. In sum, Orleanism complained that the Empire had not eliminated the last traces of Bonapartism.

In the plebiscite of May 8, 1870, the committee headed by Thiers recommended a *no* vote. In a common manifesto the *Gazette de France* similarly advised the Legitimists and *L'Union* made the same request of Catholics. So in the last hours of the regime the Right Wing groups again moved into the opposition. The Legitimist Right never had departed from its attitude of abstention, while the most fervent Orleanists retained all their suspicion of the system and its personnel. But again it was the massive fidelity of the countryside to Bonapartism which brought the success of the plebiscite in a France which still had a majority of peasants. Thus, the various positions had already been taken when the disaster came to fix them in history.

V. A Bonapartism of the Right

The attention thus far devoted to following the history of the regime's relations with its Rightist opposition has led us to defer the examination of the other side of the situation: between 1860 and 1870 what became, not of the Empire, but of Bonapartism?

Rural Bonapartism, despite the defection of the notables and the secession of the clergy, remained a force whose stability was demonstrated in the plebiscite of 1870. It continued to combine two aspects: conservative and democratic. But in any case it could not be expected that peasant opinion alone would define a political tendency. As to the Bonapartism of the notables, we have seen what the liberal movement of the regime left of it: nothing more than their conservative liberalism agreed to tolerate, that is, a discreet Bonapartism almost ashamed of its origins. As to the Bonapartism of the Church, since the events in Italy it went to rejoin in memory the other regimes which the hierarchy had abandoned to their unhappy lot.

The defection of its chance allies, in releasing it from the burden of their demands, might have left Bonapartism alone in its true nature. In fact, the initiatives taken in some areas after 1860, such as the olive branch held out to the workers, the educational policy of Victor Duruy, and the more firm and independent attitude toward the Church suggested the outlines of a policy which Bonapartism might have followed: democratic and appealing to the masses, hostile to the notables, and tinged with anticlericalism—all potentialities of the movement of 1849.

The failure to realize this possibility was due less to the increased pressure of the Orleanists already within the regime than to the evolution of Bonapartism itself. What developed was a very different kind of Bonapartism, of a reactionary character in the true sense of the word, whose entire program was the pure and simple return to the authoritarian Empire. It disapproved of everything that happened after 1860. We can see here a clear parallel to the Ultra-royalism of the Restoration. Bonapartist partisans had to abandon the seats of power but they did not despair of recovering them again. Sometimes called the *Arcadiens* after the Rue de l'Arcade where their executive committee had its office, or by a more colorful nickname, the *Ratapoils,* they still had 80 members in the Legislative Body in 1869. Their leaders included Duvernoy, Jérôme David, whom Rouher had favored to follow Morny as president of the Legislative Body, and the Cassagnacs, whose family temperament was to mark Bonapartism after 1870. In July 1870 they were the most eager for war, the victorious result of which would immediately have restored the authority of the Emperor and the prestige of the Empire and would have provided the hoped-for opportunity to send the Orleanists back to their studies, to abrogate liberalism, and to return to the constitution of 1852. The military defeat destroyed these daydreams.

The singular thing—and this is the key to the drama of Bonapartism after Sedan—was that it was this element, responsible as it was for the catastrophe and the fall of the regime, which was to survive after 1870 and assimilate all Bonapartism. Perhaps this was because it had jealously guarded its originality from the insidious contamination of the two monarchist groups on the Right. Unknowingly, before 1870, it had already fixed Bonapartism definitively on the Right Wing.

5

1871-1879: Moral Order, a Rightist Coalition

I. The National Assembly: A Resurrection of Old France

To those on the Right who, at bottom, had never fully pardoned the Second Empire for the circumstances of its birth, its nature, and its friends, and in whose eyes even the alliance with the Church was not enough to efface its original blemish, the disaster of Sedan seemed, after eighteen years, the deserved punishment for December 2. In truth the monarchists had never despaired. Hugo and the Republicans were not alone in believing in the historical retribution. For the banished it was only the expression of inherent justice. The religious spirit of the royalists was eager to recognize in it the decree of divine justice. Just as the Legitimists had had to wait eighteen years for the fall of the "faithless tutor,"[1] it was

[1] Louis-Philippe. Tr.

also after eighteen years that the notables of the Party of Order saw Caesarism collapse.

Throughout the century, intervals of from fifteen to eighteen years marked the rhythm of the successive regimes as if some mysterious law had fixed this length for their existence. After fifteen years of the Consular and Imperial period, the next fifteen years limited the duration of the Restoration, eighteen years marked off the July Monarchy and eighteen also the Second Empire. Seventeen years after September 4 the Boulangist crisis very nearly carried off the Republic and a dozen years later the storm of the Dreyfus Affair burst forth. Fifteen years, eighteen years, regimes died more rapidly than men. Perhaps this was the necessary lapse of time for the new generation whose political consciousness was awakening to forget the disillusionments of the preceding generation or draw the consequences of them and take over from the vanquished of yesterday. In this way the generation of young Republicans of 1865, positivist and realistic, followed the mystic idealism of the forty-eighters.

The analogy between February 1848 and September 1870 goes deeper than this coincidence of chronological order. The two regimes fell in the same way. The Parisian insurrection of 1848 had swept out the leadership of the July Monarchy; the Parisian "day" of September 4, 1870, dispatched into political limbo all the governmental and administrative personnel of the Empire, suddenly discredited by the disaster it had brought upon the country and which had, moreover, never rooted itself as deeply in French society as its predecessors. Thus in forty years, from 1830 to 1870, or about the length of a career in politics or government service, three revolutions successively excluded from public life three distinct leadership groups, a frightful waste. France was the only country in Europe so politically advanced and socially differentiated to be able to afford such extravagance.

February 1848 began a confused period when newcomers, parvenus as the fallen leaders scornfully called them, had to face problems aggravated by the uncertainty of the times. September 1870 began with similar endeavors of another team of improvised leaders, the men of the Government of National Defense, to assure the continuity of the State in an unfortunate war. In both cases the upheaval worked to the benefit of new men who had served their political apprenticeship in the Republican opposition. In neither instance did the Rightist opposition, the Legitimists in 1848 nor the Orleanists in 1870, try to seize power by surprise, or attempt to assume the difficult responsibilities of government. Why didn't the leaders of the Right try to carry the decision with a well-calculated move after Sedan? They certainly would have found a majority in the Legislative Body. But this hypothesis is as vain as the question. Since 1830 both branches of monarchists, accustomed to revolutions being fomented against them, dared neither to oppose them nor guide them, and left the field clear for the Republican leaders, more expert at handling crowds and speaking to the people.

But this attempt carried on by new men, in 1870 as in 1848, was short lived. The first lasted only four months, the second five; one ended in the June Days, the other ceased with the defeat; both concluded tragically with a failure in which exceptional circumstances figured. Two assemblies then undid the deeds of these two interregna, and ousted the men as well. This was the hour for the reentrance of the Rightists. We recall the formation and success of the Party of Order in 1848. In 1870 the Republicans of the capital were able, in the aftermath of the defeat at Sedan, to take by surprise a power that the Bonapartists abandoned to them without a struggle. But the assembly to which universal suffrage again delivered the destinies of the country on February 8, 1871, was an assembly with a majority on the Right.

Seven hundred sixty-eight seats were to be filled. Taking account of multiple elections[2] and resignations, the total of these elected who met at Bordeaux some weeks later was about 650. There were 400 royalists of all varieties. They garnered the four vice-presidencies; eight of the nine members of the executive committee were royalist. Although the by-elections of June 2 only gave them a dozen seats of the 118 chosen in this second batch, the majority of this "Comparable" Chamber remained monarchist.

But for once the sober language of numbers is less expressive than that of surnames. Running through the names of those elected is like leafing through a book of heraldry, or better, rereading the history of Old Regime France: La Rochefoucauld, Noailles, Broglie, Harcourt, Gontaut-Biron, Haussonville, and many others who, although more obscure, were not less substantial nobility. This National Assembly, in which even a Decazes was not lacking, was it the "Incomparable Chamber?" But moving along a little farther we see the July Monarchy miraculously revived, with the princes—Aumale and Joinville—in the first rank, then twenty names famous between 1830 and 1848, Pasquier, Casimer Périer, Thiers, Guizot, a Duchâtel, Dufaure. . . . But it is vain to

[2] The same person elected in more than one district. Tr.

look for a survivor of the regime which had just collapsed. Some of those elected doubtless harbored in the secret of their hearts a discreet fidelity to the fallen dynasty, but to all appearances nothing escaped from the wreck of the Empire. It was the hour of old France, that prior to 1850, of its families and its notables. As the erosion which removes alluvium and surface deposits bares the older strata and discloses the rock, the troubles of the *année terrible*,[3] in sweeping away the precarious Bonapartist edifice, brought to light the traditional contours, the older structures that eighteen years of the Imperial regime had been able to cover only temporarily. Beyond what seemed the accident of the Empire, continuity was re-established with the Legislative Assembly of 1849, a good number of whose members met again, twenty years older, on the benches of the Bordeaux Assembly. Ties were renewed even beyond the Second Republic to the Assemblies of the Constitutional Monarchies. Once again universal suffrage confirmed the authority of the traditional elites, the nation recognized itself anew in the monarchical Right Wing.

Unquestionably, France's unusual situation greatly assisted them. During the war the prestige of the old families grew due to the part they spontaneously took in organizing the defense. And when resistance became useless it was the local lord who was able to find the words that were necessary, who perhaps knew the language of the enemy, who possessed the habit of social relations, and whom the villagers asked to interpose himself between them and the occupant, to mediate so as to soften demands or obtain a pardon for a guerilla soldier. In a period of distress the notable took up again quite natu-

[3] 1870-1871. Tr.

rally, and with general consent, the time-honored role of protector. The Legitimists in particular gathered the fruit of their long association with the peasants. Beyond the hereditary prestige of their social function, the notables had in their favor the fact that at the moment when the issue was war or peace, they represented, against the Empire which was responsible for the defeat and against Gambetta's group which favored continuing the struggle, the desire for peace of most of the rural areas, that is to say, the majority of the country.

Nevertheless, if the circumstances had been otherwise, would the result have been very different? To think so we would have to ignore all the signs of the slow and progressive rise of the monarchists and forget the veritable Orleanist restoration which shortly preceded the fall of the Empire. The reversal of the majority did not come after Sedan, it came much earlier, at some point between Solferino and Sadowa. The only novelty of 1871, recognizing the irony in using this word to designate such an old tradition, was the return in force of the Legitimists. The reconquests of 1860's were won by the Orleanists above all; the royalists of the elder branch had scarcely any part in them. But over a hundred Legitimists came to Bordeaux, an unhoped for figure after forty years of political abstention scarcely broken by three and one-half years of public life during the Second Republic.

For the second time in a quarter century the royalists could expect an imminent monarchical restoration. Did they not have a majority which expressed the sentiments of the country? Was not the assembly sovereign, with no other power limiting its prerogatives? In fact, what possible force would prevent them from carrying out their plan? This time a Bonaparte's ambition would not frustrate them. On June 8, 1871, by 484 votes to 163, the Assembly abolished the exile law,[4] was not this the necessary preface to the restoration of the monarchy?

II. The Two Monarchical Traditions

As yet we have not considered the divisions that weakened the Right Wing; just as happened a half-century earlier to the Ultras, their internal divisions were to ruin the hopes of those on the Right. Still, bringing up the Ultra precedent puts things in too advantageous a light: for the Ultras, however divided they were, agreed on essentials. Their disputes ordinarily concerned only methods and tactics. Whether friends or enemies of Villèle, they constituted only one family, they were but *one* Right. In the days of the National Assembly there was a *coalition* of Rightist factions. This nuance is important for in it lay the history of this assembly, the fate of its plans, and the explanation for their ludicrous failure.

Coalition means a plurality of diverse and circumstantially reconciled groups. Perhaps there isn't a better example than the National Assembly to show that it is a little too schematic to think of two large homogeneous blocs face to face, to set up in opposition a Left unanimously "progressive" and a Right just as massively "reactionary," or to use less relative terms, a party of movement and one clearly labeled "old regime." This is sufficiently proved by the historian's embarrassment in classifying certain groups where he is unsure whether they lean to the Left or to the Right. We remember the ambiguity of Orleanism at the beginning and the hybrid

---

[4] This law had forbidden the Bourbon or Orleanist princes to reside in France. Tr.

character of Bonapartism in its early years. The same held true for certain groups in the National Assembly as long as a crisis did not require them to choose one or the other of the two great positions. In the alternation of periods of tension and relaxation we can make out two unequal Rights. One, more limited but more stable than the other, was composed of the established traditions—Legitimist Right, Orleanist Right, and perhaps already the Bonapartist Right. The other, larger and more precarious, temporarily included other groups brought in by the need for realignments against a common enemy.

The formation of the coalition that pulled Thiers down on May 24, 1873, offers a good example of the movement from one to another of these two types of coalition, of this step-by-step enlargement. The intrigue was concocted in the spring of 1872; it took shape with Duke Albert de Broglie's return from the embassy in London. We shall skip over the preliminary skirmishes. At the beginning of April 1873, 304 Deputies against 285 elected Buffet, an Orleanist of the Right-Center and former minister in Emile Ollivier's cabinet, to the Presidency of the Assembly in place of the old Republican Jules Grévy. We can say that on that day 304 members voted on the Right. Then came one after another the surprise election of the Radical Barodet in Paris (April 28), the election of two other Radicals in Lyon (May 11), and Thiers' reshuffling of his ministry to bring in three men of the Left-Center (May 18). These events determined the Right Wing to take the offensive. The very day when Thiers changed the composition of his government, delegates of the various groups met at the home of the Duke de Broglie, whose leadership they recognized, and agreed on the name of Thiers' successor.

The coalition was confirmed. On the 19th its leader, the Duke de Broglie, presented a request for an interpellation "on the necessity of having a resolutely conservative policy dominant in the government." Observe how this was put. It was supported by 320 signatures; note the number. On the 20th, they were 359 against 289 to re-elect Buffet (at this period the Presidency of the Assembly was a monthly office). On the 23rd, the Duke de Broglie elaborated on his interpellation—he expressed the worry of his political friends at seeing the government deviate from the policy of resistance that the size and imminence of the radical peril seemed to require and requested the formation of a ministry resolved to re-establish moral order. Having heard Thiers on the 24th, the issue was decided by the adhesion of 15 Deputies from the Target group who sat on the Left beyond the usual limit of Rightist support. By 360 to 344 votes the Assembly rejected the motion extending confidence to Thiers. The undecided rushed to the support of the victory—a few moments later the motion of censure of Thiers won 368 votes and in the evening there were 390 to put MacMahon in the Presidency. They had begun with 304. On that evening the Rightist majority reached its greatest extent. Subsequently it was only to shrink. It thus grew in one month from a few more than 300 to a few less than 400. This kind of numerical elasticity suggests that this majority included disparate elements, and that there were different degrees of being Right with regard to seniority as well as fidelity. In fact the majority of May 24, 1873, exhibited a profile in which were revealed all the successive strata in the Rightist coalition.

The various political groups in the Assembly, rather vaguely defined as they were, we consider as a secondary matter in contrast to the distribution of opinions and divisions of points of view. At that time there were neither clearly delimited parliamentary groups nor organized parties. The Orleanist princes had a network of correspondents in Paris and in the provinces to whom they sent messages and instructions which the latter disseminated. In the same way the Marquis de Dreux-Brézé managed the office of the Count de Chambord. The nature of the feelings that attached the monarchists to the pretender, the character of their convictions, the importance of personal relations, family traditions, and marriage alliances were incompatible with the existence of modern parties which imply individual equality, acceptance of the practice of universal suffrage, and the prior adoption of democracy.

The coalition of 1873 again offers us the spectacle of the three tendencies representing the three traditions whose appearance we have reviewed and whose development we have outlined. Let us take up again the familiar but always new parallel between the two families of royalists. This requires some repetition but can we do otherwise if the sons are the images of their fathers? Besides, for the Legitimists, lost in their provincial exile, time did not seem to have passed: they believed they had returned to the happy days of 1849 or 1815. The extent of changes in the strength and direction of currents of opinion wrought by thirty or forty years of normal existence emerges when one compares them with constants. The monarchists nevertheless remained as different from one another as at the beginning. At a distance, such as that from which their political opponents saw them, the two might have passed for close kin—weren't they both equally attached to the monarchical form? For a Repub-

lican, Orleanists and Legitimists were just royalists. But
there was more than one way of understanding monarchy; an apparently common opinion could disguise
radically different social and doctrinal choices, with the
latter perhaps the more divisive.

Fidelity defined the Legitimists, fidelity to the princes,
fidelity to their fathers' principles. A hundred of them sat
on the extreme Right. They took their nickname *chevau-
légers* from the name of the street in Versailles where the
hotel was where they customarily gathered when not at
the sittings of the Assembly. Their role was not as large
as their numbers; few of their names would be known
from the records of parliamentary activity. Eloquence
was not their strength, often their speech was short and
crude. Was this provincial awkwardness or the timidity
of gentlemen less clever at talking than fighting? They
were readier to brave the fire of the Sardinians at Castel-
fidardo or the Prussians at Patay than to climb the steps
to the tribune in the Assembly. It required nothing less
than crucial stakes or outrages to their sacred principles
to dislodge from their sullen reserve those who were
mockingly called *"bonnets à poil."*[5]

Their fidelity was absolute. It was neither shared nor
withdrawn. It was not one of those half-loyalties which
are also half-treasons. Incapable of guile, these men
made only one promise. Several times the Count de
Chambord put their fidelity to the test and they never
failed him. Of course, we should not make Legitimism
more homogeneous than it was. It included some rather
supple persons, with more insight, whose finesse or sub-
tlety did not fit in well with the brusque inflexibility of
their colleagues and who subscribed neither without res-

[5] An allusion to soldiers' fur caps, or bearskins. Tr.

ervations nor qualifications to the official Legitimist program. Falloux was absent from the National Assembly
but he discreetly exercised his influence and his opinions
were even solicited. A liberal Legitimist, he favored conciliation with new France and had no illusions as to the
presumptuous folly of wanting to restore the intangible
past.

Nevertheless, the idea of restoration was the dominant
note in the system of Legitimist thought. However little
taste for speculation was shown by these men, who were
of a breed more martial than verbal, all their thoughts
and their maneuvers were in terms of a system. It may be
stated in a word, which they now prefered to restoration,
counter-revolution. They inscribed it on their banners,
imagined its development, and undertook to lay its foundations. Since 1815 the word had changed but not the
program. Three revolutions in forty years only served to
reinforce their certainty. They were confirmed in their
belief of the fragility of any regime other than monarchy
and of the impossibility of building a durable society on
the principles of 1789, which experience seemed to them
definitively to have condemned. All things considered, it
was perhaps a religious document, the *Syllabus,*[6] which
presented the best statement of their system of thought,
for to its anathemas they willingly subscribed.

Monarchy was connected in their thought, their yearn-
ings, and their desires, to a form of society in which personal ties ruled social relations, where the superior
provided protection and assistance to the inferior and received recognition and devotion in return. The lord protected the farmer, the employer his employees, the
master his servants, as the father his children and the

---

[6] The *Syllabus of Errors* of Pope Pius IX of 1864. Tr.

king his subjects. A network of duties and reciprocal services linked the degrees of the social hierarchy to each other. And the fulfillment by each man of his own social function gave to civil society, because of the presence of the Church at every act, a character as much sacred as natural. A *Christian monarchy, a hierarchical society, patronage,* these were the key words and major lines of political, religious, and social belief which lay behind all their attitudes, as well as flowing from the pens of their publicists. The similarity between this thought and that of the writers of the Restoration is evident.

One fresh consideration, however, gave new life to the old Ultracism: a more lively and explicit concern over social conditions. It was natural that landlords accustomed to the respect of their peasants, but in addition always ready to come to their assistance, that feudal lords hereditarily attached to a network of personal relations, were the first on the Right to worry about what was called "the social question." They were shocked by the scandal of corporations where capitalists, preoccupied exclusively with profit, controlled multitudes of individuals of whom they knew nothing. Economic liberalism was contrary to all their principles. To this problem they proposed a solution inspired by their own experience, historical as well as individual, and in conformity with their ways of thought—patronage by the upper classes and corporative organization. This was the program of the *Catholic Workers' Circles,* of an entire generation of social Catholics, and of La Tour du Pin and Albert de Mun. The first social Catholicism had a conservative inspiration, a counter-revolutionary design, and Legitimist affinities. Later a second generation would develop out of Christian Democracy, but it is not clear

even today, ninety years later, if social Catholicism has
eliminated from its program and its spirit all traces of the
counter-revolutionary program of its precursors.

The opinions of these Legitimists were attached so
clearly to the counter-revolutionary doctrines of a Bonald, of a de Maistre, or of the early Lamennais, that they
smacked of bullheadedness. Really, there were none less
theoretical than they. Had they even read the theoreticians of counter-revolution? Nothing is less sure. Above
all, that society which they held as the ideal was that in
which they lived, that rural society whose framework
and customs were infinitely slower to decompose than
the brilliant but fragile urban civilization. They were
deeply convinced of its merits by a long familiarity with
its laws, usages, and virtues. How could they not wish to
preserve this society and extend its benefits to the entire
nation? It was less, in fact, a matter of restoring it, as if it
were necessary to create it *ex nihilo*, than of crowning it
with the monarchical institution whose presence was, for
it, a guarantee of continuation and whose absence delivered it defenseless to the insidious or brutal schemes of
its enemies.

It is unfair to deny to the Legitimists all understanding
of their era and impute to them an anachronistic view
of society. Among the several juxtaposed societies in the
France of 1873, there was a France of 1820, or perhaps
even of the Old Regime, which events had scarcely
touched and which had survived the political upheavals.
The Legitimists knew this France well; and they were
men to speak only of what they knew and liked well.
But it was clear that they scarcely knew the other Frances: bourgeois society was foreign to them, they were out
of touch with the working-class France which was be-

ginning to appear, and even a certain part of rural France was already trying to escape them. Every passing year made them a little more alien to their era and even to their country.

The Orleanist position was entirely different. They were entirely up-to-date in their history. It did not escape the best informed that Orleanism was on the eve of experiencing a kind of golden age. They did not intend to let such a good opportunity escape. The Legitimists withdrew to one side in a sulky abstention; the Orleanists were at the heart of negotiations, at the center of intrigues, and were part of all ministerial combinations. Their number (about 200) made this group the weightiest in the Assembly, its position in the hemicycle of the Chamber (closest to the Center, which made it impossible to govern without it, much less against it), and its leaders' parliamentary ability, all made it the axis of any majority. Once again the old opposition between a Legitimism aloof from governmental responsibility and an Orleanism associated in the exercise of power was confirmed.

It would be hasty and unjust to explain the Orleanists' privileged position as the result of unscrupulous opportunism. Without making them more disinterested than they were, it is to their credit that they took a more realistic and less fragmentary view of contemporary France than the Legitimists. They knew some levels of the bourgeoisie as well as a part of urban society. Also, no sentimental superstition attached them to the past, no out-of-date intransigence limited their freedom of action. Certainly, they quite justifiably called themselves monarchists and their dynastic fidelity cannot be doubted. But it remained true that if they bore a respectful affection for their princes, and the quality of this affection suggests what it cost them to rally to the Republic, above the monarchical institution they placed France. But the dilemma of monarchy as against fatherland scarcely made sense to a true Legitimist. To him fidelity to the person of the king and service to the country were not separable. This was evident in their desertion of their public careers after 1830. For the Legitimists monarchy was a person, a feeling; for the Orleanists a principle, a form of government. Experience also revealed that in the royalist camp, Orleanism represented the line of least resistance. Almost all the men of the Left-Center, headed by Thiers, who were to resign themselves to the Republic, were former Orleanists.

The basis of Orleanist thought remained a mixture of political liberalism and social conservatism. The parliamentary regime, equidistant between the arbitrariness of absolute power and the dictatorship of the masses, was the pledge and protector of civil liberties. The dictum of Augustin Cochin, a liberal Catholic with Orleanist sympathies, admirably expressed their political credo: "The social reforms of 1789 and parliamentary government, whether one likes it or not, this is what is called civilization." The position of the group in the Assembly illustrated the double nature of Orleanism. Two political arrangements required it and it gave itself to each in turn: an alliance of the centers with the Left-Center, or a Rightist coalition with the Legitimist extreme-Right. Its regular alternation between these two stances well expressed the ambiguity of its position half way between the extremes. Although pushed slightly to the Right by the rise of new political strata, Orleanism remained the party of the *juste milieu*. Between the excesses of reaction and the extremes of radicalism, and it is hard to say which was more repugnant to it, Orleanism tried to hold a middle course which, while giving democracy a role, would temper its impulses.

On the level of political institutions and the forms of society, we have already plumbed the depth of the disagreement which opposed the two royalist traditions. Far from softening with time, the conflict became perhaps even more acute. In any case there was one area where it hardened and in a way which involved men's personalities so deeply that a rapprochement would have been improbable even had other sources of discord disappeared. This was the area of religious feeling where as the opposition became stronger the terms in which it was couched were altered.

Let us recall what differentiated Legitimism and Orleanism in their attitude towards Catholicism from the very beginning. The principle of an alliance between throne and altar, although it correctly defines the basis of the relations between the Ultra party and the Church, does not describe the spirit of these relations. It puts the emphasis on the tactical or diplomatic side, thus passing over the more intimate bonds that established a kind of consubstantial unity between the monarchy and the Church. They were two parts of the same system, two elements of the same order, both spiritual and temporal. The king held his crown from God and the Church was that of the king. It would therefore be an error to speak of an alliance between two institutions which were so closely joined together. With Orleanism the point of view was quite different. Divorce had been pronounced between the Church and the secular monarchy. This new definition of their relations in no way excluded, circumstances permitting, the development of courteous and even cordial relations between them. In fact, the open anticlericalism at the beginning of the July regime rapidly lost its virulence. Yet these relations remained those which might have been established between two originally distinct powers jealous of their independence. Then too, improving relations did not wipe out intellectual antagonisms; eclecticism was hardly compatible with dogmatic orthodoxy, and the tolerant liberalism of the Orleanists did not sit well with the narrow intransigence of the Church.

Thirty years later[7] the respective positions were rather notably altered. To be sure, the Legitimists had not denied the faith of the Ultras, but the Ultras in general had favored a Gallican Church whose union with the Papal See involved considerable liberty and respect for special traditions. The Gallicanism of some went far enough to take the form of an open suspicion of Ultramontanism and a strong animosity against a Catholicism rightly or wrongly reputed to be *Jesuit*. By 1860 and even more by 1873 this variety of Gallican Catholicism was tending to become an archeological curiosity. It is hard to believe that all the Gallicans had disappeared, but in a Church becoming more and more centralized, in which Ultramontanism had won a conclusive victory at the Vatican Council of 1870, they were reduced to the state of a minority without means of expression. The bulk of the royalists was won, heart and soul, to an Ultramontanism whose sincerity was demonstrated by the sacrifice of the papal zouaves. Simultaneously, Orleanism was undergoing an even more important evolution. Repudiating the anticlericalism of its early days, it rallied to Catholicism,

---

[7] That is, in the 1860's and 1870's. Tr.

but kept its originality by taking over from liberal Catholicism. Thus the original Ultra clericalism and anticlerical liberalism gave way at the end of this series of changes to Ultramontaine Catholicism and liberal Catholicism. It would indicate a poor understanding of religious matters to imagine that this transposition which reduced the distance between the traditions was able to weaken their disagreement. By moving within the pale of the Church, the conflicts became more irreconcilable. Perhaps there is no animosity so strong as that between divergent interpretations of a commonly accepted truth.

A new kind of Catholicism caused a novel shift in these internal quarrels. It appears, in fact, that just after the defeat of 1871 a new Catholicism took shape. Let it be understood that it did not propose any new dogmas to the faithful, even that of papal infallibility only formalized a long tradition of belief and did not at all upset the architecture of dogmatic structure. The changes referred to another dimension of religious life, perhaps more important in some ways than the theological—the dimension of sensibility. If a name is required for this neo-Catholicism, we shall baptize it *Assumptionist* Catholicism. This was not the first time in the history of the Church that an order, a society, or a congregation exerted a decisive influence on an era; witness the mendicant orders in the thirteenth century and the Society of Jesus in the Counter Reformation. In France during the thirty years from 1871 to 1901 the Augustin Fathers of the Assumption, who had in their favor neither a glorious past nor renowned thinkers, put the mark of their spirit on French Catholicism; or if one prefers, in deference to the complexity of spiritual influences which came together in this period, their religious feeling and the nature of their activities were most closely suited to the tendencies and inclinations of French Catholicism after 1870.

This Catholicism borrowed some of its most character-istic traits from current circumstances. The formative factor was that it came into being just after a national disaster and a social tempest. To those familiar with scholastic analogy, practiced in deciphering the spiritual meaning of sacred texts, it seemed natural to look for the hidden meaning of every event beneath its visible causes. They were going, then, to scrutinize circumstances and make history speak, through a rather elementary process of reasoning. Besides, didn't foresighted Providence ar-range, in the margin of events, almost a translation of them? The visions of La Salette, Lourdes, and soon of Pontmain multiplied the warnings and offered an ad-vance explanation of public misfortunes. Remaining deaf to these admonitions, France was justly punished for its callousness. When free-thinkers asked what errors had been committed, preachers and theologians had a ready reply—for the last seventy-five years France had denied God, disregarded His rights, transgressed against His laws. With this theme of a France faithless to its Chris-tian tradition, the idea developed in ecclesiastical circles that France had ceased to be the Christian nation that the clergy of the Restoration had still believed it to be.

Therefore France had to atone for its life of pleasure and frivolity in Paris during the Second Empire. The preachers invited to repentence the modern Babylon whose disorders had attracted the fire of heaven, as sym-bolized by the Commune. The construction on its highest hill of a basilica dedicated to the Sacred Heart would proclaim on the Parisian skyline the capital's repentence.

Expiation, repentance, and atonement colored all piety during the 1870's. The devotion to the Sacred Heart was primarily a cult of atonement; all the sermons, hymns, and religious writings reflected this grieving, repentant, and self-abasing sensibility. Circumstances worked curiously to associate the cult of the Sacred Heart with wounded patriotism and with monarchical fidelity. At Patay and Loigny the former papal zouaves of General de Charette and the volunteers of General de Sonis fought bravely under their colors—a white flag embellished with a Sacred Heart. Their valor furnished a proud and pious reply to the exploits of the Garibaldians or the Republican flying columns in 1870-1871. The love for the defeated and mutilated fatherland, the desire to atone, the monarchical faith, the solidarity of veterans faithful to their fallen comrades, all merged into the common and easily exalted fervor that made up the psychological context of the new devotion.

Another defeat seemed to sharpen the sentiments inspired by France's misfortunes—that of the papal power. French Catholics saw more than a coincidence between the defeat of the eldest daughter of the Church and the Sardinian seizure of Rome. The pope's captivity was analogous to the king's exile. The devotion of the faithful was excited to see both causes exposed to the same enemy. Everything was an omen for those to whom the supernatural was familiar. The providentialism that ruled their interpretation of contemporary history required the notion of the Enemy. Few periods were so receptive as this one to the fascination and mirages of Satanism, whose evocation left a sulphurous trail in the literature of the period, from Barbey d'Aurevilly (a Legitimist) to J. K. Huysmans. But illuminism, proficient at deciphering omens, was not less so at reversing their meaning. Its alchemy excelled at transmuting reality, at reading into the troubles of today the victories of tomorrow. In this apocalyptical light, mystical souls believed they were living in the days heralding Judgment. Catastrophism became millenarianism; Catholic opinion awaited, with a confidence which among some replaced political sense, the double miracle which would simultaneously return pope and king.

This frame of mind could very easily, due to a lack of appropriate means of expression, have remained inarticulate and progressively wasted away. The historian would have found no trace of it. But it was expressed, displayed, and organized. Here the Assumptionist Fathers entered the scene. They did not invent this form of piety but they had the talent to create practices and exercises suitable to the religious feeling of that time and society. Their initiative can be seen at the beginning of every innovation. They knew how to discover the means of action, to use methods of influencing people at the level of the masses that universal suffrage brought into the political field. From the first they understood the power of an extensive press and refused to let the enemies of the Church have a monopoly of it. With the crowds that flocked to pilgrimages[8] they brought to the Church the equivalent of political meetings and gatherings. It is to them that the Catholicism of these years owed its popular, even plebeian nature. They operated on a big scale, addressed huge audiences, moved crowds, spoke to them in direct language. After fifty years they took up the

[8] In February 1872 the General Superior of the Assumptionists created a General Council of Pilgrimages. The publication of the *Pèlerin* began about this time. Author.

work begun by the Missions of the Restoration and revived the popular tradition of Legitimist royalism.

Although this fighting Catholicism—mystical, militant,
even military, leaguer, and ultra—considered itself to be
all of French Catholicism, outside of it there remained
another current which refused to let itself be swept
away. This was the continuation of that liberal and Orleanist Catholicism that we watched develop from 1855
to 1860. This group had little notoriety. By its natural
disposition it had an aversion to tumult and valued the
discretion which seemed equal to sincerity in belief. Men
such as the Duke de Broglie, Thureau-Dangin, or the
editors of the *Français* were not less good Catholics[9]
than the writers of *l'Univers* or the Legitimist gentlemen, but they did not have the same conception of religious life. To them the place of religion seemed to be in
the secret places of the heart and in domestic intimacy
rather than in the forum. Very significant was their silent
and stubborn refusal to consecrate France publicly to the
Sacred Heart. They feared that the Church might suffer
great harm by a mixing of two different elements. They
discreetly criticized the new devotions, the parades of
pilgrims, the alien piety which wounded all their attitudes. They were too French to appreciate the demonstrations whose theatrical character they judged was
closer to the spirit of foreign countries than to French
national character and to the traditions which formerly
were the glory of the Gallican church. The word superstition came to their lips but they refrained from pro-
nouncing it.

[9] Although Veuillot was suspicious of their Catholicism: "M. de
Broglie is half-caste, mixed blood of France and Geneva, of Catholic
and Protestant, of yes and no." Author.

Perhaps because they knew history better, they gave no credit to the apocalyptic interpretations of the visionaries. They did not think mystically and remained too intelligent to consent to throw their own judgment on the scrap heap, or too proud to admit that a sacrifice of their intellectual distaste might be pleasing to God. They believed that there were sincere unbelievers and feared the unfortunate impression the latter might get from these noisy demonstrations. Either because of human respect or apostolic considerations, they did not care to present spectacles which might repel men of good will. They also had the weakness of thinking that concrete situations often are less simple than principles, and that the interests of the Church as well as political sense required a minimum of prudence. In November 1873 the Duke Decazes made as a formal condition of his acceptance of the foreign affairs portfolio in the reshuffled Broglie ministry that it explicitly disavow the clerical campaign for the restoration of the pope's temporal power. The complaint of the *Correspondant* discreetly echoed this, "It is well to remember that there is a wise prudence in matters of faith as in those of politics."

Their opposition never went, however, beyond a mute disapproval. While they naturally disliked extreme methods (they were of the *juste milieu* even in their Catholicism), they did not dare to declare themselves too openly against the dominant view. They were a minority, a dangerous position within the Church. In a period when intransigence was on top, when dogmatic affirmations were made without restrictions, they had the misfortune to be liberals, to remain tolerant, to remember the rights of conjecture. Consequently Mgr. Dupanloup would never be raised to the cardinalate. Liberal Catholicism also had against it that it was a small elite, inbred and cut off from the mass, another trait which related it to Orleanism. Between the radical masses who cheered Gambetta and the crowds of pilgrims who chanted, "Save Rome and France," there weren't many left to be Orleanist or liberal Catholic. The spirit of the age was for extreme positions, for entrenched oppositions. Neither in the country nor the Church was there then any place for conciliation or the *juste milieu.* This discussion of religious psychology throws light on the depth of the misunderstanding which separated the majority of the Orleanists from the bulk of the Legitimists.

The temptation is strong for the present-day historian to relate these differences of thought and variations in feeling to an early difference in social origins. The composition and recruitment of the two Right Wing groups was involved. It is true that a good number of Legitimist Deputies were provincials, countrymen, lower-ranking Breton nobles, Gascon gentlemen, Angevin country squires, or great landlords from Franche Comté, a race of outdoorsmen who adapted themselves poorly to the intrigues of Versailles and were more at ease on their land than on the tribune of the Assembly. Quite to the contrary, the Orleanists seemed never to have lived elsewhere. But these contrasting pictures immediately call for some qualifying touches. The Legitimist faction was not entirely composed of rural and noble oafs; the handsome mansions of the Faubourg Saint-Germain which reopened for a while and enjoyed an Indian summer of splendor were not all won over to Orleanism. The extreme Right also included some first-rate bourgeois recruits such as Chesnelong, just arrived from Bonapartism, and whose support led to hopes of a resurgence of youthful royalism. On the Orleanist benches the diversity was even more pronounced. The éclat of the dukes did an injustice to the bulk of their colleagues. There were only three dukes out of some 200 seats. Men of the ancient nobility, recently ennobled lawyers, and moneyed bourgeois jostled and mingled with each other.

A similar prudence should prevent hasty generalizations about the comparative resources and wealth of the two Rightist movements. M. Beau de Loménie has attempted to base an entire explanation of political history on the difference between their inherited wealth, and this does contain a part of the truth. For example, it is quite certain that the Legitimists, who ordinarily lived on their estates and often personally directed their operations, had most of their fortunes in real property and knew little about the business world. The names of Orleanist notables on the other hand frequently turn up on boards of directors: the Duke Decazes, whose wealth was associated with the industrial activity of Decazeville, the Duke d'Audiffret-Pasquier, director of the Compagnie des Chemins de Fer du Nord and brother-in-law of Casimir Périer whose name was the very symbol of the "bourgeois dynasties." In this connection more than one Orleanist, even the Dukes, had more affinity with Republicans of the Left-Center such as Léon Say or Dufaure, than with his monarchist associates of the extreme Right. However, we must beware of seeing in every Orleanist a speculator on the Bourse and of looking upon the party as the recognized defender of anonymous and nomadic finance. Although keeping part of their wealth in stocks they nonetheless shared the common prejudice that land was the highest form of property. It alone conferred respect, and the profits that it guaranteed were not to be disdained.

Consequently, while Legitimists and Orleanists sat

next to each other in the Chamber and on two or three occasions made a common front behind the Duke de Broglie's leadership so as to work for the higher interests of France, of the monarchy, and the social order, they still continued to represent, sometimes unwittingly, two systems, two religions, two histories, and two societies. Between these two sectors ran an abyss which none of the Right Wing groups had the power to efface or fill in.

III. The Monarchist Groups and the Bonapartist Right

Still, the depth of their discord was not enough to leave one or the other family outside the Right. This was so for the simple and banal reason that the presence on their Left of a strong Republican group pushed them to the Right of the Assembly. They were there because their thoughts, their inclinations, and their programs fixed them on the Right. Their temporary alliance in a great coalition reflected common tendencies. Doubtless they knew better what they did not want than what they did want to do together. However, a gradual rapprochement of their political beliefs was afoot which would have worked out in practice if the Legitimists had not placed dynastic considerations above concern over political institutions.

Indeed the extreme-Right, faithful once again to the policy of the worst and through spite for the Orleanists, was able to block passage of the proposal for an upper parliamentary house called a Grand Council and destined by the Duke de Broglie to serve as a counterweight to a Chamber elected by universal suffrage. It did this even though the idea showed an obvious resemblance to Ultra proposals. Orleanism had made a clear step toward a more aristocratic conception of the parliamentary regime. The time had passed when the most ardent of them demanded and the most prudent accepted the abasement of the peerage. All the political thought of Albert de Broglie (whose father, it is true, had never approved the abolition of the hereditary peerage) tended to reconstitute it. Whatever its name might be—Grand Council, Upper Assembly, or Senate—it was all the same thing. It was now the turn of the Orleanists to insist on the strengthening of local freedoms, to plead the cause of the communes, to seek to extend the authority of the general councils[10] so as to temper the jolts of universal suffrage through the influence of the upper classes and the stability of institutions, just as formerly the Ultras extolled decentralization to weaken the administrative despotism of Napoleon. Now the Orleanists reaped the harvest of Caesarism. On the level of political institutions, the two doctrines (Legitimist and Orleanist) prepared the possibilities of agreement and mutual understanding, sketched out the points of eventual common action. No longer can we say whether the theory of *intermediary bodies* was the property of the Ultras or the keystone of the Orleanist program.

On the institutional level, two or three attempts were made on a common policy. A resolutely conservative policy, according to the terms of the resolution of May 23, 1873, was to gather, according to the vocabulary of the time, all the "decent people," the "virtuous men," around a fighting government determined to close the door to radicalism and make the spirit of social conserva-

[10] Elected bodies on the departmental level. Tr.

tism prevail. This was the program that Marshal Mac-
Mahon, whom the Right Wing elected, outlined in his
messages. What this conservative program would have
been was suggested by the measures passed by the Right
Wing during the period of coalition. In the winter of
1872-1873, a few months before the offensive against
Thiers, the Assembly adopted four laws whose contiguity
was even more significant than their content. One limited
the working day for women and children, a second restricted drunkenness and regulated the sale of alcoholic
beverages, the third brought more of the notables into
the Higher Council on Public Instruction, and the last
admitted priests to the welfare bureaus. Social good will,
moral order, clericalism, and the influence of the notables, in four legislative texts we almost have a summary
of the conservative policy where differences between
Orleanists and Legitimists were forgotten and where the
Rightist groups were reunited.

For a while one can see analogies and affinities extend
even to common behavior. The eloquence of both factions followed the same lines and found inspiration in the
same models. Its tone was perhaps more facile on one
side, more awkward and embarrassed on the other, but
solemn and formal in both cases. All these men were
grave, dignified, and filled with a sense of their responsibility. They performed their duties with precision and
reserved for moments of intimacy any confidences or personal confessions. Daniel Halévy picturesquely described
them, "Pointed collars sticking up, their wearers put on
airs." When compared to men of the Left, to the Republicans, who were more jovial, even disorderly, the kinship
between these two groups leapt into view, nobles and
notables recognized their own resemblances. Their simi-

larity is perhaps even more striking if we compare them to the small group of Bonapartists.

As yet we have hardly spoken of the latter because they were of slight importance. Bonapartism was saddled with a heavy mortgage—responsibility for the disaster, and the failure of its foreign policy. A kind of unanimity proscribed its memory and even its name; it was not wise to declare oneself faithful to the fallen regime. The Bonapartists thereby were reduced to a clandestine life. Some, however, sat in the Assembly to which they had been sent by Bonapartist fiefs, some traditional ones (Corsica), others conquered more recently but more durably (the Charentes). They neither admitted nor declared their Bonapartism yet. Whether they were 10 or 20 no one, except themselves perhaps, would have been able to say with precision.

The disaster of Bonapartism was not conclusive, however. The country, whether it was more forgetful than the notables or, on the contrary, forgot less quickly the victories, the glory, and the prosperity of the Second Empire, was less severe toward it than were its representatives. Without bluster, insidiously, Bonapartism reconquered its positions, some of which it had never lost. The Fourth of September had cleaned out the higher ranks, but the core of the administrative apparatus remained in place. In the army the Empire retained much sympathy; some generals only waited for the right moment to declare themselves. Bonapartism even had allies in the higher clergy; the name of Cardinal Bonnechose was mentioned as one of the prelates faithful to it. Soon it began to reorganize, sparked by Rouher's election in Corsica, February 11, 1872. The party soon had a press—*Le Gaulois, L'Ordre,* and *Le Pays.* It presented

candidates at the by-elections, and each one marked another step in its progress. In 1873 Colonel Stoffel tried his
luck in Paris; in 1874 in Nièvre Baron de Bourgoing,
former aide of the Emperor, won 37,000 votes to 4500
for the Legitimist and 32,000 for the Radical candidate.
The possibility which had seemed unbelievable three years
earlier, an Imperial restoration, emerged. Rumors of
plots were spread about; it was said that the Empress
was assured of Jesuit support; most important, the death
of Napoleon III (January 7, 1873) removed the victim
of Sedan from the scene and made of the young Prince
Imperial a glamorous pretender. Bonapartism rose from
its disrepute. The Bazaine case[11] hurt it less than the
constitutional uncertainty of the Assembly helped it. In
its favor was its record of being at the same time a regime severe toward anarchy and of guaranteeing equality against the fear of a monarchical restoration. The
votes that left the older Right Wing groups did not all go
to the Republicans. For a time Arthur Meyer[12] sought
his direction in Bonapartism. In July 1878 the Anzin
miners went on strike to cries of "Vive Napoléon IV!"
Today, of course, hindsight makes the prospect of a restoration of the Empire purely imaginary, but one only
has to consult the voting statistics to be convinced that it
was indeed one of the possibilities suggested by the uncertainty of universal suffrage in 1873-1874. Early in
1876 there were 75 Bonapartists in the Chamber and 40
in the Senate; many were former Imperial prefects or
functionaries. In October 1877 they returned 104 to the
Palais Bourbon; in 1881 half the conservatives were
Bonapartists.

[11] Marshal Bazaine was tried for his action in the Franco-Prussian
War and found guilty. Tr.
[12] A noted Parisian journalist in the half-century before 1914. Tr.

No eventuality was better calculated to displease the two monarchist factions. Everything opposed them to Bonapartism: past, thought, and methods. Tactical rapprochements could not hide their irreconcilable disagreements. Against Thiers, the Duke de Broglie saw his way clear to seeking the aid of 20 to 30 Bonapartist votes, which they did not refuse; he was able even to include two Bonapartist ministers in his cabinet, but neither he nor his political friends could forget the twenty years of their lives that the Empire had forced them to spend outside public affairs. They could not think of an amnesty. Too many memories set them apart: the 2nd of December and the long night of despotism and silence which followed. Men of order and moral order, the monarchists detested the easy morality, the flashiness and vulgarity of the Second Empire. Anything rather than restoration of that regime, and in fact the Orleanists would have preferred the Republic rather than witness the success of the Imperialists.

The Empire was democracy, it was the sovereign people. The neo-Bonapartist program regenerated and reorganized by Rouher put all this into a slogan which gave the party its name: *the appeal to the people*. This was the pure plebiscitary tradition of the Bonapartes. The Bonapartists continued to proclaim themselves men of 1789. In the constitutional debates of 1875 they alone wanted to affirm the principle of popular sovereignty. In competition with the Republicans they carried on an obvious demagoguery against the Orleanist Constitution of 1875. Against the traditional view of a hierarchical society they set forth the principles of a popular, egalitarian, and democratic regime; against the aristocratic and parliamentary liberalism of the notables and nobles, they advanced the authoritarian antiparliamentarism of the urban and rural masses. This was not a new conflict. Its beginnings went back a quarter of a century, for the old struggle between the Party of Order and the partisans of the Prince-President was breaking out again. The methods and tone of Bonapartist propaganda were not at all such as to dispel fears inspired by the past or by the party's doctrine. Their speakers and their press readily used a direct, vehement, familiar, and bantering style. Its frequent demagoguery contrasted strikingly with the formal and austere academism of the Orleanists. It was a Bonapartist who hurled the insolent threat at the Assembly, "We shall impose silence on you." It is easy to imagine what the great bourgeois of the Right-Center thought of the excesses of a Paul de Cassagnac.

But if the Bonapartists had Cassagnac, the Legitimists had Louis Veuillot, and it is quite difficult to choose between these two polemicists. If there was not the slightest common ground between Orleanism and Bonapartism, there were between Legitimist Ultracism and the extremist opposition of the Bonapartists more analogies, parallels, and affinities than they were willing to acknowledge. More than once between 1873 and 1875 they combined their enmities, joined their votes, or united their blows against their common enemy: Orleanism. In January 1875 a coalition of Legitimists and Republicans elected a Bonapartist in the Midi against the Center candidate. In the Assembly, Legitimists and Bonapartists voted together against the Constitutional proposal. There was, despite appearances, a similarity of spirit and temperament between them, an involuntary but incontestable relation: their secret and common approval of a policy of the worst from which one group awaited the necessary stroke of force and the other the saving miracle.

History was to grant a fine revenge to Bonapartism over the Party of Order, and this ultimately justified Thiers' warning to the head of the Rightist coalition, "The Duke de Broglie will be the creature of the Empire." Thiers accelerated history too much. The Duke de Broglie promptly broke with the Bonapartists in the Assembly, but twenty-five years later Bonapartism imposed its tone, its violence, and its plebeian tendency on the old monarchist Right.

This is the way in which elements of discord and possibilities of rapprochement were mixed together among the three groups on the Right that the coalition of May 24, 1873, presented as an anatomic section. The three traditions, initially opposed, always profoundly dissimilar, began to blend together, like the distinct threads which make up the warp and woof in a piece of cloth. But they had not yet reached that point at the time of the National Assembly. Each of the threads had not yet lost its individuality, nor each tradition its originality. The breakup of the coalition just after its success shows this emphatically.

IV. The King is Dead! End of the Right Wing?

"Do you know, what I wanted more than anything in the world was the union of the Right Wing." This ambition of the Duke de Broglie to keep the Rightist tendencies lastingly united to carry out a conservative policy was only a wish, soon dashed by events. To be sure, these groups did not haggle over their support as long as it was a matter of creating *moral order* and hindering the development of Republican propaganda by repressing political meetings, limiting secular funerals to certain hours of

the day, and forbidding the sale of Republican newspapers on the streets. But divergences emerged as soon as
they turned to the question of what institutions to give to
the country. Without even counting the Bonapartists,
who one could not reasonably expect to sell their hopes
cheaply, the dynastic fusion (summer, 1873) had not destroyed all the old germs of dissension between those
faithful to the two royal branches. The Orleanists knew
that Henry V was profoundy steeped in the sense of his
rights and feared to see him surround himself with a
group into which they had but small chance to enter.
Why not try to prolong this golden age of Orleanism? We
wager that more than one must have welcomed without
displeasure the adjournment of an eventual restoration
until the death of the Count de Chambord. The Legitimists held a grudge against the Orleanists for this lukewarm monarchism.

The coalition began to crack in the autumn of 1873.
The Duke de Broglie forbade *L'Univers* to publish for six
weeks and suspended *L'Union* for two weeks for having
published a message from the Count de Chambord. In
November the two Legitimists in the ministry, Ernoul
and La Bouillerie, withdrew. On May 16, 1874, 50
chevau-légers voted with the Republican Left and contributed to the fall, 381 to 317, of the cabinet formed
twelve months earlier by the 390 votes of the Rightist
coalition. The failure of the Broglie proposal was consummated by the maneuver which led to the Constitutional Laws of 1875 and by the rapprochement of the
two Centers. The antagonism between the two monarchist groups reached its climax at the end of 1875 when
the time came to choose the 75 lifetime Senators provided for in the Constitution. Rather than see men of the
Right-Center elected, a group of Legitimists preferred,

from resentment and at the risk of compromising the future, to reach an understanding with the Left and elect 57 Republicans, leaving only 8 seats for the Right-Center. This paradoxical combination underlined the constant fidelity of the extreme Right, from the Ultras of the Incomparable Chamber (election of Grégoire in Isère) to the *chevau-légers* of the National Assembly, to the policy of the worst.

With the end of the National Assembly the Right Wing groups lost a privileged position that they never were to regain. It took scarcely four years to bring about their decline and to confirm their fall. Universal suffrage would not renew the gesture of confidence of February 1871. In January 1876 only 180 conservatives returned to the first Chamber of the Third Republic, and 75 of them were Bonapartists, against 363 Republicans. May 16, 1877, was a final attempt to recover the majority, by means of a dissolution, and return to a conservative policy. The coalition of 1873 was reassembled for the occasion. Once again the rule was proved that in a time of crisis there is room for only two blocs, each made up of the rapprochement of the like-minded. "The struggle is between order and disorder," declared Marshal MacMahon on the eve of the election, October 11, 1877. The Rightist coalition managed its campaign like a crusade. With over-simple imagery it painted the fight of the good Marshal against the evil Gambetta. Although confident in the merit of its cause, the government did not disdain the use of the most direct methods: administrative pressure and dismissal or transfer of officials. It was not enough. The conservatives won only 207 seats out of some 600. The Marshal submitted. The country confirmed its verdict. In a few years, universal suffrage succeeded in dislodging the Right from all positions of political power. After the Chamber, the Senate escaped them. There the partial election of January 5, 1879, reduced them to 126 of 300; of the 82 seats in contention 66 went to the Republicans, 16 to the monarchists. MacMahon's resignation on January 30, 1879, removed the Right from the last of its constitutional positions. They were now completely in the opposition. That this was not due to a temporary shift of opinion was shown without doubt by the general elections for the second legislature. Ninety conservatives, of whom half were Bonapartists, were all that remained in the Chamber of 1881 to represent three traditions, three regimes, which, placed end to end, covered most of the nineteenth century.

This was the situation scarcely ten years after the resurrection of 1871. What a change in such a short time! Few decades have witnessed such a striking reversal. For almost two-thirds of the century the groups on the Right, whatever their mutual relations, except for two or three crises had always commanded the majority and held power. This long occupation of positions of power now ended. Now the three Rights were forced, all together and for an indeterminate period, into the opposition, deprived of the advantages and the opportunities of power. A new group of political personnel replaced them.

As if to complete their disaster, a series of fortuitous events suddenly struck down their dynastic leaders. On June 1, 1879, in the depths of the South African bush, in an obscure skirmish with a native tribe, the unlucky prince imperial was killed. Bonapartism did not recover from this blow. The partisans of Prince Jérôme and those of Prince Victor fought each other. In January 1882 the government had the former arrested. On August 24, 1883, in an Austrian castle the Count de Chambord breathed his last, the miracle child, perhaps the most-loved of all the sovereigns, without ever having reigned. This time the king was quite dead and monarchy with him. Henry V was the last king of France and 1883 marks the end of old monarchical France. Three years later an exile law expelled from France the heads of families that had ruled the country, and with Boulangism we see commence a collaboration in which the monarchist movements no longer recognize their tradition. The kings were gone. Discouragement crept into the hearts of the most faithful.

So far we have considered only one dimension of events: at the level of the government and the parliamentary assemblies. Thrown out of the central power, the men of the Right expected to salvage their local positions. This illusion was quickly dissipated by an event even more decisive than the others because it ruined the very foundation of their authority in the country. This was what was called the city-hall revolution. Already the January 6, 1878, election of municipal councils had assured the success of numerous Republicans. Three years later they were the masters of more than 20,000 communes while the conservatives kept only 9,500. The politics of the rest of the municipalities were not clearly defined. And then, six months later, the election of half the general councils left only 21 out of 87 to the Right Wing. This was what happened to the traditional preponderance of the notables in the departmental and communal assemblies. It was the arrival of those new social strata which Gambetta had earlier predicted. In Périgord Marshal Canrobert was defeated by a veterinarian! It was the end of an epoch.

It was not the end of a society. The Right had lost power, its leaders were in the process of losing their local positions, but they had not lost everything as long as they kept a group of administrative and social positions in which they seemed impregnable. The conservatives remained masters of the army, navy, diplomatic service, the judiciary, of many public administrations such as those finance and of bridges and highways—not the University, and the conflict between the army and the University was one key to the Dreyfus Affair. The world of finance, business, and a large fraction of the liberal professions were naturally dominated by them. Above all, and it was a substantial advantage in a regime where opinion made the law, they controlled a majority of the newspapers and possessed the support of the Church. The Republicans had doubtless undertaken the beginning of a purge, but quite timidly. To be sure, they started hostilities against clericalism and worked to gain control of education, but the last word was not spoken and the game was not yet lost. The new political power strived hard to control society but the social authorities laid siege to it from their side: of the two which would have the last word? The Second Empire had offered a foretaste of this singular situation in which society opposed the political power, but it was the society which finally won mastery over the regime. This time, however, one had to take into account the consequences of universal suffrage, of the rise of new social strata, in a word, of democracy. Of these three Right Wing movements, each of which corresponded to a long historical and ideological tradition and wrote its chapter of nineteenth century France, what would remain twenty-five years later? In the France of 1900, would there be a place for them, or had they written, with the episode of May 16, the last word of their history?

6

1899-1902: Another Coalition, Nationalism

I. Three New Right Wing groups

Let us now jump over twenty or twenty-five years, scarcely the length of a generation of politicians. Let us move ahead to the end of June 1899 when Waldeck-Rousseau had just formed his great ministry for Republican defense, or even to the eve of the elections of 1902. The leaders of the National Assembly, the protagonists of May 16 all have gone; names then unknown have replaced them. But at this time, as then, two coalitions confronted each other, between which there was conceivable neither a third party nor a middle position. The Rightist bloc was in the minority and it had been so for two decades. This was a considerable difference from the situation of the Right Wing in 1873 and it could not fail to have some consequences, even on political thought.

Powerless to stop the passage of detested legislation, perhaps desparing of regaining a majority, men on the

Right often gave in to the temptation of all oppositions: they contested the validity of the majority which imposed its law on them by appealing from the Assembly to the country, to the extent of stirring up opinion against the parliamentary regime. In 1872 and 1873 it was the Left, Gambetta above all, who appealed to the country and who denied to the National Assembly the right to choose a constitution for France. In 1899 and 1900 it was the turn of the Right to contest the Chambers' power to impose on the *pays réel* legislation contrary to its wishes, and to invoke the latter's sentiments against the *pays légal*. The roles were inverted, just as the power relations had reversed. Moreover, in the meanwhile the Republic had been founded and confirmed. At once, Republican loyalty changed its meaning. In 1873 the Republic still represented the unknown, it was an adventure; while in 1899 it was the legal government of the country, the state in being, order. "To want something else would bring a new revolution and the most fearsome of all," Thiers had declared already in 1872. Now in 1899 it would be a success of the Right which would open the gates to adventure, and the Republicans were the true conservatives. Who knows if we are not touching here one of the most telling reasons for the rapid and lasting support given by the rural masses to the new regime, and an explanation of the same group's failure to respond to Rightist orators? Psychological factors in favor of political conservatism, fear of adventure, and desire for stability, all now worked in favor of the Republic.

In 1899, just as in 1873, a coalition juxtaposed three points of view, but the analogy stops there. A survivor from the National Assembly would no longer have recognized his colleagues. Names had changed, and along with the labels the content and programs of political groups had been modified also. Time seemed to have eroded the old monarchist bloc. In the Chamber of Deputies royalist groups had seen their numbers melt away from election to election. After the revived hopes springing from the brilliant results of 1885 (176 seats taken by the conservatives on the first ballot), the unfortunate association with the Boulangist movement threw discredit on those who felt they had to sacrifice their principles to a tactical opportunity. The *Ralliement* delivered an even harder blow to the old monarchical cause. Not that Jacques Piou's Liberal Action or the Constitutional Right ever won over solid battalions, but the defection of a certain number of Catholics, often the most faithful, cut the party in two and confirmed the decline of royalism. The monarchists scarcely dared to advertise themselves as such anymore. Of course, it was even less a question of separating themselves into Legitimists and Orleanists; the gap which divided them was well filled in. The Count de Chambord's death without descendents, leaving the Count de Paris the single heir, certainly greatly contributed to calming the waters. At the news of this event, Dreux-Brézé requested the Legitimist committees to dissolve. But the general evolution of events contributed even more directly by making the ancient controversies obsolete. The 1880's marked a watershed in the second half of the nineteenth century and the disagreement between the two monarchist families seemed quite small compared with new problems. The royalists henceforth ran candidates with the label, less precise but more exact, of *Conservative*.[1] In the Chamber of 1898

[1] As early as 1878 Dufaure styled them as a party without a name. Author.

there were some 80 of them, of all stripes. Evolution was even more ruthless to the Bonapartists; they had dropped out of the picture. In twenty years they had fallen from 104 to zero. This was because they had in their favor neither solid geographic strongholds nor the traditional social bases which were still the main source of strength of the conservatives, former royalists.

Thus, it required a little under twenty-five years to reduce to simple historic survivals—and for one, to destroy—the three great traditions which had appeared, one by one, over an eighty year period, and whose rivalries and rule had composed almost all the political history of the nineteenth century. The three Rightist groups had practically ceased to count as political forces.

On the site still marked by their debris three new political groups rose, but in which one looks in vain for elements corresponding to the defunct coalition. One of them attracts attention by its novelty as much as by the blustering noise of its activity—nationalism. A phenomenon absolutely unpredictable in the political context of the nineteenth century, it transferred from Left to Right a whole combination of ideas, sentiments, and values heretofore considered the birthright of Radicalism. It is generally recognized that this crucial mutation occurred in the period 1887-1899. Boulangism drew up nationalism's birth certificate and the Dreyfus Affair its baptismal record. One of the most dramatic surprises for the historian is to measure the disproportion between the briefness of the Boulangist episode, the mediocrity of its leading character, and the ephemeral weakness of its immediate results, as against the lasting abundance of its consequences.

Nationalism brought a program to the new Right and inspired a mode of behavior. Until this point a certain kind of patriotism, vibrant, romantic, and militarily chauvinistic, was the property of the revolutionary Left. Patriotism and Jacobinism went hand in hand. In 1830 the "patriots" were the Republicans; in 1871 again, the Republicans wanted to continue the war while the monarchical Rights favored peace. By 1900 these positions were completely changed. Nationalism was now such a characteristic element of the Right that it took the place of a program, label, and flag. The reversal, however, was not total, for if the Right had become nationalist, the opposite was not entirely true. The Left was not completely synonymous with internationalism or pacifism; it would never be entirely, for the Radicals would not deny the Jacobin patriotism of their great ancestors.

This evolution has other interesting points. Nationalism, which is concerned above all with national grandeur, displays a constant interest in the army which is the instrument of that grandeur. The nationalist Right was militarist. This was new, for even in 1873 it was far from this.[2] The Gouvion-Saint-Cyr law,[3] whose democratic inspiration the Ultras had never accepted, placed the nobles in competition with officers risen from the

[2] On everything concerning military opinions and ideas, consult the excellent essay by Raoul Girardet, *La Société Militaire dans la France Contemporaine, 1815-1939*. Using the *Annuaire de l'Ecole de Saint-Cyr*, he has been able to establish the disappearance of certain names between 1830 and 1860; the proportion of apparently noble names which was about 50 per cent in 1826 fell below 30 per cent in 1833. It rose again from 1858 on. After 1870 the movement which led the aristocracy of birth toward a military career accelerated. R. Girardet points out between 1870 and 1913 six d'Humières, four Metz-Noblat, four Rouvroy de Saint-Simon, and four Rohan-Chabot. Author.

[3] The 1818 law reorganizing the army, see p. 53. Tr.

ranks for a service that their fathers had considered as an honor and a birthright. After 1830 many (about two thousand) had left the army out of fidelity to their princes and so as to avoid serving the usurper. The Second Empire had in the eyes of the monarchists ended up by compromising the army. Had it not aided, doubtless with pleasure, in the operation of December 2? After Sedan many higher- and lower-ranking officers had remained faithful to the regime to which they owed their commissions. In addition, most of the Rightist Deputies represented rural populations, those on which the burden of conscription always rested; militarism is an urban product. The Right generally was hostile to all foreign adventures, except those to restore the pope's temporal power. It wanted peace in 1871; it voted in principle against the colonial policy of Jules Ferry. In March 1885, Mgr. Freppel was the only one on the Right Wing benches to vote against the evacuation from Tonkin. Albert de Mun considered he made a great concession by abstaining.

In 1900 nothing remained of these reservations or suspicions. The successive collapse of regimes which demanded that officers swear personal allegiance to the head of the State ended the scruples of the nobles. The anonymity of Republican institutions made it possible to serve France again (only the application of anticlerical legislation gave new life to their scruples of conscience). But for all that they did not repudiate their political opinions. Thus the alliance was reconstituted between the Right and the army. The appeal to the army became a political prescription and a maxim of government. Rightist writers magnified the grandeurs and virtues of military institutions. They began to see in it the instrument of national salvation. Whoever dared to shake the foundations of its discipline was guilty of a true sacrilege. In fact the Right was hardly less severe on the enemies of the army as on those of the Church. In reality weren't the two causes equally sacred?

Religious matters had then ceased to be the only sacred things. Religious sentiment was markedly altered and its objects were modified. Never had the Legitimists nor even the Orleanists thought to place the Church of the kings and the daughter of Bonaparte, religion and the army, on the same level. They had too strong a sense of the hierarchy of values to permit this kind of confusion. By 1900 the slogan of the "alliance of the sword and the holy water sprinkler" had succeeded that of the throne and the altar. Along with the evolution of feelings, the political relations between the Rightist parties and the Church were profoundly changed. The *Ralliement* was not, to be sure, a stranger to this important shift. As soon as Cardinal Lavigerie's move[4] was known, the royalist leaders endeavored to forestall any Roman intervention. Mgr. Freppel presented to Leo XIII a memorial signed by 44 royalist and Catholic Deputies. When the papal decision was made many refused to accept it. The Count de Paris contested the Pope's right to prescribe political institutions to French Catholics. He was echoed by the *Gazette de France* and *La Libre Parole*. Some of the most renowned leaders of royalism, Lucien Brun, Chesnelong, Keller, who had fought so long for the Church and king as a unity, Baudry d'Asson, La Ferronays, Le Cour Grandmaison, La Tour du Pin, refused to separate that which they had always united. In the West as in

---

[4] It was his toast urging French Catholics to support the Republic that inaugurated the *Ralliement* in 1890. Tr.

Guienne and Provence, some important royalist strongholds ignored the papal recommendations. The conflict
between their traditional fidelity to the monarchy and
the pontifical instructions roused some Gallican inclinations and fancies, eclipsed since the Concordat. They
paved the way, thirty years later, for the Action Française's resistance to the Roman condemnation. These
royalists would continue to make defense of religion an
essential point in their program, but henceforth nourished some bitterness toward the Church. The other factions on the Right used the Church more than they
served it and their relations with it sprang more from
tactical considerations than from conviction. The new
generation of the nationalist Right was more clerical than
truly religious. For this shift of opinion certain groups in
the clergy were partly responsible, and of decisive importance were the Catholic activities we have called Assumptionist, leaguer, and popular. The tone of a Veuillot,
the excessive violence of his attacks, the injustice of his
judgments, formed a mentality which prepared neo-
Catholicism to give a warm welcome to the unqualified
extremism of the nationalist Right.

Even more militarist than patriotic, more clerical than
religious, nationalism differed on a third point from the
classic Rightist traditions: it was violently antiparliamentary. The Right Wing of 1873, except for Bonapartism,
had no basic hostility against the parliamentary regime.
Even more, along with Thiers they had claimed the necessary liberties and fought the regime which confiscated
them. It would have been difficult to find more convinced
practitioners of parliamentarism than the Broglies and
their Orleanist friends. The nationalists of 1900 had only
sarcasm for parliament; their distinctly minority position

partially explains their attitude. But above all, the prestige of parliamentary institutions, especially the Chamber of Deputies, did not emerge unscathed from the succession of scandals which had shaken public opinion over
the preceding fifteen years. The Wilson Affair[5] and Panama had lent credence to the idea that the members of
parliament were composed in large part of extortioners,
or to use a word whose coarseness is proportionate to the
violence of public indignation, of guttersnipes. Boulangism, whose poverty of thought and imprecise program
made verbal demagoguery a necessity, launched its campaign with the famous cry, "Down with the robbers!"
The questionable circumstances in which the two houses,
in an underhanded or sneaky way, decided without discussion to raise the salaries of their members from nine to
fifteen thousand francs stirred up indignant astonishment. Only two Senators of the Right protested (November 1906). The sobriquet of Q. M. (*quinze mille*
francs) followed members of parliament for a long time.
Candidates were elected on the sole program of reducing
salaries to the previous level. Nationalism was the expression of this entire movement and exploited its force.

But even if the morality and honesty of the members
of parliament had been above all suspicion, nationalism
would not have been less basically antiparliamentary. Its
origins had impressed on it an instinctive antagonism towards a regime which handed over to an elective assembly the duty of deciding in oratorical debates the interests and destinies of the country. Militaristic, nationalism
scorned or mistrusted eloquence and lawyers. While
there were, it is true, several traditions in the army

[5] In which the son-in-law of President Grévy was found to be
selling decorations of honor. Tr.

(throughout the century the scientific branches, the engineers and artillery, expressed a rather strong respect for the law and trained generations of officers and especially non-commissioned officers who were Republican), nationalism won over the simplest, the least intellectual, the most brutal, the fighters who had only contempt for the regime of babblers and speechmakers. This tradition was also that of the most aristocratic branch, the cavalry.

Nationalism found in the intellectual atmosphere of the period other reasons for scorning words and questioning their effectiveness in a world ruled by force. The poetry of Gabriele d'Annunzio, Nietzschean infiltrations, Kipling's novels, all fashioned a vast epic of action, a romance of virile energy in which nationalism was one chapter, and which exalted the values of force and the qualities of action. Man discovered himself in action and by action. A Lyautey in his grandeur perfectly incarnated this moral philosophy. Barrès, the historian and bard of nationalism, was led to Boulangism[6] by the cult of the self and it is a difficult business to say what in his development came from political convictions and what from personal motives. Already, here and there, we can see signs of some of the forces that the fascist revolution was to exploit twenty-five years later.

A burst of energy against verbalism, a revolt of emotion against reason, this nationalism carried profoundly anti-intellectual tendencies that the crisis of the Dreyfus Affair drew into the open. For, in the last analysis whose fault was it that France was torn to pieces by this unfortunate case? Would there even have been an Affair without the inopportune scruples of some officers, forgetful of

---

[6] He was elected as a Boulangist in Nancy when he was twenty-seven years old. Author.

their duty, and of some intellectuals who took it upon themselves to reopen a closed case? That eternal enemy, the critical spirit, was chiefly responsible for this Affair, that spirit of free inquiry introduced by the Reformation, used by the *philosophes* of the eighteenth century, let loose by the Revolution of 1789, and triumphant upon its ruins. Soon Maurras, in his theory of the four States, was to yoke the Protestant and the Freemason beside the Jew and the Metic. From this time onward the nationalists were suspicious of those who claimed to refer everything to the test of their reason. Moreover, the doctrinal content of the movement was very weak: what a decline compared to the systematic vigor of Ultra thought, or to the beautiful and reasonable dignity of the Orleanist doctrinaires! This nationalism had no theory, scarcely a program. It had powerful antipathies, vigorous aspirations; it was instinctive, passionate, shaken with furious gestures. And yet it inspired an abundant literature, won over illustrious writers, and mustered a number of eminent intellectuals; this was one of its paradoxes.

Militarism, exaltation of action, discrediting of words and even of intelligence, all converged in antiparliamentarism. The regime was made responsible for the party divisions which debilitated governmental authority, weakened power, and split up public opinion. Words divided, action united, force brought together. This antiparliamentarism had two outlets: street demonstrations and polemics by a newspaper press lying in wait for scandals, prompt to exploit them, and ready if necessary to invent them. The Rightist parties had always maintained such a fear of the streets that they constantly refrained from unloosing popular forces. One could say that the street and the city had been on the Left against a

Right which had depended on the countryside. These terms were partially reversed starting with Boulangism. While the peasants rallied to the Republican regime, the bourgeoisie and middle classes began the opposite move in this exchange of places. It was at this point that the Municipal Council of Paris was lost by the Left. In 1900 the Radicals lost the majority, the Socialists retained only 19, while 9 conservatives and 32 nationalists barely carried off the absolute majority (of 80 seats) that they have held thenceforth except from 1904 to 1906. In this way the long tradition that went from the insurrectional Commune of August 10, 1792, to that of March 18, 1871, including the insurrections of 1830, February 1848, and September 4, 1870, was interrupted. Paris had passed over to the Right, and the nationalist Right inherited as a consequence all the turbulence, restlessness, and whims of an urban population. From this came the taste for violent words or actions as manifested by such diverse happenings as Déroulède's attempt at a *pronunciamento*,[7] Baron Christiani's attack on President Loubet with a cane,[8] or the obstinate resistance of Fort Chabrol[9] to the police siege.[10] A new political temperament appeared, more combative, more plebeian than that of the traditional Right Wing movements. The latter were pop-

[7] In February 1898 when a regiment of soldiers was returning from President Félix Faure's funeral Déroulède vainly tried to lead it against the presidential palace in an uprising. Tr.

[8] One of the highlights of the Dreyfus Affair, this event occurred at the Auteil racetrack. Only the president's hat was damaged. Tr.

[9] A group of antisemites holed up in their headquarters on the rue Chabrol in Paris and defied arrest, forcing the police to besiege them for thirty-eight days. Tr.

[10] It was at this point that Anatole France coined the word *troublion* to express the turbulent spirit of this nationalist agitation. Author.

ular in their fashion, but the people they represented were rural. The urban character of the movement determined its appearance almost as much as its ideas. The ideas may have been more reactionary than the political thought of the late Duke de Broglie—and with a Maurras they certainly were—but this did not prevent them from being expressed in a more revolutionary fashion. The parliamentary orator gave way to the demagogue, the writer to the pamphleteer; the age of the militant began. On the ground of the old Right Wing, where only a few out-of-date witnesses remained, there now rose a new type of Right in which certainly neither Chateaubriand, nor Broglie, nor Falloux, nor perhaps Morny or Baroche would have recognized their legitimate heirs.

While nationalism had the leading role and performed on the front of the stage, it was not the entire Right; it was not even the most numerous element in it. In May 1902, of 220 Right Wing Deputies elected, the nationalists, running on the *Patrie Française* ticket, had only 59, even though they had chalked up significant gains over the preceding chamber where nationalism had been represented by 15 Deputies plus 4 antisemites. Eclipsed by the nationalists' blustering flashiness, overshadowed by the tumult of their arrogant youthfulness, two other groups on the Right adjusted themselves as well as they could to their embarrassing proximity. These two were the *Ralliés* and the Progressists.

The *Ralliés* were composed of former monarchists, more often from the Legitimist tradition than the Orleanist, who had followed the recommendations of the sovereign pontiff and had accepted the Republic. This group revived on a larger scale the attempt planned after the elections of 1889 to regroup in an independent Right a small number of Deputies elected on the conservative Republican ticket. The gesture from Rome increased the small nucleus of those who already had rallied to the Republic. In 1893 several renowned monarchists, including Albert de Mun, Count Greffulhe, the Marquis de Castellane, and the Viscount de Montfort campaigned together. Despite the defeat of some of the more outstanding of them (Albert de Mun, Jacques Piou, Etienne Lamy), the Republican Right did win some 35 seats. They rose to 50 in 1902. We have seen the consequences of this *Ralliement* on the destinies of those faithful to the monarchy.

The route which brought the Progressists into the Right next to them was not that of the *Ralliés*. The Liberal Action group of 1902[11] was the result of a movement toward the Left; the Progressists made the opposite movement. The history of this slow change somewhat resembles that of Orleanism, except that while the passage from Left to Right took a half-year for the men of resistance,[12] it took the Progressists exactly twenty years. It occurred between 1879, when the Republicans obtained control of all the Third Republic's institutions, and 1899, when the Progressists were not included in the formation of a bloc for defense of the Republic. The endpoints of this passage from Left to Right clearly in mind, we shall now trace its principal stages. Already in 1880, the Left-Center had voted with the Right against Article 7.[13] Three years later Jules Ferry proclaimed, the

[11] That is, the *Ralliés*. Tr.

[12] See pp. 100. Tr.

[13] A provision of an educational bill presented by Jules Ferry which would have denied to non-authorized religious orders (including the Jesuits) any role in French public or private education. This article was defeated in the Senate. Tr.

peril is on the Left! But then all Republicans regrouped in 1885 before the very present danger springing from the victory of 176 Rightists on the first ballot. In 1887, however, there was a second attempt at a rapprochement between conservatives and "government Republicans." Baron Mackau, leader of the Right Wing, offered neutrality in exchange for a policy of appeasement. For almost six months the Rouvier cabinet leaned to the Right. Then the Boulangist agitation changed everything. Afterward, the *Ralliement* re-established relations; the Catholics voted with and for Progressists; this was the *new spirit*. Simultaneously, division appeared in the Republican ranks, as formerly, between resistance and movement. On the issue of repressing anarchist plots, as on proposals for tax reform, the Progressists moved gradually toward a Right which in its turn had come part way to meet them. For twenty-eight months, from 1896 to 1898, Méline depended on a coalition of conservatives and Progressists. The Dreyfus Affair split the Progressist group in two. One part fell back with Waldeck-Rousseau to the Left and formed a bloc with the Radicals; the rest, led by Méline, accomplished once and for all the move to the Right. This was the third element in the Rightist coalition of 1902. André Siegfried has noted that at Brest, until 1898, moderates and Radicals had never competed with each other, so as to defeat the Right Wing candidate. This no longer occurred after 1898. With the Dreyfus Affair the moderates shifted to the Right.

They took their constituents with them, their voters, entire regions even. The passage of the moderates to the Right introduced in French political geography the most profound reversals that it experienced in the course of the nineteenth century. To the traditional map of the old

Right Wing a new map was now juxtaposed. The change in Paris was reflected in the provinces, Lorraine's adhesion to the Right dates from this point, although in 1871, for example, the department of Meurthe-et-Moselle had elected only Republicans.

Thus, in 1902 as in 1873, a coalition linked three associated Rightist groups against a Left Wing bloc. But the analogy stops there, for everything else seemed different. The men had changed, as had the names, labels, and programs. Twenty years seemed to have entirely transformed the Right Wing.

II. From One Coalition to the Other

Can it be true that the only traits of resemblance, after twenty-five years, were purely external? We can forsee the consequences that such a categorical conclusion would force on French political history. If a quarter of a century was all it took to completely renew the Right, then the permanence of political opinions is only an illusion, change is the truth and the rule. For each generation there would correspond a Right whose sole link with its predecessor was that of not being on the Left. But if we believe that states of mind are more durable and feelings more tenacious, something must remain. Perhaps an informed examination of the essential constants might uncover the hidden continuities, as it is possible to find an invisible link between two apparently separate streams of water. There are beginnings which seem to rise from nothing but which, for someone who knows how to trace subterranean passages, are only resurgences.

In 1873 we recognized three quite different political families on the Right. The coalition of 1899-1902 also included three. Let us form a hypothesis: let us suppose that the latter were the same three which survived, faithful to the essence of their inspiration. The Legitimists were continued by the *Ralliés*, the Orleanists had heirs among the Progressist Republicans, while Bonapartism experienced a brilliant change of fortune in a new role, that of nationalism. It now remains only to furnish proof of these connections and to demonstrate that these relations are not pure fancy. Let it be conceded only that in matters of political opinion, the questions of the type of the regime is not the most decisive factor. Certainly it reveals less of the underlying tendencies than social positions and philosophical convictions.

The very circumstances of the *Ralliement* suggest that the *Ralliés* were the legitimate heirs of the monarchists and the identity of the men involved confirms it. The prelate whom Leo XIII chose to pronounce the decisive words, Cardinal Lavigerie, was a traditional Legitimist. Before becoming the spokesman for the *Ralliés*, Albert de Mun was an orator of the extreme Right. Except for some conservative Republicans, they were all former monarchists whose monarchical fidelity was left empty by the death of the Count de Chambord. The papal recommendations transferred their fidelity, they did not pledge it to the Republic. Their system of thought remained unchanged. The *Ralliement* did not make democrats of them. They were conservatives and conservatives they remained. The very name they chose for themselves in 1902, *Liberal Right*, shows clearly that they remained faithful to the great liberal tradition of aristocratic royalism. Lyautey offers a good example of this attachment to the ideal, to the sentiments, and to the ways of life of his group. The young officer, whose article on the role of the officer showed his social preoccupations in 1891, belonged to a bourgeois family of notables allied by numerous links to the Legitimist nobility of the East. He was, in sum, the heir of those families that Stendhal described in *Lucien Leuwen.* Thus on both sides of the chronological break produced by the *Ralliement,* there was the same sense of responsibility, the same belief in service, and equal desire to rebuild a society which would respect the rights of God and of the Church.

The demonstration of continuity between Orleanists and Progressists is less easy; the men were not the same. The dukes did not politically survive the failure of May 16. Even before that, the coalition of Republicans and *chevau-légers* in December 1875[14] had set a forseeable end to the political career of several of them. But if the names changed (not all of them, for Casimir Périer served as a link between the two groups), opinions and sentiments did not vary nearly so much. Both turned from Left to Right. They retained from this evolution an ambiguity which made them appear sometimes as conservatives and sometimes as liberals, according to the point of view from which they were analyzed and the aspect of their program emphasized. Maintenance of the principles of 1789 and defense of order—this was how Casimir Périer defined his program. Which Casimir Périer? The one of 1831 or of 1893? With constancy they held the position of the *juste milieu.* "Neither revolution nor reaction," was the slogan of the Progressists of 1902. It could have been and in fact it was that of all the generations of Orleanists. All of them paid less attention to the form of the regime than to a set of political and

[14] See pp. 200-201. Trans.

economic liberties and the protection of society. Order and liberty always were the two complementary points of their program. The Progressists, liberals like the Orleanists, were no more concerned than they about labor problems. One finds among the Progressists the very same ritual denial of liberalism in the matter of tariffs. In this case, a man at their head like Méline, whose name is associated with the increase in tariffs and with protection for French agriculture, is more than a symbol. If one more piece of evidence were needed, the identity of religious positions would furnish it. Hardly clerical, less so than the monarchist conservatives, they disapproved nevertheless the excesses of anticlericalism and rejoined the Rightist opposition on this issue. Above all, the course of this evolution was strangely familiar. It led them from an anticlerical secularism to tolerance, and as we saw a union develop between liberal Catholicism and liberal Orleanism, we can recognize the early traces of a rapprochement between Republicans and Catholics. Finally, the sympathy of the business world did not extend to the turbulent and blundering nationalists, but to the Progressists, just as a half-century earlier the notables of Orleanism were thick with the mining firms or the budding railway companies.

Let us pass on, finally, to the last element of the Right, nationalism. Its similarities with Bonapartism are obvious to the least acute observer. The themes, sentiments, and methods were almost the same. The taste for authority, the fascination with force, the attraction to adventure and glory, the cult of the leader, antiparliamentarism, appeal to the people, all that made up Bonapartism reappeared in nationalism. Moreover, would it not have been surprising for a movement which was power-

ful enough to survive Sedan and so well-rooted as to
enjoy the speedy re-establishment that we have indicated
after 1871, to be abruptly annihilated? A great reserve of
powerful forces and feelings remained available whose
resources and energies nationalism knew how to exploit
and control. It was from the same reserve that Boulangism drew such a quick and emphatic echo. It inherited
from Bonapartism the verbal violence, the excesses of
language, and the oratorical demagoguery. Who was it,
for example, who launched these invitations to direct action: "A well-led battalion admirably supplements the
weaknesses of the Constitution. Let us clean out everything; let the broom become a symbol!" From a Boulangist sheet or an antidreyfusard pamphleteer? No, from
the pen of Paul de Cassagnac writing in the Bonapartist
newspaper *Le Pays* after May 16. The three languages
were identical. Far from being the absolute novelty that
a rather short-sighted view might detach from earlier history, nationalism moved into the Caesarian, authoritarian, plebiscitary, popular, and antiparliamentary tradition of the two Empires. Some names show a link
between these successive steps in the same tradition: Paul
de Cassagnac, who first called himself a Catholic, then
monarchist, finally Imperialist, and campaigned for the
Conservative Union which was to bring the Right Wing
into a coalition; Baron Mackau, head of the monarchist
groups at the time of Boulangism and former official
candidate of the Empire. Only one new element was
added, of which Bonapartism was innocent: antisemitism. No one can contest Drumont's credit for inventing
this although an anti-Jewish feeling had been at work in
the establishment of the Union Générale bank.[15]

[15] In 1876. Tr.

An examination of the electoral map confirms on almost every point this permanence of traditions. Except for a few changes, and Lorraine was the most notable, it was always the same regions which sent men of the Right to sit in the Chamber or Senate: Brittany, Vendée, Anjou, and Poitou in the West, the Nord, the remote departments of the *Massif Central,* certain cantons of the Midi, both in Provence and Languedoc, and Franche-Comté. As for nationalism, M. Dansette has pointed out that the results of Boulangist elections often reproduced those of the election of December 10, 1848.[16] This was the case for the districts of Paris. In Charente-Inférieure, where General Boulanger in April 1888 won 51 per cent of the votes, three years earlier the Bonapartist candidate had obtained 55 per cent.

III. *Nationalism and the Leagues*

The relative continuity of the Rightist traditions has now been verified. But despite some constants, several changes had occurred which modified the over-all picture and the balance of the internal forces of the Right. Although the three movements maintained themselves, even under new names, their relative proportions did not remain identical. The parliamentary representation of the traditionalist Right had grown thinner. In the language of the chemist we would say that only traces of it existed; in the elections of 1902 the conservatives who included all the elements of this group won only 50 seats. Even more serious, in a few years nationalism had developed so much and had carried on so strong a campaign

[16] The election in which Louis-Napoleon won the presidency of the Second Republic. Tr.

that it was able to impose its tone, style, and methods willy-nilly on the other Right Wing groups, even on those whose seniority and original tradition should have offered the best protection against such an infection. This was the posthumous revenge of Bonapartism, that recalls the prophetic warning Thiers made to the Duke de Broglie on the eve of May 24, 1873, "You will be the creature of the Empire." Clerical resistance took a militant turn which justifies allusion to the monks of the league.[17] Even Orleanism let itself be contaminated by the nationalist fever; did not the Count de Paris approve the Boulangist campaign? The switch dates exactly from the moment when the pretender was won over to the principle of the plebiscite. The manifesto of September 15, 1887, in whose compostion Arthur Meyer seems to have taken a rather important part, accepted the formula of the appeal to the people. On the tactical level, formal instructions specified the rapprochement with Boulangism. Baron de Mackau, the Marquis de Breteuil, and Albert de Mun were its principal promoters, although the Duke de Doudeauville, the Prince de Léon, and the Duke de La Trémoille financed the enterprise with generous contributions. The new royalist generation was beginning to turn away from the parliamentary regime.[18] Another indication of how nationalism "bleached" those

[17] A reference to the Catholic League of the sixteenth century French religious wars. Tr.

[18] Not all the royalists approved of or followed this evolution. The Duke d'Aumale severely deprecated this disavowal, while Eugène Veuillot made the comment, "There is no longer any king." Several Orleanist Senators did not hide their disapproval and in 1889 D. Cochin, a Catholic and Orleanist, ran against a Boulangist. Thus, an authentic Orleanist tradition was maintained and the present Count de Paris revived it after the condemnation of the Action Française by the House of France. Author.

faithful to the monarchical idea was that they let themselves be won over by the crude arguments of antisemitism.

Yet, despite its influence, nationalism represented, at least on the parliamentary level, only a limited force: in 1898 15 seats plus 4 anti-Jewish Deputies sent from Algeria. In 1902 the results were more respectable, 59 seats, but hardly more than the conservatives. First place incontestably went to the Progressists. In 1902 they numbered alone more seats (111) than the total of 50 conservatives and 59 nationalists. However, they received scarcely half the publicity. Nothing demonstrates better the divergence between the parliamentary strength of groups and the noise they make in the streets, the disparity between the political life of Paris and the opinion of the country.

A second transformation, perhaps even more important, concerned not the balance of forces among the Rightist traditions but their structure. Until the end of the nineteenth century, French political life had known only a rather limited choice of means of expression. There was the parliamentary group but it was only an accidental meeting of men brought together by their convictions or their interests, without strict discipline, without statute or rules, and without an official character or legal recognition. On two or three occasions, generally in times of trouble after long periods of constraint, in 1848, in 1870, clubs temporarily channeled the energy of opinion. On the other hand, the secret society compensated for its lack of numbers by the strictness of its discipline and the cohesion of the group. The *Congrégation* or the *Charbonnerie,* the Republican societies under the July Monarchy, are analogues to our modern parties in the sense that in both cases they respond to the same need for expression and action. Throughout the nineteenth century there was nothing that resembled parties lying between these two opposed types of organization. Can we really identify as parties the electoral committees, those essentially provisional groups which, so to speak, never survived the circumstances of their creation: committees of the Party of Order in 1848-1849, the conservative committee in 1876?

In this respect, the years 1900-1905 clearly broke new ground by introducing several new types of organization in the annals of political morphology. If the too-often used expression "turning point" retains any meaning, rarely could it be more justly applied than to the beginning of this century. In 1901 was held the convention which definitively created the Republican Radical and Radical-Socialist Party, supported heretofore by a rather loose network of local committees. This meant the entrance into political life of the militant, the committee, and the Leftist party, all at once. Even more decisive was the date of 1905 when, at the end of a half-century of quarrels, socialism came together into a unified party. The S.F.I.O. (Socialist Party) was the first strongly centralized workers' party which subordinated its parliamentary group to the control of its militants and their demands. It joined the International at the same time as the British Labour Party chalked up its first success (election of 1906). Between the dates when these two leading organizations were formed, other new ones were constituted: the Democratic Republican Alliance (1901) and the Republican Federation (1903). Also in these years two movements were born which opposed each other on everything and likewise were destined to mark

French political thought: *Sillon* and Action Française. Radical Party, Unified Socialist Party, *Sillon,* Action Française, Democratic Alliance, Republican Federation, here were grouped, with the single exception of the Communist Party, all the factors which were to govern French political life until 1939; in a half-dozen years all the playing cards for forty years were dealt out.[19]

Into this movement nationalism brought an original note with the league, the antecedents of which went back to Boulangism. A league was not a party; it differed from it by its methods as well as its objectives. It was even further removed from the older forms of political organization. It aimed to enroll great numbers of members, form crowds into regiments, keep its adherents on the alert, carry agitation into the streets. The league was the first example of the mass movement. Many of them sprang up. Following the old League of Patriots, founded in May 1882 by the Republicans to prepare the country physically and morally for revenge and swept by the Boulangist tidal wave into the nationalist camp,[20] came the Antisemitic League of Jules Guérin, then the League for the French Fatherland, and finally, the most famous

[19] To the same movement belongs the progress which the idea of Proportional Representation made in public opinion at this time, and the official recognition of parliamentary groups which received a legal existence in 1910. Author.

[20] The evolution of the League of Patriots was itself very characteristic of the birth and development of nationalism. The initial objectives were exclusively patriotic: to preserve in the country the memory of Alsace-Lorraine and the cult of the national virtues, to prepare it on the military level. The program then admitted of no political intent nor did it hide any conservative reservations. The concerns of its founder, Paul Déroulède, were close to those of Jules Ferry and the creators of Republican primary education. Only gradually did it become antiparliamentary. Author.

of all, destined to have the longest future, the League of Action Française.

It is appropriate at this point to correct a too widely spread legend concerning the supposed inability of the Rights to organize themselves. They are painted as incapable of imposing discipline on themselves, poor at winning over an undecided crowd, and thus struck with a congenital inferiority with respect to the parties of the Left which were better organized, more united, and more heedful of tactical imperatives. Partially true, it is wrong to take this view for a general truth; it needs to be qualified. In fact it is probable that non-voters were more numerous on the Right than on the Left. But it is not true that the Right Wing always had the worst of it when it came to discipline. The election of 1885 offers the best example to the contrary: in the face of the Republicans weakened by dissensions between Opportunists and Radicals, the conservatives, by uniting all their votes in each district for a single list, took in the first election 176 seats against 127 for the Republicans. A third of a century later, in 1919, the triumph of the *Bloc National* (with a different electoral system, it is true) repeated this demonstration. On both occasions the Right Wing won out over its adversaries, temporarily or permanently, due to its cohesion.

Nevertheless, the Right Wing rarely gave birth to organizations as efficient and well articulated as those of the Left such as the Radical committees or Socialist federations. But it cannot be doubted that they had something equivalent or in place of them. The Right, in fact, was always able to count on the help of other forces: the sympathy of the Church, the influence of the traditional social authorities, the spontaneous support of the economic powers. These were more than was necessary to counterbalance the use of committees. In fact, it was rather those on the Left who, since nature did not provide them with these valuable supporters, had to invent substitutes and improvise methods of attraction. The modern party was their reply.

In addition, the monarchical Rights could feel only repugnance for this form of organization and action. Did it suit the majesty of a prince, the legitimate heir to his kingdom by right of birth, and father of his subjects, to take the leadership of some party whose very existence would have implied the acceptance of democratic postulates?[21] The Count de Paris, by accepting the principle of the plebiscite, perhaps showed himself the heir of the king of the barricades; most certainly he betrayed the legitimate monarchy. The political party, whether one wished it or not, denied the social hierarchy, shattered tradition, established individual equality, and laid the foundations for democracy.

In the light of these observations the extent of the upheaval that the appearance of the leagues introduced into the traditional structure of the Right Wing can be measured. It revealed the decline of monarchical ideas, already suggested by the disappearance of the royalist groups from the parliamentary chamber. It also underlined the weakening of the framework of French society.

[21] The Orleanist pretender received the advice of some interested persons, whom he brought together in a privy council. At Paris he was represented by a political office headed for a long time by an old Norman Senator, Edouard Bocher, a devoted servant of the House of Orleans. He had administered its properties since 1848. When in 1891 he asked to be relieved of his duties because of his advanced age, the Count de Paris chose as his successor the Count d'Haussonville, nephew of Duke Albert de Broglie, and attached by family tradition to the parliamentary monarchy. Author.

Parties and leagues were new forms that corresponded to the new factors of political life and social organization— political democracy, the exercise of universal suffrage, the spread of education, the development of organized labor. At the same time a group of transformations slowly altered the face of France: the growth of cities, the rural exodus, industrialization, the formation of a single national market, all gradually shifted the center of gravity from the thousand small regional areas of rural France toward a France of workers and petty bourgeois in which the urban middle classes saw their importance expand. Concomitantly, the authority of the traditional social forces weakened. Anxieties changed, it became less a matter of fighting radicalism than of resisting socialism. The renovation of the Rightist movements reflects the consequences of all these changes. Everything worked against the old traditions for whose decline therefore there appeared to be no remedy, everything moved for the benefit of the new traditions. However, all of the past was not lost, since the new movements acquired the essence of its spirit and aspirations.

7

Action Française: A Synthesis of the Right Wing Traditions?

I. Integral Nationalism and Neo-Royalism

To these two new developments, the glamour of nationalism and the appearance of the leagues, we can add a third, just as decisive: the birth at the turn of the century, of a new movement around a new doctrine. Both the doctrine and the movement, destined for a rather fine future, together exerted on French political life and public opinion for forty years, and perhaps more, an influence which cannot be measured by the number of declared adherents; we are speaking of Maurrasism and the Action Française. They can be recognized, during the most somber days of our history, as mixed up in the intrigues of Vichy, and even today it doubtless would be premature to speak of them only in the past tense although events have dealt them a rather hard blow.

Several studies recently have established the starting

point of this curious story. The Dreyfus Affair gave birth to Action Française. It proceeded from it chronologically as well as intellectually. The hagiography of the movement goes back to April 1898 with a small group of young men, two of whom stand out: Henri Vaugeois, who taught philosophy at the College of Coulommiers, and Maurice Pujo. We shall meet them again. The official creation of Action Française has a precise date, fourteen months later: June 20, 1899. Contemporary with the Affair, Action Française was indeed the daughter of anti revisionist nationalism, the source of its inspiration. Louis Dimier[1] declares that the apology for Colonel Henry and the justification of the "patriotic error" were the point of departure for the movement and the sign by which its members recognized each other. They expected to profit from the example of the fiasco of the League for the French Fatherland which doubtless drew strength from the patronage of half the *Académie Française* and from a hundred thousand enrollments in twenty-four hours, but was feeble because of its doctrinal weakness. Its members hoped to breathe into nationalism the thought which was so obviously lacking. Action Française was never to betray the doctrinal preoccupation of its origin. Its leader was a thinker, a doctrinaire, and the will to undertake an intellectual reform, taken up from Renan, was always displayed prominently in the columns of its newspaper and also in the program of its courses at the Action Française Institute.

To start with, however, the promoters were no better prepared than the heralds of nationalism were. It was probably this absence of any doctrine which made them so ardently want to develop or find one. Observe this

[1] *Vingt Ans d'Action Française*, p. 9. Author.

vacuity at the start, it clarifies certain characteristics of the movement. Nevertheless, they clutched one absolute: the national interest, and condemned that conditional nationalism which might be willing to subordinate policy to values other than the grandeur of France. France and *only* France! Absolute, their nationalism was integral as well. They wanted to react against the anarchy which they claimed resulted from the proclamation of the Rights of Man without caution or counterpart. Henri Vaugeois' article-manifesto in the first number (August 1, 1899) of *Action Française,* which was still only a small twice-monthly magazine[2] with a grey cover, was proudly titled, and not at all provocatively, "Reaction First." This attitude was important for we see nationalism turn its back on its democratic origins and begin the break with the popular tradition from which it sprang. However, Action Française accomodated itself for the moment to the republican form of government which it did not yet judge to be incompatible with the country's interest, however little room this form left for the principle of authority. So the small group of the first months brought together in a curious fraternity Republicans, Catholics, and freethinkers.

This period of loyalty to the Republic was of short duration. An intellectual event which was decisive for the future orientation of the new movement took place in 1900. A young Provençal writer in his early thirties (he was born in 1868), smitten with literature, enamored of belles-lettres and fine literary style, undertook an investigation of royalism among leading French personalities for the very royalist and very traditionalist *Gazette de*

---

[2] The *Action Française* became a daily only on March 21, 1908; it continued to appear until 1944. Author.

France. This man, Charles Maurras, placed his own conversion to the monarchical idea in the year 1896. The *Gazette de France* had sent him on a trip to Greece, his first voyage abroad, on which he had experienced a very powerful feeling of national degradation. The forced comparison with British power and the thundering rise of Imperial Germany had persuaded him of the munificence and superiority of the dynastic institution. In his investigation Maurras interrogated writers, publicists, the notables of royalism. Many gave their support or came over to the monarchical principle as the only one capable of assuring national grandeur. From these many responses, like so many depositions, there gradually developed the notion of a hereditary, antiparliamentary, and decentralized monarchy which had the guarantee of some of the then most revered names of French letters: a Paul Bourget as early as 1900, a Jules Lemaître in 1903. The editors of *Action Française* had attentively followed the course of the investigation. They soon adopted the positions defined by Maurras and subscribed to his conclusions. The result was that the nationalism of Action Française was to be monarchist and Maurras its spokesman.

This was a decisive turn in the history of political ideas and sentiments. After the death of the Count de Chambord (1883), royalist sentiment also was cut down. Step by step, the failure of Boulangism, the imprudent collusion with the plebicitary movement, and the *Ralliement* all precipitated its decline. The death of the Count de Paris, September 8, 1894, had made his son, the Duke d'Orleans, a playboy of only mediocre ability and incapable of any initiative, the heir of the House of France. Some renowned supporters no longer hid their discouragement. The Marquis de Breteuil, Deputy from Hautes-

Pyrénées and a great name in the party, retired from political life. Royalist traditionalism was slowly withering away and the moment could be foreseen when only a few old gentlemen, loyal against all reason to the tradition of their families and to the honor of their names, would maintain the faith of their fathers to the dynastic principle. But suddenly the monarchist zeal, the stubborn conviction, and the persuasive force of a young, thirty-two year old publicist and the adherence of a handful of young men to royalism rejuvenated the old trunk and infused fresh sap into it. From the dried-up stump sprouted a younger and more aggressive neo-royalism which found again a reasonable basis for hope. The monarchist idea was not yet dead. The old tradition underwent a miracle.

Moreover, history was to show that this neo-royalism was not only the old tradition miraculously rejuvenated. It was another royalism with perhaps only the name in common with that of the Ultras, the Legitimists, and the *chevau-légers*. Action Française did indeed soon gather up the scattered faithful of the old tradition and these did represent an element of continuity from the old royalism.[3] But from one generation to another, what a change in sentiments! What remained of that quasi-religious attachment to the *person* of the king, which made young women's hearts beat faster when presented to the Count de Chambord? The allegiance of Action Française, completely rational, came from the head and went to the *institution*. Did it not even survive the disavowal of the princes? The institution was stripped of that sacred dignity with which centuries of time and the

---

[3] In the provençal Midi, the country of Maurras himself, around Aix and, the Alpilles hills, Action Française moved into the positions of the old Legitimism and revitalized it. Author.

intimate union with the national religion had clothed it.
The writers of the Action Française, those new "doctrinaires," were, however they squirmed, the sons of the
rationalist and positivist nineteenth century. Jules Lemaître saw this clearly when he announced the appearance
of a new category of royalists, which he discerningly
called positivist. Their royalism was not a faith. Maurras
and Bainville arrived at the monarchist position as the
conclusion of a critical investigation, as the most satisfactory political formula, as the type of government recommended by historical experience. Their monarchism was
the result of a geometric proof; it was the consequence of
the laws of social physics; it came from the mentality of
mathematicians, not of mystics. Nationalism led them to
the monarchy. Thus they discovered themselves to be
monarchists while the royalists of old were so by birth.
Come from nationalism to monarchism by way of logical
reflection and practical empiricism, the men of Action
Française were always to remain basically more nationalist than monarchist and more monarchist than royalist.

By 1903 then, the doctrine of Action Française was
endowed with its two fundamental characteristics. It had
amalgamated two of the three currents of the French
Right. Their fusion in a single movement was unprecedented, but this does not prevent the historian from
clearly recognizing the contributions of the two currents
to the new synthesis.

II. *Action Francaise and the Old Rightist Traditions*

From nationalism Action Française acquired its most
superficial traits, the most gaudy and noisy practices,
which also earned for it the most lasting enmities: the

taste for violence, at least in verbal form, among men all of whom, unfortunately, did not have the talent of Léon Daudet, the polemical brutality, the partisan passion which stopped at nothing, neither dangerous accusations, nor excesses of style, nor slanders. This fashion of understanding and practicing a journalism of opinion manifested a direct descendance from Cassagnac to Daudet; moreover, did not the latter come directly from the *Libre Parole*? *Action Française* took up the offensive name "slut" invented by Paul de Cassagnac to designate the Republic. Nationalism also lent its structure and forms of organization to Action Française. It was not and never would be a party, it took up the style of the league. It pretended to be disinterested in electoral battles and parliamentary struggles. When some of its leaders, in 1919 and 1924, took their chances with universal suffrage, it was only an isolated episode and the outcome, happy or unfortunate, in no way committed the movement's future. Action Française chose to act in other ways, by methods inaugurated by Boulangism. The *Camelots du Roi*,[4] founded in 1908, were soon heard from (the Thalamas and Bernstein affairs[5]). Finally, in a direct line from nationalism came that original mixture of antiparliamentarism and authoritarianism, which until this point constituted the personal note of Bonapartism in the concert of French political traditions. Even antisemitism was inherited, in form and substance. The Jews were one of those four groups united to ruin France whose sinister

[4] The strong-arm squads affiliated with Action Française. Tr.

[5] Thalamas was a history professor whose opinions about Joan of Arc caused the *Camelots* to riot against him in 1908-1909, while the playwright Henri Bernstein's youthful desertion from the army and his Jewish origin made him a target for the *Camelots* when the *Comédie Française* staged one of his plays in 1911. Tr.

combination Maurras denounced. So was that constant theme of the neo-royalist campaigns and of the Maurrasian dialectic, the opposition between the *pays légal* and the *pays réel,* which came from earlier days. Moreover, Action Française was never embarrassed, never made a mystery of these origins. It was with a pride into which entered some defiance that the newspaper called itself the organ of integral nationalism.

Although it was the original basis of Action Française and was as old as Action Française was young in French political thought, the heritage of nationalism did not exclude other influences with which it formed curious alliances. This is an additional illustration of the diversity of possible combinations and the flexibility of development in the area of the history of political ideas. Monarchical nationalism, however integral it pretended to be, or perhaps because it was integral, was an intransigent, restrictive, and exclusive nationalism. The nationalism of Barrès laid claim to the Revolution of 1789 as one of the most glorious episodes of our history; Maurras rejected it without hesitation. Despite a vocabulary which affected plebeian airs and a demagoguery which carefully remained verbal, the new nationalism was purified of all references to the democratic principle and undamaged by any infiltration from the masses. Everything that had pulled Bonapartism toward a kind of social democracy was obliterated, all that once had made it an outlet for protest against the social authorities, the Church, or the prerogatives of the ruling classes now disappeared. Action Française was the opposite of democracy. Its political philosophy, based on a hierarchical conception of society and respectful of natural superiorities, was solidly aristocratic. Its social program boiled down to the anachronistic restoration of the corporative system and came to it from the traditionalist, aristocratic, and paternalistic branch of social Catholicism, as exemplified in the name of La Tour du Pin. To affirm "politics first" was even a way of denying social problems and maintaining the *status quo*.

Action Française shared its doctrine of repudiating democratic principles and its respect for the social hierarchies with another form of thought, that of the traditionalist Right. The similarities cannot be denied. On both sides the same intransigence, the same refusal to discuss or make adjustments. Neither one nor the other admitted of compromise. Action Française called itself an integral nationalism; Ultracism was an integral royalism. The extraordinary thing, which underlines their deep relationship even better, was that these doctrines of the absolute were also systems of contingency. They built their rejection of systems into a system and elevated deference to experience into a principle of research and a rule of action. These theories of political empiricism asserted their basic repugnance to the role of universal conceptions; they aspired only to the particular and wished to legislate for only one country. "France alone" was their guiding principle well before it became a slogan. The thought of Taine at this point met the teachings of Bonald.

Ultras and neo-monarchists were also alike in making history speak; no one heard it better than they. The Ultras had awakened the memory of the ancient liberties and restored honor to the traditions of the feudal and Christian Middle Ages. The Action Française did not do less for the past. Several of its groups placed themselves under the posthumous patronage of Fustel de Coulanges and claimed the intellectual heritage of the great historian of the *Political Institutions of Ancient France*. A whole school of scholars or essayists drew inspiration from Maurrasian postulates to study the national history. The most brilliant of them was Jacques Bainville, who offered to the general public, fond of history and attracted by memories of the past, an interpretation conforming to the principles of organized empiricism. This form of propaganda and education had an influence on opinion which should not be underestimated.

As a final point of analogy with the Ultra party of the Restoration, Action Française also flattered itself as being "the party of intelligence." It boasted of a notable proportion of intellectuals in its ranks. Among the youth of the universities and the professional schools it had its most thorough success and found its most earnest militants. By the brilliance of its writers and the quality of its literary and artistic columns, the newspaper after a hundred years made a splendid echo to the *Conservateur* of 1818.

If it is still necessary to complete the demonstration, to prolong a parallel which is not a simple stylistic exercise, the long list of common political strands would complete the demonstration of the identity of thought of the Ultras and the Action Française: hostility toward Jacobin centralization, attachment to local freedoms, defense and reconstruction of intermediary bodies, the same view of the monarchy which made it the bulwark of individual liberties and of the king as the federator of the French republics. All this was more than coincidence. Action Française embraced the guiding lines of the Ultra political and social system.

And yet Action Française was quite another thing than

an identical reprint of Ultracism, and Maurras more than a belated epigone of Bonald. They diverged even on points which were not minor. Did we not recognize in Romanticism one of the constants of Ultra sensibility? But all of Action Française, excepting perhaps Daudet, fought without mercy against Romanticism in politics, society, and even literature. It considered Romanticism synonymous with mental disorder and a source of intellectual confusion. Maurras stood for doctrinal and militant anti-Romanticism and here Maurras was all Action Française, so great was the importance of his preferences, whims, and prejudices. His role as a teacher of literary taste was perhaps as decisive as his function as a leading thinker. Classicism was the basis of his system, as much political as literary, in the exact measure to which his ethic was determined by an esthetic. "The philosophical and esthetic theories of *Athinea*[6] .form the very foundation of my politics." Ten volumes, a hundred articles mark this long struggle and attest to the permanence of this preoccupation in the author of the *Amants de Venise*. This Classicism explains his unexpected fondness for the work of Anatole France, despite the latter's suspect opinions; writing well redeemed him for having thought badly.

Differences of taste and disagreement in feelings led to divergences of opinion. This Classicist had fewer motives for liking the Middle Ages than did the Romantics of the Restoration. Their predeliction did not go to the same period. Maurras saw the ideal monarchy less in the protective royalism of Saint Louis or the paternal administration of good king Henri, than in the brilliance and pomp of the Sun King, although it is not clear whether he

[6] 1901. Tr.

admired Louis XIV more as the patron of letters and arts
or as the glorious sovereign, master of Europe, served by
Colbert and Louvois, Turenne and Condé. With such
tastes, Maurras no longer had the same reasons as the
Ultras for mistrusting the influence of power. He exe-
crated the Jacobin State but a monarchical State seemed
a blessing and a necessity to him. He even admitted an
intermediate phase, rather comparable to the historic
role that Marxism assigned to the dictatorship of the
proletariat in the movement from capitalist society to
classless society, in which the monarch would step out of
his proper role as arbiter to take on that of a temporary
dictator. Nothing indicates better the extent of the liberties taken with the thought of the first counter-revolutionaries.

There was a third Rightist tradition in the French
ideological inheritance, Orleanism. But who would think
to seek out affinities between Maurrasian antiparliamentarism and the parliamentary liberalism of the notables,
between Action Française, deliberately counter-revolutionary, and Orleanism, the agreeable heir of 1789?
However, an examination without any mental reservations would turn up some peculiar surprises. For example, is it completely irrelevant that for many years
Jacques Bainville wrote a regular column in *Capital?*[7]
And that in 1919 he published a guide to saving entitled,
How to Invest your Wealth? But there was something
more significant—Action Française's choice of intellectual fathers: Taine and Renan (and not the Renan of *The
Future of Science,* but that of the later years, of the *Intellectual and Moral Reform,* and also the Renan-Prospero,
liberal and aristocratic, filled with the necessity and the

[7] A daily financial newspaper founded in 1908. Tr.

beneficence of the elites, that is, on the whole, Renan the Orleanist). Maurrasian empiricism then, was not quite so far removed from opportunism and from the *juste milieu*. The Gallican anticlericalism of Action Française after 1926 revived the tone of the anticlerical Gallicanism which had fallen off with the first Orleanism. In both cases we see the same independence with regard to dogma and moral rules; did not Orleanism adopt, even before Action Française, the rule "politics first"? To be sure, the Orleanist share in Action Française was not the most important, nor the most decisive. Its presence, although inobtrusive, nevertheless permits us to conclude that none of the three Rightist traditions was absent from Action Française and that the new movement indeed represented, in unequal proportions, a synthesis of all the Right Wing groups of the nineteenth century.

III. Internal contradictions: Failure of the Synthesis

A true synthesis or simply a chance juxtaposition? The question is not entirely without basis, however little one takes account of the sometimes violently contradictory tendencies attracted by Action Française, both in doctrine and personality. The nature of Maurras's thought was to desire to establish in the art of leading men the harmonious and classic beauty of a completely reasonable order. But French political history, however rich in contrasts and discords, hardly offers any comparable examples of factions so dominated, carried away, and sometimes maddened to the point of blindness by polemical passion and its attendant frenzies as Action Française. For forty years it dispensed insults and spewed out abuse. Its campaigns offer material for a veritable an-

thology of verbal violence, a compendium of sarcasm and
calumny. It represented the confluence of the classical
tradition and nationalist turbulence, but it appears that
the mixture was not of equal parts. Passion and its crude
impulses prevailed over rational inclinations, like the
roiled and muddy waves of a flood which submerge and
destroy the noble and peaceful arrangement of a French
garden. For every one of Maurras's readers who clearly
understood the teachings of the philosopher, ten or
twenty perhaps profited more willingly from the lessons
and invectives of the polemicist. This victory of passion,
was it the revenge of that Romanticism whose evil Maurras spent his whole life denouncing?

This manifest conflict between reason and passion,
between the head and the heart, had its expression
within the doctrine, where it compromised the coherence
of political positions. The attitude toward the modern
State betrayed the contradiction between the two tendencies most clearly. The Ultra position had been simple:
the State was evil, irremediably, immitigably. Thus, their
program was a complete reaction against administrative
tyranny and bureaucratic centralization, the wretched
daughters of Jacobinism and Napoleonic despotism.
Maurras, the disciple and admirer of Mistral, the Provençal attached to his province, renounced nothing of
this way of thinking. But nationalism contaminated and
changed the purity of the original reaction. At bottom,
the school found it hard to avoid the fascination of
power. For it the State was not only an odious monster, it
became in its way a kind of absolute. The newspaper
based part of its attacks against the Republican regime
on the weakness of the executive and constantly extolled
a reinforcement of its power. The virtues of authority
represented an essential value for the men of Action

Française. Certainly it would be unfair to lay upon the theorist of organized empiricism the sole and entire responsibility for the errors of straying disciples; and yet it is impossible not to recognize in the seduction of power on this school the vice which explains the drift of several of its initiates toward fascism in 1939-1940. Among its readers, in the ranks of the leagues, *Action Française* introduced, maintained, and confirmed some inclinations, sympathies, prejudices, and some guiding ideas which indisputably prepared ground favorable to fascism. Moreover, did not Maurras himself enthusiastically salute its appearance in Italy (*Preliminary Introduction* to the definitive edition of the *Investigation on Monarchy*, 1924)? A curious fate for a counter-revolutionary school, heir of Ultra antistatism, respectful of hierarchy and tradition, to have been the intermediary between late nineteenth century nationalism and the fascism of the 1930's!

A third contradiction came directly from the Ultra forerunners, poorly disguised by continual references to the lessons of history. Affected by positivism, Maurrasian pragmatism presented monarchy as a sensible solution, as the governmental formula prescribed by the experience of centuries. Maurras's pragmatism refrained from penetrating the ultimate secret of things and from proposing an *a priori* to political philosophy. What a striking contrast between the would-be modesty of the intention and the dogmatism of its expression. No political group, except those which used Marxism as the principle of their thought, took the tone of certainty so naturally, divided truth from falsity with such assurance, nor extended praise or excommunication so lavishly. In truth, this school had the pretentions of a Church.

Precisely this was one day to oppose it to the Church,

that is, the latent conflict within its own thought between a relative philosophy and its pretentions to the truth, between an empiricist outlook and a religion of empiricism. This was the most formidable of all the contradictions which ran through Action Française, for it managed to place in opposition the thought of the master and the fidelity of a part of his disciples. The relations between Action Française and the Catholic Church has a singular history. Political circumstances and the bad relations between Rome and the government of the Republic had the effect of postponing a decisive showdown for a quarter-century. However, it was inevitable that some day the ambiguity would out. It was not the fact Maurras personally was an agnostic (as a student at a religious college he had lost the faith of his childhood) which made this unavoidable. This was a matter of personal feelings and doubtless Rome would not have encroached on the secrets of consciences. That one politician, among others, declared that he held Christianity to be "the immense multiplier of individual whimsy," would not have led to a pontifical warning. But Maurras was more than a politician. He cut a figure as a thinker, he assumed almost the position of a spiritual father. In this area he naturally roused the traditional suspicion of the Church.

But it happened that the system of this agnostic, become the intellectual leader of a large part of the Catholic public, rested on a denial of any metaphysical absolute and on the postulate of a positivistic methodology. His political conclusions agreed with those of Christian thinkers, so what did it matter if they arrived there by different routes? Maurras was closer to the skepticism of Renan or the empiricism of Taine than to the inspiration of the author of *On the Pope*.[8] To be sure, he proposed

[8] Joseph de Maistre. Tr.

only a political system which set aside all questions of theology. But was it so easy, was it even possible for his readers to discriminate between his political declarations and his estheticism, between his system and his philosophy? The slogan "politics first," still so often misinterpreted and improperly used against its author, sounded like a defiance of the spiritual authority, an unacceptable assertion of Machiavelism. How could the Church accept what seemed to be a refusal to subordinate the choice of political means to the consideration of moral ends? In any case, if only by default, the national interest took the place left empty by the absence of another absolute and tended to set itself up as the highest end. It was perfectly clear that universal Catholicism could no longer accommodate itself to this nationalism.

Some reasons of fact suddenly appeared which gave such considerations of principle an overriding urgency: the apparent coincidence or identification of French Catholicism with neo-royalism. Very quickly Action Française took in many Catholics. In the years before the First World War adhesion to integral nationalism seemed the logical conclusion of a spiritual conversion; Jacques Maritain and Joseph Lotte illustrate this evolution. Action Française then grouped around itself a galaxy of intellects that later divergences were to disperse in all directions. The brilliance and variety of this diaspora had no equal short of the list of those writing for *L'Humanité* in 1919-1920. Action Française seemed at the time the advanced and militant wing of French Catholicism. The two causes seemed more closely linked than ever. For example, it was Action Française which spearheaded a campaign for the "Saint of the Fatherland."[9]

[9] It is curious to note that at the origin of this cult, which was soon monopolized by the extreme Right, was the great figure of liberal

There developed then between neo-royalism and one tendency of French Catholicism one of those seemingly fortuitous connections which was mysteriously prepared beforehand by hidden relationships. French Catholics have always had a choice between several orientations. "The alliance of throne and altar"[10] corresponded politically to doctrinal agreement between traditional royalism and an Ultramontanism of a theocratic character; a generation later, during the pontificate of Pius IX, a liberal Catholicism of Orleanist sympathies and an Ultramontaine Catholicism with an authoritarian disposition were opposed to each other. Forty years later Action Française brought about the conjunction of an exclusive nationalism with a Catholicism of which it was said that it was paradoxically the opposite of universalism. There were many affinities between *integral* nationalism and Catholic *integrism*. Did they not fight the same good fight, in different areas, against modernism? At the Action Française institute Maurras founded a chair of the *Syllabus*. On both sides there was the same attachment to beliefs in order, authority, and hierarchy. Similarly, there was the same accent on tradition and minimization of the necessity or the virtues of adaptation. So, more than one clergyman rejoiced in the valuable aid furnished by Action Française in the struggle against modern errors and Action Française in return found in the Church active sympathies, useful friendships, and powerful protectors, both among the theologians (Cardinal Billot, S.J.) and in

---

Catholicism, Mgr. Dupanloup, who in 1878 suggested that Catholic women parade and place flowers at the foot of the statue on the Place des Pyramides. This was to be a reply to the celebration of the hundredth anniversary of Voltaire's death. Author. (The saint is Joan of Arc and her statue stands on the Place des Pyramides. Tr.)

[10] During the Restoration. Tr.

the orders most jealously attached to tradition such as the Benedictines of of Solesmes and the Dominicans of Saint Maximin. On the other hand Action Française provided the largest audience for the denunciations which were the unfortunate specialty of the *Correspondance de Rome,* organ of the clandestine *Sodalitium Pianum.*[11]

But integrist Catholicism was not all of French Catholicism. The tendency to conciliation, the liberal inclinations, and the democratic sympathies encouraged in the pontificate of Leo XIII were neither reduced nor seduced. On the theological level, starting in 1911, Father Laberthonnière pointed out the lack of orthodoxy in the origins of Maurrasian thought (*Positivism and Catholicism*). In the area of political choices, the permanence of another group of thinkers demonstrated the possibility of another combination: that which went from the *Sillon* to the Popular Democratic Party, and the names of Marc Sangnier and Francisque Gay underline its continuity. The dividing line within French Catholicism which separated Action Française from Christian democracy, although in the last analysis it concerned only small minorities, perhaps is as important for an understanding of French political life as the dividing line between Left and Right. Few divisions cut so deeply into the national consciousness and involved such profound consequences. Both the Church of France and the French political consciousness were involved. This line divided two temperaments, two sensibilities, two interpretations of Catholicism. The quarrel which flared between these two

---

[11] A secret organization within the Church, often called the *Sapinière*, which set up a network of surveillance and denunciation of those whom it suspected of straying from its integrist view of Catholicism. Tr.

schools had the sharpness of a civil war intensified by the ferocity of a religious war.

The pontifical condemnation, of which we shall describe neither the slow growth nor the sudden proclamation (1926),[12] was the outgrowth of strictly theological considerations, but had some political consequences of capital importance. In a few years it reversed the majority in French Catholic opinion. It even modified the behavior of Action Française, for the conflict with Rome and a refractory stubbornness in insisting on its justness equal to that of the Jansenists resurrected a form of royalist Gallicanism not seen since Montlosier. Events thus brought to light a last internal contradiction, that of an ostentatiously shouted religious fidelity and practical anticlericalism whose virulence soon eclipsed that of the professionals in this line.

But neither in 1900 nor in 1925 did these internal contradictions really weaken Action Française's influence, which was considerable. It always is rash to forward an estimate of an influence of this sort. In any case let us admit that it cannot be measured by the circulation of the newspaper,[13] and even less by the number of *Camelots du Roi*. Beyond this "visible school," the teachings of Maurras won over a large segment of the youth of the time. The apparent logical rigor of the system, the elegant simplicity of its basic principles, the attraction of its toughness, the vigor of its polemics, and the prestige of some of its intellectual princes all argued in the movement's favor. It appears to be undeniable that by the eve of the First World War, Action Française had considerably changed the intellectual climate of the country and

[12] The papal condemnation of Action Française. Tr.
[13] M. A. Dansette suggests the figure of 55,000 subscribers on the eve of the pontifical condemnation. Author.

had created a new inspiration. We have some testimony on this which is not without shortcomings but which it would be wrong to neglect. It is the investigation carried out in 1913 by Agathon (Henri Massis and A. de Tarde)[14] on contemporary youth. It concerned only a limited sample, the youth in the schools, and it tells us nothing of working-class or rural youth. Besides, the authors made no bones about their own positions: Massis was a disciple of Maurras. With these qualifications, the study has a certain interest. The titles of the principal chapters confirm the congruency of the preoccupations of this generation and the characteristics of integral nationalism: the taste for action, patriotic faith, Catholic renaissance, political realism; is this not like skimming through the program of Action Française?

Finally, we must consider a broader kind of influence which operated, in diffuse, insidious, and unconscious ways, on larger sectors of opinion, and in this way perhaps even more deeply. At least the extent of it can be guessed by considering the success of the leagues in the 1930's. Of course the leagues were not Action Française and both would have rejected identification, but if integral nationalism had not traced out the path and prepared opinion, the leagues would not have experienced their early and astonishing success.

In this way the historical importance of the phenomenon takes form: Action Française at once rejuvenated a declining royalism and regenerated its doctrine, gave to the nationalist passion a system of thought, and ventured an original synthesis of their contributions, even when conflicting. It furnished the Right with a deliberately reactionary philosophy which impregnated a part of French opinion.

[14] *Les Jeunes Gens d'Aujourd'hui* (Paris, 1913). Author.

8

1919-1939: From the *Bloc National* to the National Revolution, the Classic Right Wing and the Leagues

The War of 1870-1871, brief as it was, brought important and lasting changes to the equilibrium of political forces. The First World War, on the other hand, despite its length and its extent, affected only the surface of the French political situation. The years 1914-1918 do not mark a dividing line between two epochs. Once the tragic parenthesis of four years of war was closed, the postwar period smoothly resumed the prewar development. The only visible change was that which inevitably resulted from the natural aging of generations and the turnover, scarcely more rapid, of the political personnel and the electorate. Far from shaking institutions, the war confirmed their stability. Reinforced by forty years of routine, the regime was crowned with the prestige of a victory. The Republic had the right to claim credit for this victory in the exact measure as its enemies would have charged it with the responsibility for a defeat. For the moment at least, its critics abandoned trying to overthrow it, and the republican system was not at issue.

However, the general election of November 1919, the first after the armistice, marked the most important shift of opinion during the Third Republic, since it showed a complete reversal of the majority compared to the results of May 1914. The minority of yesterday became today's majority. The Right Wing, defeated once again in Spring 1914, came back in force and its numerical superiority was such that one must go back to the National Assembly of 1871 to find its equal. Even the names of certain representatives of the Right, Audiffret-Pasquier, Cassagnac, emphasized the similarities and confirmed the strange impression that the old days had returned. It seemed as if wars, whether they were disastrous or victorious, inevitably brought a reinforcement of the forces of order and conservation. The National Assembly of 1871 had numbered 400 to 500 Rightist Deputies out of some 750 representatives; the *Bloc National* won 437 out of 613 seats. Fortune had changed sides. The Right finally won the revenge it had so stubbornly coveted, and while between 1876 and 1919 it was almost constantly reduced to the pitiable state of permanent opposition, between 1919 and 1939 it controlled the government for fourteen years out of twenty. It was a radical change, to go from 150 representatives in the outgoing Chamber to 437 Deputies in the Blue Horizon Chamber.[1]

If inspected more closely, however, the change was clearly less profound than parliamentary arithmetic

---

[1] The Chamber elected in 1919 won this sobriquet because of the many blue-uniformed war veterans who sat in it. Tr.

would suggest. All the *Bloc National* was not really
Rightist. To the 221 members who incontestably belonged to the parties of the Right because of their opinions, attachments, or constituency, were associated some
215 Deputies whom circumstances and the traditional
law of the alternation of the Centers much more than
personal convictions had pushed to the Right, after the
move to the Left in the spring of 1914. Far from con-
tradicting the prewar evolution, the autumn elections of
1919 resumed the tendency which slowly moved the center of gravity of the political system toward the Right.
Forget for a moment the results of 1914 and turn back a
year earlier: the Progressists, temporary representatives
of an older Rightist tradition, won three presidencies.
The election of Raymond Poincaré as President of the
Republic in January 1913 against the Leftist candidate
Pams was greeted by the public as a victory for the
Right. The same political majority carried Paul Deschanel
to the Presidency of the Chamber and Louis Barthou to
the premiership. The success of these men, all favorable to the three-year military service law, showed the
strength of Rightist revival. But, and nothing demonstrates the continuity better, the same Deschanel,
whose election in 1913 to succeed the Radical Henri
Brisson had marked a victory of the Right-Center, was re-
elected to the presidential chair of the new (1919)
Chamber with 473 votes. A few days later the parliament
chose him over Clemenceau to succeed Poincaré at the
Elysée. Finally, an even more significant development:
the outgoing President of the Republic, Poincaré, soon
returned to office as head of the government, upheld by a
Rightist majority to follow a Rightist policy.

Problems and slogans as well as personalities con-

verged to weave a continuous thread between the prewar
and postwar periods. However strange it may seem on
the morrow of such an upheaval, political preoccupations
and respective positions had hardly changed. At the most
there was some modification of details necessitated by
new aspects of the problems. Right and Left continued to
oppose each other on the same issues: military and financial. In 1914 the Right had conducted a campaign for
three-year military service and against the income tax.
After 1919 it fought for military security and a balanced
budget. These two articles of its program corresponded
point by point to two successive aspects of Poincaré's
policy—the occupation of the Ruhr in 1923 and the defense of the franc in 1926.

The stability of personnel, permanence of problems,
and identity of issues are all reasons which forbid us
from opening a new chapter in the history of the Right
with the elections of November 1919. But ten or fifteen
years later these reasons are no longer so strong. Changes
had occurred, subtle at first and scarcely noticeable to
contemporaries, but soon they became so manifest that
they were obvious to the least acute observer. The
rhythm of these events presents a delicate problem to the
historian who undertakes to describe the period: where
was the point at which the normal course of development
was altered? February 1934 is too late; February 6 was
already a consequence of the shift that we are seeking to
date. Earlier, 1924 or 1926 still scarcely boded its approach. It was between these two points that the passage
from one period to the following took place. We shall
adopt M. J. J. Chevallier's suggestion and set it in the
year 1929. With the retirement of Poincaré in 1929 came
the eclipse of one generation by another and a change in

personnel; 1929 also was the beginning of the great economic depression which swept the world, even if France was not to feel its first blows for another two or three years.

We see then, after a first period which went from 1815 to the Dreyfus Affair, a second extending for thirty years from the morrow of the Affair to the early symptoms of February 6th. Again, 1939 will present quite a different political situation, the result of the decade of the 1930s. From one period to another the periods became shorter, the rhythm of change accelerates, in strict conformity with the general pattern of the evolution. Did there remain through these changes anything of the earlier traditions or is it proper to conclude that the speed and extent of the renovation wiped out their last remaining traces?

I. A Third Coalition: the Bloc National

In 1919 as in 1873 it was a coalition—did it not call itself the *"Bloc" National*—which opened the road to power for the Right Wing. Union was the necessary condition for their victory. It seems to have made short work of the old discords which had divided and weakened the Right Wing for so long. Renounced in the patriotic fervor of the Sacred Union, the old rancors melted before the rays of the victory whose prestige the *Bloc* expected to monopolize. The Right was even quite willing to cross out the fatal conflicts which in the past had opposed it to the Left. Only those shades of opinion incompatible with legitimate requirements of patriotism were excluded from a coalition which extended farther to the Left than at any other time. Adolphe Carnot brought to it the adherence of the Democratic Alliance, while the bad con-

science the Radicals felt in breaking up a union sealed by
the wartime defense of the country, and their obvious
hesitation to be the ones to unearth old differences as
well as their repugnance towards waging a separate
campaign, all these were so many justifications for the
contention of the Rightist groups that they represented
more than themselves—the nation and its unity.

From this came that very revealing name of *Bloc National* in which the adjective had even more weight than
the noun. It will be objected that this attitude was not
new. Had not the Right for over twenty years gloried in
its patriotism and opposed its nationalism to the internationalism of the Left? But in 1919 nationalism sacrificed
its suffix, it soberly called itself national. From nationalist
to national may seem a negligible nuance but it was of
capital importance. At best nationalism was only one of
several ways of understanding and serving the national
interest; but when it was national, the *Bloc* was the nation. Everyone who was not with it was against the nation. The S.F.I.O, for example, excluded from the *Bloc*,
ipso facto found itself cut off from the national community. Henceforth the Right was to monopolize the word,
the idea, and if possible, the reality behind them. The
union would be *national* whenever the Right joined it
and even more when the combination was constructed
around the Right. In 1926 with Poincaré, in 1934 with
Doumergue, in 1938 with Daladier, the coalition was
formed each time under the aegis and for the benefit of
what M. Goguel has named the party of the established
order. From this postulate came the natural psychological consequence: that the national values were on the
Right. The Right saw in the Left not only political adversaries, but bad citizens; the trench which ran between

Right and Left no longer separated two blocs competing for power, it distinguished bad Frenchmen from good patriots. This conviction introduced into political struggles an additional measure of harshness and seriousness, for it involved national integrity.

Heir of prewar nationalism (the presence in its ranks of a Barrès was a sound guarantee of the legitimacy of the relationship), guardian of the "war veteran" spirit (the Chamber of the *Bloc National* also bore the name Blue Horizon Chamber), the Right exalted patriotic sentiments and celebrated the national glories. The *Bloc* made the feast day of Joan of Arc into a legal holiday and authorized the movement to turn the memory of the Maid into an official cult. At the canonization ceremony of this saint of the fatherland (May 16, 1920) by Benedict XV, 80 members of parliament from the Right and Center attended in a body behind Gabriel Hanotaux. In return the Left pretended to consider the festival of Joan of Arc as a clerical and reactionary manifestation and refused to join in the annual solemnities.

Like all sincere sentiments, the patriotism of the Right was demanding and intransigent. It had the proud austerity of the great virtues. The memory of the dead and the realization of what was owed them that their sacrifice might not be in vain inspired the vigilance of the Right in the area of national security and guarantees. It firmly meant to keep the fruits of victory for France, and with the scrutiny of a pettifogging lawyer watched over the punctual execution of the clauses of the Versailles Treaty. Wilsonian idealism always seemed suspect to it, and the League of Nations, the principal edifice of this sentiment, inspired only a limited confidence. The Right did not have faith in the spirit of Geneva which offended its disdain for legal structures or awakened its inner skepticism for everything which tried to change the natural course of events. We recognize here one of the old characteristics of the Rightist spirit, the sentiment of submission to the natural order which made it condemn revolutions, constitutions, and the very principle of structural reforms. It did not believe in the suppression of wars any more than in the elimination of inequality, and the proposal of a legal organization of peace seemed to it quite as utopian as the common ownership of property or social democracy. However, the Right willingly accepted a League of Nations which perpetuated France's privileged position and guaranteed the maintenance of the *status quo*. But its realism ultimately preferred concrete guarantees to legal assurances and utopian proposals. The trilogy *status quo,* armaments, alliance, summarizes its entire foreign policy. The line followed by Poincaré: the occupation of the Ruhr and the taking of guarantees, conformed in all points to its views. Ten years later Barthou formulated the same program in the famous note of April 17, 1934.

In domestic policy the *Bloc National*'s position was expressed in another aspect of Poincarism, strict financial orthodoxy, based on the postulates of economic liberalism.[2] The Right was opposed on principle, and perhaps also for motives not foreign to the desires of its voters, to any increase in public expenditures and to any rise in taxation. It thereby took up on its own account the theme of cheap government exploited a hundred years earlier by the liberal Left. By definition the budget was always

---

[2] This apparent budgetary rigor was coupled with a policy of financial pliancy, for can one give another name to the constant preference to borrow rather than tax? Author.

too high. Then there was the constant plaint that the government employees were too numerous. Onto the major theme of budgetary prodigality was grafted the minor theme of "budget-devouring" functionaries generously paid to do nothing. Many Frenchmen wanted nothing better than to believe this but the consequent rancor of the functionaries was expensive for the Right. In 1924 and 1936 the success of the *Cartel des Gauches* and of the Popular Front was due in part to their displeasure provoked by the Poincaré and Laval decrees.

The unity of the Right Wing was cemented by a third theme which actually belonged to its arsenal of propaganda, namely anticommunism. In this the national mystique and the attachment to the established order were joined together. The poster showing the-man-with-the-knife-between-his-teeth played a significant part in the victory of the *Bloc National*.

To develop this program the *Bloc* had at its command a machine unprecedented in the history of the Right. For the first time it put into action an organization comparable to that of the Leftists and using the same methods. The novelty of the electoral system—a mixture of proportional representation and majority vote which gave an advantage to well-organized groups—invited this and offered a premium to organization. On the local level, electoral committees federated the Right Wing groups, joined their forces and leadership, and coordinated their efforts. On a higher echelon, national committees possessing an unusual authority intervened, chose nominees, and even arbitrated differences. The *Bloc* was thus an organic reality which brought powerful means to bear. Resources were not lacking; we should point out the unofficial part played on the margin of strictly political affairs by bodies which contributed to the financing of the campaign, such as the Union of Economic Interests[3] of Senator Billiet, or in 1928 and 1932 of the *Redressement Français* of Ernest Mercier.

To these one can add the activities conducted on a wider scale, from 1927 on, by the Propaganda Center for National Republicans, under the patronage of the *Echo de Paris* newspaper, for the benefit of all groups on the Right without distinction. By its nature the Center was only a specialized body which placed its services[4] at the disposal of all groups called "national," but by force of the authority that it could bestow it in effect made choices among candidates and effected withdrawals from run-off elections. It found itself performing a role which exceeded considerably that of a service. It is not impossible that its leaders, of whom Henri de Kerillis stood out, hoped to work for the unity of the Right Wing and aspired to reinforce its cohesiveness. In any case, the presence of common organizations was a new development which both demonstrated and reinforced the unity of a bloc on the Right. A common program, identity of views, and a grouping of efforts, everything seemed to converge. For the first time the unity of the groups on the Right appeared to win out over their disagreements; would it survive electoral campaigns and tactical considerations? Were the three Rightist traditions, so differen-

[3] This was a body established by about thirty employers' associations to carry on political action. Created at the beginning of the century, it had already taken an important part in prewar electoral campaigns. In one of the pre-1914 elections it had paid or advanced part of the campaign costs for some 300 of those elected. Author.

[4] It operated a school for speakers for debates and published posters which were technically excellent. An annual fund drive promoted by the *Echo de Paris* furnished the subsidy needed for its operation and propaganda. Author.

tiated until this point by their origins and beliefs, about
to merge into one?

If progress toward unity made headway, division
nonetheless remained the deeper reality. Every bloc has
its cracks and the *Bloc National* did not eliminate its, and
as the crevices in a wall reveal the points of weakness in
its construction, the eternal subjects of dispute made the
traditional lines of cleavage reappear among kindred
spirits.

The Right Wing factions reached agreement rather
easily on the defense of the franc. Their votes were unanimous to approve Poincaré's policy of firm intransigence
toward Germany, and they also managed to reach a certain unity of attitudes on other problems of lesser importance, but they ceased to form a bloc when the religious
issue came up for discussion. Poincaré, their leader and
symbol, who maintained correct and even courteous
relations with the ecclesiastical authorities and urged the
re-establishment of diplomatic relations with the Holy
See, did not permit the slightest impairment of the secularism of the State, nor allow any question raised about
the current status in the relations of the two powers. He
was in flagrant disagreement with those of his colleagues
who favored a proportional education budget.[5] So, in
1924 as in 1873 or in 1830, the religious question continued to divide two factions within the Right. Secularism stood obstinately as a boundary between two ideological and political traditions of the Right, which remained distinct beneath the façade of unity of the *Bloc
National.*

The older of the two traditions was the conservative

[5] A Catholic proposal for the government to allocate educational
monies to all schools in proportion to the number of students. Tr.

Right.[6] It experienced a brilliant comeback which compensated for its long and disappointing wait. Above all, it was Catholic. Its voters supported it because of its program of religious defense. A number of its members, often the most conspicious, were well-known Catholics and their religious connections, their personal relations with the bishops or with Catholic institutions, were recognized. In return, the majority of the Catholic element voted conservative. It was in the regions of widespread religious practice, where the old clerical and social framework remained vigorous, where the clergy had not lost its traditional influence, in the West, Lorraine, Franche-Comté, and the southern edge of the *Massif Central,* that the conservative members of parliament had their most faithful supporters.

Officially, however, the hierarchy, converted by an unfortunate experience to a respect for the principle of separation of Church and State, now kept itself prudently outside the political arena and scrupulously abstained from taking part in the electoral campaign. Ordinarily the bishops' charges were limited to reminding the faithful of their electoral duty and advising them to "vote wisely." But old ties do not fall aside quickly; the loyalties were of long standing and it took time to change almost sacred habits. In fact, why should the Church weaken these ties, which it believed were advantageous

[6] Despite the discredit attached to the notion of conservatism, some candidates proudly hoisted the conservative banner. Generally they were monarchists. A larger number judged it wiser to present themselves under less compromising labels. In the Chamber most of the Deputies of this Right joined the Democratic Republican Entente which had taken the place of the defunct Liberal Action and Republican Federation. In 1924 the name Democratic Republican Union was substituted for this Entente. Author.

and to which it judged itself compelled as a work of gratitude? In time of peril or trial it was always on the benches of the conservative Right that it knew it could find its most earnest defenders if not its most adroit ones. So, regularly, at each crisis the Catholic voters took the road again to the conservative Right.

In 1924, worried about the success of the *Cartel des Gauches* and over the stated intention of the new majority to reaffirm the application of the separation laws and even extend them to Alsace and Lorraine, the hierarchy replied by establishing the National Catholic Federation. This was a vast assemblage of an exclusively defensive character, which aimed at mobilizing all the faithful on the civic level, outside party politics, to defend Catholic interests and stop the growth of anticlericalism. This organization did not intend to take on any political coloration. But its presidency was given to General de Castelnau, a glorious soldier with great prestige, yet by his family tradition and royalist beliefs a man of the Right. Despite the basic honesty of his character, was there not room to think that by this choice the two causes, the conservative and the Catholic, the political and the religious, would be a little more intertwined in the sight of their friends as well as their enemies? In fact, when the president of the National Catholic Federation had to make an appeal, to spread instructions, or to utter a warning, he used the *Echo de Paris* as a spokesman, a newspaper with a clear political orientation, the same one which supported the Propaganda Center for National Republicans. It was in its pages in 1932 that he took to task the Catholic Association of French Youth whose loyalty to papal instructions on peace and international relations inspired some uneasiness in the federation whose patriotism was touchy and vigilant. A quarrel among Catholic factions was thereby made known to the public by a Rightist newspaper. Finally, the leading Catholic speakers, those who in the years 1934-1936 each Sunday traveled from diocese to diocese carrying the word to meetings of parish unions, whether they were called Philippe Henriot, Xavier Vallat, Jean Le Cour Grandmaison, or Groussau, were all men of the Right. In all of them, agreement with the Church's position on education combined with the hereditary antipathy of men of the conservative Right for statism and the public schools. Proposals for a single school system[7] knew no more determined opponents.

Opposed to centralization, this Right generally accepted the regime. It was without mental reservations that it called itself the Republican Entente or Federation. Time had done its work; the arguments concerning the *Ralliement* were now far in the past.[8] Within the framework of republican institutions this Right wanted to follow a conservative policy. Defense of religion and defense of the social order were on a par. It opposed overly progressive innovations, found systematic reforms repugnant, and accused them of being utopian. Its traditional suspicion of the State made its members prefer an empirical solution to social problems. In April 1930 the Chamber voted on the bill instituting social insurance. The conservatives did not oppose the principle of

[7] This would have meant abolishing the Catholic schools. Tr.
[8] A small faction alone perpetuated monarchical fidelity. In November 1919 Léon Daudet was elected in Paris on a ticket styled National Union and supported by Action Française which calculated that some 20 others elected under various labels were in its camp. Daudet was not re-elected in 1924 but in 1932 the monarchist newspaper claimed as its own a half-dozen Deputies generally designated as Independents and sent to the Palais Bourbon by Languedoc or the Vendée. Author.

the reform, indeed many of them, won over by considerations of social Catholicism, were sincerely devoted to its generous inspiration (only 16, almost all from the rural departments of the West, joined their negative votes to those of the dozen Communists). But they feared a new intervention into these matters by the State, new administrative encroachments, and 84 (the Democratic Republican Union then included 91 members) declared their support for the counter proposal of Xavier Vallat, which organized the insurance according to regions and occupations. To them the new system would have seemed less pregnant with menace for individual liberty if it had been reduced to the scale of a decentralized organization, attached to more familiar and reassuring realities. Twenty years later the campaign for localization of social security led by *France Catholique*, the organ of the National Federation of Catholic Action, and its president, Le Cour Grandmaison, rested on the same considerations. It is not impossible either that the proponents of the Vallat bill anticipated that a very decentralized structure for the new organization would give local personalities, the regional notables, the opportunity to exercise a benevolent tutelage over the management of the local offices, an extension of the duty of patronage traditionally identified with the upper classes. Viewed in the perspective of the evolution of French politics, this conservative Right rather faithfully expressed the state of mind, the convictions, and also the fears of a certain number of essentially rural areas, as yet hardly touched by economic evolution and remaining deeply attached to old France, that is, of the West, more the Vendéan and Angevin areas than Brittany, of Lorraine, Franche-Comté, Savoy, Provence, Lozère, and the Basque country.

Whatever the cause was, whether inexperience due to its prolonged separation from governmental responsibilities, or its relative position on the fringe of possible majorities which reduced its freedom to maneuver, or even a persistent suspicion of it by the old Republicans, the conservative Right exercised power only rarely and never in its own name. Its politicians had to be content with playing minor parts or resign themselves to a representative position in National Union cabinets where Louis Marin balanced off Edouard Herriot. But how many of them became premier? Neither Poincaré, nor Tardieu, and certainly not Laval, Doumergue, nor Flandin were in this group. It voted for these men on every occasion, and they could not have done without this support, but honors and power went to another Right, less conservative or conservative in another fashion.

This other Right was not more numerous nor so much more homogeneous or better organized, but its valuable experience in the parliamentary game taught it how to exploit the advantages of its relative position in the Right-Center where it was the pivot of coalitions. It was composed, approximately, of the groups named Democratic Alliance, Left Republicans, Left Independents, and Republican Left. Such a profusion of references to the Left by these Rightist groups will surprise only those who are not aware of the secrets of political vocabulary. It will not astonish anyone who remembers their antecedents. The shift of these groups to the Right occurred between the Dreyfus Affair and the 1919 elections. The entrance of the Democratic Alliance into the *Bloc National* consummated this movement, by appearing to heal the schism which, in 1899 when the government of Republican defense had been constituted, had cut the Progressists into two opposed factions. To move from one bloc to the other, from that of the Left to that of the Right, took exactly twenty years. Now the Republican Federation and the Democratic Alliance sat side by side again, allied in the same coalition.

Though they were allied they were not merged. In fact, even though partially healed the break remained between these two varieties of the Right. To a Republican Federation which gradually absorbed the heritage of traditionalism, there were still opposed the successors of the Opportunists of the 1880's and the Progressists who followed Waldeck-Rousseau in 1899. Moreover, many had learned their political lessons under his direction. Paul Reynaud, one of the most brilliant personalities of the Democratic Alliance between 1930 and 1940, wrote an engaging and laudatory biography of the great Republican statesman.[9] They undertook to deny neither the intellectual heritage nor the spiritual traditions of the founders of the Republic. Poincaré represented them quite perfectly: a conservative Republican, an unyielding patriot, and not less unyielding on the religious question. He voted for the appropriations to re-establish an embassy in the Vatican, but the clerical Right was deluded if it counted on his aid in challenging the educational laws.

In foreign policy, however, these men leaned more than did the conservative Right toward discussion and negotiation. They also were more prone to place confidence in the League of Nations and international organizations. Briand was more to their taste. But on moving from foreign to domestic policy, from international rela-

---

[9] *Waldeck-Rousseau*, 1913. Preface by Millerand. Author.

tions to social welfare, the change was complete, the positions were reversed. The conservative Right did not raise any objection in principle to the intervention of the State so as to forestall or restrain the excesses of economic liberalism or to the development of regulations on the relations between employers and workers. On the other hand none of this was accepted by the Right-Center, whose economic doctrine as well as political thought rested on the postulates of liberalism. In this Right's attachment to liberalism there entered as much profound conviction as there was well-understood self-interest. Self-interest? This was the section of parliament which came closest to the leading circles of economy, of banking and finance. Conviction? It was undeniable. The conservative Right welcomed sympathetically the birth of social institutions, of structures intervening between the individual and the State, where it fancied to find itself as a reflection of the old cadres of traditional society and which corresponded to its organicist belief. But the Right-Center could only be unflinchingly hostile to all these attempts to create social legislation. This was a continuation of the struggle of liberal individualism against the organized framework of the Old Regime. Thibaudet was thinking of this Right when he spoke of the candidates running as Independents and from whom the Independents of today directly stem, "The word independent expresses an absolutely contrary idea to the system of dependencies implied in traditionalism." The "independent" Right corresponded to a society quite different from the old rural society; it was the political expression of the bourgeois France that emerged from the Revolution. Going back beyond the founders of the Opportunist Republic, it attached itself to the militant Orleanism of

1830, as vigilant in defending itself on its right as on its left.[10]

"Order and Liberty." The old slogan which in 1830 defined the program of the *juste milieu* was still quite suitable to characterize the governmental policy that the leader of the Right Wing, Premier André Tardieu, presented in 1930. His ministerial declaration, overflowing with projects, crackling with figures and statistics, quite concerned with economic growth, after a century's interval echoed the business cabinets of the July Monarchy, the famous speech of Guizot and his watchword, "Enrichissez-vous!" Tardieu resembled Guizot, less doctrinaire but not less intellectual. He did not teach at the Sorbonne when he was twenty-nine, but he graduated from the Ecole Normale, and instead of writing in the *Annales de l'Education* or the *Revue Française,* for several years he did valuable work for *Le Temps.* Both tasted diplomacy, Guizot at the Embassy in London, Tardieu at the 1919 Peace Conference. Tardieu appeared above all more "dynamic," as people began to say about 1930, more anxious for *efficiency,* as the English-American snobs loved to put it. Here was the principal, and perhaps the only, divergence from the *juste milieu*: Tardieu proposed an American-style Orleanism, renovated, enlarged, adapted to the new conditions of production and of the economy, affected by the mystique of prosperity. But for one Tardieu, who understood the need for modernization, how many were there in this Right who were narrow, timid, and routine-minded, living vestiges of the Chambers of the July Monarchy

---

[10] Paul Reynaud wrote an account of the *Trois Glorieuses* (the three-day 1830 Revolution) ; a significant choice. It was a thesis for his diploma in advanced studies. Author.

and evidence of a society which had fallen behind the requirements of the economy?

II. A French Fascism: the Leagues

So, with the qualifications and subtle changes naturally required by different circumstances, the traditionalist and conservative Right as well as the liberal or independent Right were exactly on time at the rendez-vous that the evolution of political regimes periodically arranged for them. Were the Bonapartist Right and its nationalist substitute alone absent? The absence or disappearance of the youngest of the three traditions would have been the more surprising because it perhaps never knew a political climate more favorable to its development than the interwar years. Exceptionally favorable in general for the blooming of nationalism, the years 1919-1939 were not invariably so. Nationalism, whose passionate nature we have pointed out and whose movements more willingly obeyed the impulses of anger than the judgments of intelligence, was closely dependent upon the currents of an unstable and volatile public opinion. When the political situation was calm Action Française was practically the only voice to make itself heard; if it was troubled, if a crisis struck the country, then the usual themes of the old nationalist program found their youth and their attraction again. The ambitious discovered their leadership qualities, the agitators became saviours, demagogues' harangues drowned out the voices of parliamentary orators, paramilitary movements sprang up like mushrooms after a storm and actively competed with the old-fashioned parties. The history of this Right was essentially discontinuous then, made up of sudden ad-

vances, of successes without consequences, followed by
collapses as abrupt as debacles. The oscillations of this
saw-tooth curve faithfully reflected shifts of opinion. The
sudden expansion of numbers corresponded to a rising of
excitement and the their decline unfailingly meant an
ebb. Yet under the apparently capricious instability of
this history it is easy to see the permanence of a fundamental tradition of French political life which was never
entirely absent during the last two decades of the Third
Republic.

It was not absent even from the *Bloc National,* if it is
true that the success of its candidates owed something to
antiparliamentarism. "Some antiparliamentary odors
spread in the atmosphere, stronger than at any time since
Boulangism or Panama," wrote M. Siegfried with reference to the election of November 1919. Antiparliamentarism seems a rather common feeling after wars. The
former soldiers retained a dislike for the Deputies for a
division of responsibilities which often kept some in the
rear areas while others risked their lives in the trenches.
The veterans who cherished a nostalgic remembrance of
their unanimity in the face of the enemy which was symbolized by the postwar slogan, "United as at the Front,"
were naturally led to associate, with the return of peace,
the resurgence of prewar political divisions with the parliamentary system.

But the first really fervent antiparliamentary movement dates from the years 1924-1927, unleashed by the
victory of the *Cartel des Gauches.* Their hopes frustrated, removed from power, men of the Right began to
despair of the voters and fell back on methods hardly
conforming to parliamentary orthodoxy. Action Française
was not the last to profit from this state of mind and it

took its share in the awakening of the authoritarian Right. In June 1927, from the 10th to the 12th, the leaguers of the Action Française entrenched themselves in the newspaper's offices near the Saint Lazare railway station, repeating the Fort Chabrol episode (resistance to a siege decidedly was a tradition of the extreme Right; one thinks of the Week of the Barricades in Algiers in 1960), and for three days withstood beleaguerment by the police who surrounded them under the direct command of Jean Chiappe, Prefect of Police.[11] Simultaneously, other organizations exploited or fed antiparliamentarism. Georges Valois' *Faisceau* appeared at this time. Most important, in 1924 Pierre Taittinger, a Deputy from Paris, founded the *Jeunesses Patriotes*, soon well enough known to be popularly designated only by its initials, even by its enemies as the song of the *Jeune Garde* testifies. This was the first of the leagues. It was to serve as a model for all these highly disciplined organizations which hoped to act directly on opinion by bringing in the man in the street to exert pressure on parliament and the government. They had nothing in common with political parties.

Their methods were hardly original. They remind us of the exploits of the *Camelots du Roi* in 1908-1909. The J.P. first gave notice of its existence by demonstrating on the occasion of the transfer of Jaurès' ashes to the Pantheon, which had been decided by a Leftist majority. A blue raincoat, a Basque beret, and the insignia of their

---

[11] The extreme Right retained a kind of sympathy for Jean Chiappe for the way in which he directed the police and negotiated the surrender of the besieged. This feeling played a considerable part in the preliminaries to the February 6 events, when his removal as Prefect of Police became known. Author.

league gave members the appearance of a uniform and a military aspect. For a while the J.P. enjoyed a certain success, especially among the university youth attracted by a taste for action, a juvenile sense of their own importance, and the noble patriotic ideal. In 1929 they claimed nearly 300,000 members, but what credence can we give to estimates, impossible to authenticate and furnished by the interested party? After 1930 the organization seemed rather to decline: the success of other leagues hurt it. However, it still played a leading role on the evening of February 6: the J.P. marched from the Hôtel de Ville toward the Palais Bourbon. The parade, led by 22 members of the municipal council, included only 10,000 demonstrators, although a good half of the leaguers were recruited from the Paris region. In 1935 the league claimed some 60,000 members in the entire country. The decline was irreparable, and the organization was scarcely mentioned in 1936.

The doctrine was no newer than the methods. The very name they chose clearly announced that the J.P. of 1924, after a victorious war, expected to continue the work of patriotic defense and national improvement which had been undertaken, after an unfortunate war, by Déroulède and the League of Patriots. In other words, they joined the tradition of French nationalism. Older still, their major issues, revision of the Constitution and reinforcement of the executive, linked them to Bonapartism. They even took up its social fancies, the ostensible interest in the world of labor. Their social program, colored with neo-corporatism like all the programs of the authoritarian Right, provided for a limit on profits, a social charter, and the association of workers. It redrew, line by line, the mixture of calculation and generosity, of illusion and demagoguery, already developed by Bonapartism. Like it, the J.P. cherished the utopian dream of satisfying the proletarians and reassuring the capitalists. Authoritarian and vaguely socialistic, it tried to play on both sides and hoped to reunite the French nation with a policy of grandeur.

Nationalism, Bonapartism, the guarantees were honorable, the references quite suitable to calm persons as touchy on the matter of doctrinal influences and prompt to suspect foreign infiltration as were the French nationalists. But chronology suggests another interpretation which does less honor to the patriotism of the leagues and offers an explanation which looks beyond the border for references and influences. In 1924, creation of the J.P.; in October 1922, the Fascist March on Rome. Did not Pierre Taittinger intend to introduce an adapted version of fascism into France, rather than reinstitute Boulangism? In this case the J.P. would be less the heirs of Déroulède than the disciples of Gabriele d'Annunzio, and more the imitators of Mussolini than the sons of Barrès. Was it not at this moment that Georges Valois named his movement the French *Faisceau*, so as to affirm the identity of inspiration with the Romagnol dictator? In April 1935 didn't a delegation from the *Jeunesses Patriotes* pay a kind of pilgrimage visit to Rome, to Mussolini's Rome?

The question is important, for it concerns not only the *Jeunesses Patriotes,* supported at this point by Georges Valois' small movement. It must be asked about all the leagues that entered political life in the 1930's and after. It is fundamental; an understanding of the period and the correct interpretation of the events which led up to 1940 depends on its answer. Formulated in general terms, the question may be posed in this way: between 1924 and 1936 French political life experienced the rise

of a number of organizations called leagues having in
common a strong antiparliamentarism. French antecedents and European analogies make it possible to attach
them as easily to a national tradition as to contemporary
foreign developments. To say that they combined the
imitation of some with the influence of others is not a
reply and only puts off the problem, for an appraisal of
the respective parts of the French authoritarian tradition
and the fascist tendencies still remains necessary as well
as a determination of which of the two streams pre-
dominated.

The problem is made still more difficult by the use, too
often without discernment, of the notion of "fascism." In
the present period few words have known such notoriety.
Everything which was not consciously on the Left was
indiscriminately reputed to be fascist, for fascism was
promoted to the role of a term opposed to "democrat" or
"progressive." This was to confuse under a single name
several very dissimilar realities, and it is exactly the function of this study to point out such differences. Political
reality is richer and more varied than abstract classification would suggest. Despite a great poverty of thought
and a doctrinal weakness which related it to nationalism,
fascism had a distinct originality, clear outlines, and an
easily recognized appearance. All the fascist movements
combined the same ingredients. On a foundation of exasperated or bruised patriotism and a "war veteran"[12]
mentality, there flourished and raged an antiparliamen-

---

[12] It almost seems to be a law of war veterans' movements that
they change into Rightist organizations. The *Stahlhelm*, the American
Legion, and the *Croix de Feu* are three examples whose similarity
offers proof. By what mystery of political psychology do the memories
of the dead, the camaraderie of combat, the desire to maintain the
fraternity of the trenches open the way to a Rightist ideology? Author.

tarism both doctrinal and practical, a devotion to the State, a passion for order, a taste for force, a cult of the leader, the dictatorship of a party, and official corporatism. In all countries this same combination reappeared.

Analyzed in this way, reduced to its constituent parts, it is clear that fascism had little in common with political and social conservatism. Only by abusing the term can it be confused with "reaction." In fact, the two notions have no common denominator. Nothing was so refractory to the seductions of fascism than the "classic" Right Wing; did not these groups on the Right rest on an opposite conception of political power? Orleanism defined itself as parliamentary liberalism; as for the traditionalist Right, it was born out of a reaction against the principles of 1789. Counter-revolutionary by nature and by system, it had strived for over a century to put together the chain of time, broken by the revolutionary "accident." But fascism did not deny the Revolution, it presupposed it; its existence and content implied the principles of 1789. Fascism could rise only after the Revolution: it put the same foundation at the basis of power as democracy did: popular sovereignty. Perhaps this relationship may be surprising, has it not been considered that fascism commandeered popular suffrage and cozened democracy? Certainly, but not before having previously rendered homage to it. As heresies can only grow out of an orthodoxy, fascism, that heresy of democracy and similar in this sense to Bonapartism, postulated democracy. Conservative traditionalism and fascism therefore recognized two contrary bases of power: on the one hand tradition, the single source of legitimacy, on the other the popular will, which fascism ultimately falsified.

When considered as to their relations with the social

structure, the two doctrines appeared even more dissimilar. The conservative Right maintained or restored the social hierarchy; the fascist party was forced by the logic of the system to enter into conflict with the traditional social authorities. German National-Socialism carried on an incessant and cunning war against older organizations, against the spirit of the *Reichswehr,* even within the new *Wehrmacht.* Fascism simply was a movement of *déclassés,* of upstarts, of adventurers, who had nothing in common with the notables. To be sure, on occasion they did ally against a common enemy, if the interests of the country or of social order required it. In such an alliance there were mental reservations on both sides and of course each hoped to win the last match. Hindenburg resigned himself to calling Hitler to power, but Hugenberg believed he could use the Nazi agitator and von Papen flattered himself as being the most clever.

Nothing is better than concrete examples. Therefore we shall illustrate these differences of principle by some cases, taken from contemporary regimes, that ignorance or prejudice arbitrarily place under the label "fascism." Certainly the Portugal of Salazar does not enter the fascist category; it is a conservative and clerical regime which has a closer resemblance to Metternich's Austria than to Mussolini's Italy. It is harder to label the Franco regime, for it has evolved considerably after oscillating for a long time between several influences. If that of the Phalange had won out to the point of establishing the national-syndicalism of José-Antonio Primo de Rivera, Franco's Spain today would add the Spanish variety to the abundant collection of fascisms. But the authority of the Church, the prestige of the army, and the influence of the social authorities firmly re-integrated the Franco regime into the family of conservative regimes, or if one prefers, reactionary ones.

With these considerations in mind, we can now return to the problem raised by the French leagues of the 1930s—fascism or reaction? As a matter of fact, the question is not exactly a new one for French political history. It was raised already, in hardly different terms, about Bonapartism.[13] Bonapartism of the Left, appealing to the masses, socialistic, and anticlerical, or Bonapartism of the notables, conservative and clerical? It was Boulangism that retrospectively supplied the definitive answer; without denying all the inspiration of 1789, Bonapartism ended on the Right with its nationalist offspring. Forty years later, the same experience was reflected with the leagues. Their evolution repeated the proof of the practical impossibility for an authentic fascism to acclimate itself in France. To see a French fascism in the leagues is to take a scarecrow for a reality. They borrowed only the ornaments of fascism, put on its finery, but threw aside its spirit. The league movement was simply the latest incarnation of the old Bonapartist tradition—Caesarian, authoritarian, and plebiscitarian—nationalism revised to fit current tastes and whose imitators did no more than replaster the façade with a whitewash of Roman fascism.

However, we should identify some organizations, noisy but without real power, which were indeed fascism in a

[13] For Bonapartism to be a French equivalent to fascism, with changes stemming from the chronological differences, only one element was lacking, but it was a fundamental one: the single party, with its powerful organization and cadres. Perhaps the dynastic link and the hereditary succession took its place to the extent that they fulfilled the functions of the party: to provide for and guarantee the permanence of the regime and to attach the masses to it. Author.

pure state, shallow copies without a glimmer of understanding. One of these was *Francism*, founded about
1934 by Marcel Bucard. Its very name cried out its allegiance; the uniform (blue shirt and tie, Basque beret)
also showed the resemblance to fascism from which it
plagiarized its program. At its first convention (June
1934), the movement which hoped to become the French
fascism sent telegrams of fellowship to Mussolini and
even to Hitler. We should place in the same category the
group named *Solidarité Française* which also appeared
about 1934 and was led by Jean Renaud, a former officer
of colonial troops. In its poverty of inspiration and inconsistent doctrine it did not even try to disguise a taste for
violence and its attraction to naked force. But the failure
of these two organizations had great significance; neither
enjoyed a real success. The adherents of *Francism* probably did not exceed ten thousand and the numbers of
Solidarité Française at best may have approached this
figure. What is twenty thousand recruits, even convinced
ones, in a nation of forty million! In Paris alone one can
always find ten thousand rowdies to acclaim anyone or
rally to any cause, especially if one can pay the price.
But *Solidarité Française* did openly profit from the
financial support of the millionaire industrialist François
Coty.[14] Only one attempt enjoyed a real success and

[14] It would be valuable to know more about the role played by this
powerful businessman who was bitten by the political bug. In the
world of the leagues his name appears at every turn. Marcel Bucard
had relations with *L'Ami du Peuple*, this perfume magnate's newspaper; we shall meet him soon at the beginnings of the *Croix de Feu*.
What was this silent partner in the newspapers *Gaulois* and *Figaro*
looking for? Did he only want to arouse public opinion to prepare for
a national regeneration? Or was he personally interested and was he
trying to develop an instrument for an eventual putsch? Did this
Birotteau dream of becoming Caesar? Author.

may be considered a serious venture of fascism, that of Jacques Doriot and his French Popular Party [P.P.F.— *Parti Populaire Français*]. But this was undertaken in the atmosphere of 1936, in the midst of an international crisis, by a personality of quite a different order. We shall return to him presently. In sum, before 1936, nothing justifies the legend of a French fascism.

Not even the day of February 6. Nothing has done so much to give currency to the idea of a fascist peril than this evening of Paris rioting. Yet its scenes were far from resembling the classic lines of the "putsches" which so many foreign capitals experienced at this time! The unfolding of events reminds one more of Boulangist agitation than the March on Rome. To be sure, the intentions of those who organized it still today remain poorly understood. What role did their plans conceive for the riot: a simple demonstration in the streets meant to exert pressure on the Chamber and extort from it the resignation of the Daladier cabinet, or a putsch against the political institutions? Reversal of the majority or of the regime? We don't know, but in the present state of research on the question, no evidence suggests a preference for the second interpretation over the more limited hypothesis of a disturbance that went awry. There is nothing to prove that a precise objective was determined in common. Quite to the contrary, each organization had its own rallying point and exercised a jealous care to avoid being mixed up with the others. Then too, the number of those who responded to the appeals of the leagues was not high. In adding them up according to the information given in Right Wing newspapers,[15] whose sympathy for the agitators cannot be questioned, one arrives at a figure

---

[15] *Echo de Paris,* the *Jour,* the *Journal, Paris-Midi.* Author.

that hardly exceeds 30 thousand.[16] To this should be added the usual crowd of curiosity seekers, idlers, passers-by, and malcontents. The bulk of the demonstrators came without a clear notion of what they did want but with a precise notion of what they no longer wanted: scandals, suppression of the truth, and the consequences of the economic depression (the National Taxpayers League was one of the organizations that prepared the demonstration). The old Boulangist cry was taken up, "Down with the crooks!" and it well expressed this crowd's anti-parliamentarism, but it is going too far to see in this the sign of a fascist peril. In the course of the day, the only insurrectionary thing was the pseudo-revolutionary language of the summons by the *Jeunesses Patriotes,* but this group worshipped a verbal tradition. February 6 was not a putsch, not even a riot, only a street demonstration that history soon would have forgotten if it had not turned into tragedy and if subsequent events had not later reflected back on it a quite unwarranted importance.

Nothing more surely confirms the shallowness of the movement and the absence of any revolutionary inspiration—for fascism, at least in the beginning, was revolutionary—than the solution of the crisis. It was a rather ridiculous conspiracy if simply the return from his farms of an "emeritus" politician could appease it![17] It took only an old man's smile to dissipate so much emotion. All this agitation to bring back into harness and to elevate to the premiership an old hand at party politics

[16] Between four and ten thousand *Jeunesses Patriotes*, 7 thousand *Croix de Feu* divided in two columns, and above all, the veterans of the *U.N.C.* (*Union Nationale des Anciens Combattants*) estimated at between 10 and 20 thousand. Author.

[17] The reference is to Gaston Doumergue. Tr.

who had served as President of the Republic from 1924 to 1931. To be sure, Gaston Doumergue went about with the leagues and he donned the Basque beret and attended a parade of the *Croix de Feu,* but his program was in fact limited to reviving the proposals made eleven years earlier by his unlucky predecessor at the Elysée Palace, Alexander Millerand. Instead of denouncing, in the rapprochement of Doumergue and the leagues, the collusion of an ambitious man with fascism, is it not more reasonable to see there a clear-cut indication of the lack of seriousness in this so-called fascism? Fascism was a leap of youth; Rightist opinion eagerly accepted an old man,[18] and the feelings that it revealed had nothing in common with the climate of revolutionary fever in which fascism bloomed. Fascism dreamed only of upheaval. The Right wanted to be reassured and aimed at stability.

III. From The Croix de Feu to the French Social Party

In truth, our demonstration still admits of a large gap: it has overlooked a capital element in the question. We have said nothing about the *Croix de Feu,* although this movement mustered perhaps two million Frenchmen and had an importance which the other leagues never approached, even at the height of their development. Here is the crux of the whole debate then: if Colonel de La Rocque's organization shows us unimpeachable bonds of relationship with fascism, it would be impossible not to

---

[18] On February 9, 1934, Henri de Kerillis, linking Doumergue, Clemenceau, and Poincaré, wrote, without suspecting the confirmation that later circumstances would bring, "It has become a sort of rite with us to appeal to an old man, to a father of the country," (*Echo de Paris*). Author.

conclude that a strong fascist movement appeared in France. But in the opposite case we would hold decisive proof that French fascism was only a myth. Without question there is no better verification of the impossibility of fascism establishing itself in France than the course of development of the *Croix de Feu* between 1928 and 1936. Therefore it is not out of place for us to elaborate in some detail the history of this movement which did, for a brief moment, excite the hopes of a large portion of Right Wing opinion.

It unfolded in three stages. Little is known of the rather obscure beginnings of the organization. Founded in 1928 by Maurice Hanot, known as Hartoy, to unite veterans decorated during the war for their bravery under fire, from which came the name, and supported in the following year by the *Association des Briscards* which was open to all those who had spent at least six months at the front, the *Croix de Feu* at its origin had no announced political program, nor any hidden one either. The aim was to gather the best of the veterans, and, on a basis of common memories and camaraderie, to form a knighthood of military courage, to lay the foundation for a new kind of Legion of Honor.

However, François Coty already had directed his interest toward the young organization. His press encouraged its first steps. He favored the rise to responsible positions of Lieutenant Colonel de La Rocque, who made his way upward rather cleverly. A member of the executive board in 1929, elected to the vice-presidency in the following year, in 1931 he became president of the movement. His ascent provokes some surprise, for nothing appeared to destine this officer for a great political role. Graduated from Saint-Cyr in 1907, he had first served in the Moroccan campaign, then for two years on the Western front. He returned to Morocco after a period on Foch's staff. Most likely touched by the wave of discouragement which affected the post-war army reduced to inaction and where the pay was mediocre, he retired prematurely with the rank of major which gave him in the reserves the rank of lieutenant colonel which in political history was henceforth associated with his name. Returned to civilian life, he joined the Compagnie Générale de l'Electricité where Ernest Mercier, the electricity magnate and founder of the *Redressement Français,* reigned as master. Mercier later would aid the *Croix de Feu.* Coty and Mercier, valuable supporters, but also compromising friends. Nothing yet attracted attention to this former officer, neither markedly original political thought, nor the gift of outstanding oratorical powers, nor even a personal style. At the most he had in his favor the prestige of rank, a youthful mien (in 1931 he was only forty-five), the upright carriage of a former officer, a handsome appearance, and a smile that inspired confidence. His fabulous success repeated the eternal and surprising enigma of the sudden popularity of men seemingly devoid of originality whom the favor of public opinion carries with a bound up to the threshold of power.

Under his leadership the *Croix de Feu* experienced a rapid rise. It had begun slowly: some five hundred in 1928, to whom were associated the three thousand *Briscards* at the end of 1929. There were fifteen thousand in 1930, thirty-six thousand at the end of 1932. The organization developed branches which spread over the country a whole network of associations aimed at the various types of Frenchmen. In 1932 came the Sons of the *Croix de Feu,* to enlist the younger generation which all the leagues were beginning to worry about, and in 1933 the National Regroupment and the National Volunteers, open to all without restrictions. The multiplication of satellite organizations around the initial nucleus paralleled the expansion of the program. The society of former wartime comrades was now superseded; political ambitions were obvious. The transition was completed from the association founded on the cult of memories to the political movement which looked toward the future. This change seemed to be de La Rocque's work. At the moment of his accession to the leadership the *Croix de Feu* took part in a political demonstration. It was at the end of 1931; Pierre Laval was returning from a trip to the United States. At Saint Lazare station where his train arrived, five hundred *Croix de Feu* welcomed him with cries of "Vive Laval! Vive Chiappe! Vive Gouraud!"[19] Some months later, with the obvious complicity of the police, they sabotaged a pacifist meeting held at the Trocadero with Edouard Herriot in the chair. This was the period when, according to the testimony of André Tardieu at the La Rocque-Pozzo di Borgo trial (1937),[20] the president of the *Croix de Feu* every month obtained money from the government's secret fund, as the *Jeunesses Patriotes* may have during Poincaré's ministry. The truth requires us to add that La Rocque always protested with extreme vigor against these charges. True or false,

[19] The last episodes of his political career, nor the first, should not hide the fact that Pierre Laval was for a long time a leader of the Right Wing. The posters of the Propaganda Center for National Republicans depicted him then as the heir presumptive and the one who would continue the policy of Poincaré and Tardieu. Author.

[20] These former associates in the *Croix de Feu* had fallen out and charged each other with slander. Tr.

there is no question that the *Croix de Feu* had now deliberately entered on the Rightist political path. In the elections of 1932 its chief urged the members to vote "national."

The group of related organizations at the end of 1933 included about sixty thousand members, yet their existence, their object, and the name of their leader were still hardly known to the public at large, much less so than the J.P. The period of their greatest development began after February 6 on which they did not play the most prominent part. On that day Colonel de La Rocque had jealously retained his freedom of action. His columns, concentrated at the Invalides and the Grand-Palais and maneuvering with precision, had pressed forward up to the Place de Bourgogne, where they threatened to take the Palais Bourbon from behind. In the following months recruits flooded into local chapter headquarters. Tens of thousands of Frenchmen increased the ranks so much that the *Croix de Feu* became by 1935 a powerful mass movement, the largest of the leagues, capable of gathering considerable audiences, of leading large crowds, of setting up, with its exact, efficient, and meticulous organization, impressive rallies. The *Croix de Feu* then offered the picture which conformed most closely to the model of the paramilitary league. Its success made it what the other organizations had hoped to become but had not. Its methods, its strictly disciplined administration, its centralized structure were indeed what one expects of a league. Authority came from above, undivided. It was Colonel de La Rocque who selected those responsible at each echelon, from the members of the executive board down to the president of the lowest local chapter. All of them submitted to him an undated resignation. The league's deliberations were held in the strictest secrecy and the transmission of decisions was surrounded with detailed precautions.

In the face of the success of this organization and of its methods the time has come again to ask the basic question, fascism or reaction? It is useless to expect the content of its doctrine to instruct us on this. As vague as possible, it could just as easily be reconciled with an unquestioned republican loyalty as serve as a front for disaffection with the regime. Reform of the State, strengthening of the executive branch, extension of the President of the Republic's powers, a family policy, reconciliation of capital and labor, legislation in favor of the workers, regulation of the right to strike, all this came directly out of the same well from which, without fear of repetition, the authoritarian Right and the conservative Right drank. There was nothing in all this to convict this "factious group" of fascism.

We know nothing of the underlying aims of the leader. Lacking this, perhaps some human psychology furnishes an indication of the movement's meaning. Here we have an association which for months saw its membership regularly increase by several tens of thousands of new recruits. What motives impelled them? How can we determine the respective shares of disinterested patriotism, of the less pure fear for the social order, of high-minded idealism, of poorly enlightened good will, or perhaps of adults' enthusiastic feeling for reliving their childhood by participating in a kind of boy scout game, or of the pleasure impenitent warriors experienced in playing soldier? Political psychology should not neglect this minor aspect of the leagues' agitation: political boy scoutism for grown-ups and civilian war games were a part of its success.

In the absence of reliable information on the real orientation of the movement in the years 1931-1936, it does not seem arbitrary to proceed by retrospective extrapolation and move from what the *Croix de Feu* became after June 1936, where it is easier to understand its inspiration, to what it was before that date. In fact, the year 1936 opened a third chapter in its history. In turn a veteran's association and a paramilitary league, it now transformed itself into a political party. A change more forced upon it than deliberately chosen, but which it seemed to accept without regret or reservation. On June 18, 1936, Léon Blum's Popular Front government declared that all leagues were immediately dissolved. This measure hit first of all the French Social Movement (*Mouvement Social Français*), the new name for the *Croix de Feu* organizations since October 1935. From the ashes of the *M.S.F.* was immediately born the *P.S.F.*, the French Social Party (*Parti Social Français*). A simple camouflage? Unquestionably the change of initials was only a way of circumventing the law and diverting its thunderbolts away from the movement. But to the change in name seemed also to correspond, in this rather short time, a significant change of methods and aims. Its adversaries and even neutral observers were often suspicious of the sincerity of this conversion. We consider it authentic, however. Developments occurred as if Colonel de La Rocque and his closest advisors had become convinced by experience of the uselessness of league methods and of the power of the regime, and had rallied to the democratic principle and the parliamentary game, confidently expecting to win out on this ground. After all, did not the Communist Party at the same time make the same calculation? In any case the new party went to work to prepare for elections, began the political education of the masses whom it influenced, and set up a whole network of local organizations and services. This was an important change which pulled it away from the sterile and vain antiparliamentary agitation and from the nationalist leagues. But it did not immediately bear fruit, because it came too late, six weeks after the general election (May 1936) in which the French Social Movement was, for itself, quite disinterested. Consequently, this large party, the most numerous with some two million adherents, had at its command throughout the life of this legislature only a ludicrous representation, 8 or 10 Deputies elected in May 1936 under other party labels, or afterward in by-elections. It was far from the 80 or 100 representatives that it had the right to expect. The disproportion was particularly marked between the Right which sat in the Chamber without organized support in the country and this Right, very strong in numbers but practically deprived of parliamentary expression, between the "legal" Right and the "real" Right.

Still more decisive against the hypothesis of a French fascism was the fact that it was after its transformation into a party that Colonel de La Rocque's movement enjoyed its greatest success. It took on the proportions of a tidal wave. In 1938 it claimed to have three million members. This figure probably was inflated and doubtless did not take into account memberships which had lapsed, but even when deflated the order of magnitude remains respectable. Was this a passing enthusiasm or the birth of a force destined to last? The events of 1939-1945, the dissolution of the French Social Party, the death of Colonel de La Rocque, have in some way begged the question by interrupting the experiment.[21] It remains

[21] All has not disappeared. The French Reconciliation Party, included in the Rally of the Republican Left, and which has some repre-

true nevertheless that the French Social Party found its greatest echo from the public once it appeared to rally sincerely to the political institutions of the Republic. This implicit approval by the rallying of the *Croix de Feu*, when added to the chronic and general failure of all the movements too obviously inspired by the foreign totalitarian regimes, prescribes the conclusion that there was no true French fascism. Of this movement France experienced only some squalid imitations, shallow copies, and plagiarisms without talent or honor. She had her Moseley but not her Mussolini.

This failure of fascism stemmed from an even more basic reason. There was no French fascism because it was difficult to establish it in France. Public opinion was, despite appearances, especially refractory before the bewitchments of fascism. It could, for a while, present the illusion of letting itself be won over, but these moods did not last. The leagues lost strength, their members left them, or they returned to the straight and narrow path of legal action. In France there was not then, and doubtless never was, any serious chance for a fascist type of dictatorship. This stability will be ascribed, and rightly, to the wisdom of the French people, to its long experience, to its political maturity. But it would not be erroneous to bring up another kind of stability, rather exceptional, that of French society. Fascism was a revolt of *déclassés,* a movement of those on half-pay, civilian and military. Everywhere it came to power through social upheavals. In Italy it established itself in a country where society was less differentiated; in Germany it erupted by surprise due to an economic and social turmoil whose sudden

---

sentatives in the parliament, remains faithful to the memory of Colonel de La Rocque and continues to publish the *Flambeau.* But this is only a rivulet. Author.

magnitude cracked the traditional framework. Nothing like this happened in France where, comparatively, the social composition remained surprisingly stable and was affected only very superficially by the wake of the war and the depression. France had no one on half-pay and it had five hundred thousand unemployed when Germany counted them in the millions. So it was much less fascism than conservatism or reaction which courted the French Right. Along with a handful of fascists, there was a minority of reactionaries and a great majority of conservatives.

IV. The Shadow of Fascism

A handful of fascists. . . . However, in critical periods this handful might be inflated with the disaffected, the embittered, and the anxious who betrayed an unexpected inclination for revolutionary activity. A phenomenon of this kind appeared in 1936. If fascists existed then, they were certainly in the French Popular Party (P.P.F.). The P.P.F. was Doriot; the party drew its distinctive characteristics from its leader. Jacques Doriot was a man of the people and managed to remain one. Son of a blacksmith, a metal worker himself in his youth, he was a wholly self-made man. Powerfully built, with a mighty voice and direct gestures, he spontaneously found the tone and words which won popular audiences. He had even, to complete the resemblance to this or that dictator, spent a period as a Communist before becoming one of its more redoubtable enemies. For a long time Doriot worked in the extreme Left and held high positions there. A militant trade unionist, a member of the Socialist Youth and then of the Socialist Party, in 1920 he naturally followed the majority of the Left and found himself in the Communist Party where he rose in the scale of responsibilities. In 1923, secretary of the Communist Youth, representative of the French Communist Party in the Third International, in 1931 mayor of Saint-Denis which he represented in the Chamber of Deputies and where he held an almost impregnable personal position, member of the central committee of the party, he then was the *bête noire* of the bourgeoisie which later adopted him with an enthusiasm comparable to its former fear.[22]

But Jacques Doriot broke with the Communist Party in 1933. Henceforth he fought it with the fervor and violence of a powerful character, of a single-minded personality. In 1936 he founded the P.P.F. whose sole aim was anticommunism. Its program was poor, its thought weak. No matter! Doriot was not a man to concern himself with ideas,[23] he was a leader, the head of a gang. In another age he would have been a condottiere. He signed up fanatics and recruited rowdies in large numbers. The P.P.F. may have totaled up to 250 thousand menbers. A façade of anticapitalism balanced the militant anticommunism. A flame of revolutionary romanticism gave life to the troops: "The P.P.F. will conquer!"

Not at all surprising—but wasn't this a common char-

[22] The Right always has welcomed deserters from the Left with open arms. Some of the most popular men of the Right came from the extreme Left. General Boulanger first made his reputation as the only Republican general before being supported by the monarchists. Nor did Poincaré, Millerand, or Doumergue begin on the Right either. Author.

[23] In Doriot's entourage there were some intellectuals, Bertrand de Jouvenel, Alfred Fabre-Luce, and Paul Marion, a vigorous thinker who became Minister of Information in the Vichy regime, and who tried to lay down the lines of a doctrine in *Refaire la France* and *La France et Nous* (1937). Author.

acteristic of all fascisms?—was the extent and variety of support which Doriot received: considerable financial aid, partly foreign, subsidies from Rome, which in May 1937 gave him control of an evening newspaper, *La Liberté*. The Pozzo de Borgo-La Rocque trial threw an interesting light on these unexpected relationships. It revealed that these Right Wing groups divided themselves into two camps which carried on a secret and continual battle with each other. Almost alone on one side was the French Social Party (Henri de Kerillis was one of the few to come forward to testify in favor of its leader), which the other groups did not pardon for having moderated the style of its opposition; on the other side, the hope of overthrowing the regime brought its adversaries together: the P.P.F., Action Française, which did not inspect its allies too closely when it was a matter of bringing democracy down, the small dissident group which published *Je Suis Partout* and had moved to the most outspoken fascism, and also that small core of conspirators, baptized the Cagoulards by the general public, but which named itself the Secret Committee for Revolutionary Action (C.S.A.R.). Founded by Eugène Deloncle,[24] a former *Camelot du Roi*, to root Communist agents out of the army, this committee practiced a policy of the worst well suited to its tradition. Extreme methods did not frighten it, and it did not flinch from deeds of provocation (attacks on the office of the General Confederation of French Employers). When necessary, some of these conspirators did not disdain to render small services to foreign fascisms with which the C.S.A.R. had close relations. They were even willing to do the dirty work of Italian fascism by assassinating the two Rosselli

[24] After 1940 he founded the Social Revolutionary Movement. Author.

brothers, militant antifascists. As if by chance, we find in this camp the name of Duke Pozzo di Borgo who had broken with Colonel de La Rocque. It is more surprising to find beside Maurras, Doriot, and Deloncle the name of a representative of the liberal Right, André Tardieu. His political evolution during the last years of his life presents a strange and poorly understood case. This great politician, conservative but liberal, led a campaign for an institutional reform and developed a program which would not have been out of place above the signature of a spokesman for the plebiscitary tradition. Moreover, he was seen with the leagues and drew close to elements whose republicanism was rather dubious.

However singular this was, and certainly explicable in part by personal reasons (bitterness over not having shown his ability as a statesman), the case of Tardieu demonstrates a change which modified the usual relationships within the Right Wing. From 1934 on, something developed which resembles what we saw at the time of Boulangism and the Dreyfus Affair. As then the nationalist turbulence beguiled even the pretender whom it diverted from the authentic monarchist tradition, and extreme antisemitism set the tone for all the Rightist opposition, between February 6, 1934 and 1937 a part of the classic Right let itself be won over by the vocabulary, and taken in by the propaganda, of fascism. This betrayal of their ideas, this denial of what they represented, offered a counterpart which was the exact reverse of the itinerary of the *Croix de Feu*. While Colonel de La Rocque renounced the paramilitary decor of a league for the public activities of a political party, a number of members of parliament, including some of the best known, adopted the themes and methods of antiparliamentarism. The concomitance of these two changes of position undoubtedly explains the bitterness of the struggle which pitted the P.S.F. against its Rightist opponents. Two names taken from twenty, and significant in their differences, illustrate this shift. One was Philippe Henriot, the great and holy Catholic orator, the recognized defender of the private schools and religious liberties. This man, shaped by everything to be an opponent of absolute power, a partisan of decentralization, genuine liberties, and intermediary bodies, became sympathetic to authoritarian regimes and embarked on the political evolution which was to make him accept a position as a minister of the Vichy regime in 1944, the Vichy of the Militia and of Laval.[25] The other name was precisely that of Pierre Laval, formerly leader of the Right Wing, premier of a republican government, and whose end is well known.

Politicians were not the only ones to permit themselves to be taken in. Important sectors of conservative opinion drifted from a moderate attachment to parliamentary institutions to a sympathy, at first discreet and qualified, but then more and more open, for the authoritarian regimes of neighboring countries. The press, even that supposedly non-partisan in politics, at the same time reflected and accentuated this drift, the magazines and weeklies more than the dailies. The responsibility of *Gringoire* and of *Candide*, whose political line was less clear but which had a larger circulation, was heavy in the movement of public opinion in the critical years 1935-

---

[25] The changes during the years 1940-1944 were so great that we must very strongly emphasize that there were steps in the rapid degradation of the French State (Vichy regime). Vichy experienced three or four successive regimes to which there corresponded different personnel and as many political philosophies. Author.

1938. The *Revue Universelle* of Henri Massis, the *Revue Hebdomadaire* of François Le Grix, the *Revue de Paris*, less closely involved, the *Revue de France* of Marcel Prévost and Raymond Recouly, whose evolution is especially revealing because ideology had never taken a significant place in it and which defended Poincaré in 1926 and Fascist Italy in 1935—all these in their own ways and in varying degrees, prepared French opinion to adopt in the face of the fascist thrust in Europe some attitudes that the nationalist tradition of Déroulède and Barrès should have rendered unthinkable. Finally, we should not neglect, in the background, the influence, everyday, insidious, unnoticed, but concerted and continual, of the daily press of which a majority were Right Wing organs. To the *Echo de Paris, Jour,* and *Figaro,* newspapers of the political Right which, by a 1939 estimate, had 19 per cent of the total circulation, should be added the 60 per cent of the so-called non-partisan press (*Le Matin, Le Journal*) which was dominated by the same passions, held the same prejudices, and saw the world through the same spectacles. Public opinion was moulded by a Right Wing press. It is not an exaggeration to say that the Frenchman, even if he voted on the Left, most often read a newspaper of the Right which had an inclination towards fascism that became more and more evident.

V. The "Great Schism": from Stresa to Munich (1935-1938)

Only this slow fascination of French opinion by the prestige of foreign dictatorships and authoritarian ideologies can explain the incomprehensible and disconcert-

ing spectacle of its fluctuations on foreign problems.
From 1935 on, some of the axioms on which domestic
French politics rested lost their basic validity. It was no
longer true that the Frenchman was indifferent to foreign
policy, nor that the latter did not divide public opinion.
The opposite became the rule. Foreign considerations
henceforth affected political emotions so closely, ideological frenzies vied so strongly over concern for the national
interest, that they brought about a general rearrange-
ment at the end of which the two traditional camps, Left
and Right, found themselves fighting on reversed fronts.
The outbreak of the World War caught them in these
unforeseen positions.

At the end of 1934 the parties were still divided in
general conformity with the usual distribution: the Right
favored a policy of firmness and aggressiveness. To maintain our primacy on the Continent and prevent Germany's rearmament it hardly counted on the Genevan
institutions which had always seemed to it to be inspired
by utopian notions. It depended more upon the power of
the French army and on our system of alliances in the
East (Poland, Little Entente). In the Doumergue cabinet the two names of Louis Barthou at the Foreign Ministry and Marshal Pétain at National Defence symbolized
the two complementary aspects of this nationalist policy.
But during 1935 French diplomacy's initiative and Mussolini's ambitions threw Rightist opinion into confusion
by raising almost simultaneously two issues of principle:
was it expedient to ratify the Franco-Soviet Pact? Should
Italian aggression against Ethiopia be approved? For the
moment National-Socialist Germany was not directly
involved in either of these two problems, but the name of
Pierre Laval was associated with both of them. He was

premier at this time and was the man who had succeeded Barthou at the Quai d'Orsay.

The search for a military ally in the east to attack German power from the rear and threaten it with the menace of a second front was a strategic imperative called for by geography and was a historic tradition of French diplomacy. Against the mounting National-Socialist peril Louis Barthou reaffirmed our alliances in Eastern Europe and sponsored the U.S.S.R.'s entrance into the League of Nations. The military chiefs assented to a proposed Franco-Soviet Pact which our diplomats proceeded to negotiate. In May 1935 Pierre Laval journeyed to Moscow for the exchange of signatures. At the moment of ratifying the pact, Right Wing members of parliament discovered scruples which had not kept the Very Christian King from making an agreement with the Turks nor stopped the Republicans from allying with the Russian autocrat.[26] There was an unhappy conflict between the prudence of political realism and ideological repugnance. Did the national interest give them the right to betray the cause of civilization? Did the country's defence really require them to make this sacrifice to reasons of State? Neither Pierre Laval's signature, nor Stalin's declaration recognizing the usefulness of our military program, nor the sudden conversion of the French Communists to rearmament seemed to be sufficient guarantees. Forty-five Right Wing Deputies tried to reconcile the two kinds of obligation by abstaining, but 164 voted against ratification (February 27, 1936). This was a vote of major importance which set a date in the political evolution of the national Right. Henceforth

[26] References to Francis I in the sixteenth century and the Franco-Russian Alliance of 1894. Tr.

voices were raised on the Right which—we should like to believe unconsciously—imprudently echoed the German propaganda that used the Franco-Soviet Pact as a pretext to justify its policy of force.

The Ethiopian affair raised a problem of a different character but identical in its fundamentals. Italy made herself guilty of aggression against a member state of the League of Nations. The international organization decided to apply economic sanctions against Italy as provided in the Covenant. Would France participate? The issue divided the Right much less than the expediency of an alliance with the U.S.S.R. It was almost unanimously hostile to the sanctions, for motives which did not always coincide. The national interest: Italian friendship must be preserved at any price and the Stresa Front maintained against the German threat (only the rapid movement of Italian divisions to the Brenner Pass forestalled an *Anschluss* on July 20, 1934); ideological and sentimental sympathies for Italy: the Latin sister, mother of civilization, for her regime of order and grandeur. Several hundred writers, journalists, and professors signed a Manifesto of Intellectuals for the Defence of the West which affirmed their solidarity with Italy. The other side returned blow for blow and opposed argument to argument: the English alliance was worth more than Italian friendship. What sentiment should prevail, gratitude for past contributions to civilization or the ideal to make justice respected and to promote international order? But the Right hardly loved England and in the final analysis never believed in Genevan pacifism. Henri Béraud revived the old Anglophobian chauvinism of the Fashoda period and published in *Gringoire* his famous article with the provocative title, "Must England be Reduced to Slavery?" All the Right Wing press adopted the language of realism against the puritan hypocrisy of England and the ideological utopia of the League of Nations.

The Spanish Civil War did not modify these positions; the camps already were established. But the analogy between the political situations on both sides of the Pyrenees, the symmetry between *Frente Popular* and *Front Populaire* contributed not a little to stirring up passions and inflaming the animosity which opposed Left and Right. The two blocs thought they saw our own drama being played out in the catastrophies of the frightful Spanish Civil War and the unwilling spectators sided with the "nationalists" agains the "Reds," or with the "Republicans" against the "rebels." All the Right had the eyes of Chimène[27] for the cadets of the Alcazar. Their resistance inspired a whole literature of exhortation, while the *Echo de Paris* raised a subscription to offer a sword of honor to their chief, General Moscardo. Not for a moment did the Right doubt the legitimacy of the uprising. The inability of the regular government to maintain public order rendered it necessary. No more was it prepared to admit the danger of a Franco victory for French security. Discreet about the intervention of Italian "volunteers" and German aviators, it loudly denounced the Soviet aid, the participation of international brigades, and made much ado about any evidence of aid to Republican Spain. Ideological affinities completely eclipsed national considerations although some rather naïvely imagined they could make them coincide. There was one exception to this unanimity of conservative and national opinion: the massacres of Badajoz, the bombing of Guernica, the executions by the Phalange, the role of the Moorish soldiers in this strange crusade,

[27] Great admiration and love. A reference to Corneille's *Cid* and the controversy its first production aroused in Paris. Tr.

all led a number of Catholics, grouped around the weekly *Sept*, to denounce the scandal of a collusion between the nationalists and the Church. Maritain, Mauriac, Bernanos broke the silence, expressed their doubts, vented their sorrow. We owe that startling work, *Les Grandes Cimetières sous la Lune,* to Bernanos' indignation.

The Franco-Soviet Pact, the Ethiopian "affair," the Spanish War, these were still only the preliminaries to the great debate. Up to this point Germany, even if she was the principal beneficiary of the Franco-Italian rupture or pulled the strings in the Spanish conflict, was out of the limelight. But Germany was the leading actor in the great Czechoslovak crisis. Its tragic provisional dénouement at Munich was one of the most serious events of French political history. Certainly one would have to go back to the difficulties produced by the Dreyfus Affair to find an equivalent. Forty years apart, the "Affair" and Munich shook to the depths the foundations of the French political conscience. In 1898 it was a domestic problem, a man's liberty was in the balance. In 1938 it was at first a matter of foreign policy, a nation's safety was at issue. But there was something quite different also. The highest values were at stake and twenty debates confused the issues: the national interest and the respect for one's pledged word; the delights of peace and the inexorable fatality of war; the price of life and the causes which should be valued above it.

For the Right this was of capital importance. Except for a small group of revisionists, after the *Anschluss* it had reestablished its unity, not without some evasions, on the basis of a firm foreign policy. The Czech crisis broke this fragile unity apart. Previously foreign policy had been the area where Right Wing groups, divided over

social, political, and religious preferences, had spontaneously found their unity again. Now it divided them even
more seriously and superimposed its own divisions on the
traditional ones. A new cleavage came to slice obliquely
through the old classifications, to pass through all political families. The break between the Munichois and Antimunichois became the key to a reclassification of Right
Wing opinion between two temperaments and two systems of belief.

On the Right the Antimunichois were such primarily
because of their lucidity and their fidelity to the national
interest. They had become convinced of the German
ambitions and of Hitler's will for domination. What
could be gained by trying to appease or satisfy them?
Either Hitler's threats were only bluffs and, if so, what
risk was there in opposing them, or he expected to carry
them out, and why postpone the inevitable test of force?
By always giving in we would lose our allies and the
confidence of Great Britain, and we would encourage the
enemy. To these considerations of cold logic were added
the patriotic refusal to consent to a national abdication, a
feeling of honor which felt ashamed at the thought of
abandoning an ally in peril, and the best tradition of
nationalism. Ideological motives had only a small role in
this group's decision.

Without being decisive, such motives had more weight
with the Munichois. Let us put aside a handful of mis-
guided persons, perverted intellectuals, willing in advance to make every concession as long as it profited
National-Socialist Germany. These were the "collaborators" of the future in occupied France, the *Francists* of
Marcel Bucard, Doriot's P.P.F., the journalists of *Je Suis
Partout,* and the lawyer who was gaining some notoriety,
Maître Jean-Charles Legrand. Hitlerian propaganda

knew how to play very cleverly on the prejudices against Genevan ideology and how to use against Benes' Czechoslovakia arguments which the antidemocratic Right found it hard to answer. The Right Wing press delighted in pointing out the composite nature of this Wilsonian creation, the cunning of this democratic and masonic structure aimed to prevent the reconstruction of a good and Catholic Austria-Hungary. Really, should Frenchmen die for the Czechs, to stave off the inevitable collapse of that unviable State? This was the doubt sowed in men's minds. Then more realistic arguments came to reinforce it: who knows, perhaps Hitler is in good faith, why not take him at his word? And more than one really believed, after Munich, that peace was saved for twenty years. Some others, less naïve, believed that France needed to gain time, for she was not yet ready. Finally, several, and not the least, with Pierre Etienne Flandin at their head, resigned themselves to a retreat behind the Maginot Line and believed it very clever to divert the menace by letting Germany have a free hand in the East.[28] We see then two complete systems of argumentation and thought which confronted each other.

It is not easy to determine how Rightist opinion divided between them. We can assert, however, that most of the politicians as well as the majority of the press were found in the Munichois camp, some by resignation, some by conviction, others by that "cowardly relief" of which Léon Blum spoke, and still others against their

[28] It is not without interest to know that at its convention in November 1938 the Democratic Alliance approved by 1626 votes out of 1650 M. Flandin's position. Who knows if the difference between P. E. Flandin and Paul Reynaud at the time of Munich is not behind the notorious opposition between their friends Pinay and Laniel? One of the latter was to sit on Vichy's National Council, and the other was a member of the National Resistance Council. Author.

better judgment. In October 1938 only a minority declared itself Antimunichois, made up of a small number of personalities who were courageous enough to resist the general enthusiasm.[29] In parliament, Henri de Kerillis, the only Right Wing Deputy to vote against ratification of the Munich agreements, Louis Marin, and in the government Paul Reynaud disapproved their spirit. Some newspapers, the *Ordre* of Emile Buré and *L'Epoque* founded by Henri de Kerillis who at this point broke with the *Echo de Paris* (Léon Bailby soon bought the latter and merged it with the *Jour*) echoed them. Subsequent events which justified their predictions increased their ranks. The coup of Prague (March 15, 1939) opened the eyes of more than one Munichois and they yielded to the evidence. The surprising German-Soviet Pact facilitated the regroupment of the Right which drew a breath of unexpected relief to see Hitlerism and Communism in the same camp and to no longer have to choose between enemies. A loose union could be reconstructed but it could neither erase the misunderstandings nor the dissensions. At least in spirit the distinction remained between the partisans of conciliation and those of firmness. It reappeared, without many changes, when the time came to decide for or against the armistice, to accept Vichy or to "resist." The resigned acceptance of Munich by a part of the Right prepared it to accept June 25 and July 10, 1940.[30] Munich heralded Vichy just as the refusal of Munich foreshadowed the Resistance. Munichois, Vichyssois, Antimunichois, Resistants, was this the end of the Right Wing traditions?

[29] We do not consider here the small Popular Democratic group, its representative in the government, Champetier de Ribes, and the writer on the *Aube*, Georges Bidault. Author.

[30] The dates of the armistice and the creation of the Vichy regime. Tr.

9

1940-1968: From the French State to the Fifth Republic

I. The Right Wing and the National Revolution (1940-1944)

The importance of the Vichy episode in the history of the Right Wing demonstrates that the historic signifi-cance of events is not necessarily proportionate to their duration. Although the Vichy regime lasted only four years and the Liberation caused the disappearance of both its personnel and its institutions, the National Revo-lution[1] nevertheless had important consequences for the destinies of the Right. It revealed the permanence of aspirations and ways of thinking that were believed out-worn by the longevity of the Third Republic; it incar-nated a hope of the Right. It left memories and regrets

---

[1] This term frequently is used to describe the policies of the Vichy government, especially in its early years, while The French State was its official title. Tr.

which even today are not completely dead: currently one faction of the extreme Right Wing can be distinguished by its loyalty to the government of Marshal Pétain and its unquenchable faith in the legitimacy of the French State is the basis for its anti-Gaullism. Above all, the public's identification of the Right with the unhappy Vichy experiment discredited this faction for a long time. It dealt a blow that may be fatal to one form of extreme Right Wing nationalism. Has the Action Française ever fully recovered from the bad luck which brought into power through a defeat the ideas of a school which had set up nationalism as a religion? Thus, for better or for worse, the burden of Vichy still weighs upon the Right.

And yet it would be unjust to reduce the Vichy system to the pure and simple expression of the Right. The equation Vichy equals Right Wing suggests only a superficial understanding of their relationship. We should first remember one distinction whose evidence time has gradually revealed to impartial observers: Vichy should not be confused with Collaboration, as the history of their quarrels clearly shows. Moreover, Collaboration was far from being the monopoly of the Right. Michèle Cotta's recent study[2] demonstrates that among the Collaborators we meet almost as many men coming from the Left— from neo-Socialism, from pacifism, or from syndicalism— as from the Right. The same was true for Vichy; we find more there than the Right Wing alone. Men from the Left believed in the National Revolution, rallied to Marshal Pétain, and even participated in the Vichy government. On the other hand, Vichy did not include the entire Right Wing. Several representative personalities of the Right stubbornly refused to support the Marshal. Al-

[2]See Bibliography, section II F 1. Tr.

though Pierre-Etienne Flandin did occupy an important position for several months, his leading rival in the Democratic Alliance, Paul Reynaud, was interned by the same government. Louis Marin, the outstanding figure of the Republican Federation, never recognized the new regime. The Resistance recruited successfully among the Right Wing, beginning with its first inspirer, if it be true that the future General de Gaulle's background and convictions ranged him somewhat on the Right. If the Action Française did help to form the Marshal's entourage and furnished some of the leading ideas to the National Revolution, the Resistance also owed some of its pioneers to this group. The unprecedented seriousness of the defeat burst all political groups asunder; preconceived ideas could not withstand the harshness of the shock. The Munich crisis already had profoundly upset the map of French political opinion. Then, the military disaster, the "divine"[3] or infernal surprise of the defeat, and the abrupt collapse of the regime threw the political spectrum into further confusion. Some apparently unforeseen rearrangements took place, and they stemmed from more fundamental loyalties than those which tied persons to groups and to parties. The choices of individuals, because they committed thereby their innermost souls, expressed their basic orientations. So Vichy was far from coinciding with the Right Wing.

Another factor points to the same conclusion. The Vichy experiment was not homogeneous: the phrase conceals several realities. Brief as it was, the course of this strange government was nevertheless changeable; it reduced into four years the sequence of several regimes.

[3] Charles Maurras termed the debacle of May-June 1940 as a divine surprise. Tr.

André Siegfried has insisted upon the distinction between the Vichy of Pétain and the Vichy of Laval, and rightly so. But the Vichy of Darnand and of the Militia[4] was scarcely less distant from that of Laval than the latter was from that of the Marshal. From one to the next, about the only thing in common was the connection with the Head of the State, but the invariability of the sign covered quite different merchandise. These successive Vichys were distinguished not only by their foreign policies—their greater or lesser submission to the conqueror—but among them ran basic antagonisms whose principles came from opposed ideological systems.

And there was more. At any particular moment several tendencies confronted each other and combined in proportions of unceasing variety. From this sprang the French State's contradictions in both domestic and foreign policy. Not only was Vichy not entirely Right Wing, or made up of all the Rightist factions, but it was not the same throughout its career. In gerneral terms, its evolution progressed from the traditionalist Right toward a fascistic Right. Actually, the liberal Right never played or demanded the leading role. Its interests were well represented in the Organizing Committees which took control of the direction of the economy; some of its intellectuals such as Lucien Romier were associated with the exercise of power; and one of its statesmen, Pierre-Etienne Flandin, even accepted the office of prime minister. Nevertheless, it did hardly more than lend its aid to the National Revolution.

By the number and weight of these indispensable dis-

[4] Darnand was a pro-Nazi totalitarian and the Militia was his supplementary police force used to track down Resistants and Jews. Tr.

tinctions one can gauge the injustice and inaccuracy of
the popular identification of Vichy with the Right. But
this identification is inalienable and for a long time
public opinion will continue to see in Vichy a phase of
the eternal Right. In politics, however, what is believed
to be true is as important as what actually is true. In this
sense, the identification of the Right with the National
Revolution is a clearly observable fact. Also, it is not
entirely without foundation, for if the relationship is not
completely exact, the Vichy regime nevertheless does
present some undeniable affinities with the Right, with
its members and ideas. There remains to be explained
how this restoration happened and which of our Right
Wing groups benefited from it.

First of all, it was the result of an exceptional—
although not unprecedented—situation. The defeat was
the essential cause of the change of regimes, as had been
the case seventy years earlier. Overwhelmed by the
defeat and no longer believing in the possibility of continuing the war, the country, as in 1871, hoped for peace.
It paid no more attention to General de Gaulle's appeal
than it had to Gambetta's; it gave its confidence to the
victor of Verdun. The Right was not alone in July 1940 to
fall into line behind Marshal Pétain. Sometimes from rea-
soned conviction, sometimes from resignation, the great
majority of the country gave him its approval. And then
why not move from the effects back to the causes? It was
quite a natural reaction to ascribe to yesterday's leaders
the responsibility for the disaster without always distinguishing clearly between the initiative for the war and
the lack of military preparation. Public opinion applauded the trial of the parliamentary figures and parties
who had failed. The Right read into events the tragic

justification of its opposition to the Popular Front. All those who still remembered fearfully the strikes of June 1936 prepared to avenge themselves.

Once primed, the reaction did not halt on this fine path: from the Popular Front the criticism was extended to the governments and parliaments that had preceded it. It jumbled together the Radical ministries, Freemasonry, the public school system (the normal schools training public school teachers were closed). From the immediate past, the chase after those responsible went back to the origins of the Third Republic and even to the Revolution of 1789. In this retrospective investigation, it was natural that the last word would go to the most reactionary, to those who challenged modern society and dreamed of abolishing a century and a half of history, in other words, to the heirs of the earliest Right, the only absolute Right, the counter-revolutionary Right of the Ultras as carried on by the school of Maurras. This group in fact did furnish to the new regime the essentials of its inspiration, grafting its political philosophy onto the trunk of resignation which characterized public opinion at this time.

The phenomenon was not new. It oddly recalls what happened in 1871. The Terrible Year had brought the old Right up from the depths; the disaster of 1940 revived it a second time. The analogy extends to the intellectual and moral climate which prevailed at the beginning of the new regime. The same atmosphere of moral order, the identical invitation to do penance, similar exhortations to strive, to work, and to be austere. As before, there was talk of necessary reforms. There was self-questioning on the methods of an intellectual and moral reform.[5] The

[5] An allusion to *La Réforme Intellectuelle et Morale* published by Ernest Renan in 1871. Tr.

National Revolution even believed that it had found its Taine or its Renan in the person of Gustave Thibon whose thought is typical of traditionalist organicism and whom the press, with a straight face, presented as the Pascal of the twentieth century. The major themes of the National Revolution confirm this resurgence of the oldest Right and show that the National Revolution was another name for the counter-revolution. It laid all the blame on the principles and institutions of political democracy. The circumstances of course forbade general elections, but Vichy did not even think of consulting the voters when designating city officials. The National Council[6] was at best only an assembly of notables whose powers were more symbolic than actual and whose selection was completely in the hands of the authorities. No more elections, no more deliberative assemblies, no more political parties; those who had never accepted '89 finally took their revenge.

The counter-revolutionary Right did not limit itself to destroying, it also expected to restore. Vichy sought to rebuild a new social order on foundations that it judged more in comformity with the nature of things, with eternal values, and with the national interest. The slogan Work, Family, Country, sums up this program, and its substitution for the Republican triptych has a symbolic value. Against abstract principles which generate dissension, the National Revolution was pleased to oppose concrete and elementary realities which form the warp and woof of existence. It reproved so-called sterile and corrosive intellectualism; it preached a return to actuality— this was the title of a book by Gustave Thibon. Of the

[6] An appointed body supposedly to draft constitutional and other reforms. Tr.

three elements in the Republican triad, equality undoubtedly attracted the most vigorous criticism—did nature offer many examples of this equality? Can society then be constructed on foundations other than those of reality? Vichy intended to rebuild the social order on natural groupings, so dear to the counter-revolutionary tradition and to La Tour du Pin's school of social Catholicism: the family, the profession, the province. The institution of the family was an integral part of the program of the National Revolution, which revived Frédéric Le Play's accusations against the individualism of the Revolution and the crimes of the Civil Code, allegedly responsible for the division of inherited estates. Although the authorship of the Code of the Family belonged to the Third Republic, a policy promoting the family was not yet separated from a basically counter-revolutionary attitude. Vichy also exalted labor, but its spontaneous sympathy clearly extended more to work on the land and to artisanry than to industrial activity. Although the needs of the moment required the regime to make use of all the nation's resources, the theme of a return to the land was in tune with the basic direction of the agrarian feelings and thought that went to make up traditionalist organicism. It was the ancient rural society that emerged from the depths of the past. Vichy distrusted the forms of a modern economy, as it condemned both the class struggle and the abuses of capitalism. The Marshal abolished unions and trade associations and reproached big business interests. There was an attempt to organize a corporative society: the Farmers Corporation and the Labor Charter were established on the principle of a single and obligatory occupational association. Instead of departments—the artificial creations of an overly systematic attitude—

there were dreams of breathing life into the old provinces as guardians of the past, and the cult of local patriotism was celebrated. This restoration of the institutions of pre-Revolutionary France was to find its justification and its consecration in the alliance of political power and religious values. As in the time of Moral Order, the political and social reaction was extended by clericalism. The regime gladly invoked the patronage of religious authorities and was not at all stingy in granting to the Church both attentions and honors. For example, it gave financial support to the Church's educational system.

So the true nature of the National Revolution becomes clear. It was not fascist; it was even the opposite if it be true that fascism begins with a reaction against the established order. It was scarcely nationalist; it was rather an Old Regime patriotism mingled with a loyalty to the sovereign. It was conservatism triumphant, reaction in its pure state, a mixture of paternalism, clericalism, moralism, militarism, and boy scoutism. The regime mobilized traditional values and feelings in its service: love of the soil, attachment to the land, family solidarity, the taste for craftsmanship—all the old loyalties. It buttressed itself with the social, natural, religious, and moral authorities—the local notables, the clergy, the army, the veterans. And so the National Revolution created nothing, brought no innovations, opened no new vistas. It was a sudden and anachronistic return to the past. Vichy was antimodernism erected into a social system and a way of government.

The National Revolution, however, was not the only thing at Vichy. This ideology of the first Vichy, and the most characteristic, was gradually obliterated, overcome

by others less enamoured of doctrinal fidelity. Pierre
Laval certainly was less encumbered than Raphael Alibert
or Jacques Chevallier with ideological considerations. He
was a creature of action who had slight interest in recon-
structing a social order. Besides, circumstances were
hardly favorable for this kind of enterprise. The continuing deterioration of the diplomatic and military situation
heightened the unreality of these theoretical views.
Above all, the Vichy government never ceased to harbor
divergent tendencies; for example, at a time when the
Head of the State criticized the egoism and blindness
of big economic interests, the creation of the industrial
Organizing Committees, partially required by the needs
of the moment, had the result of restoring big business to
its control over the economy. One can detect already at
this point in the administration of the French State a pre-
technocratic aspect which curiously foreshadows certain
tendencies of the Fourth and Fifth Republics. Vichy
praised intermediary institutions, extolled decentralization, exalted liberty, but when a plurality of organizations should have been the logical corollary of these
views, the Vichy policy insisted everywhere on the unitary and statist principle. A government decision substituted this system for a multiplicity of associations, extending from the Red Cross societies and the Veterans
Legion to trade unionism. Some at Vichy dreamed of
making the unitary solution triumph in the youth movement; this project was not a minor factor in bringing a
change in the good relations between the regime and the
Church. Consequently, the experiment of the French
State was far from being identical with its initial inspiration; in the end it went down as a tragic and ludicrous
parody of fascism.

Inevitably the crimes of the last stage of Vichy reflected on the policy of the first, and in 1944 public opinion joined together in a common proscription all who had intimately or remotely participated in the experiment of the National Revolution. One cannot expect the public to have drawn at that time the distinctions that the historian can establish twenty years later. There were also those who had an interest in maintaining a fatal entanglement among their enemies on the Right. The Liberation then, appeared to mark the end for the Right Wing. Just as the defeat in 1940 had seemed to be the revenge of those vanquished in 1936, the shameful collapse of the regime established in 1940 appeared to signify the irrevocable condemnation of the French Right Wing.

II. Disappearance and Restoration of the Right Wing (1944-1954)

In 1945 the hour finally seemed to have arrived when "the End" could be written to the history of the Right. Everything was conspiring against it. Personnel suddenly was lacking. Its leaders were struck down: several were dead and others had let themselves be compromised with Vichy. All members of parliament who had voted full powers to Marshal Pétain on July 10, 1940—and that included all of the Right Wing—were ousted from political life. Even those whose conduct had been irreproachable did not wholly escape suspicion and were required to justify their conduct, as if simply belonging to the Right was disreputable. Paul Reynaud, opposed to the armistice in June 1940 and later deported to Germany, had to engage in a difficult debate in order to validate his election to the Constituent Assembly. The Right Wing showed itself to be short on personalities. Young people abandoned its banners; only a few members of parliament too old to change allegiances remained faithful. In the Provisional Consultative Assembly[7]—where the Right numbered only 23 delegates out of 248—there was the elderly Joseph Denais, along with the obscure Joseph Laniel, who alone expressed the Right's hostility to structural reforms. It sought spokesmen whose names might be a warrant of patriotism. Michel Clemenceau therefore was carried to the presidency of the Party of Republican Liberty (P.R.L.). To come from the eastern provinces was another recommendation, as was the case for Louis Marin and Pierre André.

The organizations of the Right were equally hurt. Neither the P.S.F. nor the Action Française were represented on the National Resistance Council. The Republican Federation and the Democratic Alliance, in spite of their official representation (one sending Jacques Debu-Bridel and the other Joseph Laniel) lacked influence in the face of the large Left Wing parties. The time seemed ripe for mass parties, basing their strength on the support of hundreds of thousands of militants. In contrast, the groups on the Right—which had never been more than parties made up of cadres joining together some notables —appeared to be outdated. Less able to operate clandestinely, they were not prepared to gather political fruits from the individual participation of their members in the Resistance. They were slow to build up their organizations again. Experience did not seem to have cured them of their congenital inability to overcome their divisions. Although the requirements of political

[7] This appointive body sat from November 1944 until August 1945. Tr.

strategy commanded them to oppose the great Left Wing
parties with a substantial organization of their own, we
see on the eve of the October 1945 elections a number of
small groups sprouting up: the Agrarian Party of Paul
Antier, the Republican and Social Party of French
Reconciliation, which included some elements from the
P.S.F., and the Monarchist Rally. To be sure, we can
record one attempt at reorganization by means of the
"Union of National Republican Movements" (this was a
revival of a name commonly used before the war to
designate the Right) which brought together the representatives of a half-dozen parties or movements: the
Republican Federation, the Democratic Alliance (but
only as observers), the Party of Republican Renovation
headed by André Mutter, a leader of the internal Resistance, the Patriotic Republican Union, which included
some former P.S.F. Resistants led by Charles Vallin,
some Independent Radicals and some Resistants organized in a Free French Party. But these groups intended to
keep their autonomy and the effort had no sequel.

The unfortunate results of this chronic disintegration
were aggravated by the change in electoral procedures.
Proportional Representation benefited the large parties.[8]
The Right Wing, whose strength came principally from
its personalities and from loyalty to men and families,
was bereft of its usual assets when voting was by list and
constituencies were enlarged to the scale of the department.

Lacking organized and capable machinery, the Right
Wing did not even have recourse to a newspaper press
which might amplify its voice. Most of its pre-war organs

[8] The voters chose among party lists; except for the seven most
heavily populated departments, the constituency was the entire department and each constituency returned two or more deputies. Tr.

had disappeared or fallen under the ban of the ordinance decreed against newspapers which had continued to appear under the occupation. It had at its disposal little more than *Figaro* and, for a few months from June 1945 on, *Epoque*, which was somewhat further to the Right.

But neither the dearth of manpower nor the weakness of organizations and means of expression approached in importance the discrediting of the Right's ideas and the disaffection of the public toward them. Here are the basic causes of the weakening of the Right. To everyone its ideas seemed beyond recall. Who would dare refer to them anymore? It was not only tactical prudence that prescribed this caution; the truth is that its ideas were no longer believed. Public opinion considered itself to be unanimous in desiring a radical change—all Frenchmen hoped for a thoroughgoing renovation of society; they shared the hopes of the Resistance which wished to prolong itself in a revolution. Now in this regard the Right had nothing to offer. Its spokesmen in the Consultative Assembly and in the two Constituent Assemblies were reduced to fighting a delaying action against all reforms, nationalizations, social security, and the Solidarity tax.[9] It was recognized that opinion turned away from these representatives of the past and gave its votes to the parties of the Left or to the Popular Republican Movement (M.R.P.). The emergence of this new group which was born of the Resistance and whose religious interests tempered its boldness on economic policy in the eyes of ordinary Right Wing voters, dealt considerable damage to what remained of the Right. So the Right lost even its voters.

[9] This tax of 1945 was a special levy on capital and on war-time income. It was strongly demanded by Left Wing and Resistance groups. Tr.

The results of the first elections organized after the Liberation showed the extent of its decline. We do not refer to the referendum of October 21, 1945, for if most of the moderates were basically favorable to a return to the Constitution of 1875, the Democratic Alliance finally decided not to take a position on the first question and the Republican Federation recommended yes on both questions so as not to seem to oppose General de Gaulle.[10] But the election results were not equivocal. In the municipal elections of April 29 and May 13, 1945, the moderates lost control of 7000 communes. In Paris their percentage fell from 39.5 per cent in 1935 to 22.3 per cent. This was not accidental; for in the cantonal elections of September 23 and 30, 1945, combining the votes of the Democratic Alliance, the Conservatives, and the Independent Radicals, the total number of general councilors elected by the Right fell from 826 to 306. Finally, in the Constituent Assembly chosen on October 21, 1945, the classic Right won a total of only some 60 out of 545 seats from Metropolitan France and North Africa. Consequently, it could not attempt to play the slightest role in the government and in the preparation of the new institutions. Already the Provisional Government as recast at the beginning of September 1944 had included no one from the Right. The Popular Democrats[11] or Radical-Socialists were as far to the Right as

[10] There were two questions posed on the referendum. The first asked the voters if the Assembly they chose should be constituent, i.e., should write a constitution to replace that of the Third Republic; and the second asked if some specific limitations should be placed on the legislative authority of this Assembly. De Gaulle favored a yes to both questions and the voters did also, by proportions of 96.4 per cent and 66.3 per cent. Tr.

[11] Forerunners of the M.R.P. Tr.

the Government wished to go. The moderates were not included in the negotiations of November 1945 which preceded the election of General de Gaulle,[12] and the party bargaining in the formation of the cabinet took place without them. If one of their number, Louis Jacquinot, figured in the new ministry, it was more a personal triumph, due to his presence in London with de Gaulle during the war than as their representative. Disavowed by the electorate, abandoned by its usual supporters, excluded from power, distrusting the changes demanded by the public, the Right had, it seemed, nothing more to expect of the future. After one hundred thirty years alternation of success and misfortune, the history of the Right ended with a disaster, unprecedented as much by its size as by its apparently irretrievable character. Had not the moment come, this time, to place a final period to this long and capricious history?

Such was, at that time, the general feeling; many did not hesitate to announce the definitive end of the Right as a political force and even as an ideology. To what extent this was a hazardous prediction was revealed by the sequel which recorded quite the opposite. Ten years later it was possible for Marcel Merle to write, "Weighing everything carefully, perhaps the most important political phenomenon of the regime's [Fourth Republic's] history was this reconstitution of a Right that everyone, hopefully, or scornfully, had agreed to condemn."

We must now try to make clear how such a recovery

[12] The First Constituent Assembly, itself elected October 21, 1945, chose him President of the Provisional Government of the Republic. Tr.

could be accomplished. The explanation is complex and takes in several lines of development. With the passage of time we can begin to form a better understanding of the exact extent and limits of the disaster of 1945. With perspective, the climate of the Liberation appears in its true light—as an exceptional interlude which for a moment suspended the operation of the laws of political physics. Since then these laws have regained their ascendency. In terms of the subject of this book, the entire history of the ten years which followed the Liberation is that of a slow and gradual restoration of the Right Wing.

It will be recalled that at least one Rightist Group did not disarm itself at all in 1944-1945: the one which believed to the very end in the National Revolution and which put its hopes in Marshal Pétain. Failure did not change its mind. It continued to maintain that the Vichy government was the only legitimate one and challenged the legitimacy of all *de facto* regimes. The policies of the Provisional Government and the presence of Communist ministers in it were not calculated to change this judgment. If the bulk of its voters fell in behind the M.R.P. before turning to the Rally of the French People (R.P.F.), the leadership remained unchangeable in its loyalty to the past and in its opposition to the institutions springing from the Resistance. In 1945 this hard core was reduced to silence and struck down by penalties, but the rigors of the purge only hardened its feelings which were still ardent twenty years later. When they could, the faithful began a campaign for an amnesty, for the suppression of political ineligibility, and for the liberation of Marshal Pétain. A committee was formed in April 1948 to effect these changes; it gathered around Louis Madelin, some of his fellow members of the *Académie Française*, a handful of retired generals, and a cardinal. Even the death of the Marshal on July 23, 1951, did not end their efforts. Thereafter they tried to rehabilitate him and carry out his desire to rest among his soldiers at Douaumont. All allowances being made, the memory of the Head of the French State gave rise to a cult similar to that of the guillotined king. In the election of June 17, 1951, some lists won the votes of those faithful to Vichy under the banner National Unity and Republican Independents (U.N.I.R.). Their candidates included Maitre Isorni, Admiral Decoux, Loustanau-Lacau, Leroy-Ladurie, and Trochu; some were elected.

Another indication of the persistence of this Right and a sign that its eventual support was not unheeded was its winning of some unexpected allies. One of these was General de Gaulle himself who, in a press conference of March 29, 1949, evoked the drama of a man to whom he returned the title of Marshal. "It is a great human and national drama, . . ." said de Gaulle. "Today there is an old man in a fortress to whom France owes much. Why should this old man die without being able to see again a tree or some green grass?" A year later he reiterated, and more categorically, "It is shameful to keep a man ninety-five years old in prison." The head of the Resistance brought up only the human aspect of the Pétain case and thought of the need for national reconciliation. One of his followers went further. Colonel Rémy published an article in *Carrefour* on April 11, 1950, which went as far as justifying the action of Marshal Pétain. "France in June 1940 needed both Marshal Pétain and General de Gaulle, a shield as well as a sword." The reaction was lively; the double game was rehabilitated, especially as

Rémy let it be known that he was expressing the thought of General de Gaulle, from whom he even quoted this remark, "France had to have two strings for her bow." Was the R.P.F. claiming the heritage of Vichy? Disavowal by his leader cut short the discussion, but Rémy's move suggests the relative position of the R.P.F. as its struggle with the Fourth Republic brought it closer to those faithful to Vichy. Some months later, Louis Terrenoire, another notable of the R.P.F., offered a motion in the National Assembly proposing to end Pétain's detention. It was rejected but those who voted in its favor included the R.P.F., the P.R.L., the Independents, and the Peasant Party—a Right Wing bloc.

These advances did not break up the unyielding hostility of the Vichy faithful toward General de Gaulle. They chose every opportunity they could to fight him; and if, in 1958, some of them were able, for a moment, to combine their action with that of the Gaullists, it was only a chance encounter while engaged against a common adversary. The Algerian policy of the Head of State soon pushed them into a total opposition that some did not fear to extend to an assassination attempt—is it a simple coincidence that J. M. Bastien-Thiry[13] had married the daughter of the first Undersecretary for Youth in the Vichy government? In any event it is clear that the conspirators of Petit-Clamart had drawn the motives for their actions from a political ideology inspired by the same philosophy as the National Revolution.

We shall presently examine the ups and downs of this Rightist faction over the past twenty years. Since the Liberation, no sector of public opinion has been less atsame philosophy as the National Revolution. Even today, the transfer of the ashes of the victor of Verdun to Douaumont remains a major and distinctive demand of this nostalgic Rightist group.

Since the Liberation, no sector of public opinion has

[13] The organizer of the plot to assassinate General de Gaulle in Petit-Clamart, near Paris, in August 1962. Tr.

been less attracted by the prestige of General de Gaulle and it is probably the only one never to have been beguiled by him. If this Right, that we can indeed call extremist, is the most steadfast component of anti-Gaullism, the reason for it does not arise in a simple incompatibility of personalities. There is no question that their antagonism has roots in another sort of fundamental opposition, that of two ideologies, which we shall have the opportunity to examine more closely and which has animated the contemporary history of the Right.

By its very nature a minority, this extreme Right as defined in regard to Vichy was quite unable to upset the situation. It was also too doctrinaire, too much a prisoner of its own resentments to constitute a political force. If the decade 1945-1954 gives the impression of a restoration of the Right Wing, this cannot be the work of the Vichyite Right. We must look beyond, toward another Right, more classically parliamentary, the one that the interwar period so often had seen in power. This was the only one capable of mobilizing big battalions of voters because it was also the least identified with the Right Wing. In fact it was by the action of this Rightist group that the situation was going to change completely. Quietly, by gradual stages, it recovered its spirit, gained confidence, found spokesmen if not leaders, recovered a following, and step by step it gained back its positions to the point of finding itself perhaps stronger ten years after the Liberation than it had ever been since the beginning of the Third Republic.

Actually, the disaster this Right Wing group suffered at the Liberation had not been so large as the electoral results, judged solely by the distribution of parliamentary seats, seemed to indicate. For in the election of October 21, 1945, the various slates affiliated with one or another of the Right Wing parties won almost three million votes. This was the starting point for the future reconquest of the ground lost. The Right Wing's situation above all was going to be changed by developments which were to transform the system of political relationships. Tripartism[14] isolated the Right and imprisoned it in a sterile opposition. The breakup of tripartism eventually opened the road to power. In the referendum of May 5, 1946, concerning the first proposed constitution, the moderates and Radicals were no longer alone; beside them the M.R.P. and U.D.S.R.[15] also campaigned against the proposed draft. The victory of those opposed to the constitution was partly the Right's. On the morning after, Pierre Brisson write in *Figaro* that this victory had a fundamental significance: "It shows that the idea of liberty remains alive in the country." Now the Right's opposition took as its banner precisely the idea of liberty.

The movement continued. The number of ministerial portfolios and the level of responsibilities given to the moderates, commonly called Independents, marked out the steps of their reascension. Paul Ramadier brought two of them into the first government of the Fourth Republic. The Communist Party's move into the opposition created an entirely new situation, for, reduced to their own resources, the Socialists and the M.R.P., even with Radical support, did not constitute a majority. Therefore, they needed to add reinforcements from the Right. This marginal aid was not granted by the Right without recompense. At each ministerial crisis its role was more

---

[14] The postwar political alliance of Communists, Socialists, and Popular Republicans. Tr.

[15] Democratc and Socialist Union of the Resistance. Tr.

weighty and apparent. It can be measured by the part taken by Paul Reynaud in the opening and resolution of ministerial crises. Although his influence on the moderates was strongly contested in a sector where rivalries in personal influence are almost congenital, nevertheless he did act as a leader of the liberal parliamentary Right. He played a part in the fall of the Ramadier cabinet. In July 1948 he entered the Marie government as Minister of Finance and Economic Affairs. This political reappearance had a symbolic value, since it was, after the parenthesis of the years 1940-1948, a continuation of the pre-war period. The choice of cabinet portfolio implied also a change of economic policy and the abandonment of the socialist line. This reversal was still premature, for the André Marie cabinet fell after a month, precisely over financial policy. The second appearance of Paul Reynaud, in the ephemeral Queuille cabinet of July 1950, was even shorter. But the issue was only postponed.

The Right Wing consolidated its strength. It was also in 1948 that for the first time in its recent history it began to establish a national structure in the National Center of Independents (C.N.I.)[16] promoted by Roger Duchet. The Republican Party of Liberty had failed in its attempt to establish a fourth party capable of confronting the three large ones. Several groups had refused to join with it and by 1948 it was an obvious failure. The C.N.I. formula was destined for more success. It was also more flexible. Recognizing the inherited repugnance of the moderates to an imposed discipline, it based their agreement on exactly this denial of dictatorship by party leaders and established the freedom of voting in parliament into a rule. The National Center did not try to

[16] Soon joined by the Peasant Party and abbreviated C.N.I.P. Tr.

recruit supporters: it formed an alliance among departmental organizations which grouped local notables, mayors, general councilors, and senators. But little by little, with patience and ability, Roger Duchet succeeded in making it the nucleus of a powerful force. Soon the Center began bestowing endorsements. It granted or refused the right to run on the Independent ticket, which became a kind of registered trade mark. By means of these designations the Center was able to make choices and to develop a greater cohesion. On the parliamentary level, through the many twists and turns which showed the inability of the Right to rise above its disagreements, the Center ended by joining together in a compact group almost all of the Right Wing.

With confidence renewed and strength recovered, the Right regained its independence. Formerly it had had to accommodate itself to the patronage of other groups and to accept the protection of powerful parties. These helping hands ceased to be needed. It took back from the M.R.P. a part of the voters that it had formerly ceded to it. Above all, it became possible to escape from the arrogant protection of the R.P.F. whose patronage it had accepted only from necessity.

The year 1952 substantiated these important changes and offered striking demonstrations of the restoration of the parliamentary Right as a force of the first magnitude. Indirectly, this was the consequence of the June 17, 1951, election. The law on electoral alliances did not cause trouble for the Right; on the contrary, for although it gained few votes over 1946 (some thirty thousand) and was only the fourth largest group with 13.1 per cent of the vote, the coalition of all kinds of moderates, including Independents and Peasants, won more than 100 seats.

Immediately it made known to the candidates for the premiership what it demanded: eight Independents and four from the Peasant Party took seats in the Pleven ministry. Its success in the cantonal elections of October 7 and 14, 1951, when it obtained 21 per cent of the votes and gained 142 seats in cantonal councils, emboldened it. At the fall of the Edgar Faure cabinet, an Independent was asked to form a ministry for the first time. Somewhat by surprise, Antoine Pinay carried off the Assembly's investiture on March 6, 1952, when he obtained 324 votes. For several reasons this event was important for the history of the Right.

It was first a sign that the tacit barrier which had kept the men of the Right out of power now was lifted. It proved also that the Right again had found its electoral strength and parliamentary positions. The way in which A. Pinay won his majority was not less significant. He could not have done it without the defection of 27 R.P.F. Deputies who ignored General de Gaulle's orders and who voted in favor of the Independent candidate. And so the moderate Right now was not only strong enough to dispense with the Gaullist guarantee, but it was of such a nature that it could split the R.P.F. bloc; it exerted on some of the elements of the latter an attraction stronger than the cohesion of the Rally and the authority of the General. In fact, the 27 dissidents were not slow to break with the R.P.F. and establish a new parliamentary group called the Republican and Social Action (A.R.S.), which allied with the National Center of Independents and Peasants. This latter group was on the way to becoming the true rally, joining all the groups on the Right together again.

The Pinay experiment finally was an outstanding event

in the recent history of French public opinion. Its rever-
berations spread far beyond the parliamentary circle.
The name of M. Pinay was, with those of Pierre Mendès-
France and perhaps Guy Mollet, the only one to have
enjoyed a real popularity under the Fourth Republic.
The reasons for this popularity are directly related to our
investigation of the Right Wing. They were, actually, the
same which a quarter of a century earlier had called for
the personality of Poincaré. The average Frenchman
identified himself with M. Pinay, who was not a professional politician and who had the average man's ideas on
the management of public affairs and financial policy.
His desire to fight against inflation, to re-establish price
stability, to reduce public expenditures, and to defend
the franc need only be recalled. Antoine Pinay suddenly
focused on his person and his policy all the common fund
of ideas, prejudices, and biases that the public piously
transmits from generation to generation and which form
the body of thought, half liberal and half conservative,
that has continued since the July Monarchy. So the Pinay
experiment betokened something beyond itself; it symbolized not only the recovery of this Right Wing group's
political strength, but also the restoration of the essential
mentality and ideology of the Orleanist Right. As if to
show that the investiture of the Independent leader was
not simply the effect of a freak vote, several months after
his fall another moderate succeeded him as head of the
government, Joseph Laniel, another member of the Democratic Alliance. To be sure, this membership in the
same party did not hinder them from diverging on several points or from having followed different paths: Antoine Pinay had agreed to join the National Council of
Vichy; Joseph Laniel had represented his group in the

National Council of the Resistance. Insiders knew that the first was a friend of Pierre-Etienne Flandin, the second a protégé of Paul Reynaud, and they marveled to see continued by these interposed persons the old quarrel which for twenty years had opposed the two leaders of the Democratic Alliance. But it was true nonetheless that the struggle for power hereafter unfolded between moderates even though several years before they had all been shut out from holding political responsibilities. Some months later, at the end of 1953, another event gave great moral satisfaction to the classic Right. One of their own, Senator René Coty, assumed the Presidency of the Republic, succeeding the Socialist Vincent Auriol. The Right held both the Presidency and Premiership; in less than ten years what a revenge for the humiliation of the Liberation and what a change in the alignment of political strength! It had moved from a feeble opposition to grasping the reins of power. It had acquired a unity which it had never before attained. In 1954 the A.R.S. group decided to join the National Center of Independents and Peasants, which, with 132 deputies, now became the largest group in the National Assembly. After the transitory aftereffects of the war the Right had resumed the ascent begun on the eve of 1914.

III. Regression and Multiplication of the Rights (1954–1968)

Although the year 1954 marked a high point on the curve of the Right Wing's strength, it also brought signs indicating a reversal of the situation and introduced elements which were going to complicate the arrangement of political forces. In the first place, the Right lost the direction of the government which passed to the Radicals Mendès-France and Edgar Faure, and then even back to a Socialist, Guy Mollet. Although some moderates did agree to enter the cabinet of Mendès-France, the investiture of the Radical Deputy appeared as a defeat for the Right since Mendès-France followed Laniel. The center of the majority shifted to the Left-Center, unless it was that the forces of the Left were shifting toward the Right. Moreover, in the election of January 2, 1956, Radicals and Socialists joined together under the name Republican Front, and with support from the U.D.S.R. and even from the Social Republicans (the remnants of the R.P.F.), they carried off a partial victory.

Although this modification of political strength was of great consequence in the exercise of political power and directly concerned the party leaderships, it was less decisive in the history of Right Wing ideas than the changes which then occurred in the area of values and feelings, changes which had as their first result to confuse the situation.

At this point we note the reawakening of a phenomenon—nationalism—which already has had an important place in the history of the Right Wing. The year 1954 marked a turning point, for it was when Dien-Bien-Phu fell, when the negotiations at Geneva ratified the loss of Indochina, and when the Algerian War began. French nationalism, which traditionally had defined itself with respect to Germany and paid attention only to Europe, now was going to define itself essentially in relation to Africa and the decolonization movement. In the Resistance, patriotic feeling was rather on the Left; with the colonial wars it seemed to return to the possession of the Right, which made good use of this identification.

Military defeats and diplomatic concessions revived patriotic sentiment and then exasperated it. At this point there reappeared a phenomenon already seen several times since Boulangism: in a period of nationalist fever, the disease spreads gradually to all of the Right Wing. The minority for whom nationalism is the only *raison d'être,* and for whom it constitutes the entire program, imposes it on the rest of the Right Wing which ends by borrowing its themes and adopting its style. So we see from 1954 to 1962 a section of the Independents competing with the pure nationalists in verbal demagoguery and polemics. At the conventions of the National Center of Independents a turbulent handful laid down the law and reduced to silence those members of parliament hostile to this and any other kind of demagoguery. Paul Reynaud for a time broke his contacts with the Center and its executive secretary, Roger Duchet.

Nationalist exaltation even aroused some new forces outside the normal channels or brought some substance to organizations seeking a program. We see Poujadism—until this point pledged to defend shopkeepers and artisans against the tax collector and the State—change itself into a political party only when it rallies to the nationalist position. It was this very adherence to the defense of the Empire that marked its passage to the Right and that permits us to mention it in a description of the Right Wing. Although the movement may have disappeared as quickly as it had emerged, we should not forget that the candidates of the Union to Defend Retail Merchants and Artisans (U.D.C.A.), the Poujadist movement, won some two and a half million votes and 50 seats in the election of January 2, 1956. Those small youth groups and veterans associations whose virulent antiparliamentarism, forms of agitation, and taste for conspiracy recall the climate of the years of the *Cartel des Gauches* and of the Popular Front also multiplied. (Concerning them one is tempted to speak of French fascism.) It was this current of nationalist thought that weakened the regime and prepared its overthrow for the benefit of General de Gaulle.

The appearance of this name brings up the question, what about Gaullism? Where should it be placed with reference to the preceding tendencies? Is it not a faction of the Right Wing? Without for the moment settling a question whose solution determines one's whole interpretation of contemporary political life, it behooves us to point out that the R.P.F. at first, and the Social Republicans later, often made common cause with the other groups representing Rightist nationalism. In return, the explosion of national vanity provoked by decolonization turned to the advantage of Gaullism which channeled it, before their two paths diverged.

The changing relations among all these groups from 1954 to 1962 admirably illustrate the effects of nationalism on political ideas. It served as a link among the diverse Right Wing groups that it temporarily joined together. It also upset the balance of their relationships by assuring supremacy to the most aggressive. It drew toward Right Wing positions some men and groups that until this point were counted on the Left—as we see in the Radical Party and among the Socialists in connection with the Algerian War. It caused shufflings and introduced into the political topography an element of confusion and disorder, undoubtedly because nationalism is itself more an emotion than a doctrine. And so, from 1954 on the landscape changed, its pattern became more intricate, familiar vistas clouded over.

By confirming the elections of 1958, those of autumn 1962—the constitutional referendum on the selection of the President of the Republic by universal suffrage and the legislative election—not only consolidated the regime born of the accident of May 13, 1958, but they made it clear that Gaullism's success was more than a brief episode analogous to the Poujadist skyrocket. The presidential election of December 1965 and then the legislative election of March 1967, when correctly understood and freed from superficial or partisan explanations, convincingly demonstrated that Gaullism, shoving its way onto the political horizon, seriously threatened the various Right Wing groups. The Independents had successfully held off the competition of the Gaullist Union for the New Republic in 1958, for its electorate had increased by a million votes, but in November 1962 it was cut to pieces, for half of its voters now deserted it. They apparently left without thought of returning, for the Independents in March 1967 did not retrieve their disastrous losses of 1962. As for the extremist faction which forced itself on the other Rightist groups by the fury of its invective and the dogmatism of its nationalism, the successive elections brought it back to a clearer understanding of its essential weakness. Despite a campaign for the presidency in 1965 in which he began earlier than all the other candidates and which he conducted with intelligence and courage, the extreme Right's Jean Louis Tixier-Vignancour could not win more than 5 per cent of the vote. In the legislative election of March 1967 the extreme Right, in which we include the candidates of the Republican Alliance for Liberties and Progress led by Tixier-Vignancour along with Dominique Venner's European Rally for Liberty, saw its percentage of the vote drop to

0.87, almost nothing. The extreme Right no longer figures as a political force. In these circumstances should the historian of Right Wing groups henceforth concentrate all his attention on the U.N.R.? In a general picture where should be placed a new movement that emerged from the ruins of the National Center of Independents after the 1962 election? a group with the name Independent Republicans and under the baton of Valéry Giscard d'Estaing? Its name indicates the tactical step of attempting to appear at least in part as the heir of the liberal Right, but unlike that group which had given way to the anti-Gaullist current, the Independent Republicans distinguished themselves by their support for Gaullist institutions and their decision not to break with the Gaullist majority. According to the characteristics one wishes to emphasize, should one maintain that they are the descendants of the Independents, a particular strain of Gaullism, or finally an original family whose creation would mark the appearance of a new star in the firmament of political constellations? All these questions force us to take another inventory of the Right Wing.

Some quite different reasons run parallel to this in diversifying the panorama of the Right Wing. Concerning alliances contracted, positions taken, policies applied when in power, is it not proper to place this or that group or school on the Right which formerly one had not considered to belong there? If it is true, as we have observed for the Orleanist Right and for Bonapartism, that the Right Wing in general is formed of Leftist traditions that have moved to the Right, did not the moment come in 1954 or later to mark the passage of new groups to the Right? The question must be asked especially of Radicalism, which made common cause with the Right between 1945 and 1954 and which could be distinguished from it neither on constitutional problems nor on financial, economic, or labor policies. In both cases the same hostility to statism, to the nationalizations, to social welfare measures; the same passionate—and perhaps self-serving—defense of individual initiative, liberalism, and private property. Until 1954 did not the Democratic Alliance join with the Radical Party in the Rally of so-called Left-Republicans? The question might also be asked about the M.R.P., well before its attempt at a rapprochement with the Right, because of its long participation in ministries and because of its ties with Independent ministers. But since 1964 when it helped to torpedo the proposed broad federation extending from the Socialists to the Moderates, and chose instead to form an exclusive alliance with the politicians coming from the National Center of Independents within the Democratic Center, for the benefit of which it agreed to give way in September 1967, the question can no longer be evaded and there remains no doubt about the answer. It would not even be absurd to ask this question about the Socialist Party, for if its current opposition to de Gaulle's personal power and its leading position in the Federation of the Left make such a query inappropriate for the moment, were not those in 1956-1957 who denounced "National-Molletism," charging the Socialists with following a Right Wing policy?

Recent years offer, therefore, the spectacle of a multiplication of Rightist factions, sometimes through the creation of apparently new forces such as Poujadism and Gaullism, sometimes by a movement from the Left to the Right. But can we enumerate these groups? In the presence of such a proliferation, one is tempted to paraphrase

André Gide's famous remark about God's Command-
ments: Rights, are you ten or twenty? In such calculations what then remains of our tripartite distinction? Is it
useful anymore? And beyond, does the traditional distinction between Right and Left retain any meaning? Or if
the Left itself has become the Right should we not put
the term in the museum of historical usages? Recent developments have called into question the very principle
of this traditional division.

IV. A Search for Criteria that Divide Right and Left

The issue is not a new one. It will be recalled that it
was raised at the beginning of this work. On every occasion when one tries to consider the Right, or even to
describe it—and the problem is identical for the Left—
one stumbles over the same entanglement of difficulties.
If it is indispensable to have a definition which distinguishes the Right even if one wants only to take its
measurements at a given moment, how much more important is it if one wants to classify its constituent parts.
How can it be differentiated from the rest without the
aid of such criteria? So, a definition of the Right, an
estimation of its strength, and an analysis of its constituent
parts, are three closely interwoven exercises, each depending on the completion of the others. The untangling of
this confusion would be rather simple if we established
a preliminary definition, deduced from a kind of eternal
idea antedating all historical experience. But this entire
book tends to prove that if the Right-Left division has
any meaning, there is no eternal Right Wing essence.
Except perhaps for the counter-revolutionary Right,

which from its beginning was enrolled in the camp of those opposed to change, no movement was born on the Right. They moved to the Right through the effect of time that shifted the whole system of relative positions that orders currents of thought in ideological space. It is not possible therefore to begin with an *a priori*. Consequently, the only possible approach, however, unsatisfactory it may be to minds anxious for rigorous logic, is to examine experience and discover empirically the several Rightist groups. If for the last few years the raw material seems more widespread and more diverse, fortunately we have at hand the guidelines furnished by the past.

Considering the importance of certain questions in political life and certain debates about ideas, we shall discuss those that put Right and Left in opposition. They will suggest the criteria capable of marking the boundary between the two camps.

Let us first consult the criteria tested by time. That of the social order is not disappointing, for it was indeed the conception of society that in 1945-1946 opposed the remnants of the Right to the tripartite alliance. In reference to the structural reforms, nationalizations, and the State-directed economy, the divided segments of the Right Wing found themselves united to defend free enterprise and personal property against the intervention of the State (even so, there was an authoritarian Right for whom the State should be a driving force in the promotion of the general welfare and which assigns a major responsibility to the public powers). But behind this negative unity we see the Right Wing lose its unanimity as soon as it tried to define the ideal society. One group continued to dream of restoring the Old Regime. The other was attached to the liberal society that emerged from the

Revolution. Both were nostalgic, but not for the same historical past. In addition, these two groups were no longer alone in carrying on the struggle. In their battles they were almost always aided by the representatives of Radicalism. The movement that took shape at the end of the Third Republic was completed: on issues of the social order at least, the Radical family joined liberal conservatism and formed its third variety, following the heirs of the Orleanists and the posterity of the governmental Republicans.[17]

For a long time religion was another decisive criterion. There used to be no surer touchstone in dividing the Right and the Left. At present its significance is much less certain: not that the question has entirely ceased to have its political side; to declare that the quarrel over the lay state is completely and definitely ended would be to anticipate what is only probable. Besides, the future may unexpectedly reactivate passions. We have seen the school question[18] became in 1951, and once again in 1959, a great national controversy and reopen old cleavages. In the eyes of many men of the Left it was the issue of the lay state that hindered the M.R.P. from appearing as a real force on the Left Wing. But two factors have greatly weakened the political significance of this criticism. For one thing, as all the subjects in dispute gradually have been amicably settled, the religious question affects the government and political movements only sporadically and over limited stakes. The debate today deals only with the amount of tax funds for private educational institutions

[17]The faction of the Progressists who followed Waldeck-Rousseau, see p. 219. Tr.

[18]The debate over using public funds to support Church-run schools. Tr.

in return for public supervision. On the other hand, except for those persons who continue to live in the exclusive remembrance of the past, the division between Catholics and laics has ceased completely to coincide with the division between Right and Left. A group on the Left can include authentic Christians in its ranks, who can even act according to religious considerations without being relegated to the Right, while the positions adopted by the Church, especially since the Second Vatican Council, have aroused a Rightist anticlericalism whose virulence does not yield to that of its rival on the Left. So, the religious issue operates to divide Left and Right less than ever, and it no longer serves as a force of unity among the Right Wing movements. The boundary between Right and Left follows a line situated within Catholicism, and in reciprocal fashion the Radical deputies split when they have to decide on a method of aid to private education. The religious touchstone is the type of criterion which is on the verge of losing its significance and, in so doing, losing all utility in identifying the Right.

Recently in its stead another problem—decolonization—has played a decisive enough role so that it might be regarded as separating a Right from a Left. It is not illegitimate to believe that the refusal to grant independence to colonial peoples and the desire to preserve the integrity of the Empire defined an attitude of the Right; while an acceptance of the movement for emancipation characterized a policy of the Left. In practice the division was approximately this, at least in its general lines. But each time that an unprecedented issue arose, unexpected rearrangements occurred: men of the Left fought for the retention of Algeria in the Republic, and clarification became even more difficult when some people's passionate anti-Gaullism and others' unquestioning support for the General became involved. The stands taken since the Algerian affair on aid to underdeveloped countries may be even more revealing of basic attitudes, because they are less affected by day-to-day political maneuvering. But if so, can we consider Cartiérism[19] as characteristic of the Right? A part of the Left does not hesitate to resort to egotistic everyone-for-himself demagoguery in attacking the candidates of the regime, and it is in the *Canard Enchaîné*[20] that we discover in its pure form the expression of the crude belief of French superiority over the formerly colonized peoples.

Foreign policy, which had taken such an important part in the lacerations of the years 1935-1939, seemed rather secondary in comparison with the passions aroused by disagreements over Algeria. Foreign policy did not clearly demarcate a Right. Except for the Communists, all the parties agreed to hold to the Atlantic Alliance during the Cold War. The Right Wing in particular was not unanimous, as foreign policy was an additional reason for divisions. Its positions with regard to plans for European integration show this. Although a Paul Reynaud, faithful to his maverick character, was won over to the European idea from 1947 on, some of the most determined opponents of the Schuman Plan came from the ranks of the Independents and Peasants. Not less divisive was the European Defense Community. The Social Republicans formed a coalition with the Communists against it. Finally, the European idea was by no means the property of the Right—the M.R.P. (but perhaps this group already was

[19] A reference to the prominent journalist Raymond Cartier, who has opposed French foreign aid programs. Tr.

[20] A satirical weekly generally considered to be Left Wing. Tr.

on the Right in an indefinite sort of way) and the Socialists adopted it also. Like the idea of the nation, the notion of "Europe" is an empty vessel whose political significance ultimately depends on its contents. Considered as an unrestricted field open to the activities of big business, "Europe" would move to the Right; as a democratic manifestation of the peoples it becomes more a construction of the Left. In effect, except for the Communist Party and some Left Wing personalities, all the opposition joined to fight General de Gaulle's foreign policy, but by mixing together Right and Left this removed all the usefulness of this issue for our purposes.

The numerous allusions to Charles de Gaulle suggest that this inventory of criteria that has developed out of issues and situations would be incomplete and awkwardly unreal if we did not mention General de Gaulle's person and policy, without at this point anticipating what will be said later of the connections between Gaullism and the Right Wing. It seems to be one of the characteristics of this man's destiny, that while impassioned for unity, he has been the subject of discord and a cause of division. Or, to be more exact, his historical character has followed a curve along which have alternated periods of national unity and stages of discord. Considering only the Fifth Republic, he was restored to power in May 1958 by an explosion of nationalism and he appeared almost as a unifier of all the Right Wing factions. Five years later anti-Gaullism was, in the main, the only trait which joined in a common opposition those nostalgic for Vichy, the heirs of the Action Française, integrist Catholics, the ultras of *Algérie Française,* the remnants of Poujadism, the few germs of fascism, and the representatives of the liberal parliamentary Right. If General de Gaulle did not encounter so much opposition on the Left, one could make anti-Gaullism one of the contemporary criteria of the Right.

This inventory has shown the limitations of an inquiry which, in an effort to define the area of the Right, includes only objective criteria drawn from political issues. The oldest of these are no longer applicable. Even anti-Semitism doesn't distinguish the extreme Right any more since this group discovered that it had some sympathies for Israel growing out of its animosity against the Arabs and from its resentment against Egypt or independent Algeria. This sudden reversal remains one of the most singular turnabouts in the history of ideologies. The new criteria that can be developed from the most recent political debates are not any more satisfactory. Certainly none of them, old or new, separates in a clear-cut fashion a Right presumed to be unanimous from a Left deemed uniform. The positions that at one point appeared to be appropriate to the Right can be recognized on the Left, and we soon learn that the Right itself does not line up solidly behind them. We have to recognize the disappearance of what the authors of the study dealing with the contemporary political families in France[21] call the traditional keys revealing Left and Right. They found no political theme—except for authority—on which at least three-fourths of the voters who considered themselves on the Right had the same view. Not any more than these authors should we conclude that the Right-Left division is out of date and that the ideas it sets against each other have lost all their significance. Rather, we should return, once again, to the assertion that justifies this whole work:

[21]A reference to Emeric Deutsch, *et al, Les Familles Politiques Aujourd'hui en France* (Paris, 1966). Tr.

there is not simply one Right, but several groups whose number varies over time. We have now only to try to examine them, this time beginning with the observation of political realities.

V. Metamorphoses of the Right Wing Groups

To do this we shall refrain of course from identifying the Right Wing elements according to the number of established political groups. We have often pointed out heretofore that ideologies and organizations do not regularly coincide. Sometimes divergences on minor points have led the same tradition to split into several groups. On other occasions the reverse happened as several distinct traditions coexisted within the same movement. Perhaps this was the case of the Peasants being neighbors with the Independents in the C.N.I.P. Also, it sometimes occurs that ideologies are scarcely represented at all by political groups. In general, however, the number of organizations, parliamentary groups, or parties considerably exceeds the different strands of thought. At some periods of the Fourth Republic the Deputies of the liberal Right were distributed in at least four competing groups, but among them there were no substantial differences in doctrine. Our interest is in the basic trends, of course, and for this investigation it seems clearly indicated that we should follow the several Rightist groups in the order in which they successively established themselves. Perhaps this is also the order in which they may disappear.

What then befell the traditionalist and counter-revolutionary Right whose first lineaments were furnished by the Ultra party of the Restoration? It is still present. To be sure, one would look for it in vain among the large parties; its philosophy inspires none of the forces which for several years have struggled for power. In the most recent legislative election (1967), the total of votes won by all the candidates of the extreme Right did not even reach one per cent of those cast, and this total includes the votes for several candidates who did not adhere to this Right. But actually, except for some rare moments, when did it ever give birth to a powerful party? Its weakness is congenital and often aggravated by internal divisions. One of its characteristics is an inability to play the game of modern political society. The Legitimists, sometimes by moral scruples—the refusal to take the oath—and sometimes by rigid adherence to principle, have remained almost constantly outside active political life. This Right Wing group found its strength in a section of society where it furnished the natural philosophy, and in a system of thought. Neither one nor the other have completely disappeared. There are still areas rather protected from social transformations and sectors of society that have stayed faithful enough to their traditions to continue to see in traditionalist philosophy the most finished expression of political wisdom. On the fringes of these dormant sanctuaries, where adherence is no longer contagious, knots of more doctrinaire intellectuals churn about, sects, schools, and political sheets, whose effervescence contrasts sharply with their weakness as organized movements. It is among these little groups and not in the leadership of the parties that one must look to find the reality of this Right. This characteristic is not unique to it, however. Is not the same thing true of a certain nonorganized Left which is reluctant to enter into the conformity of political machines? Overflowing with intellectual activity, speaking and writing, this Right furnishes ideas to other Rightist movements that are in short supply of significant thought. This fact permits the counter-revolutionary Right to extend its influence well beyond its own limits; it explains the spread of some of its views into regions where one would hardly expect to see them. The same phenomenon occurred under the Third Republic when the thought of the Action Française thrust itself into large areas of the Right Wing.

It would be incorrect to describe this extreme Right as inexorably wasting away and destined to vanish as the Old Regime retreats in time and the society that perpetuates it declines. As a result of circumstances and especially of crises of regime, and because of its close relationship with nationalism, recently it has gained strength in some areas and improved its position in others where there already was some sympathy. Currently its principal strength rests in two sectors: the most intransigent segment of French Catholicism and a part of the army officer corps, these two centers often being the same. Once again there is a link between the most rigid and strict interpretation of Catholicism and the authoritarian, counter-revolutionary aspect of the Right Wing. As in the days of Louis Veuillot or the Action Française, integrist Catholicism and integral nationalism find themselves allied in a common struggle. They have the same enemies and, even more, they have great intellectual similarities.

The process was a little different for the soldiers. Fighting against Communist subversion, left without orders by the political leadership, obliged to invent a system of values in order to justify their struggle in their own eyes, they believed they had found it in the defense of Christian civilization against Marxism. To those most anxious for results, Catholicism, approached through a systematic presentation, appeared as the only thing capable of offering an antidote to the seduction of Marxism. So it is in a movement of thought and indoctrination such as the *Cité Catholique*[22] that posterity will find the most authentic expression of contemporary counter-revolutionary ultracism, or perhaps in M.P. 13, a movement founded by an Algerian *colon,* Robert Martel, and whose enigmatic initials signify popular movement and May 13.[23] The symbol of the Sacred Heart that M.P. 13 adopted from *chouannerie*[24] eloquently demonstrates the continuity of thought, as does the program which extols a State based on the restoration of natural social groups and on corporatism. Isn't it equally significant that in the split which tore apart the Secret Army Organization[25] after its defeat, the founder of M.P. 13 turned up at the side of Colonel Château-Jobert at the head of a faction which first called itself the Counter-Revolutionary Army and then the Army of Christ the King, and which was in opposition to the authoritarian and fascistic wing? Names, political itineraries, and programs clearly display the intimate alliance between counter-revolution and Catholicism which has been from its beginning a basic trait of the traditionalist Right. With *Verbe* it returns to the positions of Bonald and de Maistre.

This resemblance is not fortuitous or superficial—it

[22]A movement sponsored by the magazine *Verbe* which receives support from the more traditionalist members of the French hierarchy. Tr.

[23]The Algerian uprising that ultimately toppled the Fourth Republic began on May 13, 1958. Tr.

[24]A counter-revolutionary movement in Western France in the 1790's. Tr.

[25]Abbreviated O.A.S., this was the last ditch movement of officers and *colons* to reverse General de Gaulle's Algerian policy and retain the area for France. Tr.

extends to the substance of the doctrine. The aversion for democracy has not diminished. It is still viewed as an absurd and impious system, contrary to nature as well as to the will of Providence. There is one new note, anti-communism, but a way has been found to join this to the purest counter-revolutionary tradition. For our integrists there is in fact only one revolution, that stemming from the arrogant revolt of man against the order willed by God. The Revolution of 1917 sprang from that of 1789 and it prolonged it: such are the poisonous fruits of the liberal error. Without letting itself be fooled by the mortal struggle which today pits against each other those two presumed children of the same father, democratic liberalism and Marxism-Leninism, counter-revolutionary integrism thinks it recognizes in communism the satanic vision of Evil, just as some Catholics at the beginning of the Third Republic fought all democratic endeavors in the name of the rights of God.

Since all that is bad comes from the Revolution of 1789, the remedy will come from the restoration of a society based on contrary principles. The traditionalist Right continues to distrust the State, a secular rival of the Church and an instrument of all despotisms. It places its hopes in the rebirth of natural social groups: family, profession, and province. It preaches against the class struggle and against the excesses of capitalism, and holds up the merits of occupational corporatism.

But on one point at least the present representatives of the oldest of the Rightist groups have renounced tradition. They are no longer monarchist, or not very strongly so. Dynastic loyalty, which once was almost enough to fully define Legitimacy, long ago evaporated due to the lack of a prince about whom to rally. After the death of

the Count de Chambord, which ended the direct hereditary line, this Right has not found a prince true to its
heart. Its support of the Orleanist pretenders sprang more
from political calculation or resignation to the inevitable
than as a movement of the heart. Then with Action
Française monarchism took quite another character, more
positive and cerebral. For a few the transformation of the
royalist idea by Maurrasian thought and its change by the
fusion with nationalism seemed in retrospect to be responsible for the weakening of monarchical sentiment. This
shift from personal allegiance explains how a Jean Louis
Tixier-Vignancour could in all sincerity use the name
Republican Alliance for the group he established just after
his campaign for the presidency of the Republic in 1965,
and in so doing deny nothing of his political beliefs—
everything depends on what one means by Republic. It
also explains how one-time royalists can rally to the
support of General de Gaulle in whom they salute
the embodiment of a true monarchical power. As for
the Count de Paris,[26] because he favors the trends of the
twentieth century and is a supporter of democracy, he is
too Orleanist to attract the transplanted loyalty of the
descendants of yesterday's Legitimists. In despair, or by
a narrow interpretation of the principle of legitimacy,
some have transferred their allegiance to the Spanish
Bourbons, but this only an archeological fantasy that cannot hide the decline of royalist faith. If monarchy is ever
restored in France it would certainly be on the initiative
of democrats, and the event would not at all signify the
victory of the principle of hereditary legitimacy.

The political thought of the extreme Right has been

[26]The Orleanist pretender since 1940. Tr.

marked in another way by its recent past. Since its regeneration by the Action Française it has retained close ties with nationalism. Although prejudicial to its doctrinal purity, the mingling of counter-revolutionary thought with the fevers and passions of nationalist sentiment in truth forms the strongest part of its power of attraction and accounts for perhaps three-fourths of its success with the public. Consequently, it is difficult to trace the boundary between the authentic heritage of traditionalism and pure nationalism. Ideological topography permits such easy communication between the two that nationalism, naturally rather short of ideas, does not hesitate to draw heavily upon the inheritance of counter-revolutionary extremism. This is an unstable mixture, however, and produces disagreements. Closely allied as they may be, these two nationalisms do not mix. One trait differentiates them: pure nationalism sets up the national interest and the grandeur of France as absolutes. For the traditionalist Right this interest is subordinated to a higher end: France will find its true grandeur in serving moral values, in the defense of Christian civilization.

The continuity of descent of our counter-revolutionaries is proved by their very actions. There is no need to strain for similarities. How can one fail to notice the kinship between the Ultras in 1815 who had scruples against taking the oath to the Charter because its fifth article authorized freedom of religion, and the integrists in 1958 who urged voters to oppose the proposed Constitution under the pretext that it declared the State to be secular? For both the same intransigent attachment to principles taken in the most literal sense, the same fundamental refusal to face realities. With a century and a half's interval, the two meanings of the word "ultra" conceal a close similarity of temperaments. The more one observes these two types of people, the more one is struck by their resemblance. They are both émigrés, in the moral sense of course; the Ultra of the Restoration refusing to accept the Revolution, the current one likewise refusing to accept decolonization. Both live outside their own time and even their own country. Secluded on his rural estate, the Legitimist of 1830 scarcely understood his century. Is not the situation somewhat the same for those army officers who lived outside the country for fifteen years and who upon their return felt themselves to be foreigners in a nation they no longer recognized, in a nation whose basic qualities they sometimes knew nothing about? Is it not significant that counter-revolutionary thought scored its only successes among the *colons* of North Africa and the colonels of the Army of Algeria, that is, in two groups either geographically or professionally on the fringes of the nation? We therefore presume a continuity and suggest that we are dealing here with a philosophy of refusal and emigration, worked out in opposition to and by reaction against the development of political society. This is also why its followers traditionally seek their points of departure outside their own time or country—in an idealized Middle Ages or a modern Portugal, that are confidently admired and are assessed more on their principles than on their practical achievements.

If it were any other country than France and if it were not a matter of ideologies, this striking failure to adjust to contemporary life would be mortal, but a century and a half of persistence seems to offer proof to the contrary. The danger weighing on the future of this Rightist faction comes from elsewhere—the risk that two of its principal areas of support may soon fail it. Its strength for a long time has rested on the loyalty of rural society and the support of the Church. But the rural world has experienced an unprecedented transformation since the Liberation. Its numerical importance is rapidly declining and its way of life is changing. Labor on the land is ceasing to be a style of life and is becoming merely a job like others. In particular, the interests of the elite are changing. A younger generation is rising which refuses to bind the defense of its interests to a traditional social order, a generation which wants to profit from all the potentialities of technical progress and which is trying to separate family values from agricultural activity. This is cutting one of the tap roots of traditionalist thought. Such developments are closely related to those in the Church and they are going on with the encouragement of rural Catholic action.[27] For the last third of a century, with advances and retreats, the Church has worked to dissolve the bonds that held it to the past and to the old ways. This evolution completes the movement begun over forty years ago with the condemnation of Action Française. It is now too far advanced to be reversed. It goes beyond support for a particular political system, for the basic issue is its attitude toward history, and upon this the Second Vatican Council reached decisions which irretrievably committed the Church. So it is not by chance that this extreme Right found itself in the course of a struggle against the tendencies of the Council, and that its attacks on progressivism served as a common denominator for its supporters. But it cannot expect to reverse the current. Can it even survive this breaking of the age-old alliance, as an ideology henceforth without any support from social or economic groups? This is all the more true as the ideology itself is in trouble. Its philosophy has been so deeply im-

[27]A generic term for several Catholic Action groups active in the agricultural milieu. Tr.

pregnated with religious considerations, it has had such close relations with a theology, that one wonders if it can survive the indifference that the Church expresses for it.

As a cause or consequence, the thought of the extreme Right has experienced still other misadventures. It suffers not only from a growing anachronism, but it has to endure the annoyance of seeing this or that theme pass over to the enemy. Such is the case with the intermediary bodies, a keystone of its system. Against Revolutionary individualism and Jacobin Statism, the natural groups were to safeguard personal liberty and set up a bulwark against egalitarian democracy. But today we see the idea of pluralism, the praise of active civic organizations, and the defense of private association—the general theme of intermediary bodies—taken up by democrats. The traditionalist Right sees at the same time then, its strongest supporters disappear and the originality of its doctrine vanish. As this happens the nationalist aspect fills the void.

We have now discovered the heirs of the first of the Right Wing groups. Will we have as much luck with the posterity of the second? This is quite another problem, for the two movements always have been very different. Over the years their disparity has even grown, especially in the area of demeanor. As it saw its troops drift away, the Ultra Right developed its doctrinaire leanings and its literary activity. Conversely, the moderate Right, with its brilliant history of reflective thought, gradually has let itself be diverted from intellectual efforts by its exercise of power, by the defense of its interests, and by attention to day-to-day events. Today it presents a shabby figure in the sphere of political thought and it is scarcely represented in the reviews and weeklies. So there seems to be little to say

about it, but it does have what is more and more lacking
to the extreme Right, it has supporters.

At first sight it appears to lack any unity. The maze of
parliamentary groups is bewildering; one becomes lost in
the network of their estrangements and reconciliations.
Personal rivalries among possible candidates for the premiership and disagreements over whether to participate in
a government always have raised obstacles to the formation of a large conservative party characterized by intelligence, reasonableness, and liberal attitudes. The absence
of such an organization traditionally is viewed with alarm
by moderate writers. The breakup of the National Center
of Independents at the end of 1962 simply crowns a long
series of failures, from the Propaganda Center of National
Republicans and de La Rocque's P.S.F. to the P.R.L. After
a promising beginning on the path blazed by the brilliant
effort of Jean Lecanuet in his 1965 presidential campaign,
it does not appear that the Democratic Center is going to
be more successful in its attempt to unite all the progressive
and pro-European democrats. But it is not in this area, on
the level of organizations, that the fundamental unity of
this Right emerges. One must step back a little from the
vicissitudes of party politics. Then when the general trend
of its thought and its actions are considered, the profound
unity lying beneath the tactical disagreements stands out
with indisputable clarity. At the same time there appears
the continuity of tradition linking it to Orleanism by way
of the government Republicans at the turn of the century.
We see the same themes, with the same mixture of implications, some positive and some negative.

For this Right, as in 1830 or in 1895, liberty still remains the key word. But its meaning changes with circumstances. When the Right demanded it against tripartism,

liberty had a clearly conservative content; but if the group asserts it against the pretensions of one-man rule or activist temptations, it takes on a clearly democratic character. Such is the basic ambiguity of this Right that cannot be better defined than by applying the double label of liberal and conservative. It is the very interdependence of these two aspects which constitutes it and makes it unique. Liberty for the voter to select his deputy as he desires, without ready-made slates established by party managers—from this comes the campaign for the return to the single-member constituency. Liberty for the deputy to vote according to his conscience without having to bind himself to the dictatorship of the party (the Independents developed out of a reaction against party rule). Liberty of education against the possibilities of State monopoly. Liberty of the producer against bureaucratic controls and fiscal inquisitions. And liberty to work against a strike organized by trade unions. All these are demands with a conservative tenor. But we also hear calls for the liberty of members of parliament from overly insistent pressure from the executive branch; for liberty of the press from censorship or arbitrariness; for liberty of justice and respect for the rights of the defense against extraordinary procedures. All these positions are included in a contrary attitude. If, within this Right there are those who lean more toward the most conservative conclusions and there are others who let themselves be swayed to a greater degree by a more advanced interpretation, it is not possible to present the doctrine as completely liberal or purely reactionary. It depends upon the political situation, which sometimes stresses the defense of order and sometimes the defense of liberty.

This ambiguity in fundamental beliefs is repeated on the level of strategy as well as in the choice of allies and

enemies. Like their distant ancestors of the *juste milieu,*
the moderates fight on two fronts, opposing both extremes.
The slogan, "neither reaction nor revolution," which defined the line of the Progressist Republicans in Méline's
day, still represents very accurately the middle-of-the-road
position of our Independents. Even if they lean to the Right
they are in the Center. M. Lecanuet's Democratic Center
rejects and denounces the polarization of politics into
two extreme positions, around the Communist Party and
around Gaullism. Doesn't this suggest that it leans toward
the Right? With the same impulse the men of the Right-
Center spurn demagoguery and authoritarianism, dictatorship of the masses and dictatorship by an individual, communism and fascism.

Can one still deny that they are the direct heirs of
liberal and conservative Orleanism? Let us examine their
financial and economic policy; what are its axioms? Protect property and the fruits of labor; encourage private
initiative; defend savings; fight inflation; preserve the pur-
chasing power of money; prefer borrowing to raising
taxes; and re-establish confidence. All this is joined to an
attitude distrusting the State and to the cult of the balanced budget. The policy that made M. Pinay so popular
with a great part of the public (because it saw here a
return to good sense and the victory of tested precepts
over illusions) resembles like a brother the policy of
Premier Poincaré, which in turn hardly differed from that
applied by the finance ministers of the Opportunist Republic, itself heir to the policy of the Bourgeois Monarchy.
In this domain, which is considered essential by the leading classes, the continuity is striking.

Does the policy favored by M. Valéry Giscard
d'Estaing differ very much from that of these eminent

predecessors of his at the Finance Ministry? It is easy to see how one might object to such a conjunction, first of all pointing out some different political choices. While most of the classic Independents are in the opposition, the Independent Republicans of Giscard chose to remain in the majority. The first group opposes the regime; the Giscardiens appreciate it for upholding stability and authority. But is this a fundamental difference or does it instead spring from divergent analyses of the immediate political context and of variations in tactics? Without any question Pinay and Giscard have basically different styles. But if in politics as elsewhere, style is the man, politics cannot be reduced to personalities alone, for ideas also have their weight. And the program of the Giscardiens is that of the liberal Right, updated to include the key words and intellectual fashions appropriate to a generation of supervisory employees and technicians. They talk more about expansion than economizing, more about modernity than tradition, but Valéry Giscard d'Estaing is no less vigilant than M. Pinay in his defense of orthodoxy. As Minister of Finance didn't he identify himself with the return to a balanced budget, ending the deficit, and holding the growth of public expenditures to a rate parallel with the expansion of the national income? Who can doubt the similarity, when this group upholds the right of discussion within the majority, or the independence of the parliament vis à vis the executive power. If one accepts our identification then, the tradition of the liberal Right is represented in part by a group within the present majority.

This continuity is confirmed even in its internal contradictions. Acceptance of the liberal theses always has involved some interesting exceptions. The Independents are opposed to State intervention, except to aid agriculture or artisans by artificially keeping prices high. Similarly their liberalism often stops at the frontiers of the national market. For them liberty of education means State financial aid to private schools. And finally, their attachment to liberty for political parties does not always go as far as persuading them not to demand the prohibition of the Communist Party.

Above all it is the same bourgeois mentality based on the exaltation of the average Frenchman's virtues, the same anxiety for order and stability, the same praise for common sense rather than Utopias. The moderate Right condemns adventure, all adventures, whether domestic or foreign. It chooses the possible, the reasonable, the lesser evil, as against the policy of the worst or the recourse to mighty strokes. From this comes its temperamental incompatibility with the doctrinaires of the extreme Right, and from this also stemmed its aversion for the policy and methods of the R.P.F. Valéry Giscard d'Estaing remained faithful to his principles when he held himself somewhat aloof from what he called the solitary exercise of power. This Right preaches moderation and respect for legality. In every case it prefers makeshift to radical solutions. It is fundamentally opposed to extremism. All these characteristics go to make up a mental portrait as much as a system and a type of personality strangely resembling the description of the Orleanist, or the Méline or Poincaré type of Republican. Under successive regimes, through changing party names, we perceive the essential continuity of a tradition whose basis has scarcely changed in one hundred thirty years. Other points corroborate the argument of a connection: the geographic and sociological similarity of its voters, and the analogy of structures (or to be more precise, their parallel absence). There is also the sympathy for the same political institutions—representative assemblies, the existence of a second chamber to counterbalance the caprices of an assembly chosen by universal suffrage, the balancing of governmental powers, the responsibility of the executive to the parliament, and an electoral system that allows personalities to play a role and preserves the influence of the notables.

The unchanging persistence of this ideology for nearly a century and a half, the fact that it has withstood political upheavals and outlasted social transformations, gradually thrusts forward as a certainty a thought that at first was only a conjecture: is Orleanism a kind of second nature of the French body politic? Every regime seems dedicated to return to it. The Second Republic after a few months, the Second Empire at its end, the Third Republic in its fashion during the major part of its life, and the Fourth Republic as well, in spite of an upheaval of unprecedented magnitude, returned to it with the Pinay experiment in 1952. With reservations as to the conclusions that we shall draw from the analysis of Gaullism, from the success of the U.N.R., and from the course of the Fifth Republic, it is not at all an exaggeration to say that this Right, liberal and conservative at the same time, equally attached to order and to liberty, expresses one of the permanent desires of the French body politic and that everything happens as if it corresponded to the center of gravity of our political life, "a kind of dead center," as Georges Burdeau puts it, "where after each impulsion the motor rests."

Another observation points in the same direction. Despite its relative poverty in doctrinal matters—or who knows, perhaps because of it—this tradition now sees

approaching it, sometimes hesitantly and sometimes irre-
sistibly, movements which for a long time were its avowed
opponents. This is the case for Radicalism and Christian
democracy. At their births each of these political families
defined itself in part as opposed to classical liberalism.
The Radicals criticized its oligarchic nature, Christian
democracy its hardheartedness and inhumanity. The general curve of their development has brought them so close
to the moderate Right that their originality often appears
about to disappear. We use the phrase general curve of
their development advisedly, and emphasize that we are
thinking of the very long term, analogous to the secular
trends studied by economists. If instead one takes a closer
perspective and considers the short term, the fluctuating
records of these two movements confuse the scene. It is
not clear at all if they belong on the Right or the Left,
but this very uncertainty has significance. For several
decades the Radicals and Christian democrats have
carried on a series of curious maneuvers with the Right-
Center that has complicated the game of musical chairs
that they have played with each other. It appears that
these two political groups and the constituencies they represent maintain a sort of mysterious reciprocity which requires them to exchange their positions. When one tries
to make a move toward the Right, the other quickly remembers its leftward inclinations, and vice versa.

Consider the Radicals. On the morrow of the Liberation nothing, except their party organization, differentiated them from the moderate Right. They mingled
together in opposition; and on the issues of political institutions, tripartism, the basic law of the French Union,
structural reforms, the electoral system, freedom of the
press, nationalizations, or social welfare, in other words,

everything, the positions of the Right and of the Radicals were identical, as were their votes in parliament. This similarity continued in the legislatures which followed. The moment seemed to have come in 1945 or 1951 to note down the irreversible passage of Radicalism to the Right Wing: a century after it finally re-enacted the transfer which had then moved liberalism from the Left toward the Right. Once again, time and the exercise of governmental responsibility, by extinguishing the subversive fervor of an ideology and by carrying out the essentials of its program, would have enriched the Right to the detriment of the Left. But while the transposition of liberalism gave birth to a new group on the Right— Orleanism, the movement of the Radicals did not create an additional Rightist faction. They simply caught up to the liberals and lined up on their positions.

Actually, hadn't the passage to the Right Wing begun long before the Liberation? These kinds of movements are difficult to date, for they develop over a long period and the transitions come with an artful prudence. At what point did the attraction to the Right begin to win out over the pull from the opposite direction? In 1924 the Radical Party was the prime mover of the *Cartel des Gauches;* in 1936 it was still part of the Popular Front; but in 1938 it brought about the ruin of that coalition. So one might be tempted to date its final break with the forces of the Left from the formation of the Daladier Cabinet (April 1938) and the Marseille Party Congress (October 1938); but it should be mentioned that the Radicals already had participated in the Doumergue Government in 1934 and the Poincaré Government in 1926, and even took their place in the *Bloc National* in 1919. In the legislative election of 1928, 250,000 to

300,000 electors who had voted Radical on the first ballot, exercised their suffrage on the run-off for a moderate in a better position. Doesn't this indicate that for at least a fraction of the Radical supporters, the reflex of Republican defense already had lost its imperative character? The ambiguity of the Radical policy, its successive reversals, indicate that during the interwar period Radicalism already straddled the line dividing Right from Left. It moved in this direction as the pressure of more advanced parties on its left began to push it toward the Center. The contradictory pulls that it experienced thereafter, as does any party in the Center such as the Orleanists and the Progressists before it, finished the operation and the post Second World War period made the result official.

While such shifts extend over long periods of time, we can never be certain that they are irreversible. In 1953 there was every reason to suppose that the Radicals consisted of only a branch of the great tree of conservative liberalism; everything joined them together: program and constituency, allies and opponents. A few months later the political movement led by the Radical Pierre Mendès-France threw out all these interpretations. It will be recalled what became of this attempt to regenerate Radicalism by carrying it back to the Left. Doubtless it came too late. Moreover, it was not the first try but the latest in a long series of analogous attempts, from the Young Turks of 1932 to the Progressive Radicals of 1945, to take Radicalism back to its initial sources and restore its originality to it. These efforts were the counterpart of the slow movement that drew it to the Right. But the failure of Mendès-France's movement, while it showed experimentally that the Radical Party no longer was a Left Wing force, should not lead us to conclude that it has passed over fully to the Right. More recently, opposition to Gaullism encouraged its leftist orientation—the Radical Party joined the Federation of the Democratic and Socialist Left. Is this enough to decide that Radicalism has eliminated its rightist tendencies and that we should consider it as an authentic Left Wing group? Only if we forget its hesitancy to ratify the charter of the Federation, its internal debates, the regrets of several of its leaders that the agreement could not be made with the M.R.P. instead, and their unexpressed desire to do this some day. In fact, within the Radical organization, which until now has maintained its autonomy, two dissimilar ideologies coexist, after a fashion. Leaving the one on the left aside, that on the right wing of the Radicals long ago took the plunge: nothing now separates it from the liberal tradition, it has become only a variation of the moderate ideology. Just as in 1899 when the Progressists split and their right wing moved in to settle down with the descendants of the Orleanists and the recent *ralliés,* those on the right wing of the Radicals, whether they have remained in the party or have left it, today cease to differentiate themselves from the Independents and Peasants.

The case of Christian democracy, and especially of the Popular Republican Movement, which was its organized political expression from 1944 to 1967, offers both similarities and differences when compared with the Radicals. It differed in its origin and its initial inspiration, for it laid out a course in the opposite direction, coming from the Right and steering to the Left. Did it not propose to cut the hereditary ties between the religious interests and the Right Wing parties and resume the dialogue with the parties of social progress? In fact, although the school question has periodically pushed it to the Right and obstructed its admission to the Left on a basis of equality, it followed an economic and social policy close to that of the Socialist Party. Upholding the structural reforms, it clearly established itself to the left of the Radical Party between 1945 and 1953. But in its turn the M.R.P. experienced the problem facing all Center groups, to choose between moving to the Right or the Left. It is risky to hope to retain a constantly equal balance between pressures coming from each direction. Sooner or later the balance beam tilts to one side, and experience shows that it is most often to the Right. Its militants pulled it somewhat to the Left, as did the hope of attracting the more "politically aware" groups. But its voters drew it rather to the Right, as did the hope of spoils to be reaped from the U.N.R. after General de Gaulle left the scene. The failure of the effort in 1965 to build a grand federation, in which Gaston Defferre was so involved, and for which the M.R.P. must take some of the responsibility, dashed the possibilities of a leftward movement. From the moment that the Radicals did decide to move to the Left and chose to enter the small Federation, the M.R.P. had to turn to the Right and deal with the Independents. Already its leaders had called upon M. Pinay to be their candidate for the presidency of the Republic. They did not find it inappropriate that the name of this former premier and that of their own president, Jean Lecanuet, should be offered as complementing each other— the candidate of prudence and the candidate of youth. The constitution of the Democratic Center, the places that people with typically moderate views hold in its leadership, the political coloration of some of the candidates it endorsed in legislative elections, the neutrality it displayed toward candidates of the extreme Right, and finally the decision to put the M.R.P. to sleep, all force us to conclude that, despite friction and without prejudging the future, the bulk of Christian democracy today has returned to the Right-Center and has taken up the positions of Orleanist liberalism.

The permanence of this Orleanist Right, its ability to rebound from its defeats, its power to attract other groups, and the convergence of several movements around its leading principles all contribute to make it a dominant trend of French political life. Where does Orleanism get its capacity to resist the eroding effect of time? From time itself, whose action slowly snuffs out the subversive ferments in each political doctrine and reveals the forces of conservation. And also from the evolution of society which continuously expands the middle classes: government employees, white collar workers in banking, commerce, and the nationalized firms, supervisory personnel in commerce and industry, engineers and technicians, people whose feelings, interests, and political or social prejudices probably find their most adequate expression in the liberal and conservative ideology. Does this mean that the development of society itself should have as a direct consequence the steady growth of this form of the Right Wing?

This view has been considered and written about. The regular progress of the Independents after 1946 justified such an interpretation. In the election of November 1958, did not the National Center of Independents gain a million more votes despite the success of the Gaullist U.N.R.? But four years later another election came along to remind us how imprudent it is to build general hypotheses on momentary results. This election was a disaster for the moderates. Their vote dropped from four million to less than two million; their parliamentary representation was cut by two-thirds; and they no longer had any deputies from Paris,

Lyon, or Marseille. The usual consequence of a defeat, schism, split the National Center into those who accepted the new Gaullist institutions and those who chose opposition. The patient fifteen-year effort was utterly destroyed and this Right was pushed back to the positions it had held at the beginning of the Fourth Republic. The election of 1967 brought no significant change for these moderates. For the Christian democrats this election had the same effect as that of 1962 had on the moderates; their parliamentary delegation was reduced exactly to the number that their forerunner, the small group of Popular Democrats, had under the Third Republic. Nevertheless, it would be as excessive to infer from this defeat the immediate disappearance of these political attitudes as it was rash yesterday to extrapolate an indefinite progression from their earlier electoral successes. For one thing, their disaster is very largely the consequence of the U.N.R.'s victory. Nothing guarantees that it will recur in other circumstances. There are even reasons for thinking that as the thrust of Gaullism weakens, many of the voters who deserted the moderate Right will return to it. Second, inspecting basic attitudes rather than membership in organizations reveals a less gloomy balance sheet. Added together, the loyal Independents, or what is left of them, the Independent Republicans, the democrats with a Christian point of view who have supported the Democratic Center, and the right wing Radicals, make up a total that is far from negligible, and which still can look ahead to better days. Yet, with reservations as to the accidental and unpredictable, one can ask if this defeat of the liberal Right does not signify that the liberal ideology has been overtaken by the evolution of public attitudes. The adherence of popular opinion to the themes of expansion, economic development, and social

progress, the almost unanimous acceptance of the theses of
a concerted economy and of planning, do they not radically
outmode the ideas that brought success to Poincaré and
Pinay? In comparison to the normal persistence of mental
attitudes, the sudden shift from a value system based on
the primacy of stability to an ethos emphasizing development and expansion gives the appearance of an intellectual
revolution and can have profound consequences on ideologies. Supposing that sociological evolution is working in
favor of the liberal and conservative Right by steadily en-
larging its social base, who knows if developments in
thought are not tending to ruin its intellectual positions?
In the light of this, we can see the significance and import
of M. Giscard d'Estaing's strategy, which tries, without
disturbing the basic postulates of the doctrine, to rejuvenate
its appearance and revise its techniques.

Having thus recognized the lineage of two of our
Rightist groups and confirmed their parentage, ideological
space is reduced to some order. It is not fully clarified, however. For one thing we have not yet identified the presumptive heirs of our third Right; also the field remains littered
with tendencies and movements still awaiting a name. Do
these things fit together? It would be tempting to believe so.
To avoid anticipating how the facts will respond, we shall
adopt the opposite procedure to that which we have followed for the traditionalist and liberal groups; instead of
investigating the survivals of the past in our own time, let
us begin with the observation of contemporary data.

Several movements attract attention either by analogies
with older phenomena or because the Rightist tag has been
hung on them. Such is the case, for example, with Poujadism, which offers a good illustration of the difficulties

we experience in classifying this type of movement. Its brief existence is no objection—it is the nature of these phenomena to vanish almost as suddenly as they appear. They are flashes in the pan, but they can ignite great conflagrations. Because of its suddenness and its violence, it falls into a series—Boulangism was like this. Was Poujadism on the Right or the Left? Launched here and there by men of the Left, sometimes encouraged in its beginning by the Communist Party (as the Radicals had at first applauded the early success of Boulangism), it subsequently drew recruits from the Right. Intellectually impoverished, its program was a mixed bag. It has been argued that its hostility to the government, its suspicion of the State, its impulsive and disorderly protests against taxes, bureaucracy, and technocrats link it to Alain;[28] this conjunction is justified in the sense that the Radical philosopher articulated in rational terms an instinctive reaction of the average Frenchman. But these reactions and prejudices, don't they lead us to think of the positions of the Independents over the last twenty years as much as to Radicalism? Right here we clearly hit upon the exact spot where Radical ideology meets that of traditional liberalism in a common attitude. From the point of view of its program, we can then justifiably attach Poujadism to one of our Rightist groups. It also offers more than one common characteristic with the Taxpayers League which made common cause with league agitation in the period around 1934.

There was in Poujadism's success a second element as important and perhaps even more decisive than this anti-statism: its nationalism. As much as a defense reaction by

[28]The pen name of the Radical Emile Chartier (1868-1951), a lycée professor and columnist who upheld the freedom of the individual against the tyranny of organization. Tr.

social groups who believed themselves menaced by the State's fiscal and economic policies, it expressed a reaction of humiliated national pride. It is in this area that it allied itself closely to certain Rightist movements that we have already met: Boulangism and the leagues. By its vocabulary, its subject matter, and its phobias, it was indeed the descendant of that form of temperament with which French nationalism has identified itself since the defeat of 1870— a defensive and introspective nationalism, a nationalism that a feeling of decadence renders aggressive, an ill-tempered and combative nationalism that turns to chauvinism, xenophobia, and anti-Semitism. In Poujadism there wasn't enough intellectual power or magic of style to hide the poverty of thought or the anachronism of the program. So it appeared as the monstrous exaggeration of the possibilities included in the nationalist tradition. It was this meeting of antistatism with exasperated nationalism that drew Poujadism to the Right and brought it the support of the die-hard opponents of the Republic. Neither antiparliamentarism nor nationalism alone suffices to place a movement on the Right, for there are antiparliamentarisms of the Left and nationalism is not the exclusive property of the Right. But the union of the two is a rather sure criterion that we are dealing with a force on the Right, even one on the extreme Right.

It was also nationalism that, starting in 1954, roused a number of small movements which all upbraided the regime for betraying the country, and nationalism plunged them into all kinds of activity in which street agitation ran parallel with clandestine actions. This mixture of desires created among all these bodies an indubitable relationship which was often expressed on the level of action by the creation of common fronts. But was it enough to establish an original Right, distinct from the others, which would take its place next to the traditionalist and liberal movements? To be sure, they were attached to the nationalist line which descends from Bonapartism, but nationalism, because it is more sentiment than doctrine and because it is determined by reference to other things does not alone suffice to generate a movement. It sets forth a framework and projects a silhouette while waiting to receive some substance before taking a final form. This vacant frame can support very dissimilar doctrines. It can serve as the outline for a Leftist inspiration as well as a philosophy of the Right. This is why nationalism is peculiar to no party; it appears in all political movements, including the Communist Party, only the degree varies.

This explains why, in periods of nationalist strain, men of a clear Left Wing background, and even Left Wing groups, succumb to the general enthusiasm and support a policy that superficial observation presents as Right Wing. Because it cannot exist by itself and urgently requires a complementary political philosophy, nationalism is an unstable substance analogous to those bodies that the chemists say are in suspension; it is its association with a political doctrine that precipitates it. Depending on the tone of the doctrine with which it is joined, nationalism produces compounds of different colors. This diversity can be found even within Rightist nationalism. Sometimes it is associated with counter-revolution and forms those compounds of Catholic integrism, corporatism, and nationalism that we have discussed when describing the heritage of the Ultra Right and to which the name National Catholicism has been given. Sometimes it turns toward authoritarian formulas and dreams of social revolution. This last variety is that which, in contemporary France, comes closest to fascism. Leagued against parliamentary democracy, these nationalisms do not remain permanently associated. Success as well as failure separates them, and the dissensions in the Secret Army Organization which tore it apart, the divisions between the counter-revolutionary faction of Château-Jobert and the fascistic wing of Argoud, show the powerlessness of nationalism to offer a positive program of action on which centrifugal tendencies might join together. This can also be seen in the break up of the nationalist opposition after it had been allied behind J. L. Tixier-Vignancour, for personal disagreements and rivalries among cliques were not fully responsible. Between the Republican Alliance for Liberties and Progress and the European Rally for Liberty there were more fundamental differences springing from the instability of the mixture that makes up Right Wing nationalism. So the components of nationalism, as soon as the momentary synthesis that they created breaks up, go back to their intellectual origins.

Now the moment has come to attack head-on a final and capital question: that of the nature of Gaullism and its relations with Right Wing groups. Until this point we have gone around Gaullism, discussing it in connection with its effects on the action of this or that Right, or considering its influence on the over-all configuration of political forces. This peripheral description just will not do for a current which, even before achieving power, held such a leading place in political life. It is at least since 1947, when the Rally of the French People was constituted, that it claims our attention. This is even more true since 1958, for haven't we shown that with Gaullism occupying the entire ground the earlier Rightist groups no longer had room to spread out, and that the electoral victories of the

U.N.R. were, at least indirectly, responsible for their repeated defeats? All this raises a major question—is Gaullism Right Wing? If the reply appears to be positive, this will not solve the issue, for we still have to decide if it belongs to a Right Wing tradition older than itself and of which it would be only the most recent form, or if its entrance into political life marks the appearance of a new Right, the birth of one more tradition in the diversity of groups on the Right Wing.

These are essential questions, but the answers are not evident. Gaullism lends itself badly to the analyses these questions imply; the difficulties inherent in its examination spring from its very nature and also furnish a good example of the obstacles to be overcome in reducing to some accepted principles a political phenomenon that is still close to its origin. The basic difficulty comes from its diversity and heterogeneity. How can it be grasped? There is no unique, stable, and permanent Gaullism. The profound thought of General de Gaulle is not the whole of Gaullism. In a study of political ideologies perhaps it is not even the most essential element. In any case we cannot restrict ourselves to studying the documents in which General de Gaulle has recorded his political opinions. On the contrary, the motives which led five, six, or seven million voters to choose the U.N.R. in 1958, 1962, and 1967 sometimes have only rather loose connections with the essence of Gaullism.

If there are reasons for hesitating over the most appropriate level at which to understand the most authentic Gaullism, the choice of time period leads to still more uncertainty, for Gaullism has changed. It is only too clear that the Gaullism of 1940, of the first Free French, and the Gaullism of 1960, of the supporters of a party in power, are not the same. The U.N.R. is not the R.P.F., although here a comparison is more justified since both are party organizations. Is this because one was in the opposition? The Rally emphasized potentialities that the U.N.R. does not develop to the same degree: violent language, provocative style, combative temperament, and indulgence toward street agitation. One's estimate of the nature of Gaullism changes considerably according to the time considered. Finally, Gaullism presents itself as an ideology promoting unity, and reality does partially correspond to this claim. It not only rallies together by means of its structure and followers, but it also tries to do so in its doctrine and program. It challenges traditional divisions and above all Right-Left distinctions. It maintains that these are obsolete and it accuses them of keeping sterile oppositions alive. It claims to take merit wherever it finds it and to borrow indifferently from Left or Right. It seeks to work for national unity, the symbol and necessary condition of the country's grandeur. Actually, its list of members, the disparity of their origins, and the distribution of support indicate a widespread following in which Gaullists of the Left and Gaullists of the Right are neighbors. Gaullism at election time is a rally; Gaullism in the parliament is a coalition. This being the case, is it not tempting failure to try to insert such a composite political current into the rigid structure defined by the antagonism of Left and Right? So we shall not be hasty in classifying it. For example, because all the organized groups on the Left are today in the opposition does not automatically make Gaullism a Right Wing force.

We shall, nevertheless, proceed despite this objection. Such a scruple would be legitimate and even conclusive if Gaullism were the first case of this kind, but it has had precursors. Other movements before it, sometimes with sincerity, more often by calculation, also have aspired to transcend the old division and effect the reconciliation of the national idea and social justice. If we consider only the movements which had a wide response, this was the ambition of Boulangism and of the French Social Party. For a while they even succeeded in that aim, but the sequel was to show that it was not possible to ignore persistently the Right-Left opposition. Even if at the beginning the denial of this duality does not always hide some underlying Rightist tendencies, this sort of venture unfailingly ends on the Right Wing; Leftist alibis do not prevent them from having their centers of gravity on the Right. Why should Gaullism be an exception?

But assuming Gaullism to be, in consequence, on the Right does not fully settle the question of its identification. For each time that we have tried to describe a new movement, the question has actually been twofold. Once agreed that we are in the presence of a Right Wing faction, it remains to be decided if it descends from some recognized and classified Right, of which it enriches the genealogical tree, or if it is the first bud of a new species. There is no other way to classify the nature of Gaullism than to compare it with the Right Wing groups with which we are familiar and by successive approximations to delineate its true reality.

Is Gaullism then in the oldest of the Right Wing traditions? There are reasons for thinking that it revives the Ultra doctrine, that it joins to the old traditionalist trunk a graft analogous to that of Maurrasian doctrine which regenerated a declining royalism at the turn of the century. Is it not commonly said that the keystone of the Fifth Republic is a monarchical power? Has not General de Gaulle, by restoring a disguised monarchy, granted the ancient vow of the extreme Right? This is, in point of fact, the view of some royalists such as Pierre Boutang who have come to support General de Gaulle as the only possible king in the present circumstances. Is it not admitted that his political thought has felt the impression of Maurrasian positivism? These analogies, all shallow, are quite fallacious; the personal nature of power is less decisive than the form of the State and the organization of society. Where can one see in the present regime the least indication of that decentralization to which the counter-revolutionary theoreticians ascribe so much importance and which in Maurras' thought was to be the counterpoise of the authoritarian monarchy? Where in the thought of General de Gaulle can be detected the slightest sympathy for the rebirth of the intermediary bodies and the smallest trace of indulgence for corporatism? There is no philosophy more Statist, more centralizing, more unitary, less inclined to share power with other institutions. Charles de Gaulle is too much the Jacobin—or too modern—to give credit to the archeological dreams of counter-revolutionary doctrinaires. He is also too realistic, too aware of the force of facts and the weight of history to imagine that one can reverse the changes brought by time. Far from believing that a century of history can be wiped out capriciously, his political action is guided by the idea that evolution is irreversible. Nothing is more contrary to the thoroughly reactionary philosophy of the extreme traditionalist Right than General de Gaulle's modernism, his interest in adaptation, his gamble on economic development, his will to bring France up to date, and his bias in favor of progress, whether it be in military affairs or production techniques. Without question, Bergson more than Maurras has affected his thinking.

As to the nationalism which seems to establish a link between Action Française and Gaullism, it will be recalled that there are several kinds of nationalism; General de Gaulle's repudiates no chapter of the French epic and stems as much from Michelet and Barrès as from Bainville; it also is a nationalism of unity, guardian of a composite heritage. Finally, if we add that Gaullism does not deny democracy and bases itself on the legitimacy conferred by popular support, we can see what is left of the attempt to identify Gaullism with the Maurrasian or traditionalist Right—nothing is left. Besides, the representatives of this Right know it well, for they never have recognized General de Gaulle as one of them. Their absolute and unconditional opposition is neither a banal clash of temperaments nor a disagreement over particular issues; it is entirely the expression of a fundamental and irreducible difference. The counter-revolutionary Right fights Gaullism just as for a century and more it has fought all those who accepted the evolution of the social order.

Does Gaullism then attach itself to the Orleanist tradition, liberal and parliamentary? This was thought and said in 1958 in discussions of the Constitution of the Fifth Republic. It is easy to see which of the new institutions lent themselves to such an interpretation: the dual conception of power, the preoccupation with equilibrium, the double confidence needed by the cabinet, and above all the oligarchic nature of the college responsible for electing the President of the Republic that was to make him "the choice of rye and chestnut";[29] in a word everything which after a century appeared to restore the July Monarchy or

[29] A phrase coined by Georges Vedel suggesting the over-representation of the relatively retarded economic areas in this electoral college. Tr.

the Constitution of 1875 as the latter's authors conceived of it.

On the margin of institutions, there were aspects of General de Gaulle's policies, personnel, and the regime which furnished some evidence to support the equation Gaullism equals twentieth century Orleanism. Thus the presence of bankers among the entourage of the Head of the State or in the leadership of the U.N.R. gave some credence to the thesis that claimed to see in Gaullism the tool of high finance. With the Pompidous and the Chalandons, did not the Fifth Republic find its Casimir Périers and its Laffittes? Once again the bourgeois dynasties had known how to turn the outcome of a political crisis to their own best interests. When a Roger Duchet, architect of the revival of the Right Wing, executive secretary of the National Center of Independents during its days of glory, came over to Gaullism, wasn't this of major significance? Can we not detect some analogies in the events by which the two regimes were established: thanks to a revolution, through the device of a solution negotiated with a parliament that in both cases accepted the results most likely to preserve public order and civil peace? Without extending the parallel with Louis-Philippe too far, who knows if a *juste milieu* politician does not slumber within General de Gaulle? His persistence in putting the two political extremes on the same level and in condemning "the two gangs" with equal severity, his inveterate taste for intermediate solutions, and his desire to link together the new and the reasonable, are not these the distinctive characteristics of an Orleanist temperament?

But other symptoms forbid us from pushing this comparison too far. Let us begin with the very institutions which suggested the resemblance and which should offer empirical confirmation of the equivalence between Gaullism and Orleanism. If a reading of the constitutional texts lent itself to such an interpretation, the usual changes that such documents experience in practice soon ruined this view, for the Gaullist regime deviated on all points from the liberal parliamentary tradition. The weakening of parliament soon broke the equilibrium of powers; the growing authority of the Head of State removed the direction of general policy from the control of the legislators; and the constitutional revision that transferred the President of the Republic's election to universal suffrage dispelled the last remaining similarities with the *monarchie censitaire*. Above all, the practice of the referendum brought into political usage a principle of direct democracy incompatible with parliamentary liberalism.

These changes are far from being the result of fortuitous events; actually they are consistent with Gaullist political philosophy. Not only is its behavior antiparliamentary, so is its inspiration. Based on the spontaneous agreement between those in power and the people as expressed through referendums, it distrusts the assemblies which interpose a screen between them, which arrogate power, and which are impotent either to make clear a definite will or to favor the general interest over a multitude of special interests and conceits of groups and parties. The campaign of the R.P.F. did not avoid verbal excesses in expressing this antiparliamentarism and the Constitution of 1958 institutionalized it. Gaullism abhors intermediaries, whoever they may be, party managers, trade union leaders, or newspapermen; it pushes aside representatives and hustles corporate bodies out of the way in order to seek direct contact with the people whom it wants to know only in its undifferentiated mass. Its relations with the political, social, and other elites feel the effects of this: except for some transient alliances required by momentary parallel interests, they are nonexistent or openly bad.

The history of relations between the Independent members of parliament and the successive political expressions of Gaullism is most eloquent in this connection. The Independents, kept out of the ministries headed by General de Gaulle between 1944 and 1946, joined him in the same camp in opposition to the Constitution of the Fourth Republic. In the period of the R.P.F. some of them made common cause with the Rally, but as their electoral and parliamentary situation was re-established they kept their distance and freed themselves from a tutelage they judged too coercive. The break was completed when 27 R.P.F. deputies broke discipline to vote for M. Pinay's investiture in 1952. General de Gaulle regarded this dissidence as an insult.

The Fifth Republic repeated the same cycle. On the morrow of May 13, all the moderates rallied to General de Gaulle. In succession they broke away: some because of his Algerian policy; others due to his conception of political power and the movement of the regime toward a personal and authoritarian government. Therefore the agreement between the liberal Right and Gaullism could rest only on an ambiguity that events soon undertook to expose or on a transitory coincidence of strategic interests.

The sometimes dubious device that illustrates the interaction between ideologies through the relations of leading personalities is fully justified when General de Gaulle is one of those considered. What is more indicative than

the history of his relations with the two outstanding
figures of the parliamentary Right, Antoine Pinay and
Paul Reynaud? These two men's paths, starting from
opposite points of the compass, finally joined in the end.
M. Pinay owed the beginning of his career to his success
in shaking the cohesion of the R.P.F.; he was saluted as
the man who was able to dispense with recourse to the
head of the R.P.F. But in 1958 the Independent leader
was the first to make the trip to Colombey[30] and helped
to prepare the reversal of the majority which then permitted General de Gaulle's investiture. He entered de
Gaulle's government with the responsibility for economic
and financial policy. But after several months of collaboration, relations grew too tense or too distant and the
departure of ex-premier Pinay from the government was
interpreted as the signal foreshadowing a divorce between the moderates and the regime.

The case of Paul Reynaud is an even better example,
because this former premier was bound to General de
Gaulle by a very old friendship. In the 1930's he had
been the first to present to the Chamber of Deputies
Major de Gaulle's arguments on the armored force and
the professional army; by making de Gaulle Undersecretary of State for War in June 1940 he unknowingly prepared one of the foundations for the General's claims to
political legitimacy. Subsequently their relations remained
cordial, although the politician disapproved of this or that
posture and did not hide his concern over the autocratic
direction in which the Fifth Republic was moving. But the
cordiality of their friendship did not withstand the most

[30]To consult General de Gaulle on his terms for taking power. Tr.

recent constitutional innovation[31] of the Chief of State; Paul Reynaud was one of the first to lead the opposition to this change. The incompatibility is simply unshakable between the liberal view of political power that inspires the parliamentary Right and the kind of democracy that flows from Gaullist political philosophy. As in May 1870 when the Orleanists who had lent their support to the semiparliamentary Empire felt they had been gulled and left the government, so Paul Reynaud and his friends were convinced in October 1962 that there was no agreement possible with the partisans of Gaullism. Implicit or articulated, this was the same reasoning of the voters who in the presidential election of December 1965 preferred Jean Lecanuet to General de Gaulle, and then in the run-off voted for François Mitterrand. Even more recent events add another element to this analysis. If one agrees with us that fundamentally the Independent Republicans also are part of the posterity of the Orleanist Right, the distance that their leader gradually placed between himself and the levers of power demonstrates the unavoidable disagreement between orthodox Gaullism and the conservative liberalism of the Right-Center. After Antoine Pinay and Paul Reynaud, Valéry Giscard d'Estaing was led in his turn, as much by the logic of his views as by calculation, to separate himself from a conception of power and a political philosophy that differed too much from his own. Three times in less than ten years the same route was outlined or covered.

A conclusion clearly emerges at the end of this comparison. If Gaullism is on the Right, it neither grows out

[31]The proposal in October 1962 to elect the President of the Republic by universal suffrage and de Gaulle's alleged short-cut in obtaining this constitutional revision. Tr.

of the organicist and traditionalist Right of the counter-revolution, nor can it be identified with the parliamentary and liberal Orleanist Right.

Before deciding whether Gaullism constitutes a new species in the political spectrum and an original variety in the Right Wing, a third key remains to be tried, that of the tradition born with Bonapartism and continued under the Third Republic by a certain type of nationalism. At the very first some areas of agreement stand out, more numerous and more obvious than with either of the other two Rightist groups and they permit at least a presumption of kinship. Thus, sixty years later, the R.P.F. presented some similarities with the Boulangist movement and these parallels did not escape some of its opponents. If we disregard vulgar polemics and the differences due to time and situation, then we are dealing with two groups that are similarly variegated. The ambiguity of the programs maintained a heterogeneity of support. A current coming from the Left (Radicals in both cases) mixed with a mass recruited more from the Right. In parallel fashion the two movements fought the established regime, the parliamentary Republic that they accused of weakness in defending the national interest. Safety would be found in a revision of a harmful constitution which would be replaced by a regime in which power would gain a leader. Revision meant that the assembly then in existence would be dissolved before the end of its term. General Boulanger and General de Gaulle both campaigned for dissolution. The slogan Dissolution, Constituent, Revision,[32] could be

[32]That is, the present legislature should be dissolved and a constitutional assembly elected to revise the constitutional framework of the country. Tr.

either that of the Boulangists of 1887 or the Gaullists of 1947. Polemics and agitation assumed very similar forms: they reached the same level of violent insults and insolent sarcasm. As did Boulangism in its day, the Gaullism of the Rally showed some fancy for social reform and roused some echoes in the masses. Finally, geographical comparison furnishes its contribution to this parallel. The R.P.F. carried off some of its most brilliant victories in the cities and regions that formerly had rallied to Boulangism, beginning with Paris, which, in the municipal election of October 1947, gave 40 per cent of its votes to the Rally's candidates.

It always is profitable to go back to the origin of movements: being purer at their sources, they present an image still untainted. But readers who have come this far will remember that Boulangism was not a foundling, it was one incarnation of a political temperament that had found its name and personality in Bonapartism. To render the proof more convincing, we shall submit Gaullism to a comparison with Bonapartism, such as its second appearance, that of the Second Empire, finally developed it. The parallel with Boulangism must necessarily be limited: the latter scarcely lasted more than three years and was unable to emerge from the opposition; Gaullism on the contrary passed from the opposition to win power, as did Bonapartism. In consequence, the analogies stand out more readily between their methods of government and their policies. When the Fifth Republic's Minister of the Interior encourages the prefects not to remain neutral in politics, how can we keep from thinking of the political activity of the Imperial prefects and of the recommendations that they received from Persigny? Is not the present government prone to use the monopoly that the law gives it over television in the same way the Imperial regime acted toward the press a hundred years ago? The two regimes reassured the property owners, satisfying the desire for public order and the need for stability; they seemed to provide safeguards against nineteenth century Radicalism and twentieth century Communism.

They are not, for all this, purely reactionary regimes, they should not be identified with the unchanging maintenance of the status quo. They proclaim a concern for social issues; they interest themselves in labor problems and in workers' conditions; they abrogate regulations making strikes illegal or encourage a closer association between capital and labor by profit sharing or even by labor representation in management; and they find friends and guarantors among labor's elite. While Napoleon III had his cousin Prince Jérôme, General de Gaulle has the Democratic Union of Labor (U.D.T.), Léo Hamon, and Louis Vallon.[33] Their economic policies in particular are related, and this is one of the areas where they moved furthest away from the liberal Right. They used their authority to carry out reforms; they launched innovations. Among the Saint-Simonians of 1860 and the technocrats of 1960 there is the same confidence in autocratic initiative, the same desire to break the cake of custom and to ignore obstacles. This reformism is an essential component and prevents us from reducing this tendency to the conservative Right. Its union with stability perhaps is the most acceptable definition of this political phenomenon and the key to its success with the public. Yesterday's Bonapartism and today's Gaullism reconcile order and progress in the eyes of their voters; or to borrow a phrase

[33]The U.D.T. is a Left Wing Gaullist political organization, with Hamon and Vallon among its leaders. Tr.

from General de Gaulle himself, in which he summed up his program since 1945, the new and the sensible.

Once in power the two regimes preferred to resort to men with no political past, using the services of big businessmen, of high-level civil servants, of technicians or men who appeared to be such. The Baroches and Rouhers have their counterparts under the Fifth Republic.

The parallel even extends into areas where one might not have expected it. Does not Louis Napoleon's policy of an Arab kingdom foreshadow in a way the Algerian policy of General de Gaulle, when he still envisaged some kind of association between the two countries? His decolonization policy, although it resulted in freeing some of the territories that the Second Empire had made into colonial dependencies, did not differ so much from it in its philosophy. And foreign policy? It presents material for some very interesting comparisons: in its formation the same secretiveness surrounding the key decisions; if the term "reserved area" had not been invented for use in the Fifth Republic,[34] it might very well have been imagined for the Second Empire. The policy of encouraging all nations to achieve their independence and supporting the countries of the Third World against the imperialism of the great powers may well recall Napoleon III's policy of nationalities which aided young Italy against Austria.

We shall stop the parallel at this point, even though there is material to extend it further. Tempting as it may be, this is a dangerous exercise. Historical comparisons ordinarily are only the most subtle form of anachronism,

[34] A reference to the provisions in the Constitution of the Fifth Republic which restrict the parliament's legislative power to certain areas and reserves others to the executive. Tr.

and the highest virtue of historical intelligence is to know how to detect differences. Therefore we want to be clearly understood: it is not our hidden motive to show that Napoleon III continues to govern France behind the person of General de Gaulle and that the Fifth Republic is the restoration of the Second Empire. We shall leave these oversimplifications to the polemicists. Too many differences separate the two experiences—that between the Heads of State being an essential and decisive one in a regime of a personal type. In a century France also has changed too much in its political life as in its social situation for these changes not to have had some effect on institutions. The political support also is different. The Second Empire found its most faithful supporters in the countryside, while it is in the cities and regions of economic growth that the R.P.F. and then the U.N.R. have won their most solid successes. The two regimes are differentiated finally by their evolution. Bearing in mind the 1958 Constitution and the circumstances in which it was written, one might almost assert that the Fifth Republic began where the Second Empire ended.

But the quantity of similarities between the two movements, some superficial and others more fundamental, constitutes a presumption too strong not to accept the invitation to penetrate further into what shapes the essence of their political traditions, their basic principles, and their fundamental postulates.

Now, when distilled through the refinery of ideological analysis, to what elements can the essence of Gaullism be reduced? A passion for the grandeur of France, a yearning for national unity desired for its own sake as much as a precondition for grandeur, and direct democracy. If one turns back to our presentation of Bonapartism the con-

cordance cannot fail to be impressive, especially if one
notices that the same elements take the first place in the
scale of values. At once the similarities appear for what
they really are, the symbol and result of a real kinship of
inspiration. It is in the logic of the two systems to find
support among the people consulted as a mass rather than
through representative assemblies. As with Bonapartism,
Gaullism incarnates a certain idea of direct democracy as
expressed by means of the referendum. In some ways it
achieves that mixture of authority and democracy, of
appeals to the masses and antiparliamentarism, which is
so characteristic of the authoritarian Right. Yet it is to
go too far to speak of the Right, for it is in the very
nature of this tradition to try to avoid the dualistic framework. We cannot insist too much on the impossibility
of reducing Gaullism purely and simply to the Right
Wing, whether it be liberal, conservative, or reactionary.
Actually, it is the very ambiguity of Gaullism, our difficulty in pinning it down, and the diversity of aspects that
it presents (extending from a social Gaullism through a
gamut of variants to one quite authoritarian), that cer-
tifies its relationship to the tradition. The same thing can
be said of Bonapartism. Allowing for differences of
persons, period, and circumstances, in our view Gaullism
is the contemporary version of the tradition which, on
its first appearance in France, assumed the countenance
of Bonapartism, a Bonapartism that has been filtered and
adapted, and those faithful to the Appeal to the People
of the 1870's perhaps would consider quite changed. But
it is the nature of traditions to evolve; indeed, what remains today of the initial monarchism of the most loyal
and traditionalist of the Right Wing traditions? It is
only at the price of these transformations that they can

endure. Gaullism has interpreted, amended, and corrected; still it has kept the essence, the alliance of democracy and nationalism. By emphasizing as it does the deep-rooted approval of the country, by patting itself on the back for having given the people back its voice, by expanding the practice of democracy through the referendum and the election of the President of the Republic by universal suffrage, it has even brought the Bonapartist tradition back to its origins. After the Boulangist crisis the inordinate growth of the nationalist strain at the expense of the other components had accelerated the movement of nationalistic sentiment to the Right. Nothing remained any more of the democratic aspects that had been associated continuously with it since the Revolution. Now Gaullism tends to reconcile them. Perhaps this is a hidden, but decisive, cause for the implacable opposition to Gaullism by the extreme Right which had used nationalism for the profit of a counter-revolutionary ideology that was totally inconsistent with nationalism's democratic origins.

What has just been said refers to the essence of Gaullism and to its ideology. Actual practice often corresponds only distantly to it. Not only does Gaullism assume many forms, but reality pulls it in other directions. It has even succeeded in bending Gaullism toward a course that is somewhat parliamentary. Without being overly schematic, we can say that just like the Second Empire it fluctuates between the Bonapartist and Orleanist traditions. Also, in this double and contradictory attraction there may be a presentment of a mysterious law whose power extends not only over Gaullism but in addition governs all the Right Wing and perhaps by extension or by analogy, all French political life.

Placing the extreme Right aside (for it involves only minorities incapable of acting effectively or of changing the development of political society), the Right Wing is torn between two types of political organization which express two dissimilar conceptions of the social order and of political philosophy when dealing with the relations between governmental power and the citizen. One raises above all the liberty of the individual and ultimately the liberty of organizations. It places its confidence in private initiative, either individual or collective, and expects personal happiness and social development to come from it alone. The effective operation of institutions implies the supervision of governmental power by elected representatives. Equally distant from personal dictatorship and from the despotism of the masses, this system grants the key responsibility to intermediaries, a small elite characterized by ability, experience, wealth, or education. It interposes halfway houses between the State and the individual.

The other system gives the leading role to the State. A society cannot do without a concentrated, active, and efficient authority. Democratically inspired, it acknowledges that power must be delegated by universal suffrage. Anxious for efficiency, impassioned for unity, it is suspicious of all bodies that threaten to erect a barrier, to weaken the central power, to slow down decisions, to break up unity, to maintain particularisms, to make the interests of a group prevail over the general interest of which the governmental power believes itself to be the only judge. This conception tends to reduce the political game to a dialogue between the governors and the governed, and as the initiative in this dialogue belongs exclusively to those who hold power, this exchange of opinions runs the strong risk of becoming a monologue. On a more profound level, the choice between these two systems concerns the opposition between a social philosophy based on discussion and argument, and one granting primacy to action.

These two systems were formulated in the course of the nineteenth century. The conflict between the Legitimist Right and the Orleanist Right implied a fundamental disagreement over the principles of '89. But the two chief currents of the contemporary Right Wing both propose to accept the society issuing from the Revolution and to adhere to its basic principles. Their divergences are located within democracy. For a century the alternatives have been clear.

In the November 1962 election in the twelfth district of the Nord department, the Bergues region, the race pitted against each other, along with some other candidates, three personalities whose past, name, or allegiance turned them into symbolic figures: former premier Paul Reynaud had taken the leadership of those opposed to personal power and to the authoritarian evolution of the regime in the name of the necessary liberties and the rights of parliamentary representation; Emmanuel Beau de Loménie, historian of the bourgeois dynasties and disparager of Orleanism, ran on the slate of the National Peoples Party, a new name for the Poujade movement, but he really represented the extreme Right tradition as much opposed to the power of a leader elected by the people as to that of the members of parliament; and finally there was a U.N.R. candidate who guaranteed the presence of Gaullism. The three Right Wing traditions lined up side by side. One hundred years earlier, in 1863, under different names—Legitimist, Orleanist, Imperialist

—the choice scarcely would have been different. When Valéry Giscard d'Estaing chides the Pompidou government and criticizes the "solitary exercise of power," one might believe it is an Orleanist disapproving of Napoleon III for using the plebiscite and attacking Emile Ollivier. A century later the three traditions which as a group ordinarily are called the French Right Wing are still alive, even if their relative strengths have changed.

This extraordinary permanence does not mean that nothing changes or that change is only a misleading outward appearance. It would be to interpret badly the lessons of history if one drew from it an argument to support the rather limited vision that sees nothing new under the sun. On the contrary, the stability of these tendencies takes all its significance from being part of the general movement. Men pass on, regimes disappear, problems change, but ideas remain. There will always be a Right and a Left. What they will be tomorrow is the future's secret. Heirs of the past, they will be the answer that the men of tomorrow give to questions raised by future society. What such a permanence of traditions of thought ultimately reveals, over and above the stability of those combinations constituted by our great political systems and by their marvelous ability to last, is the power of ideas upon men's minds, and in return men's loyalty to those ideas which have won their hearts and their intelligence.

Epilogue
The Right Wing in the
Light of the Events of Spring 1968

Just as the third French edition of this book was about to appear, there occurred what political modesty almost immediately came to call the events of May 1968. Modesty, and perhaps prudence also, for to give a name to these events would be rather venturesome for some time to come. Until they have worked out all their consequences, their ultimate significance will remain uncertain. It is not clear that we have seen a revolution, whatever may be said, but there is no doubt that France has experienced one of the most serious crises of its recent history. It was a crisis of the political system, of the society, perhaps even of the civilization, in which we have seen movements originally quite distinct join and work together, but after their brief convergence they will undoubtedly separate again. It was also a crisis in the universities—its most original feature—and a labor crisis, of a more classic nature, and finally a test of political strength. Whatever one may think of its causes and its motivations, this crisis raises questions for the historian, especially for one who is interested in political movements and ideologies.

It is in the nature of crises, even if they are not direct products of disruptive or revolutionary theory, to challenge traditional analyses. Every crisis changes reality quite as much as it displays it. It reveals and upsets things at the same time. So this is a good point at which to confront our pattern of explanation with the teachings of this recent crisis. It is more than a favorable occasion, for intellectual honesty requires us to ask what remains of our patiently constructed distinctions and relationships after the storm which has swept over our political universe. It is not fair to dodge this confrontation. Three questions emerge from this affair, and none of them is really new. Does the bi-polar distinction of Right and Left retain any validity after these weeks in which the two traditional camps split up and their members fought shoulder to shoulder with partners coming from the opposition? Has there been any change in the relative strengths of Right and Left? Have the content and meaning of these two notions significantly changed since the beginning of May 1968? Old questions to be sure, but made relevant once again by present circumstances.

In order to examine them separately, we shall first distinguish the May crisis, which broke out and developed outside normal channels—through agitation in the streets, strikes, and the occupation of factories—from the election of June 23 and 30 which brought a partial response in a classic form to the questions raised by the earlier movement. We also want to dwell upon both the originality of this crisis and then clarify the resemblances that it may present with others. Some observers quickly pointed out reminiscences of 1848, analogies with the beginning of the Commune of 1871, recollections of June 1936, the parallel with the Liberation, or even the similarity with the great strikes of the autumn of 1947 and the summer of 1953. All these relationships have some justification and each throws light on one aspect of an especially complex crisis which was a synthesis of many quite different phenomena. Without moving so far back in the past, let us stop with the most recent change of regimes, that of May 1958, from which emerged the Fifth Republic. Considerations of the calendar are not the only ones which inspire this comparison—the most recent crisis unfolded ten years almost to the day after the preceding one—for there are more profound analogies. In both cases the crisis began outside the legal institutions and procedures; the seizure of the main government buildings in Algiers had as its counterpart the occupation of the Sorbonne. The actors in these two affairs resembled each other; in Algiers, university students and older lycée pupils played a decisive role, and there is a tempting parallel between Pierre Lagaillarde and Jacques Sauvageot.[1] In both cases the government had a majority in the Assembly but of what use was it in the face of the growing agitation in the streets? When we move beyond these common factors the two situations begin to diverge: while in 1958 the government lost control of the army, in 1968 it was the educational system (and it is quite true that for educational institutions and teachers the recent events have been

---

[1]Lagaillarde was a leader of an Algerian university student organization in 1958, while Sauvageot headed the French university student union in 1968. Tr.

as severe a test as the Algerian War was for the military). In 1958 the center of the subversive agitation lay on the other side of the Mediterranean and the government should have been able to rely on metropolitan France if the personality of General de Gaulle had not held a formidable influence over its activity and even its legitimacy. In 1968 the heart of the revolt beat in Paris itself and General de Gaulle was its target. But primarily —and from our point of view isn't this the major difference?—ten years ago the Right was the principal source of inspiration for subversion against an assembly and a majority oriented more to the Left; in 1968 the opposition took its arguments from the Left against a regime that it cast on the Right.

The progress of this crisis offers some lessons that the history of political ideas would do well to ponder. The first concerns the power and vitality of ideologies. In recent years what has not been said about their decline and expected death? The time apparently having come for a politics determined exclusively by objective facts, the future would have room only for realistic programs, calculated scientifically. But in this month of May were people ever so little concerned about what was possible and what wasn't? Whatever one may think of the motives of the movement, whether one considers them completely unreasonable or on the contrary sees in them the promise of a wonderful future, they certainly did express a contempt for the objective factors that ordinarily restrain initiatives, a refusal to take into consideration the constraints that spring from the order of things, and a reaction against forecasts based on rational analysis and programming. By dint of believing or wanting to believe that anything was possible, a part of France acted as if it were in a state of levitation. These events have refuted the allegation that our age would see the death of ideologies. A brief eclipse was taken for the proclamation of their final disappearance. We now know that there is a future for ideologies and in particular for those which take a place in the Right-Left system.

This unexpected resurgence of the utopian imagination in our industrial and technical society brings into the spotlight one essential dimension of this Right-Left division that too intellectual an analysis of the various themes might tend to minimize. Both the Right and the Left define themselves to a great degree by their fundamental attitudes toward existence, society, history, power, and politics. In these matters, the line of division separates not only those who hope for change from those who wish to retain the status quo, nor even those who support change by the revolutionary path from the evolutionists who favor progressive reforms enacted legally; it sets in opposition the will to believe that anything is possible against the conviction that there are objective forces among which political action is required to choose; it opposes those who believe that in all situations novelty is always worth more than the heritage of the past against those who maintain that a society neither can nor ought to break with the continuity of its collective experience. The disagreements rooted around this general issue are more profound than ordinary quarrels over the form of the regime or the content of a policy.

The crisis also upset the normal distribution of opinions and jumbled the political topography to which observers had become accustomed after ten years of the Fifth Republic. So we have seen faithful Gaullists such as David Rousset and René Capitant side with the student movement and even approve its acts of violence. Even more striking was the almost constant parallelism of the policies of Gaullism and Communism, equally alert to head off a disaster, and both fighting desperately against the recklessness of the Left. This spontaneous convergence, which one might call a pragmatic alliance between them, can be explained without recourse to plots of the romantic or mystery novel type. Communism found all its traditional enemies, anarchism, Trotskyism, Maoism, Guevarism, allied in a coalition of violent opposition. For its leaders there could not have been the slightest hesitation as to the line to follow—a fight without quarter against the heresies that challenged its orthodoxy. But here, and for the first time, appears the suggestion that the day may come when it will be appropriate to ask, as we have of Radicalism and of social democracy, if orthodox Communism is not about to pass from the Left to the Right, as have so many other movements before it. In May 1968 this question, which hitherto was only a scholastic hypothesis, ceased to be purely speculative and became an anticipation.

This, because for the first time the Communist Party ceased to be the movement most to the Left in the French ideological spectrum. To the left of it appeared something else, which automatically pushed it a little to the Right. The birth of an ultra Left perhaps is the most consequential event of the crisis. This extreme Left managed to join together, at least for the duration of a crisis, some very disparate components—in addition to several revolutionary coteries whose audience suddenly swelled beyond all measure, the Unified Socialist Party (P.S.U.), a section of the French Democratic Confederation of Labor (C.F.D.T.), the current spokesmen of student unionism, and a significant fraction from the teachers' unions. It reforged the alliance of workers and intellectuals, present in all revolutionary enterprises. All other things being equal, it takes the place and plays the role that the Communist Party did when it was Bolshevized and before 1935 when it began to move toward quite a different style of organization. Instead of taking its orders from Moscow, however, this new extreme Left looks to Cuba and tries to find its models in the Third World. Another difference with the Third International is the active presence of Christians in the midst of this coalition, which reveals a great deal about the path that the churches have traveled in the last half-century in defining their relations with politics. The revival of a fighting extreme Left which extols the role of active minorities, which challenges the most solemnly consecrated practices of parliamentary democracy in the name of real democracy, and which appeals to the militant rather than the voter, suddenly reminds us that antiparliamentarism is not the exclusive property of a certain group on the Right Wing; there also is an antiparliamentarism on the Left. The struggle against fascism and the communist acceptance of the principles and practices of "bourgeois democracy" almost made us forget it. And so the mechanism that produces new groups on the Left, which apparently stopped because the Communist Party for a half-century had so effectively worked to prevent such activities, now has begun to operate again.

But if this is so, shouldn't we draw up our report and conclude that the traditional Right-Left distinction has now broken down? To the ultra Left nothing distinguishes the Communist Party from the Gaullist regime; why then retain a frontier between them that they themselves have eliminated? To accept this claim would be rather boldly to anticipate the future. This analysis is as yet held by minorities that are too small to convince public opinion generally of their views. Following the history of the Right Wing for over a century and a half has taught us that the appearance of new lines of division does not erase older cleavages—the movement of the liberal ideology to the Right did not in consequence either abolish or absorb into it the militant counter-revolutionary Right. If the electoral campaign of June 1968 did appear to be a struggle of the Left against the Right (and rarely has an election presented such a clear cut two-sided character, accelerating the movement by which the Fifth Republic had led French politics toward a bi-polar system), the Left Wing was a group of several movements, associating Radicalism, Socialism, and Communism in a joint struggle against the Rightist groups.

If the Right-Left division still retains its relevance, nevertheless, the voting of June 1968 did reveal some changes in the composition of these two camps and in their internal as well as external relations. It is both a virtue and a function of elections to substitute incontestable arithmetic evidence concerning the relative strengths of various movements in place of self-serving estimates. In particular, successive elections show the changes that occur in the balance between contrary forces and the shifts that affect the distance between allied political groups. It is important, therefore, after drawing lessons from the May crisis, to examine what the election of June 23 and 30, 1968, can tell us of each of our Right Wing groups.

The first conclusion concerns Gaullism and is simply arithmetic: the astonishing growth of its voting strength

in one year. The numbers speak for themselves. Added
together, the votes of the Union for the Defense of the
Republic, the present name of the orthodox Gaullists, and
the Independent Republicans, who are a special group
within the Gaullist majority, came close to ten million on
the first round. The total is unprecedented in our series of
legislative elections. The proportion of 47.79 per cent
came very close to a majority of the votes, so their electoral plurality is close to catching up to their parliamentary majority. If we look at these matters from the point
of view of the various kinds of electoral Gaullism, legislative Gaullism, which for a long time was the weakest
of the three types, has caught up to and even surpassed
presidential Gaullism (General de Gaulle won only 45
per cent of the votes in the first round of the presidential
election of December 1965), and is in a good position
to overtake referendum Gaullism. These figures show how
legislative Gaullism is taking root in the electorate after
ten years of the Fifth Republic.

The Gaullist majority in the Assembly is without
precedent in our parliamentary history. The Incomparable
Chamber of the Second Restoration has been suggested as
a parallel, but it will be recalled how it was chosen by a
small fraction of the population, some tens of thousands
of voters with high property qualifications. As to the
Chamber of the *Bloc National,* its majority had far less
homogeneity, for it comprised a coalition of groups where
each retained its independence, and the difference between
it and the opposition was not so marked.

We see then that the result of the upheaval of May,
this crisis that seriously shook the structure and values of
French society, was to permit those in power to obtain
a "clear and massive" majority and to improve on their

mediocre and uncertain results of 1967! It was an unexpected consequence of the student movement, the sort of
trick that history often plays! The result requires an
explanation. In this case, wasn't it determined by the very
course of events? Violence in the streets, fear of subversion, and abhorrence for revolution threw the voters into
the arms of Gaullism. This interpretation, suggested immediately, has spread so widely that it has assumed the
appearance of truth. Gaullism would be the most recent
embodiment of that party of fear which in the past gained
power in 1849, in 1851, and in 1871. "The polls full of
fear," read the headline of the newspaper *Combat* the
morning after the first round of the election, a newspaper
that from the beginning of the crisis had lined up in the
camp of the most determined opponents of the Gaullist
regime.

One cannot deny that fear, or something approaching
it, played a part in the electoral results. It is certainly not
we who would be tempted to forget the role that simple
emotions—hope, the need to admire, confidence, and
fear—play in political life, and especially in voting motivations and behavior. Although contemporaries do not
always see this clearly, such feelings are at the basis of
the great stampedes which punctuate the upheavals of the
classical topography of political forces. Unquestionably
fear operated in June 1968, as it did in 1958, in 1940,
and in other circumstances. But to stop at this point really
says nothing. To reduce the victory of Gaullism or of the
Right (in a moment we shall examine their possible
assimilation) to a simple reflex of fear suggests that its
triumph is based only on an identification of the Left as
the party of hate or of envy. But negative feelings never
amount to more than the lower foundations of a mental

system which joins to them positive values, idealistic hopes, and constructive aims. Supposing that fear indeed was the mortar holding the victorious coalition together, we still have to determine whom and what the voters feared and for what reason they were so shaken. No doubt they feared less for their goods, property, and incomes, than for the values on which they believed society was and should be founded. They defended material interests less than social values, responsibilities, and a place in the scale of esteem. This difference is not unimportant; it completely changes the significance of the electoral surprise.

Wrongly or rightly, the voters also believed they were defending legal procedures against subversion, normal institutions against an effort to substitute street violence for the verdict of the polls. At this point in the analysis a parallel comes to mind, that some will believe quite incongruous, but which may clarify the motives of some of the voters who shifted over to support the candidates of the Union for the Defense of the Republic. Our analogy concerns the political situation in the years 1934-1936. The antiparliamentary agitation of that period, the little street war that the students of the Latin Quarter carried on against the police and which reached a climax on the evening of February 6, 1934, the belief—it doesn't matter whether it was true or not—that republican institutions were threatened by actions of reputedly seditious leagues, these events and beliefs pushed a significant number of republicans and democrats of the Center, acting in the name of antifascism and defense of the Republic, toward an alliance with the socialists and even the Communist Party. Their support contributed greatly to the electoral triumph of the Popular Front in

April–May 1936. Who can say if, over thirty years later, similar motives operating in an inverse fashion did not cause similar reflexes, this time pushing many Left Wing republicans more to the Right? To this suggestion two facts seem to bring at least a beginning of a confirmation. For one thing, Gaullism clearly recovered some labor votes in the traditional strongholds of the Left, such as the Nord, the Pas-de-Calais, and even Meurthe-et-Moselle. In addition, it progressed in the southern part of the country where the traditional political attitudes include respect for republican legality.

The size of the Gaullist increase (an 8 per cent improvement on the first round in 1968 over the first round in March 1967), and the closeness of the election to the events of May, which naturally suggest a cause and effect relationship between the two occurrences, should not hide the continuity that can be seen in a graph of voting statistics. Beneath the contingencies of daily events, broad subterranean movements continue to operate, that only the surprise of the run-off of March 1967,[2] magnified by the analyses of the moment, hid from sight. In the ten years from November 1958 to June 1968, from election to election, orthodox Gaullism continued to gain votes and strengthen its positions in the country. Starting out with little, in 1967 it attracted 37 per cent of the votes and raised this to 46 per cent in June 1968. If one excepts the accident that took place in the run-off in 1967, its parliamentary forces, running under different names and initials in succeeding elections, progressed continually—in 1958, 194 U.N.R., in 1962, 229 U.N.R.-U.D.T. who were joined by 20 Independent Republicans after the breakup

[2] In this election the Gaullists and their allies lost 40 seats while the Left Wing parties gained 60 seats. Tr.

of the National Center of Independents, in 1967, 224
U.N.R. and Independent Republicans, and finally in the
triumph of June 1968 almost 300 U.D.R. and affiliated,
plus some 60 Giscardien Republicans, or about three-
fourths of the new Assembly.

If the result of June 1968 is put into the pattern of successive elections, it already appears less as an accident
related to an extraordinary situation. Then, examination
of the map gives even more support to the hypothesis of
continuity. Gaullism in the period of the R.P.F. and even
at the beginning of the Fifth Republic was a northern
French phenomenon. Its bastions lay in the East, the
West, the Paris region, and the Nord. This was still true
in the presidential election of December 1965. The geographic distribution of the vote shows a clear contrast between a northern France where the majority voted for
General de Gaulle and a southern France—approximately
the unoccupied France of 1940—where the single candidate of the Left, François Mitterrand, enjoyed his greatest strength. The election of 1967 announced a change:
Gaullism had cut into certain traditional Left Wing
strongholds, especially on the periphery of the Massif
Central. Then in the June election they were not only cut
into but carried. The classic map has been completely upset and the specialists in electoral geography can no longer
recognize their familiar patterns. The candidates of the
majority won all the seats in Dordogne, Isère, and
Vaucluse. They gained both votes and seats in the South-
West (Landes, Lot-et-Garonne, Basses-Pyrénées, Hautes-
Pyrénées, Haute-Garonne) and on the Mediterranean
coast both in Languedoc and Provence. In none of the
seven departments which for generations were a kind of
red garland in southeastern France did the Gaullists fail

to gain strength, at the expense of the Radicals sometimes, but more often of the Socialists and Communists
(Pyrénées-Orientales, Aude, Hérault, Gard, Bouches-du-
Rhône, Var, Alpes-Maritimes). This advance also manifested itself in the Rhône Valley where the vote had been
shifting from Right to Left since the Second Empire
(Vaucluse, Ardèche, Drôme). This accelerated advance
south of the Loire, joined to the regaining of positions
shaken or threatened in the north, explains the size of the
victory of June 1968. These general gains indicate that
if Gaullism, stronger in the north, seemed in decline there,
it was a long way from losing its power of penetration
south of the Loire. There it continued to make forward
progress. This situation brings about two consequences,
linked together in their nature and their effects: the nation-
alization of Gaullism and the increased uniformity of the
electoral map.

In any electoral analysis, the political origin of new
voters is not less important than their actual numbers.
The increase in the size of the Gaullist vote implies losses
elsewhere. Whatever may be the number of votes cap-
tured from the Left that are shown by the changes in geographic distribution that we have just pointed out, the
most substantial increase, nevertheless, came from the
Right. The major fact demonstrated in the election of
June 1968 is the action of the whole of the Right Wing
in closing ranks around Gaullism. This is new. Until this
point, in fact, a good share of the Right was sulky with or
fought against General de Gaulle and his friends. Even
a group that accepted an alliance with him strove to retain its autonomy. In November 1958 the first electoral
success of the Gaullists running on the U.N.R. ticket did
not prevent a substantial advance of the Independents

organized in their National Center. Ten years later Gaullism has dissolved the Rightist groups, broken up their organizations, and gathered up their electoral clientele. After several years it carried out the prediction of Maurice Duverger and became the "federator of the Right Wing groups."

Evidence for this has multiplied. Certain persons have come over to Gaullism: after Pierre Poujade, Jean Louis Tixier-Vignancour agreed to sacrifice his resentments on the altar of anticommunism. Several members of parliament who in 1967 campaigned against Gaullists this time ran under the U.D.R. banner: Pierre Baudis, one of the earliest organizers of the Democratic Center for Study and Liaison, Bernard Lafay, and others. The old disagreements have been put aside, at least for the moment. Algeria—which had cut an apparently uncrossable division within the Right Wing between those who subscribed to self-determination and those who fought against it, even to the extreme position of the O.A.S.—has now become history. The expected liberation of General Salan, head of the O.A.S. and condemned to death six years ago, has a symbolic meaning,[3] as does the governmental proposal for a total amnesty. Not only does this satisfy in part the stubborn demands of the extreme Right, but it demonstrates the obliteration of old divisions and the reconciliation of the Right Wing groups against a common enemy, the danger of revolution.

By its issues and by its tone the election campaign illustrated and evidenced the regrouping of the Rightist factions against the Left. In deciding to direct his attacks against communist totalitarianism—although the Com-

[3]General de Gaulle pardoned General Salan and thirteen other O.A.S. leaders in June 1968. Tr.

munist Party has never been so innocent of this charge as at this time—Prime Minister Pompidou was able to awaken old reflexes. He appealed for order against anarchy. In some ways the electoral situation and the line-up of the forces confronting each other recalled 1849 or 1919, or more recently 1936. The parade organized by the Gaullists from the Place de la Concorde to the Etoile on May 30 awakened a host of reminiscences in any observer with a memory. First he probably remembered earlier epochs of Gaullism, recognizing both persons and themes from the R.P.F. But he detected something more than Gaullism there, personal loyalty to the Head of the State was no longer, as formerly, the primary tie among these hundreds of thousands of marchers. It also suggested as an echo the demonstrations which occurred on the same spot ten years earlier in favor of *Algérie Française*. More than anything else, the spectator who was not born yesterday might believe himself carried thirty years back in time, watching a parade of the French Social Party. Here was the same mixture of young people and war veterans, united around the cult of the tricolor, of supervisory types and middle class people, with a sprinkling of blue collar workers, the same combination of patriotism, of anticommunism, and of social goodwill that characterized the Right Wing at the rare moments when it broke down its internal divisions and rose above its dissensions to unite in a collective enthusiasm—Boulangism in 1888, the P.S.F. in 1938, and Gaullism in 1968. These also are the only circumstances in which the Right can pull hundreds of thousands of marchers into the streets and so balance off the demonstrations of the political and labor movements of the Left. There is a final analogy with the earlier movements: its ability to transform crowds into an electoral force. Usually the agitation of Right Wing leagues scorns elections, but putting aside this rule, Boulangism methodically courted voters and won the success with which we are familiar. If circumstances had allowed an election in 1940 one can easily believe that the P.S.F. would have run candidates everywhere and a reasonable estimate of political strengths leads us to believe that it would have sent a hundred of its members to the Chamber of Deputies, that is, about the same number of R.P.F. candidates that General de Gaulle succeeded in having elected to the National Assembly in 1951. If in 1968 the U.D.R. managed to win more than half the seats, this is because it gained for its candidates nearly all the votes of the Right and the Center as well.

On this point it is particularly worthwhile to compare the last two run-off elections, just fifteen months apart. Political science for a long time has neglected to study run-off elections, and for easily understandable reasons. Since they involve only a share of the districts it is difficult, if not impossible, to establish relationships between the first round and the run-off. But they do reveal something that the first round cannot—second choices, that is, preferences that determine where the votes will go, and by the direction in which these votes move the relative distance that separates or joins the various political movements. The run-off of 1967 showed that when voters in the Center had to choose between Gaullism or the Left, many then preferred to vote for the Left Wing candidate, sometimes even if he were Communist, rather than contribute even a little to maintaining the Gaullists and their regime in power. Dislike for one-man rule, resentment over the Algerian or European policies of the Fifth Republic often won out over all other considerations, as in December 1965, and quieted, in particular, the recurring fear of revolution. This movement to the Left placed General de Gaulle in difficulty already in 1965, and caused the surprising outcome of the 1967 run-off. But the phenomenon did not recur in 1968. On the contrary, the U.D.R. and the Independent Republicans won most of the votes of the Right and Center in the run-off. The line of separation that always divides Right and Left within the system of alliances and conflicts, sometime so difficult to detect because it shifts around, in 1967 isolated Gaullism from the Centrist voters; but after the events of May 1968 it jumped to the other side of the Center that was now in the Right Wing camp. The Left, consequently, was reduced to its own hard core, without additional votes coming from elsewhere. Gaullism did in fact act as the federator for all those who refused to line up on the Left.

Does this mean that Gaullism has finished traveling the road that leads all movements of this nature to identify themselves with the Right? Is an observer justified in stating that Gaullism and the Right henceforth are simply one, the former having unified the latter? M. Waldeck Rochet, Executive Secretary of the Communist Party, proclaimed this thesis when on July 9, 1968, he declared to the central committee of his party, "Henceforth there is no political movement on the Right except Gaullism." Examining the situation more closely, it does not seem that things are so simple or that the situation is so rigid. Several factors require us to recognize that Gaullism still objects to considering itself as one of the poles of the classic Right-Left relationship.

First of all, the entire Right Wing did not rally to the Gaullists. While the bulk of the liberal and parliamentary Right, conforming to its principles and usual habits, made common cause with the established order against disorder and presumed subversion, one cannot say the same of the Rightist group that has joined the heritage of counter-revolutionary thought with the exaltations of nationalism. When Tixier-Vignancour asked his political friends to close ranks behind his successful competitor for the presidency of the Republic, his move brought on a crisis in the Republican Alliance and an irreconcilable faction managed to suspend him from his position in it. Resentments that are now a quarter of a century old have not died away. If Gaullism grants an amnesty to the O.A.S., those who are nostalgic for Vichy have not amnestied the disobedient general. Jacques Isorni did not support the Gaullists, and Alfred Fabre-Luce urged his readers to take up the cause of Pierre Mendès-France, against whom in other days he built up the legend of M. Pinay.[4] Neither Georges Bidault nor Jacques Soustelle has pardoned his former leader. The professional anticommunist Georges Sauge decided that the seriousness of the revolutionary peril did not justify joining a man and a movement that he still saw as the very precursors of communism.

The situation of the Rightist faction we have called Orleanist, this family attached to both order and liberty, is scarcely less confused, particularly since 1962 when the National Center of Independents lost its unity and cohesion. Two branches grew out of it. One decided to enter the Gaullist majority—the Independent Republicans who found their center in the personality of their leader Valéry Giscard d'Estaing. The other chose a stance of moderate opposition and merged with a part of Christian democracy; after Jean Lecanuet decided not to run for a

---

[4] A reference to his book *Mendès ou Pinay* (Paris, 1953), that he published under the pseudonym Sapiens. Tr.

seat in the Assembly in 1967, it formed a group there
around the figure of Jacques Duhamel. Although these
two branches have grown out of the same tree, their relations with orthodox Gaullism appear rather different according to whether one examines them at the level of their
parliamentary leadership or in the behavior of their
voters. On the electoral level they appear to differ decisively: one group belongs to the majority, the other
fights it. What else matters? It is doubtful whether the
voters detect the nuances which distinguish the U.D.R. on
the one hand and the Independent Republicans on the
other. The Giscardien group appears as a variant within
the majority. But when carefully examined, the positions
of M. Giscard d'Estaing's Independent Republicans and
M. Duhamel's Center for Progress and Modern Democracy are very close to the same thing. The only matter
that separates them is a tactical disagreement on the best
way to be heard by the majority.

Curiously, the game of parliamentary arithmetic that
once divided them now tends to push them together and
perhaps will lead to a reconciliation. The 1967 election
disappointed the hopes of the Democratic Center's leader,
for the Gaullists, aided by the Independent Republicans,
having won an absolute majority by a narrow margin,
could manage without the Center's votes. The parliamentary representatives of this group, Progress and Modern
Democracy, which expressed in the Assembly the continuity in the country of a distinct Right-Center position
at the point where the Independents and Christian democrats meet, were now pushed outside the governmental
majority, and thereby bereft of the key position which
would have given them the role of arbiter in close votes.
Fifteen months later the same mischance occurred to the

Giscardiens. Although they gained votes and increased the number of their Deputies by almost half, the unexpected inflation of the seats held by orthodox Gaullists over the threshold of an absolute majority threw them outside this majority, in the same position as the Democratic Center. The Gaullist U.D.R. has no need tomorrow of M. Giscard d'Estaing as it yesterday did not need Jean Lecanuet or Jacques Duhamel. Neither of these two groups can expect to act as the keystone of the majorities of tomorrow. Will this analogous situation lead them to come together to rebuild a homogenous force? Whatever happens, such a development would conform to their characters. Their decision does not depend less on Gaullism than on their own desires. Gaullism's attraction for the supporters of the moderate Right has divided that group. Gaullism has lastingly weakened this Right, it has partially absorbed it, but still it has not succeeded in carrying off all of it. So, whatever Rightist group that we consider, we come to the conclusion that although it has honestly tried, Gaullism has failed to unify them all. One group continues to maintain an undying animosity toward it; the other has, for better or for worse, retained its uniqueness.

But have Gaullism or its leaders ever really wanted to federate the Right Wing? There is reason to doubt this, for all the while they have never ceased trying to gain voters on the Left. This is the second factor that at present frustrates all efforts to reduce the Gaullist phenomenon to a simple expression of the Right Wing. It has too many potentialities that pull it in the opposite direction, beginning with General de Gaulle himself, who denies neither his past nor his personality. The motives ascribed to him make somewhat believable the declaration he made only a few days after the height of the May crisis, "I also am a revolutionary!" The shocks of his foreign policy, which experience broad approval on the Left, and his inclinations toward social reform do create a barrier between the classic Right and himself. If the composition of its voters has a decisive influence on determining the nature of a movement, those who support Gaullism contribute to maintaining this ambivalence. François Goguel has analyzed the presidential election of 1965 using two different methods and he arrived at the same result—about three million voters from the Left preferred General de Gaulle over the candidate recommended by the party they usually favored. While the election of March 1967 revealed a slackening of this flow from the Left, in that of June 1968 it became a torrent, for not only did Gaullism win over a part of this electorate but it probably increased its share. Any other conclusion could not explain why so many seats changed hands. This phenomenon is nowhere so noticeable as in the departments south of the Loire and we have mentioned some of the symptoms of this. The Left Wing parties lost some of their votes on the first round in 1968 and in the run-off they did not recover all of them, some abstaining and others going to the U.D.R. This shows the gradual weakening of the Left. Since the Liberation and its overturning of political forces, the Left has never recovered the majority which under the Third Republic seemed to come to it almost by statute. We have examined some reasons for this weakening, which may come from social changes as well as ideological shifts. But since 1958 the Left's numerical importance has rarely stopped declining; together, Communism, Socialism, and Radicalism, even with the addition of small parties such as the P.S.U. and the stimulation of the clubs, have seen their percentage of the vote decrease regularly: 43.41 in 1958, 42.82 in 1962, 43.51 in 1967, and finally 41.22 in 1968.

For two reasons at least, then, the opposition between Gaullism and its adversaries does not match line for line the Right-Left division. Gaullism has not wholeheartedly attempted or succeeded in effectively unifying all the Rightist groups; and second, it has tried hard and partially succeeded in attracting a fraction of the Left. This observation, one may say, is not a novel one. Of course, but isn't the result of elections often to reintroduce as evidence certain elementary truths that parliamentary debates or party controversies cover up? The real novelty is that this conclusion is still true ten years after it was first stated. In 1958 no one took the risk to predict such a longevity. It is difficult to believe that such persistence cannot leave some posterity behind it.

Bibliography

(The place of publication is Paris unless otherwise noted.)

I. General Works

A. GENERAL HISTORIES

In the "Clio" series with its emphasis on interpretation and bibliography, the appropriate volume is *L'Epoque Contemporaine,* Part 1, *Restaurations et Révolutions (1815-1871)* (1953), by J. Droz, L. Genet, and J. Vidalenc, and Part 2, *La Paix Armée et la Grande Guerre (1871-1919)* (1939), by P. Renouvin, E. Préclin, and G. Hardy; while the relevant volumes in the "Peuples et Civilisations" series include Félix Ponteil, *L'Eveil des Nationalités et la Mouvement Libéral (1815-1848)* (1960); Charles Pouthas, *Démocraties et Capitalisme (1848-1860)* (1948); P. Benaerts *et al, Nationalité et Nationalisme (1860-1878),* new ed. (1968); Maurice Baumont, *L'Essor Industriel et l'Impérialisme Colonial (1878-1904),* 3rd ed. (1965); P. Renouvin, *La Crise Européenne et la Grande Guerre (1904-1918),* 4th ed. (1962); M. Baumont, *La Faillite de la Paix (1918-*

418

1939), new ed. (1967-1968); and Henri Michel, *La Seconde Guerre Mondiale*, Part 1 (1968).

Still valuable for France are the volumes in Ernest Lavisse (ed.), *Histoire de France Contemporaine depuis la Révolution jusqu'à 1919* (1920-1922): S. Charléty, *La Restauration (1815-1830)*, and *La Monarchie de Juillet (1830-1848)*, C. Seignobos, *La Révolution de 1848. Le Second Empire (1848-1859), Le Déclin de l'Empire et l'Establissement de la IIIᵉ République (1859-1875)*, and *L'Evolution de la IIIᵉ République (1875-1914)*.

In E. Perroy *et al, Histoire de la France pour tous les Français*, 2 vols. (1950), vol. 2, *De 1774 à nos Jours*, the chapters covering the years 1815-1950 by Charles Pouthas and Maurice Baumont constitute an informed statement of the most recent research and often suggest new viewpoints on political developments. Jean Jacques Chevallier, *Histoire des Institutions et des Régimes Politiques de la France Moderne (1789-1958)*, 3rd ed. (1967), which discusses politics, men, and ideas, contains more than its title promises. G. Bertier de Sauvigny, *The Bourbon Restoration*, trans. Lynn Case (Philadelphia: University of Pennsylvania Press, 1966), is an excellent synthesis of the period in which the first Right was formed.

Six brief studies are useful: F. Ponteil, *La Monarchie Parlementaire (1815-1848)* (1949), and *1848* (1937); Jean Vidalenc, *La Restauration (1814-1830)* (1966); P. Vigier, *La Monarchie de Juillet* (1962); M. Blanchard, *Le Second Empire* (1950); and G. Bourgin, *La IIIᵉ République* (1939). That of M. Blanchard corrects more than one prejudice, enlightens our knowledge of the regime, and opens penetrating insights on its relations with the various elements of French society.

The Third Republic is the subject of two long works:
Jacques Chastenet, *Histoire de la IIIe République,* 7 vols.
(1952-1963); and Georges and Edouard Bonnefous,
Histoire Politique de la IIIe République, 7 vols. (1956-
1967). The second of these centers narrowly on politics
and tries to fill the gap left when publication of the annual
volumes of *L'Année Politique* ceased after 1905. Every
year since the Liberation a volume of *L'Année Politique*
has again appeared. These recapitulate events in domestic, foreign, and economic affairs. They are an indispensable guide.

To these general works we add studies in English by
two able students of our history: D. W. Brogan, *The
Development of Modern France (1870-1939),* new ed.
(London, 1967); and Gordon Wright, *France in Modern
Times: 1760 to the Present* (Chicago, 1960). Our history
gains from being observed from England or the United
States with viewpoints that renovate our customary
interpretations.

Geographic localization being as important as chronological position, one can profit from consulting an atlas;
see R. Rémond (ed.), *Atlas Historique de la France
Contemporaine* (1966).

B. HISTORY OF POLITICAL THOUGHT

Two textbooks offer a complete survey of political
philosophies: Jean Touchard *et al, Histoire des Idées
Politiques,* 2 vols. (1959), vol. 2, *Du XVIIIe Siècle à nos
Jours,* has sections relevant to our subject; and Marcel
Prélot, *Histoire des Idées Politiques* (1959). A discus-
sion of contemporary movements can be found in J.
Touchard, *Le Mouvement des Idées Politiques dans la*

France Contemporaine, 3 mimeographed fascicles of a course given in 1962-1963. J. J. Chevallier, *Les Grandes Oeuvres Politiques de Machiavel à nos Jours* (1950), has chapters on Burke and Maurras, while J. Droz, *Histoire des Doctrines Politiques en France,* 4th ed. (1963), is a brief survey. Henry Michel, *L'Idée de l'Etat* (1896), includes some rather summary discussions of Right Wing ideas. In English there are Charlotte T. Muret, *French Royalist Doctrines since the Revolution* (New York, 1933), and Roger Soltau, *French Political Thought in the Nineteenth Century* (London, 1931).

Robert Pelloux (ed.), *Libéralisme, Traditionalisme, Décentralisation* (1952), includes essays on the political thought of Tocqueville, Taine, Thibon, and a suggestive discussion on the conservative origins of Christian democracy. Jean B. Duroselle, *Les Débuts du Catholicisme Social en France (1822-1870)* (1951), is standard. In Albert Thibaudet, *Les Idées Politiques de la France* (1932), there are chapters on traditionalism, liberalism, and industrialism in a book that is provocative, sensitive, and delectable, with many allusions. The series of publications, "Idées Politiques," edited by Jean Touchard, performs a valuable service by presenting the leading ideologies and systems of political philosophy through readings and comments on them.

C. POLITICAL PARTIES AND SOCIAL STRUCTURE

Maurice Duverger, *Political Parties, Their Organization and Activity in the Modern State* (New York, 1954), undertakes a morphological study of parties. There is little about the Right Wing because of its weakness in organization, but comparisons with more highly structured groups lead to reflection. Georges Lavau, *Partis Politiques et Réalités Sociales* (1953), a reply to Duverger's work just cited, insists on the priority of social structures in the development of political forces. When read in conjunction these two works have even greater interest.

Emmanuel Beau de Loménie, *Les Responsabilités des Dynasties Bourgeoises,* 4 vols. (1943-1963), extends from Napoleon to Hitler. The point of view, curiously anachronistic, is Legitimist. The proofs are not always convincing or equal to the novelty of the working hypothesis. An *Almanach de Gotha* of Orleanist society, it sometimes becomes pamphleteering. From quite a different political position, Augustin Hamon, *Les Maîtres de la France,* 3 vols. (1936-1938), often arrives at conclusions similar to the pre-cited. Jean Lhomme, *La Grande Bourgeoisie au Pouvoir (1830-1880)* (1960), views the social framework of nineteenth century history and tends to identify political movements with classes.

M. Duverger (ed.), *Partis Politiques et Classes Sociales en France* (1955), is a symposium in which "Les Modérés," by Marcel Merle is especially interesting. Part of the same series is Jacques Fauvet and Henri Mendras (eds.), *Les Paysans et la Politique* (1958). While already partially outdated by the rapidity of rural evolution, this work is the first general study and systematic investigation of this essential aspect of French political society. American scholarship in this area is demonstrated in Gordon Wright, *Rural Revolution in France* (Stanford, 1964).

Raoul Girardet, *La Société Militaire dans la France Contemporaine (1815-1939)* (1953), is a penetrating and elegant essay, rich with insights on military ideas and political parties, the army and nationalism. David Thomson, *Democracy in France,* 4th ed. (London, 1964), has much on social changes.

D. RELIGION AND POLITICS

Aline Coutrot and F. G. Dreyfus, *Les Forces Religieuses dans la Société Française* (1965), is an excellent synthesis of recent research on this subject. R. Rémond (ed.), *Forces Religieuses et Attitudes Politiques dans la France Contemporaine* (1965), is the product of a colloquium on the period since 1945. Other works on religious matters include André Latreille and René Rémond, *Histoire du Catholicisme en France,* vol. 3, *La Période Contemporaine* (1962); Edouard Lecanuet, *L'Eglise de France sous la IIIe République,* 4 vols. (1907-1930), with a liberal Catholic viewpoint; A. Dansette, *Religious History of Modern France,* 2 vols. (New York, 1961), a measured and informed account that is continued in his *Destin du Catholicisme Français (1926-1956)* (1957). In English there is William Bosworth, *Catholicism and Crisis in Modern France* (Princeton, 1962), on the contemporary period. Michel Darbon, *Le Conflit entre la Droite et la Gauche dans le Catholicisme Français (1830-1953)* (Toulouse, 1953), discusses a good subject but does not exhaust it or basically change it. In addition, Emile Léonard, *Le Protestant Français* (1953), has some information about the Protestant Right; and Stuart R. Schram, *Protestantism and Politics in France* (Alençon, 1954), covers the period 1802-1954 with emphasis on the Gard.

E. THE PRESS AND LITERATURE

E. Hatin, *Histoire de la Presse Politique et Littéraire en France,* 8 vols. (1859-1861), and especially the same author's valuable *Bibliographie Historique et Critique de la Presse Périodique Française* (1866), which contains descriptions, often in detail, of the most notable journals. In the "Kiosque" series there are Charles Ledré, *La Presse à l'Assaut de la Monarchie (1815-1848)* (1960); and Roger Bellet, *Presse et Journalisme sous le Second Empire* (1967). Hardly a volume in this series does not have something on Right Wing publications. For the following period one may consult H. Avenel, *Histoire de la Presse Française depuis 1789 jusqu'à nos Jours* (1900), which unfortunately lacks an index. *Le Livre du Centenaire du Journal des Débats* (1889); and André J. Tudesq, "Un Journal Gouvernemental au Temps de Guizot: le 'Journal des Débats'," *Politique,* II (1959), 138-164, revive the career of one of the most important Right Wing journals between 1815 and the end of the Second Empire.

Albert Thibaudet, *Histoire de la Littérature Française de 1789 à nos Jours* (1936), attempts to show the relationships between political activity and literary production. It distinguishes generations of writers and politicians. Jean Touchard, *Littérature et Politique,* 4 fascicles (1954-1955), studies literary evidence on political events and writers' attitudes on politics and provides us a valuable and suggestive contribution to the history of political thought. A briefer discussion is R. Rémond, "Les Intellectuels et la Politique," *Revue Française de Science Politique,* IX (1959), 860-880.

Some literary works present a better introduction to the

Right than do scholarly and laborious historical studies. A novel can recreate a sensibility marvelously, can recall a society, can open up a whole world of anxieties and feelings, and can present in one stroke an understanding of a period. The work of Balzac presents a political philosophy close to the Ultra traditional monarchism in action. The fine thesis of Bernard Guyon, *La Pensée Politique et Sociale de Balzac* (1948), offers an orderly analysis of it. Inspired by the opposite point of view in politics, Stendhal's novels describe with a mocking precision the persons and the atmosphere of the Right. *The Red and the Black* shows the *Congrégation* and the Ultra Party, *Lucien Leuwen* presents a picture of provincial Legitimist society and the notables of the *juste milieu*.

In the following generation Armand de Pontmartin and Barbey d'Aurevilly present two complementary aspects of provincial Legitimism. The gentleman from the Comtat Venaissin (Pontmartin) made the Whites of the Midi live again, while the Norman gentleman (d'Aurevilly) evoked a strange world in Lower Normany. Their literary criticism, Pontmartin in the *Gazette de France* and Barbey d'Aurevilly in *Le Pays,* was not less Legitimist than their novels.

For nationalism and the Dreyfus Affair what better guide is there to consult than the works of Maurice Barrès *(L'Appel au Soldat, Scènes et Doctrines du Nationalisme, Leurs Figures)* or those of Paul Bourget? Novels such as *Les Déracinés* (Barrès) and *L'Etape* (Bourget) offer the most penetrating commentary on the psychology of the Right and its political philosophy. On the thought and work of Barrès, Jean M. Domenach, *Barrès par lui-même* (1954), is the best introduction and demonstrates the reality of his nationalism.

At present, the novels of Jean de La Varende, especially the series which traces the exploits of the La Bare
family, despite some imaginative extremes, give a rather
precise idea of *fin de siècle* Legitimist society. Under the
light veil of fiction one can see surviving the habits, feelings, and principles of a world which today is disappear-
ing, and which had its charm and its nobility.

F. POLITICIANS

Recalling that the traditions of the Right were of men
as much as ideas, one should place great weight on
memoirs and biographies. We shall mention especially
those politicians whose career or personality were typical
of one or another Right. From the very abundant literature of memoirs we can select F. A. R. de Chateaubriand,
Mémoires d'Outre-Tombe, 4 vols. (1948), with an
English translation in 6 volumes (London, 1892); F.
Guizot, *Mémoires pour Servir à l'Histoire de mon
Temps,* 8 vols. (1858-1867); A. de Tocqueville, *Souvenirs* (1942), with an English translation as *Recollections* (New York, 1949); Granier de Cassagnac, *Souvenirs du Second Empire,* 3 vols. (1879-1882); F. de
Falloux, *Mémoires d'un Royaliste,* 2 vols. (1888); A. de
Broglie, *Mémoires,* 2 vols. (1938-1941), and his *Dis-
cours,* 3 vols. (1909-1911); C. de Meaux, *Souvenirs
Politiques (1871-1877)* (1905). The memoir literature
has recently been enriched by a masterpiece of this genre
with the publication of Charles de Remusat, *Mémoires de
ma Vie,* edited in 5 volumes by Charles Pouthas and covering the years 1797-1875 (1958-1967). They are an incomparable account of the succession of regimes by an
acute observer and remarkable writer from an Orleanist

family. The study of a family, such as that of *Les Broglie* by J. de La Varende (1950), contributes to our knowledge of Orleanism for the generations of Dukes Victor and Albert.

There are biographic notes of politicians in A. Robert *et al, Dictionnaire des Parlementaires Français . . . depuis le 1ᵉʳ Mai 1789 jusqu'au 1ᵉʳ Mai 1889 . . . 5* vols. (1891), and recently continued by Jean Jolly (ed.), *Dictionnaire des Parlementaires Français de 1889 à 1940,* 4 vols. so far (1960–   ). The composition of parliamentary groups can be found in *L'Annuaire du Parlement,* signed by R. Samuel and Bonet-Maury. From 1910 the *Journal Officiel* has published the list of groups each year. Finally, since 1881 the statements of principles and electoral programs of candidates for the legislative elections are compiled for each election in a volume commonly called the Barodet, from the name of the author of the proposal.

II. *Works on Special Periods*

A. ULTRACISM, 1815-1830

On the antecedents of the counter-revolutionary Right: Jacques Godechot, *La Contre-Révolution: Doctrine et Action (1789-1804)* (1961), where the two aspects are separated in the exposition and the reader must set the formation of the doctrine in its social and political context; Paul H. Beik, *The Revolution Seen from the Right: Social Theories in Motion (1789-1799),* in vol. 46 of the *Transactions of the American Philosophical Society* (Philadelphia, 1956); Nora E. Hudson, *Ultra-Royalism and the French Restoration* (Cambridge, Mass., 1936);

and André Mater, "Le Groupement Régional des Partis Politiques à la Fin de la Restauration (1824-1830)," *La Revolution Française,* XLII (1902), 406-463, which is one of the first works on electoral geography. It contains a table by departments and electoral colleges of Deputies from the parliamentary sessions of 1824 through 1830.

On political thought F. Baldensperger, *Le Mouvement des Idées dans l'Emigration Française,* 2 vols. (1924-1925), is an elegant synthesis of the experiences and reflections from which Ultra political thought emerged. J. Droz, *Le Romantisme Politique en Allemagne* (1963), is interesting for the relationships and ideological similarity between Ultras and German counter-revolutionaries in the Europe of the Restoration. Dominique Bagge, *Les Idées Politiques sous la Restauration* (1952), is a conscientious review with many citations and a partisan point of view which at least shows the permanence of Ultra thought until the present. Another account is J. J. Oechslin, *Le Mouvement Ultra-Royaliste sous la Restauration* (1960).

An essential aspect of Ultra political thought is described in A. Rousseau, "L'Idée Décentralisatrice et les Partis Politiques sous la Restauration," *Revue de Bretagne,* XXIX (1903) and XXX (1903); while C. Pouthas, "Les Projets de Réforme Administrative sous la Restauration," *Revue d'Histoire Moderne,* I (1926), 321-367, shows that when the Ultras were in power they were in no hurry to carry out their decentralization policy. The later career of this theme is described in A. J. Tudesq, "La Décentralisation et la Droite en France au XIXᵉ Siècle," in *La Décentralisation: VIᵉ Colloque d'Histoire* (Aix-en-Provence, 1964), 55-67; and Thiébaut Flory, *Le Mouvement Régionaliste Français: Sources et*

Développements (1966). On another basic theme of organicist thought Raymond Deniel reconstructs *Une Image de la Famille et de la Société sous la Restauration* (1965), as seen in several contemporary newspapers. Henri Moulinié, *De Bonald* (1915), is the most complete study of the counter-revolutionary philosopher, while Paul Bourget and Michel Salomon, *Bonald* (1905), is a book of readings.

The figure of Chateaubriand dominates the period by the multiplicity of his activities—journalist, member of parliament, minister, diplomat—and by the range of his enterprises. Consequently, he has inspired many studies of parts or the whole of his career. Among them consult E. Beau de Loménie, *La Carrière Politique de Chateaubriand de 1814 à 1830*, 2 vols. (1929); Georges Collas *et al, Chateaubriand, le Livre de Centenaire* (1949); Philippe A. Vincent, *Les Idées Politiques de Chateaubriand* (1936), with a rather dry and systematic presentation; Bernard Chenot, "La Pensée Politique de Chateaubriand," *Mercure de France,* CCCIX (1950), 687-702; and Marcel Reinhard, "Chateaubriand et la Question Constitutionnelle au Début de la Première Restauration," *Revue Historique,* CCI (1949), 72-79. An excellent selection of his writings organized around the theme of loyalty is G. Dupuis *et al, Politique de Chateaubriand* (1967).

G. Bertier de Sauvigny, *Un Type d'Ultra-royaliste: Le Comte Ferdinand de Bertier (1782-1864) et l'Enigme de la Congrégation* (1948), is an important and admirable thesis which resurrects a typical intransigent Ultra and illuminates the whole period. Of recent works this has probably done the most to increase our knowledge of the Restoration. It gives the clue to an almost century-old

enigma, that of the *Congrégation*. On other personalities
there are E. de Vitrolles, *Mémoires,* 2 vols. (1950-1952),
rather disappointing; and Jean Fourcassié, *Villèle* (1964);
while we have two studies of Montlosier, A. Bardoux,
*Etudes Sociales et Politiques: Le Comte de Montlosier
et le Gallicanisme* (1881); and Joseph Brugerette, *Le
Comte de Montlosier et son Temps (1755-1838)* (Auril-
lac, 1931). Finally, Jean P. Garnier, *Le Sacre de Charles
X et l'Opinion Publique en 1825* (1927).

B. LEGITIMISM (1830-1848)

G. Bertier de Sauvigny in *La Conspiration des Légi-
timistes et la Duchesse de Berry contre Louis-Philippe
(1830-1832)* (1950), publishes secret correspondence
and other documents which throw new light on the prepa-
rations for the 1832 expedition and the differences within
the Ultra Party. See also Jean R. Collé, *La Chouannerie
de 1832 dans les Deux-Sèvres et la Vendée Orientale*
(Bordeaux, 1948). F. Gadrat, "Les Journaux Légiti-
mistes de Lyon et leur Personnel sous la Monarchie de
Juillet," *Revue d'Histoire de Lyon,* IV (1913), 302-320,
clarifies the quarrels between *old France* and *young
France*. A. J. Tudesq, *Les Grands Notables en France
(1840-1849): Etude Historique d'une Psychologie Sociale,*
2 vols. (Bordeaux, 1964), is the first general study on
French Legitimism in this period. There are many biographies of varying worth. Among them are E. Lecanuet,
Berryer, sa Vie et ses Oeuvres (1790-1868) (1893);
Paul Bastid, *Un Juriste Pamphlétaire, Cormenin* (1948),
which presents a typical case of a movement from Legitimism to the Republican Party. Among the mass of
memoirs and recollections, T. Muret, *A Travers Champs:*

Souvenirs et Causeries d'un Journaliste (1862), merits being recovered from oblivion; the author worked for several Legitimist newspapers and made the trip to Goritz. He recounts his recollections with much sincerity and a point of view quite favorable to the Duchess de Berry.

C. ORLEANISM (1830-1848)

The liberal and parliamentary Right has interested historians much less than the Ultras. This is common for those groups that achieve power; historians are more attracted by opposition forces. We recommend the memoirs of Guizot and Remusat, the outline by Vigier on *La Monarchie de Juillet*, and especially the thesis of Tudesq on the *Grands Notables*, all cited above. Other works include Paul Gerbod, *Paul-François Dubois: Universitaire, Journaliste, et Homme Politique, 1793-1874* (1967); Vincent Starzinger, *Middlingness, Juste Milieu: Political Theory in France and England, 1815-1848* (Charlottesville, 1965); and Douglas Johnson, *Guizot: Aspects of French History, 1787-1874* (London, 1963).

D. BONAPARTISM (1848-1870)

First mention must go to the thesis of Louis Chevalier, "Les Fondements Economiques et Sociaux de l'Histoire Politique de la Région Parisienne (1848-1851)," unpublished (1951). No student of the political history of these years can henceforth dispense from consulting this work. For political thought consult Paul Bastid, *Doctrines et Institutions de la Seconde République,* 2 vols. (1945). Three shorter studies examine elections: A. Tudesq, *L'Election Présidentielle de Louis-Napoléon Bonaparte*

(10 Décembre 1848) (1965); Gisela Geywitz, *Das Plebiszit von 1851 in Frankreich* (Tubingen, 1965); and Louis Girard (ed.), *Les Elections de 1869* (1960). We mention again the excellent little book of M. Blanchard, *Le Second Empire* (1950). Marcel Prélot, "La Signification Constitutionnelle du Second Empire," *Revue Française de Science Politique,* III (1953), 31-56, is a penetrating study. A recent analysis in English is T. Zeldin, *The Political System of Napoleon III* (New York, 1958). The long thesis of Jean Maurain, *La Politique Ecclésiastique du Second Empire, de 1852 à 1869* (1930), is outstanding on the relations between the regime and the Church. Several recent biographies clarify the character of Bonapartism or the nature of its relations with the notables: J. Maurain, *Un Bourgeois Français du XIXe Siècle: Baroche, Ministre de Napoléon III* (1936); Robert Schnerb, *Rouher et le Second Empire* (1949); and the fine thesis of Pierre Guiral, *Prévost-Paradol (1829-1870)* (1955), is a valuable contribution to the history of the Orleanist opposition. One will read with as much pleasure as profit the paper of Louis Girard, "Histoire et Constitution, (1851-1855)," *Bulletin de la Société d'Histoire Moderne,* April–June 1963, pp. 6-7, as well as "Les 'Photographies Politiques' de Verax: un Manifeste de l'Union Libérale (1865)," *Revue Historique,* CCXXIX (1963), 365-396. On the same subject consult "Il y a Cent Ans: le Libéralisme Catholique," *Politique,* IV (1961), 309-412.

On some forms of the opposition, see Robert Reichert, "Antibonapartist Elections to the Académie Française during the Second Empire," *Journal of Modern History,* XXXV (1963), 33-45; and R. Bellet, *Presse et Journalisme,* cited above.

E. THE THIRD REPUBLIC (1870-1940)

1. General Works

François Goguel, *La Politique des Partis sous la IIIe République,* 3rd ed., 2 vols. (1958), is fundamental, the first important study in French on the entire period. For the earlier years see also Léon Jacques, *Les Partis Politiques sous la IIIe République* (1913). In the years 1925-1932 there appeared several works belonging to the category of the essay as much as to that of observation: Albert Thibaudet, *La République des Professeurs* (1927); André Siegfried, *Tableau des Partis en France* (1930); Emmanuel Berl, *La Politique et les Partis* (1932), which is written with much talent and trenchant phrasing. Abel Bonnard, *Les Modérés* (1936), is a study of a temperament and a society that sometimes becomes a plea for the defense and a pamphlet, by a moderate. Jean Labasse, *Hommes de Droite, Hommes de Gauche* (1947), is a brief and penetrating essay pointing out the plurality on the Right Wing and showing that the appearance of the division between Right and Left came prior to any economic antagonism.

2. Regional Studies

André Siegfried, *Tableau Politique de la France de l'Ouest* (1913, reprint 1964), opened the way to research in political geography. It includes interesting observations on Legitimism and Imperialism in the West. Among recent works stemming from Siegfried's classic, we mention the important theses of Georges Dupeux, *Aspects de l'Histoire Politique et Sociale du Loir-et-Cher (1848-1914)* (1962); and Pierre Barral, *Le Département de*

l'Isère sous la IIIe République (1870-1940) (1962); as
well as A. Olivesi, "La Droite à Marseille en 1914,"
Provence Historique, VII (1957), 175-199.

3. The National Assembly

In Louis Teste, *L'Anatomie de la République (1870-
1910)* (1910), the second chapter is called, "Ce qui Restait
du Monarchisme en 1870." Arthur Loth, *L'Echec de la
Restauration Monarchique en 1873* (1910), is the first
detailed account, conscientious, and tinged with monarchist
sympathies that the author does not try to hide. In particular there are the two fine books of Daniel Halévy,
La Fin des Notables (1930), and *La République des
Ducs* (1937). Few works have with such felicity resurrected a society, revived a group of politicians, and restored a soul to the documents. Jacques Gouault, *Comment la France est Devenue Républicaine* (1954), describes movements of public opinion and contributes to
solving the enigma of a monarchist assembly adopting
republican institutions.

4. Nationalism, Boulangism, and the Dreyfus Affair

Raoul Girardet, *Le Nationalisme Français, 1871-
1914* (1966), includes both an excellent collection of
documents and an historical sketch. Mermeix (pseud. of
Gabriel Terrail), *Les Coulisses du Boulangisme* (1890),
is a collection of articles that first appeared in *Le Figaro.*
Concurrently with the events, he divulged the circumstances and methods of the collusion between the monarchists and Boulangism. Arthur Meyer, *Ce que mes Yeux
ont Vu* (1911), are the recollections of the editor of *Le
Gaulois* about Boulangism, anti-Semitism, and Dreyfusism.

A. Dansette, *Le Boulangisme* (1946), is a recent account and explanation of the nature of the movement.

For a deeper understanding of Boulangism in its political and social context, one should not fail to consult the theses of Jacques Néré, still unfortunately unpublished, "La Crise Economique et Sociale de 1882 et le Mouvement Boulangiste" (1959), and "Les Elections Boulangistes dans le Départment du Nord" (1959). Even if this research does not fully demonstrate that Boulangism came directly from the 1882 economic depression, it does show the movement's mass appeal and social content. The essence of these works can be found in J. Néré, *Le Boulangisme et la Presse* (1964).

Marcel Barrière was the personal secretary of the Duke d'Orléans in 1890-1891 and in *Les Princes d'Orléans* (1933), he judges the princes without indulgence and characterizes their entourage. Robert F. Byrnes, *Antisemitism in Modern France* (New Brunswick, N. J., 1950), is on the origins of this movement. Pierre Sorlin, *La Croix et les Juifs* (1967), describes the roots and the motivations of Catholic anti-Semitism and its decisive role in the rapprochement of nationalism and religion.

There are a number of studies dealing with the *Ralliement*. See Henri Rollet, *Albert de Mun et le Parti Catholique* (1947), which describes the Count de Mun's attempt in 1885 to establish a Catholic Party and its failure; Mermeix, *Le Ralliement et l'Action Française* (1927); Jacques Piou, *Le Ralliement et son Histoire* (1928), by one of its promoters; and David Shapiro, "The Ralliement in the Politics of the 1890's," in his *The Right in France (1890-1919): Three Studies* (Carbondale, Ill., 1962). Shapiro tries to determine the political origin of the *ralliés* and finds Orleanism represented as well as

Legitimism. Other studies in the same collection are D. R. Watson, "The Nationalist Movement in Paris (1900-1906)," and Malcolm Anderson, "The Right and the Social Question in Parliament (1905-1919)." Two other recent works on the *Ralliement* are Xavier de Montclos, *Le Toast d'Alger: Documents (1890-1891)* (1966); and Alexander Sedgwick, *The Ralliement in French Politics, 1890-1898* (Cambridge, Mass., 1965).

Works on militarism and the place of the army in nationalist doctrine include Emile Faguet, *Problèmes Politiques du Temps Présent* (1900), and *Le Pacifisme* (1900); Jules Lemaître, *Opinions à Répandre* (1901); Charles Maurras, "Armée," in his *Dictionnaire Politique et Critique,* 5 vols., ed. Pierre Chardon (1931-1934); Agathon (Henri Massis and Alfred de Tarde), *Les Jeunes Gens d'Aujourd'hui* (1913); Eugen Weber, *The Nationalist Revival in France (1905-1914)* (Berkeley, 1959), a good survey indicating that after 1905 nationalism found a growing audience. One might also wish to consider Herbert Tint, *The Decline of French Patriotism, 1870-1940* (London, 1964), in which the search for originality leads to some questionable views; and on the man who symbolized, on the eve of the war, the nationalist revival, *Poincaré,* by Pierre Miquel (1961).

5. Royalism and Action Française

Philippe du Puy de Clinchamps, *Le Royalisme* (1967), is a brief introductory survey. Some recent works that have revised our knowledge of the subject come from American historians: Samuel Osgood, *French Royalism under the Third and Fourth Republics* (The Hague, 1960), underlines the continuity and describes the forms of the royalist idea although it tends to overestimate the influence of the present Count de Paris in politics; and especially Eugen Weber, *Action Française: Royalism and Reaction in Twentieth Century France* (Stanford, 1962), the first extensive and objective study of the school that holds such a large place in the twentieth century French Right. Other studies include Henri Massis, *Maurras et Notre Temps,* 2 vols. (1951); Marquis de Roux, *Charles Maurras et le Nationalisme de l' Action Française* (1928); W. C. Buthman, *The Rise of Integral Nationalism in France (New York,* 1939); D. W. Brogan, *French Personalities and Problems (1900-1940)* (London, 1946), a collection of articles, some of which deal with Barrès, Maurras, Léon Daudet, and Jacques Bainville; and Louis Dimier, *Les Maîtres de la Contre-Révolution au XIXe Siècle* (1907).

Action Française has generated an abundant literature of studies, recollections, essays, defenses, and attacks. Political passion rarely is absent from these works. All of them therefore constitute more the materials for history than a first approximation of it. Among them are Louis Dimier, *Vingt Ans d'Action Française et Autres Souvenirs* (1926); Maurice Pujo, *Les Camelots du Roi* (1933); and Robert Havard de la Montagne, *Histoire de l'Action Française* (1950), in which one should not expect from the fervor of the hagiographer and the passion of the polemicist the objectivity of the historian. The author was the former editor of the newspaper *Rome.* Philippe Ariès, *Le Temps de l'Histoire* (Monaco, 1954), is a sincere and engaging account of one aspect of Action Française, with relevant comments on the conservative interpretation of history, Bainville's philosophy, and the influence of Action Française's historical school.

On the condemnation of Action Française and the two

Catholicisms: Louis Dimier, *L'Action Libérale dans les Elections* . . . (1914); Georges Bidault, *L'A.J.C.F. et les Mouvements Politiques de Jeunesse* (Besançon, 1926), which defines the position of the most important association of Catholic youth toward the leagues, a warning against "politics first"; Jacques Maritain, *Une Opinion sur Charles Maurras et le Devoir des Catholiques* (1926); *Les Pièces d'un Procès: L'Action Française et le Vatican* (1927), with a preface by Maurras and Léon Daudet; Mgr. Paul Rémond, *Ce qu'il faut Répondre aux Objections de l'Action Française: Conseils d'un Evêque à des Prêtres* (1927), and *L'Heure d'Obéir: Réponse aux Difficultés de l'Action Française* (1928); V. Bernadot *et al, Réponse aux Thélogiens d'Action Française: Le Joug de Christ* (1928); P. Doncoeur *et al, Pourquoi Rome a Parlé: Le Livre des Six* (1928); Maurice Pujo, *Réponse au Livre des Six* . . . (1929); Nicholas Fontane (pseud. of Louis Canet), *Saint-Siège, Action Française et "Catholiques Intégraux"* (1928), an attempt at critical history. A later discussion is Jacques Julliard, "La Politique Religieuse de Charles Maurras," *Esprit*, XXVI (1958), 359-384. On Bernanos' split with Maurras and the polemic that set them against each other in 1932, see "Bernanos et Maurras," *Bulletin de la Société des Amis de Georges Bernanos,* numbers 17-20. Y. Congar, "Mentalité 'de Droite' et Intégrisme," *La Vie Intellectuelle,* XVIII (1950), 644-666, discusses Right Wing thought within the Church, as does "Document sur l'Intégrisme," in the same journal, September 1952. The principal controversies among the tendencies of Catholic opinion in the interwar period are set forth as seen in their publications by René Rémond and Aline Coutrot, *Les Catholiques, Le Communisme et les Crises (1929-*

1939) (1960); while Xavier Vallat describes "La Fédération Nationale Catholique," in *Ecrits de Paris,* XI (November 1954), 65-74.

6. From the *Bloc National* to the National Revolution (1919-1939)

G. Bourgin *et al, Manuel des Partis Politiques en France* (1928), is a valuable compilation of organizations and their programs; Pierre Frédérix, *Etat des Forces en France* (1935) evaluates their relative importance. New suggestions on the intellectual climate of the period are made by J. Touchard in "L'Esprit des Années 1930," pp. 90-120, in P. Guiral *et al, Tendances Politiques dans la Vie Française depuis 1789* (1960). There are three relevant unpublished theses done at the Institut d'Etudes Politiques at Paris: H. Maizy, "Les Groupes Antiparlementaires de Droite en France de 1933 à 1939" (1951); J. Philippet, "Les Jeunesses Patriotes et Pierre Taittinger (1924-1940)" (1967); and Olivier Gaudry, "Henri de Kerillis" (1966). Of the same type is Harold M. Thewlis, "French Authoritarian Movements of the Right (1924-1940)," unpub. M.A. thesis, Columbia Univ. (1952).

The existence of a French fascism distinct from the conservative or traditionalist Right during the interwar period is a matter of controversy. On this fundamental issue we first cite an article that is now old but where we raised the question: R. Rémond, "Y a-t-il un Fascism Français?" *Terre Humaine,* II (1952). Since then, the issue has led to a number of publications: R. Girardet, "Note sur l'Esprit d'un Fascisme Français," *Revue Français de Science Politique,* V (1955), 529-546; J. Plumyène and R. Lasierra, *Les Fascismes Français, 1923-*

1963 (1963), where the authors tend to underestimate the importance of fascism in France. They include useful facts and documents. Two thoughtful American studies are Eugen Weber, "Nationalism, Socialism and National-Socialism in France," *French Historical Studies,* II (1962), 273-307; and Robert Soucy, "The Nature of Fascism in France," *Journal of Contemporary History,* I (1966), 27-55; and a German analysis, Ernst Nolte, *Three Faces of Fascism* (New York, 1966). On the founder of the only movement whose affiliation to fascism cannot be questioned because he called it fascist, see Yves Guchet, "Georges Valois ou l'Illusion Fasciste," *Revue Française de Science Politique,* XV (1965), 1111-1144. Fascism did exert an attraction of an esthetic sort on a number of intellectuals, as indicated in Paul Serant, *Le Romantisme Fasciste: Etude sur l'Oeuvre de Quelques Ecrivains Français* (1960); and in the recollections that Robert Brasillach charmingly recounted in *Notre Avant-Guerre* (1941), where he explains the mentality of those seduced by fascism and illuminates the attraction it exercised on a part of the youth.

The February 6, 1934, affair is described in Chambre des Députés, *Rapport de la Commission d'Enquête sur les Evénements du 6 Février 1934* (15th Legislature, Session of 1934, Documents 3383-3393); Georges Imann, *La Journée du 6 Février* (1934); Philippe Henriot, *Le 6 Février* (1934), a Right Wing version; and Georges Suarez, *La Grande Peur du 6 Février au Palais-Bourbon* (1934). Retrospective accounts include Max Beloff, "The Sixth of February," in *The Decline of the Third Republic,* ed. James Joll (New York, 1956); and R. Rémond, "Explications du 6 Février," *Politique,* II (1959), 218-230, that eliminates the plot theory but finds much still to clarify;

Maurice Chavardès, *Le 6 Février 1934* (1966); and Marcel Le Cléré, *Le 6 Février* (1967).

On war veterans and the *Croix de Feu* consult R. Rémond, "Les Anciens Combattants et la Politique," *Revue Française de Science Politique,* V (1955), 267-290; F. de La Rocque, *Service Public* (1934), in which the head of the *Croix de Feu* tries to express his political ideas and outline a reform program; two of the organization's pamphlets, *Pourquoi J'ai Adhéré au P.S.F.* (1935), and *Manifeste Croix de Feu: Pour le Peuple, Par le Peuple* (1936); François Veuillot, *La Rocque et son Parti comme Je les ai Vus* (1938); Paul Creyssel, *La Rocque contre Tardieu* (1939), favorable to the head of the *Croix de Feu;* Edith and Gilles de La Rocque, *La Rocque tel qu'il Etait* (1962), by his family, rectifies some errors. The history of what was one of the most important movements in the interwar years still remains to be written.

On Jacques Doriot and the P.P.F. see Paul Marion, *Refaire la France: La France avec Nous* (1937), and *Programme du P.P.F.* (1938). One can also refer to the portrait, scarcely veiled by a change of names, that Jules Romains drew of Doriot in vol. XII of his *Men of Goodwill* (New York, 1945), pp. 193-216 and 240-253. Douvrin resembles Doriot like a brother. They had the same fief, Saint Denis, their origins were identical for they both came from the extreme Left, they had the same strong talent for popular oratory and as the leader of a gang. Tardieu is described in Rudolph Binion, *Defeated Leaders: The Political Fate of Caillaux, Jouvenel and Tardieu* (New York, 1960). Georges Dupeux, *Le Front Populaire et les Elections de 1936* (1959), is an analysis with maps.

The "Great Schism" of 1935-1939 can be approached

through Yves Simon, *La Campagne d'Ethiopie et la Pensée Politique Française* (1936), in part a study of opinion; Henri Béraud, *Faut-il Réduire l'Angleterre en Esclavage?* (1935), a passionate indictment by a talented pamphleteer; and Pierre Milza, *L'Italie Fasciste devant l'Opinion Française, 1920-1940* (1967). On Anglophobia in Rightist opinion there is valuable material in the fine thesis in comparative literature of M. F. Guyard, *L'Image de la Grande-Bretagne dans le Roman Français (1914-1939)* (1954). Right Wing sympathy for the Spanish nationalists can be seen in Robert Brasillach and Henri Massis, *Les Cadets de l'Alcazar* (1936); and Robert Brasillach and Maurice Bardèche, *Histoire de la Guerre d'Espagne* (1939). Charles Micaud, *The French Right and Nazi Germany, 1933-1939* (Durham, N. C., 1943), is a useful collection of newspaper opinions, but the positions are not closely enough examined through men, parties, and groups. Part of the "Kiosque" series, *Munich, 1938,* by Geneviève Valette and Jacques Bouillon (1964), emphasizes newspaper opinions.

F. FROM THE FRENCH STATE TO THE FIFTH REPUBLIC (1940-1968)

A very useful survey for the whole period is Jacques Chapsal, *La Vie Politique en France depuis 1940* (1966).

1. Vichy, the National Revolution, and Collaboration

Robert Aron, *The Vichy Regime* (New York, 1958), is the first attempt at a lengthy objective history of this recent period that will remain the subject of passionate controversies for a long time. The chapter on political ideas is not the best. The sagacious views of André

Siegfried are presented in his *De la IIIe à la IVe République* (1956). Stanley Hoffmann, "Quelques Aspects du Régime de Vichy," *Revue Française de Science Politique,* VI (1956), 46-69, and "The Effects of World War II on French Society and Politics," *French Historical Studies,* II (1961), 28-63, offer such a wealth of interpretation that we are impatient to see his forthcoming book on the entire period. Several recent studies are: Claude Gounelle, *De Vichy à Montoire* (1966); Henri Michel, *Vichy, Année 40* (1966), which argues that the choice made in foreign policy determined the whole of domestic policies; Jacques Duquesne, *Les Catholiques Française sous l'Occupation* (1966); and Robert Paxton, *Parades and Politics at Vichy: The French Officer Corps under Marshal Pétain* (Princeton, 1966).

Marquis d'Argenson, *Pétain et le Pétinisme: Essai de Psychologie* (1953), is an explanatory essay that relates the mystique of the National Revolution to its antecedents. Michèle Cotta, *La Collaboration, 1940-1944* (1964), in the "Kiosque" series and the outgrowth of a thesis, attempts to trace the political trail of the collaborators in the Parisian press. Right Wing thought in the Resistance and how it was affected there is described in the thesis of Henri Michel, *Les Courants de Pensée de la Résistance* (1963).

2. The Fourth Republic

The best study on the period is Philip Williams, *Crisis and Compromise: Politics in the Fourth Republic,* 3rd ed. (London, 1964). Jacques Fauvet, *La IVe République,* 2nd ed. (1960) is especially well informed on the parliamentary level. The development of electoral geography —one of the most flourishing branches of French political science—has produced many recent studies relevant to the study of the Right Wing. We mention as an example A. Olivesi and M. Roncayolo, *Géographie Electoral des Bouches-du-Rhône sous la IVᵉ République* (1961). Foreign policy and in particular the questions raised by decolonization had an important enough place in the politics of the Fourth Republic to throw doubt on the traditional axiom that issues of foreign policy play no role in domestic politics. Therefore, one should examine Alfred Grosser, *Le IVᵉ République et sa Politique Extérieure* (1961). Jean P. Chevènement, "La Droite Nationaliste devant l'Allemagne" (1960), is an unpublished thesis done at the Institut d'Etudes Politiques at Paris, rich and intelligent.

Among several essays on politics and the Right Wing we cite Jacques Fauvet, *La France Déchirée* (1957); Raymond Aron, *Espoir et Peur du Siècle* (1957); and Simone de Beauvoir, "La Pensée de Droite, Aujourd'hui," *Le Temps Modernes*, X (1955), 1539-1575, 2219-2261. The issue of *La Parisienne* on "La Droite," (October 1956), has little weight but is a significant document showing the views of a youthful literary Right. The magazine *Evidences* published some contributions on the theme "Structures et Positions de la Droite," in its issues 76 and 77 (1959); and Paul Sérant asks *Où Va la Droite?* (1958). Armin Mohler, *Die Französische Recht* (Munich, 1958), briefly examines the extreme Right, while the essential study of "Les Modérés" remains that of Marcel Merle, cited in section I. C. above. Under the pseudonym "Sapiens" Alfred Fabre-Luce has contributed to the description of Antoine Pinay in *Mendès ou Pinay?* (1953); while the Executive Secretary of the National Center of Independents and Peasants, Roger Duchet, published some of his newspaper editorials in *Pour le Salut Public* (1958). Raoul Girardet, "L'Héritage de l'Action Française," *Revue Française de Science Politique,* VII (1957), 765-792, tells all that one needs to know about the different branches into which the Maurrasian current has divided. On Gaullism and the R.P.F. Nicholas Wahl is preparing a full scale study. In the meantime we do have Christian Purchet, *Le Rassemblement du Peuple Français* (1965). On fascism, a special number of *Esprit,* "La Pause des Fascismes est Terminée," XV (December 1947); and R. Rémond, "Droites Classiques et Droite Romantique," *Terre Humaine,* I (1951). Stanley Hoffmann, *Le Mouvement Poujade* (1956), is a model of contemporary analysis and shows what can be done in this genre.

On the relations between the Right Wing and Catholicism, R. Rémond, "Droite et Gauche dans le Catholicisme Contemporain," *Revue Française de Science Politique,* VIII (1958), 529-544, 803-820; Jean M. Domenach, "Le Regroupement de la Droite et le Renouveau de l'Intégrisme," *Synthèses,* VII (1953), 107-116; Madeleine Garrigou-Lagrange, "Intégrisme et National-Catholicisme," *Esprit,* XXVII (1959), 515-543; J. F. Henry, "Eléments pour une Etude des Survivances de l'Intégrisme dans le Catholicisme Français Contemporain depuis 1945," unpublished thesis at the Institut d'Etudes Politiques at Paris (1958), which attempts to understand the three currents of contemporary integrism; "Catholiques de Droite? Catholiques de Gauche?" *Chronique Social* (December 1956), pp. 585-749, an interesting collection of opinions; and finally, "Chrétien de Droite ou de Gauche?" *Verse et Controverse,* No. 2 (1966).

3. The Fifth Republic

The contemporaneousness of this regime has not yet allowed the appearance of many scholarly studies. One can begin with the survey by Jacques Chapsal cited at the beginning of section II F. above. On elections there is the series published by the Fondation Nationale des Sciences Politiques: Maurice Duverger *et al*, *Les Elections du 2 Janvier 1956* (1957); Association Française de Science Politique, *L'Establissement de la Ve République: La Référendum de Septembre 1958 et les Elections de Novembre 1958* (1960); F. Goguel *et al*, *Le Référendum du 8 Janvier 1961* (1962); Centre d'Etude de la Vie Politique Française, *Le Référendum du 8 Avril 1962* (1963); and *Ibid., Le Référendum d'Octobre et les Elections de Novembre 1962* (1965). No research on contemporary political life can be done without using these analyses. The later volumes, by going down to the level of the canton, have allowed a much closer examination of reality and have advanced our knowledge. Research is turning toward an investigation of voting shifts that have become unusually large in recent years.

On the present spread of political opinions as revealed by a survey of public opinion, see Emeric Deutsch *et al*, *Les Familles Politiques Aujourd'hui en France* (1966), which concludes that one can distinguish between a political Center and a floating vote in the middle that moves in either direction and that the Center is distinct from the Right. Guy Michelat and Jean P. Thomas, *Dimensions du Nationalisme* (1966), uses similar methods.

On the intellectual antecedents of the regime, an article by one of the ablest students of Gaullism, Nicholas Wahl, "The French Constitution of 1958: the Initial Draft and

Its Origins," *American Political Science Review*, LIII (1959), 358-382, is valuable, as well as the entire March 1959 issue of *Revue Française de Science Politique*, IX. For the party that has incarnated Gaullism for some ten years, see R. Rémond, "L'Enigme de l'U.N.R.," *Esprit*, XXXI (1963), 307-319; and in particular the thesis by Jean Charlot, *L'U.N.R.: Etude du Pouvoir au Sein d'un Parti Politique* (1967), along with his "L'Après-Gaullisme," *Revue Française de Science Politique*, XVIII (1968), 68-76.

Marie T. Lancelot (ed.), "L'Organisation Armée Secrète," is an unpublished collection of documents at the Fondation Nationale des Sciences Politiques. Another such collection is Anon. (ed.), *O.A.S. Parle* (164).

The Independents of several obediences and successive generations are discussed in articles that have all appeared in the *Revue Française de Science Politique:* Janine Bourdin, "La Crise des Indépendants," XIII (1963), 443-450; Marielle Bal, "Les Indépendants," XV (1965), 537-555; Marie C. Kessler, "M. Valéry Giscard d'Estaing et les Républicains Indépendants, Réalités et Perspectives," XVI (1966), 940-957; *Ibid.*, "M. Valéry Giscard d'Estaing et les Républicains Indépendants: Juillet 1966-Novembre 1967," XVIII (1968), 77-93; and Roland Cayrol and Jean L. Parodi, "Le Centrisme, Deux Ans Après," XVIII (1968), 93-106. On the person around whom the Independent Republicans are grouped, see Michel Bassis, *Valéry Giscard d'Estaing* (1968). Two personal accounts suggest the permanence of a common fund of ideas and feelings that goes to make up the liberal Right: André François-Poncet, *Au Fil des Jours: Propos d'un Libéral, 1962-1965* (1966); and Pierre Marcilhacy, *Ce Que Je n'ai pas Dit* (1966).

Some commentaries and analyses of the crisis of May–June 1968 have begun to appear. Among them we mention the entire issue of *Esprit,* June–July 1968; Jean C. Kerbourc'h, *Le Pieton de Mai* (1968); Raymond Aron, *La Révolution Introuvable: Réflexions sur la Révolution de Mai* (1968). Alain Touraine, *Le Mouvement de Mai ou le Communisme Utopique* (1968); André Philip, *Mai 1968 et la Foi Démocratique* (1969); and in English, Patrick Seale and Maureen McConville, *Red Flag Black Flag: French Revolution 1968* (New York, 1968).

Index

Titles of periodicals and names of imaginary persons are italicized.